A CONCISE HISTORY
OF THE COMMUNIST PARTY
OF THE SOVIET UNION

A CONCISE HISTORY
OF THE COMMUNIST PARTY
OF THE SOVIET UNION

Revised Edition

By JOHN S. RESHETAR, JR.

FREDERICK A. PRAEGER, *Publishers*
New York • Washington • London

FREDERICK A. PRAEGER, PUBLISHERS
111 FOURTH AVENUE, NEW YORK 3, N.Y., U.S.A.
77–79 CHARLOTTE STREET, LONDON W. 1, ENGLAND

First published in the United States of America in 1960
by Frederick A. Praeger, Inc., Publishers

Revised edition, 1964

All rights reserved

© 1960, 1964 by Frederick A. Praeger, Inc.

Library of Congress Catalog Card Number: 64-23544

This book is Number 88 in the series
Praeger Publications in Russian History and World Communism.

Printed in the United States of America

This is the ninth in a series of studies to be published by Frederick A. Praeger, Publishers, under the auspices of the Foreign Policy Research Institute at the University of Pennsylvania, established under a grant of the Richardson Foundation, Greensboro, North Carolina. The views expressed in A CONCISE HISTORY OF THE COMMUNIST PARTY OF THE SOVIET UNION are those of the author.

To my wife, Helene

PREFACE

In spite of the vast army of scholars, publicists, and archivists maintained by the Soviet Union's rulers, conditions preclude the writing in Russia of a truly objective account of the development of the ruling elite, the Communist Party of the Soviet Union. Stalin's absurd *Short Course* history, which first appeared in 1938, was subsequently denounced in 1956, but the problem of preparing a successor volume (which appeared in 1959) was complicated by the inability of the Party to describe and appraise its own past honestly.

This volume, though modest in size, represents my attempt to make a contribution to that end by way of a concise treatment based upon primary sources. Since this is a study of the development of the Soviet Communist Party rather than a history of Russia since the 1890's, many events and personalities that would be treated fully in the latter type of work are considered here only to the extent that they pertain directly to the Party. I have attempted to ground this study on the ascertainable record; I have avoided areas of rumor and have not attempted to equate speculative constructs of events with established facts. I have not undertaken to provide definitive or glib answers to questions which remain unanswerable at present.

I owe a considerable debt of gratitude to various persons who aided me during the course of writing this account. The active support and advice provided by Professor Robert Strausz-Hupé, Director of the Foreign Policy Research Institute of the University of Pennsylvania, and by Professor Stefan T. Possony were indispensable. Dr. Elsa Bernaut provided valuable assistance in much of the research which underlies this volume and also gave generously of her wealth of personal knowledge. Dr. Constantine Krypton rendered essential research aid in a variety of ways. Various parts of the manuscript were read and commented upon by Col. William R. Kintner and other associates of the Foreign Policy Research Institute, which is planning other books on the Soviet Communist Party with special reference to the post-Stalin era. Erasmus H. Kloman, Jr., in his capacity as Assistant to the Director of the Institute, provided necessary liaison and tended to many administrative matters related to the economic aspects of the project from which this volume emerged. Walter F. Hahn made numerous editorial suggestions, as did Arnold Dolin. Professor Donald W. Treadgold, my colleague at the University of Washington, generously provided advice on several matters. Various staff members of the Slavonic Division of the New York Public Library, of the Library of Congress, and of the Library of the University of Washington were most helpful in many ways. Finally—and most important—my wife provided constant encouragement and understanding, and also assumed many essential burdens connected with the manuscript.

—JOHN S. RESHETAR, JR.

University of Washington
Seattle, Washington
December, 1959

Preface to the Revised Edition

The many significant events that have occurred since the publication of the first edition have made it advisable to add a ninth chapter dealing with the policies and problems of the Khrushchev regime in the Party. Apart from minor corrections and addenda, the eight original chapters remain unchanged. Revision of these chapters would be necessary if the Party were to open its archives or if leading Soviet politicians were to publish meaningful memoirs. In the absence of such developments, the present effort must stand.

—J. S. R., JR.

June, 1964

CONTENTS

A CONCISE HISTORY
OF THE COMMUNIST PARTY
OF THE SOVIET UNION

CHAPTER I

FROM MARXISM TO FACTIONALISM

And if the revolutionaries "seize power" and make a social revolution? In this it [the bourgeoisie] does not believe, and soon the revolutionaries themselves will cease to believe in it. Soon they will all understand that if people open umbrellas when it rains, it does not follow that rain can be evoked by opened umbrellas; soon they will become convinced that if the "seizure" of political power is the inevitable result of the development of the working, as of every other, class, it cannot be concluded from this that it is sufficient for "revolutionaries from the privileged milieu" to seize power in order to make the toiling population of Russia capable of achieving a socialist overturn. Soon all of our socialists will understand that it is only possible to serve the interests of the people by organizing and preparing the people for the *independent struggle* for these interests.
—Georgii V. Plekhanov, *Our Divergencies* (1884).

For Lenin the Party is his "plan," his will, leading the realization of the plan. It is the idea of Louis XIV: *L'état c'est moi*—the Party, it is I, Lenin.
—Vera Zasulich, in *Iskra*, No. 70 (July 25, 1904).

The political and social environment of Russia at the turn of this century was singularly favorable to the rise of Communism. Bolshevism and its child, the Communist Party of the Soviet Union, did not spring full-blown from the head of Lenin, although he is properly regarded as their creator. His precursors were already active in 1870, when the future Lenin was born as Vladimir Ilyich Ulyanov, the son of a nobleman-bureaucrat, in the provincial Volga River town of Simbirsk (since then, appropriately renamed Ulyanovsk).

Politicians who achieve stature during their lifetimes invariably tend either to pass over in silence or to deny their precursors who may serve as a source of embarrassment. Conversely, they tend to magnify the contributions of those who, however remotely, can serve to legitimize their present acts. For the party of Lenin and Stalin, the acknowledged ideological precursors were the nineteenth-century radical Russian intellectuals. These outspoken literary critics—particularly Vissarion Grigor'evich Belinsky, Nikolai Gavrilovich Chernyshevsky, and Nikolai Alexandrovich Dobrolyubov—were either radicals or utopian socialists. Soviet historians have made much of the few words of praise which Marx bestowed upon Chernyshevsky, who had outspokenly criticized the 1861 reforms in Russia on the grounds that they were inadequate. Lenin, for this reason, praised him in 1894 in one of his first works (*What Are the "Friends of the People" and How Do They Fight Against the Social Democrats?*). This did not mean, however, that Chernyshevsky—who, among other things, had translated John Stuart Mill's *Principles of Political Economy* into Russian—was a Marxist.

Chernyshevsky's philosophy, in fact, resembled in many significant aspects that of the Populists (the *Narodniki*), who placed an almost mystical faith in the peasant form of communal landholding (the *obshchina*). However, Chernyshevsky did not share the Populists' opposition to Russia's industrialization; he favored the advent of industry, but maintained that the historical period of capitalism could be shortened appreciably. That he recognized the inevitability of Russia's industrialization pleased Lenin, as did Chernyshevsky's utopian novel *What Is to Be Done?* (1863)—the title of which Lenin appropriated for his own important but somewhat dissimilar work of 1902 in which he advocated a party of professional revolutionaries. Chernyshevsky's imprisonment and exile in Siberia from 1862 to 1883 endowed him with the halo of martyrdom. Yet, he was neither a political thinker nor an activist but, rather, an economist of sorts and a writer on literary aesthetics and social issues. His materialism was philosophical rather than historical and dialectical.

It could be argued, perhaps, that Lenin inherited from the Russian radicals of the 1860's the desire to jettison the Russian past, to liberate and remake man, to slough off all traditions, social conventions, alleged falsehoods, superstitions, and prejudices. In the view of these radicals, every belief had to be challenged. Their most important exponent was Dimitrii Ivanovich Pisarev, whose philosophy was embodied in the later battle cry of the "Internationale": "No more tradition's chains shall bind us." Like the Bolsheviks who were to follow them, these radicals rejected existing moral standards in the name of a "higher moral."

Two of the most significant precursors of Bolshevik method and organization have been ignored in official Party histories. These two Russian revolutionaries of the 1860's and 1870's—Sergei Gennadievich Nechaev (1847-82) and Peter Nikitich Tkachev (1844-86)—wrote and conspired along lines that later re-emerged in Bolshevik doctrine as expounded by Lenin.

Nechaev, an erratic and eccentric man who died at the age of thirty-five after ten years of Czarist imprisonment, bequeathed to Bolshevism his *Catechism of a Revolutionary*. This document—accidentally discovered in a police raid on the living quarters of one of Nechaev's associates in November, 1869—contains a number of Leninist principles. Chief among these is the need for a professional type of revolutionary. Article One of the *Catechism* describes this revolutionary as follows: "The revolutionary is a consecrated man. He has neither his own interests, nor concerns, nor feelings, nor attachments, nor property, nor even a name. All of him is absorbed in the single exclusive interest, in the one thought, in the one passion—revolution."[1] Lenin's concept of morality was succinctly stated in Nechaev's Article Four: "Moral for him [the revolutionary] is everything which facilitates the victory of the revolution. Immoral and criminal is everything which hinders it." The revolutionary, according to Nechaev, must be prepared constantly to meet death and to withstand torture. The need to exercise great self-control and to avoid emotionalism is expressed in Article Six: "Rigorous with himself, he [the revolutionary] must be rigorous with others. All tender, effeminate feelings of kinship, friendship, love, gratitude, and even honor itself must be crushed in him by the single cold passion of the revolutionary cause." In Article Seven, Nechaev demanded that "revolutionary passion . . . unite with cold calculation." He advocated, in Article Fourteen, that the revolutionary be able to "feign to be entirely that which he is not" and to infiltrate into the various strata of society, including the "merchant's store, the church, the seignioral manor, the bureaucratic world, the military, literature, the Third Division [of His Majesty's Own Chancellery], and even the [Czar's] Winter Palace." In dealing with "liberals," the revolutionary could enter into arrangements with them "on the basis of their programs, making it appear that you are blindly following them, but meanwhile taking them in hand, mastering all their secrets, compromising them to the point of no return, and, by means of their hands, muddling the state."

Nechaev was a fanatic who could inflict punishment as readily as he could bear it himself. His was a genuinely nihilistic creed based on the assumption that the revolutionary "knows only one science, the science of destruction." The fanatical one-sidedness of his approach thus distinguished him from Lenin, who was as much concerned with the establishment of a new type of dictatorship as he was with the destruction of old political forms. Nevertheless, Nechaev presaged the form of party organization which Lenin was to advocate so fervently—conspiratorial, illicit, and subject to absolute centralism and iron discipline. Both men stood for the complete denial of the self in the name of the "higher" value of the revolution. Nowhere in Lenin's voluminous writings is there mention of Nechaev, and this silence may be significant in view of the fact that Nechaev's extremism had estranged him from most of his fellow revolutionaries in Russia. Yet, Lenin undoubtedly knew of Nechaev, although the latter died in prison when the future ruler of Russia was only twelve years old. Nechaev's role in the assassination of Alexander II in March, 1881, had made him a legendary figure. Nechaev was in prison at the time of the assassination, but the bars of his cell did not prevent the resourceful revolutionary from maintaining contacts with the outside world and serving as a "consultant" to the *Narodnaya volya* (the People's Will), a terrorist Populist group which committed the act of regicide. Other circumstances make it clear that Lenin knew of Nechaev. His older brother, Alexander Ilyich Ulyanov, was a follower of the *Narodnaya volya* and was hanged, in May, 1887, for his part in the unsuccessful attempt on the life of Alexander III. It is known also that Lenin himself, when he was practicing law in Samara in 1892, had contacts with members of the then-defunct *Narodnaya volya* who lived in the town; he learned much from them about their underground methods and the techniques they had employed to foil the Czarist secret police. The presence in Lenin's works of so many fundamental principles found in Nechaev's *Catechism* indicates that Communism's debt to the youthful and fanatical Russian advocate of conspiracy and terrorism is greater than the Party is willing to acknowledge.[2]

Nechaev also adhered to the belief that "who is not for us is against us"[3]—a tenet of pure Leninism.[4] Although arrested in 1872 at the age of twenty-five and extradited to Russia from Switzerland for allegedly having killed a student accused of being an *agent provocateur,* Nechaev had a very active—if brief—career in which to apply this tenet. He first visited Switzerland in 1869, returning to Russia in the autumn to establish a narrow conspiratorial organization, the People's Justice (*Narodnaya rasprava*). The rapid suppression of this movement caused his hasty return to Switzerland in December, 1869.

It was in the late 1860's that Nechaev met Lenin's other Russian precursor, Peter N. Tkachev, in St. Petersburg. The two men participated briefly in the student unrest which characterized that period. Tkachev was a literary critic of no mean talents. As a student at the University of St. Petersburg, he had been arrested on a number of occasions during the 1860's; in 1862, he received a three-year sentence for writing revolutionary verses and a proclamation entitled "What the People Need." In 1865, Tkachev began a career as a writer which he continued until the late 1870's, although it was interrupted by arrest in 1869 and by a prison sentence of sixteen months in 1871. Tkachev's prison term was to have been followed by Siberian exile, but his mother interceded with the authorities and was able to have her son "exiled" to the family estate at Velikie Luki. (Lenin's mother was to be similarly resourceful in 1890, when she obtained for her son permission to take the

examinations in law on the basis of independent study after he
had been expelled from the University of Kazan.) Tkachev
lived at Velikie Luki until December, 1873, when he fled to
Switzerland. There he became associated with the veteran Populist leader Peter Lavrovich Lavrov, publisher of the journal
Vperyod. It was at this time that Tkachev asserted the views
which Lenin was to expound later.

One of the basic beliefs of the *Narodniki* was that the peasant masses, with some leadership on the part of the intelligentsia,
somehow could be expected to revolt. On this issue, Tkachev
attacked both Lavrov and another prominent *Narodnik*, Nikolai
Konstantinovich Mikhailovsky, whom Lenin was to criticize so
harshly in his early writings. Tkachev became convinced that
the peasant masses were incapable of independent action, and
in April, 1874, he charged Lavrov with forsaking revolution for
peaceful progress. Tkachev expressed the need for a conspiratorial minority endowed with a centralized and disciplined
organization—a notion which was not popular in the Russia of
the 1870's, when the Populists were enjoying their brief heyday.

Lenin's debt to Tkachev is indicated in the program of the
latter's journal, *Nabat* ("The Tocsin"), which began to appear
in Geneva at the end of 1875, modestly calling itself the "organ
of the Russian revolution." In it, Tkachev declared: "The
struggle can be conducted successfully only by combining the
following conditions: centralization, severe discipline, swiftness,
decisiveness, and unity of action. All concessions, all wavering,
all compromises, multileadership (*mnogonachalie*), and decen-
tralization of the fighting forces weaken their energy, paralyze
their activity, and deprive the struggle of all chances for victory."[5] The similarities between this view and Lenin's position
at the Second Party Congress in 1903 are too obvious to require
comment.

Another feature common to Tkachev and Lenin was the
extreme doctrine of voluntarism which each preached and which,
in Lenin's case, appeared somewhat incongruous alongside his
historical determinism. Tkachev expressed his concept of voluntarism in a letter written in 1874 to Lavrov's journal, *Vperyod*,
in which he asked the eminent Populist: Is it possible that you
don't know "that the revolutionary always regards and must

regard himself as having the right to summon the people to an uprising; that in this way he differs from the philosopher-Philistine; that, not waiting until the current of historical events itself indicates the minute, he selects it himself; that he is aware that the people are always ready for the revolution?"[6] Lenin expressed a similar view in his letter of November 6, 1917, to the Central Committee, written on the eve of the Bolshevik seizure of power, when his plans were opposed within the Committee: "It is impossible to wait!! All can be lost!! . . . The Government is wavering. It must be *beaten to death* [Lenin's italics] at all costs. To delay the move is similar to death."[7]

Both Tkachev and Lenin were antifederalist in their views on revolutionary organization. Both stressed solidarity. Both held utopian ideals concerning fraternity and equality and the re-education of mankind by a minority. Tkachev claimed that society had to be changed if the individual was to be reformed and if life was to be divested of "inequality, enmity, jealousy, [and] rivalry." "This great task," wrote Tkachev, "can, of course, be accomplished only by people who comprehend it and who sincerely strive for its solution—people who are intellectually and morally developed—i.e., a minority."[8] This later became Lenin's concept of the Party as the "vanguard of the proletariat," although the leader of Bolshevism concealed his minority rule under the meaningless and misleading slogan of the "dictatorship of the proletariat" and denounced as Blanquism the view that the revolution must be fashioned not by the class struggle but by a small conspiratorial minority.

Lenin's debt to Tkachev has often been obscured by the latter's association with the French revolutionary extremist Louis Auguste Blanqui and his collaboration on the Blanquist newspaper *Ni dieu, ni maître* in 1880. Two years later, Tkachev became mentally ill and was hospitalized; he died in France on January 4, 1886.* (Ironically, Lavrov, whom he had attacked so vehemently, delivered an oration at his funeral.) It is errone-

---

* Dates for events occurring in Western Europe are given according to the Gregorian calendar, while the dates of events in Imperial Russia prior to the collapse of the monarchy in March, 1917, are given in both the Julian and Gregorian calendars. All subsequent dates appear according to the Gregorian calendar.

ous to classify Tkachev either with the anarchists or—as some
Soviet writers have done—with the terrorists, however much the
Narodnaya volya terrorist group was indebted to him. Tkachev
wrote of the introduction by the minority of "new progressive
Communist elements into the conditions of popular life."[9] Unlike
the anarchists, however, he did not wish to abolish the state;
instead, he preceded Lenin in favoring the creation of a revolutionary state. While Lenin did occasionally use the term
"Tkachev-like" in a critical sense—as, for example, in *What Is
to Be Done?*, where he accused one Evgenii Osipovich Zelensky
of impatience and of advocating terror—it is nevertheless clear
that Lenin's debt to Tkachev is a substantial one. If Lenin was
hesitant in acknowledging the debt, as he was also in the case
of Nechaev, this can be explained in terms of his anxiety to
make the Bolsheviks appear to be the party of the masses—as
contrasted with Nechaev's and Tkachev's concept of the minority
conspiratorial party.[10] Lenin was not opposed to conspiracy—
he recognized it as a necessary element in combatting an autocracy—but he felt impelled to mask it as the "vanguard" of the
future and the voice of the masses.

If any Russian party could be said to have enjoyed popular
support at the time of the Bolshevik seizure of power in November, 1917, it was the Socialist Revolutionaries. In the elections to
the All-Russian Constituent Assembly held at that time, the
Social Revolutionaries received a plurality of nearly 16 million
votes out of a total of more than 41 million cast. The Bolsheviks
received fewer than 10 million votes, while their erstwhile
Menshevik comrades polled only about 1.3 million.[11] It was
understandable that the Socialist Revolutionaries, as a peasant-
oriented party, should have received this support in an over-
whelmingly peasant country. Yet, this party—as well as its
predecessor, the Populists—was severely attacked by Lenin. His
first important polemical work, *What Are the "Friends of the
People"?*, was directed against the prominent *Narodnik* Nikolai
K. Mikhailovsky (1842-1904) and his *Russkoe bogatstvo* group.
This work was written and mimeographed in 1894, but it was
not printed until 1923 when it was discovered, in part, in Russian police archives. Stripped of all its verbiage, Lenin's quarrel

with the Populists was based on their mystical belief that the people (*narod*) and, in particular, the peasantry were endowed with virtues and an ideal way of life not possessed by the guilt-ridden Russian intelligentsia. The Populists were not sufficiently class-oriented to please Lenin, and he could not stomach their belief that Russia's future lay in the decaying peasant *obshchina*, or communal form of landholding—a system involving redistribution of land every decade—which the Populists regarded as the foundation of a purely Russian agrarian socialism. The Populist view was essentially anticapitalist, antiurban, and antiindustrial; it held that Russia could, because of her uniqueness, escape the rigors of the Industrial Revolution and that the role of the factory proletariat could be ignored.[12] Lenin dismissed this view as "romanticized fantasy" and disputed Mikhailovsky's assertion that Russia could not have a working class in the European sense of the term because the peasant who worked in industry could always return to his native village during periods of unemployment. Populism was a broad concept, and Zinoviev accurately characterized it as "a phenomenon of many calibers and motley to the highest degree—[ranging] from anarchism to liberalism"[13]—one that included both revolutionary and nonrevolutionary elements.

The more active Populist group, which adopted terrorist methods, came into existence in the autumn of 1879 following the Voronezh Congress, when the Populist revolutionary center (*Zemlya i volya*) split into two groups: the Black Repartition (*Chernyi peredel*), composed of those who did not admit the need for political struggle, and the People's Will (*Narodnaya volya*), which was bent on terror and the assassination of Alexander II. This group of terrorists, the most prominent of whom was Andrei Ivanovich Zhelyabov, succeeded in accomplishing the latter objective on March 1, 1881. Their rash and fruitless act, which destroyed the autocrat but not the autocracy, was later to exert a profound influence upon Lenin's thought. The fact that such terrorism (which led to his elder brother's execution) produced no lasting results caused Lenin to think seriously about the principles upon which a successful revolutionary organization would have to be based.

The Populist schism in 1879 was important to the advent of Marxism in Russia, because from it emerged a group calling itself the Emancipation of Labor. This group was composed of former Populists of the Black Repartition wing who had fled to Switzerland and were attempting, from the safety of Geneva, to "liberate" the Russian toilers. Foremost among its members were Georgii Valentinovich Plekhanov (to whom Lenin owed so much), the future Menshevik Paul Borisovich Axelrod, and the noted revolutionaries Vera Zasulich and Leo Deutsch.[14] Although Plekhanov is generally regarded as the "father of Russian Marxism," Marx himself took a dim view of the Russians in Geneva who were to found the Emancipation of Labor in 1883, the year of his death. Marx put greater stock in the terrorists of the *Narodnaya volya*, who gave the appearance of a going concern and who undoubtedly took greater risks at greater sacrifice than did the Russians in Geneva. In a letter of November 5, 1880—written to Friedrich A. Sorge, a German Marxist *émigré* in New York—Marx described the Geneva *émigrés* as follows:

> The majority of these people [in Geneva], although not all, left Russia voluntarily and, in contrast with the terrorists who risk their own heads, are organizing a so-called "party of propaganda" (to carry on propaganda in Russia, they go to Geneva!). . . . These gentlemen are opposed to all revolutionary activity: Russia must, in their opinion, leap in one jump directly to the anarchist-Communist-atheist millenium.[15]

Thus, ironically, the terrorists who were later to be vilified by Lenin were, in Marx's own analysis of the contemporary Russian scene, more Marxist than was Plekhanov. Later, in 1923, during a series of lectures on the Party's history, Zinoviev explained this apparent contradiction and the disagreement over the use of terror:

> In actual fact, Marxists have never, in principle, been against terror. They have never taken the position of the Christian legacy: thou shalt not kill. On the contrary, Plekhanov himself repeated on more than one occasion that

not every killing [*umershchvlenie*] is murder, that to kill a reptile [*gad*] is not to commit a crime. . . . Marxists have emphasized that they are advocates of violence and regard it as a revolutionary factor. There is too much in the world that can be destroyed only by weapons, by fire and sword. Marxists [as distinct from the Populists] spoke for mass terror. But they said that the assassination of one or another minister will not change matters; it is necessary to raise up the masses . . . And only then, when they organize themselves [*sic*], only then will the hour of decision strike, for then we will employ terror not retail but wholesale [*ne v roznitsu, a optom*] . . .[16]

Thus, it was not the issue of terror itself which caused the break between the Populists and the new Russian Marxists, but rather their respective prognoses regarding Russia's economic development. In the industrial ferment which was beginning to make itself felt in the 1880's, it is difficult to discern any organization that can be regarded as the Party's harbinger. The several small workers' groups which did emerge, such as the South Russian Union of Workers in Odessa in 1874 (whose organizing group owned a library and a cooperative bathhouse), were short-lived. The Union's membership (fewer than 200) included only two intellectuals, and one of these, Evgenii Zaslavsky, received a ten-year sentence when the organization was smashed by the gendarmery in December, 1875.[17]

Another early organization was the Northern Union of Russian Workers, established in St. Petersburg in late 1877 or early 1878 by an ironworker, Victor Obnorsky, who had participated in the Odessa group, and a carpenter, Stepan Khalturin. This group did not accept intellectuals as members since the latter were predominantly Populist in their views—a fact that becomes significant when it is recalled that the new Russian *raznochinnaya* intelligentsia (representing varied social strata) was to play a dominant role in the Social Democratic movement from which Bolshevism sprang. The Northern Union stood for political struggle and for freedom of speech, press, and assembly. By March of 1879, it was crushed by the police; Obnorsky received a ten-year sentence, while Khalturin joined the terrorist *Narod-*

naya volya and, in February, 1880, arranged an explosion under the Winter Palace. Khalturin was apprehended and executed in Odessa in 1882 for having assassinated the local prosecutor. In view of Khalturin's defection to the Populist terrorists, Party historians cannot regard the Northern Union of Russian Workers as the first Marxist group.

The distinction of being the first Marxist group in Russia is usually bestowed upon the openly socialist Emancipation of Labor group, founded in Geneva by Plekhanov in 1883. The orientation of this group was toward the working class and industrial development, and against the Populists. Plekhanov, as its spokesman, poured scorn upon the heads of the Populists as early as 1884 in his work *Our Divergencies*, written a decade before Lenin's attack upon Mikhailovsky. The group's 1884 program was avowedly anticapitalist; it demanded "agitation for a democratic constitution," including equality in the right to vote and to be elected, salaries for people's representatives so that the poor might qualify, "the inviolability of the person and home of the citizen," "unlimited freedom of conscience, speech, press, assembly, and association," "freedom of migration and occupation," and the "replacement of the standing army by a general arming of the people."[18] Plekhanov's group not only wrote off the peasantry as an instrument of revolution, but also considered the Russian middle class too weak to take the initiative in combatting absolutism. It held, instead, that "the socialist intelligentsia must stand at the head of the contemporary liberation movement." In this respect, at least, it can be regarded as a forerunner of the Leninist program.

Nevertheless, it is not easy to determine the actual date of the founding of the Bolshevik Party. Grigorii Zinoviev, in his lectures on Party history, discussed a series of events, each of which he felt could in some sense be regarded as signaling the "founding" of the Party. While ruling out the Northern Union of Russian Workers of 1878, he termed the Emancipation of Labor as the "first Marxist organization." Yet, fifteen years were to elapse between the founding of the Emancipation of Labor and the First Congress of the Party in March, 1898, and even this meeting produced no concrete results. Measured in terms of its consequences, the Second Congress, which met in August, 1903, might be considered the "founding" conference of the Party; its significance is unquestionable because from it emerged the Bolshevik-Menshevik schism which was to plague the Party for nearly two decades. Yet, Zinoviev also conceded that it might be more proper to assign the title of "first" to the Third Congress of April, 1905, as the first exclusively Bolshevik conclave at which no Mensheviks were present. At the same time, he noted that—while the Prague Conference of January, 1912, provided the "complete break" with the Mensheviks—it was not until the April, 1917, Party Conference that Lenin categorically refused to unite with the Mensheviks. Finally, the Party can, in a sense, be said to date from the Seventh Congress in March, 1918, when it abandoned the Social Democratic label and renamed itself the All-Russian Communist Party (of Bolsheviks).[19]

The difficulty in dating the Party's beginning attests to the fact that the Bolsheviks constituted merely one current in the total stream of Russian revolutionary politics. If, in the end, the Bolshevik wing of the Russian Social Democratic Labor Party constituted itself as a separate party and came to dominate the entire revolutionary movement, it was due both to unusual circumstances and to the unique form of leadership exercised by Lenin.

As the son of a deceased nobleman-bureaucrat and the brother of an executed would-be assassin of the Czar, Lenin found himself in a somewhat awkward position at the University of Kazan in the autumn of 1887. It was a short-lived one, however; within three months after entering the university, he was arrested and expelled from that institution for having participated in a student protest. This led to his being placed on police probation and restricted to a family landholding at Kokushkino, forty versts from Kazan, until the autumn of 1888.

After being denied permission to go abroad, ostensibly for study, in September, 1888, Lenin settled in Kazan. It was here, during the winter of 1888-89—so maintains his sister, Anna Ilyinichna—that Lenin first imbibed the heady wine of Marxism, although he was obviously still under the influence then of the Populist tradition and could not be regarded as a pure

Marxist. Leaving Kazan in 1889, Lenin played the part of a country squire on á 225-acre holding at Alakaevka (fifty versts from Samara), which his mother had acquired for him by selling the family home in Simbirsk.[20] As a landowner and "exploiter of peasants," Lenin wanted to resume his education at the age of twenty. When his mother obtained the right for him to take the examinations in jurisprudence in the summer of 1890, he set about preparing for them and completed four years' work in little more than a year. He received his diploma and began to practice law in Samara in January, 1892. It was probably during this brief period in Samara—from January, 1892, until the autumn of 1893, when he moved to St. Petersburg—that the conviction regarding the inevitability of both the rise of capitalism in Russia and its overthrow began to take hold of Lenin's mind, and the break with the Populists became complete.

While in St. Petersburg, Lenin devoted much of his time during 1894 to participating in Marxist study groups in the capital and particularly to combatting the anticapitalist and exclusively peasant-oriented views of the Populists. It was during this period that he wrote his famous work *What Are the "Friends of the People"?*, in which he boldly attacked the influential Populist N. K. Mikhailovsky, twenty-eight years his senior. Later that year, he attacked Peter B. Struve's *Critical Notes on the Economic Development of Russia* for not going far enough; while Struve agreed with Lenin in his opposition to the Populists and his recognition that capitalism was inevitable and highly desirable in Russia, he did not share Lenin's conclusion that revolution was also inevitable.

This was the brief period of so-called "Legal Marxism," which first manifested itself between 1893 and 1895. Its principal proponents, in addition to Struve, were the prominent Ukrainian economist Michael Ivanovich Tugan-Baranovsky and, for a time, even Nicolas Berdyaev, who was to acquire great fame as a philosopher and as one of the most astute interpreters of Russia to the West. Legal Marxism, which included Lenin and Plekhanov among its practitioners, involved the use of Aesopian language in the propagation of Marxist views in order to facilitate passage by the censors. The movement reached its height in the period from 1895 to 1897; its publications dealt primarily with "scholarly" analyses of Russian economic development, the philosophy of history, and political thought. It was during this period that Plekhanov, under the pseudonym of N. Beltov, legally published (in 1895) his *On the Problem of the Development of a Monistic View of History*, a plea for historical materialism. Lenin, in Siberian exile from 1897 to 1899, participated in Legal Marxism by publishing articles on economics under the pseudonyms of Ilyin and Tulin.

Lenin's arrest in December, 1895, resulted from his Marxist activities in the capital and from his visit to Europe during the spring and summer of 1895. He had been refused permission by the government to go abroad on two previous occasions—in September, 1888, and October, 1891. It was only on the third try—in April, 1895, following a bout with pneumonia (sometime during which, legend has it, he was wrestling with the third volume of Marx's *Capital*)—that he received permission. Lenin quickly departed for Switzerland, where he contacted Plekhanov, Axelrod, and Vera Zasulich of the Emancipation of Labor group; he discussed with them future activities and the problem of smuggling illicit political literature into Russia. After visiting Paris and Berlin, he returned to Russia in September, 1895, a marked man in the eyes of the Czarist police authorities.

Lenin's arrest resulted also from his activities in St. Petersburg in what was to become the Union for the Struggle for the Emancipation of the Working Class, a small group of Marxist intellectuals who prepared propaganda leaflets for distribution among the workers in the capital. Lenin's wife, Nadezhda Konstantinovna Krupskaya, later recalled her husband's talents as a conspirator—talents which had manifested themselves as early as 1894: "Of our entire [Marxist] group, Vladimir Ilyich was best prepared in the field of conspiracy: he knew his way about, was able to dupe spies superbly, taught us how to write with chemicals in books, how to write in code, how to employ signs, [and] invented all sorts of pseudonyms."[21] Upon being arrested in spite of all this proficiency in conspiratorial activities, Lenin immediately set about planning the single scholarly piece of writing among his great flood of polemics—*The Development of Capitalism in Russia*. He began actual work on this weighty volume in June, 1896, while still in prison, and completed it during his period of Siberian exile. In January, 1897, Lenin received a sentence of three years to be served in Shushenskoe village in Minusinsk county of Yeniseisk province. It was a unique feature of Czarist prison and exile—not duplicated by their Soviet counterparts—that revolutionaries could carry on research and that during exile they actually received, to use Krupskaya's term, a "salary" from the government. In Lenin's case, this amounted to eight uninflated rubles per month, with which he easily financed his food, lodging, and incidentals.

The work of establishing provincial counterparts of the Petersburg Union for the Emancipation continued in 1896, but it also put Krupskaya in jail temporarily in August of that year. This subsequently enabled her to join Lenin in exile and to become his wife in order to avoid being exiled alone to Ufa. Despite serious setbacks—particularly the arrest of Lenin and the future Menshevik L. Martov—an effort was made, in March, 1898, to unite these pitifully small groups into a Russian Social Democratic Labor Party. On March 1-3 (13-15),* 1898, what is regarded by Soviet historians as the First Congress of the Party met in Minsk. Represented at the Congress were four local unions—those of St. Petersburg, Moscow, Kiev, and Yekaterinoslav—the Jewish Social Democratic Bund, founded in September, 1897, in Vilna and representing the Jewish Pale of Settlement in the western part of the Empire; and the Kiev newspaper *Rabochaya gazeta* ("The Workers' Paper"). The Minsk Congress formed a "party" in which each nationality was promised the right to self-determination. All local organizations of the Party were granted a large measure of autonomy and were permitted to implement the decisions of the Central Committee in a manner best suited to local conditions; they could even refuse to carry out a decision by the Central Committee

---

* There was a difference of twelve days between the Julian and Gregorian calendars in the nineteenth century, and a difference of thirteen days in the twentieth century.

if they could explain convincingly the reason for doing so. Clearly, Lenin's touch was not in evidence, as the Second Congress in 1903 was to show by way of contrast. The Union of Russian Social Democrats Abroad was declared to be a part of the new Party, and *Rabochaya gazeta,* which had published only two issues in 1897, was designated as the Party's official organ. The first Central Committee, elected by the Congress, was composed of Boris L'vovich Eidelman (*Rabochaya gazeta*), Aron Iosifovich Kremer (the Bund), and Stepan I. Radchenko (representing himself and the other three members of the St. Petersburg union); it was empowered with the authority to add new members to its ranks.[22] Peter B. Struve, a Legal Marxist, wrote the manifesto of the Congress, although he was not a delegate and had remained in St. Petersburg following a trip abroad during which he saw Plekhanov and Axelrod and collaborated on their journal, *Rabotnik.* Struve's manifesto called for the overthrow of autocracy and for a social order not based on the exploitation of man by man.

The nine delegates went home from Minsk, and the organization was hit by a wave of arrests; all the delegates except Radchenko were jailed, and nothing remained of the deliberations of the First Congress. The solitude of exile and an unwillingness to become involved in quarrels within the small community of exiles enabled Lenin to turn his thoughts to the kind of Party organization which he came to regard as necessary. Lenin revealed his preoccupation with the idea of a so-called "proletarian party" at the end of 1897 in a pamphlet entitled *The Tasks of Russian Social Democrats,* which was published in Geneva during the following year with a foreword by Axelrod. He also expressed here his dissatisfaction with and distrust of the Russian intelligentsia:

> Who does not know how easily there is accomplished in Holy Russia the transformation of the radical intellectual and socialist intellectual into a functionary of the imperial government—a functionary consoling himself with the "good" which he brings within the bounds of office routine— a functionary who by this "good" justifies his political indifference, his servility before the government of the knout

and whip? Only the *proletariat* [Lenin's italics] is unconditionally inimical to absolutism and to Russian officialdom,
only the proletariat has no *ties* linking it to these organs of
nobiliary-bourgeois society, only the proletariat is capable
of an irreconcilable enmity and decisive struggle against
them.[23]

Yet, ironically, the noble Lenin himself was far removed from
the proletariat whose virtues he had begun to extol. Nor were
other spokesmen for this new movement any closer to the industrial worker: Plekhanov was the son of a landowner; Felix
Dzierzynski, who was to establish Lenin's secret police, was the
son of a "petty landowner"; Elena Stasova, who joined the
Party in 1898 and was to serve in the Secretariat and Comintern
and even survive Stalin's death, was the daughter of a civil
servant and lawyer; Alexandra Mikhailovna Kollontai, who was
to lead the Workers' Opposition within the Party, was the daughter of a Czarist general.

Nevertheless, Lenin's convictions regarding the proletariat
were reinforced by the advent of "Economism" in the late
1890's—the Russian heretical equivalent of Bernsteinian "revisionism" which denied the need for carrying on a political
struggle and rejected the idea of the political hegemony of the
proletariat. Economism became the first of the numerous great
deviations in Russian Marxism-Leninism. Events were contrib-
uting to its popularity, since workers were succeeding in improving their wages and working conditions by means of strikes and
purely economic weapons. The Economists actually took over
the newspaper *Rabochaya mysl'* ("Workers' Thought") in
St. Petersburg, and in quiet Geneva, the center of Russian
émigré politics, they published *Rabocheye delo* ("The Workers'
Cause"). The Geneva newspaper did not deny the need for
political struggle and actually criticized Bernsteinian revisionism;
it advocated economic struggle on the grounds that this would
lead to political struggle. The Petersburg newspaper was also
the official organ of Lenin's Union for the Struggle for the Emancipation of the Working Class during his exile. Both Lenin and
Plekhanov—the former from Siberia, the latter from Geneva—
gave battle to the popular doctrine of Economism, which was

eventually embraced by the majority of Russian Social Democratic organizations.[24]

The Economists emphasized the determinist side of Marxism and argued for goals which were possible within the existing conditions of autocratic Russia. Lenin, on the other hand, stressed voluntarism, urging political action instead of passive reliance upon economic processes. Ironically, it was Lenin's own work, *The Development of Capitalism in Russia* (published legally in March, 1899, under the pseudonym V. Ilyin), which, with its welter of statistics directed primarily against the Populists, provided the Economists with data for certain of their conclusions. Lenin, of course, invoked the Marxist formula regarding the "reserves of unemployed," without which capitalism supposedly cannot exist; nevertheless, the book succeeded in passing the censor. Yet, the importance of his book as a landmark in the development of the discipline of economics in the Russian Empire has been exaggerated somewhat, especially in light of the fact that M. I. Tugan-Baranovsky's classic work, *The Russian Factory, Past and Present*, was published one year earlier.

The indefatigable Lenin wrote a tome of more than 500 pages analyzing the development of capitalism in Russia, although he was convinced at the same time that the subject of his study would disappear. In his *Tasks of Russian Social Democrats*, Lenin had donned the oracle's robes and declared: "One need not be a prophet to predict the inevitability of a crash (more or less sharp) which must follow this 'flourishing' of capitalism . . . [in which factories are growing] like mushrooms after a rain."[25] Lenin accurately described this growth which, between 1890 and 1902, was marked by an increase of 141.5 per cent in the number of factories employing more than 1,000 workers. However, it was precisely this spectacular growth which gave birth to Economism and appeared to provide little basis for Lenin's "reserves of the unemployed" argument.

A statement of the Economist position was somewhat hastily written by Mme. Ekaterina Kuskova, who later became the wife of another Economist, Sergei Nikolaevich Prokopovich. This statement, although not intended for publication, reached Lenin in exile during the summer of 1899. Somehow, en route to Lenin,

the manuscript had been given the title "Credo." Lenin became
so incensed that he immediately drafted a "Protest of Russian
Social Democrats," signed by fifteen of his fellow exiles as well
as by himself and Krupskaya. Mme. Kuskova, without intending to be heretical, had merely observed that it was desirable
to "aid the economic struggle of the proletariat and participate
in liberal-opposition activities." Her so-called "Credo" closed
with the warning that "the political innocence of the Russian
Marxist-intellectual . . . can play a mean trick on them."[26] Lenin
argued in his "Protest" that the Economists were wrong in contending, as Mme. Kuskova had done, that Marxism in the West
was an economic and not a political movement and that labor
had not participated in the struggle for political freedom. He
invoked the critical attitude of the *Communist Manifesto* toward
apolitical socialism and contended that Marxism was a response
to such doctrines as Owenism and Fourierism. He cited the
First Congress of the Russian Social Democratic Labor Party,
held fifteen months earlier. He denounced the authors of the
"Credo" (not knowing that it had but one author) as "opportunists," accusing them of "taking a colossal step backward," and
demanded that Russian Social Democrats "declare war" on
them. The much more tolerant editors of *Rabocheye delo* in
Geneva published both the "Credo" and Lenin's "Protest."

It was during the last year of his exile that Lenin, infuriated
by the course events were taking under the influence of the
heretical Economism, began to formulate the views upon which
he was to base his demands at the fateful Second Congress of
the Party in August, 1903. In an article written in 1899 entitled
"Our Program," Lenin declared that what was needed was
"not the formulation of plans for reforming society, not the
preaching to capitalists and to their hangers-on about improving
the condition of the workers, not the organization of conspiracies,
but the organization of the class struggle of the proletariat and
the *direction of this struggle, the ultimate aim of which is the
conquest of political power by the proletariat and the organization of a socialist society* [Lenin's italics]."[27] This article—not
published until 1925, because the Party organ *Rabochaya gazeta*
had become defunct—reveals Lenin's uncompromising attitude,

the fact that he played only for the highest stake—the seizure of power—and his refusal to settle for anything less. Lenin correctly noted in this article that, as a result of these views, there would descend upon his head a "heap of accusations: they will shout that we wish to transform the socialist party into an order of 'true believers' persecuting 'heretics' for deviating from 'dogma,' for all independent opinions, etc." While declaring that there was "not a drop of truth" in these charges, he recognized, significantly, that his views would elicit such accusations and felt it necessary to reassure his fellow members that he was not an "enemy of all criticism."[28] Lenin also took this occasion to assert that "we do not at all look upon Marx's theory as something complete and inviolable"; rather, he defined it as having "placed only the cornerstones of that science which social- ists *must* move forward in all directions . . ." Giving himself *carte blanche*, Lenin declared: "We believe that an *independent* [Lenin's italics] elaboration of the theory of Marx is necessary for Russian socialists because this theory provides only the general *guiding* [Lenin's italics] theses which are applied in particular to England differently than to France, to France differently than to Germany, to Germany differently than to Russia."[29]

Armed with these revisionist views, Lenin completed his exile in March, 1900, determined—as Krupskaya tells us—to establish an "all-Russian newspaper" which would be the rally- ing point for his new Party organization. Krupskaya had yet another year of exile, but she readily consented to Lenin's leaving her in Ufa so that he might return to Russia proper and push his new plan. He went to Pskov to renew contacts, and Martov visited Poltava; when they arrived in St. Petersburg, they were arrested. Lenin had 2,000 rubles in his vest—a subsidy from "Auntie" Alexandra Mikhailovna Kalmykova, the bookstore owner who was to finance the new venture in political journalism well into 1903. He also carried a list of addresses (written in chemicals) of individuals abroad, but the police did not heat the paper and discover this list; had they done so, it is unlikely that Lenin would have gone to Germany to edit the all-Russian newspaper.[30] Lenin was released after ten days; he returned to Ufa to bid his wife good-by and then left for Europe.

One of Lenin's first tasks was to visit Plekhanov in Switzerland in order to discuss with him the plans for the newspaper. It very quickly became evident to Lenin that collaboration with the *eminence grise* of Russian Marxism would not be an easy task. Two decades of European exile had left their mark on the forty-four-year-old Plekhanov, and he had become distrustful of communications from Russia. Undoubtedly, also, Plekhanov did not relish the challenge which the great plans of the thirty-year-old Lenin might present to his position of leadership. Lenin, for his part, was somewhat disappointed in Plekhanov's having permitted a split between the pro-Economism *émigrés* and Plekhanov's own group, the old Emancipation of Labor. This break occurred in April, 1900, when the majority of the *émigré* Union of Russian Social Democrats, including the newspaper *Rabocheye delo*, adopted a pro-Economist stand and obtained control of the Union. Plekhanov, Axelrod, and their small group of followers established the Russian Revolutionary Organization of Social Democrats.

The new newspaper, as Lenin conceived it, was to have a didactic role: to unite and convert all revolutionary groups by persuading the advocates of terror to abandon their weapon and by purging the Economists of their Economism. Lenin, fresh from Siberian exile and from Russia, wanted to avoid open breaks within the *émigré* ranks. Yet, three years later, at the Second Congress, he was to engineer the greatest break of all— that between the Bolsheviks and the Mensheviks.

The newspaper with which Lenin hoped to ignite all of Russia made its appearance in December, 1900, under the name *Iskra* ("The Spark"). It fought Struve's *Osvobozhdenie* ("Liberation") and the newly formed Russian Socialist Revolutionary Party; its principal task, however, was to lay the groundwork for a new congress which would re-establish the defunct Russian Social Democratic Labor Party along Leninist lines. As a propagator of ideas, *Iskra* was to be distributed by means of a network of agents within Russia organizing local groups which would provide the necessary cadres for the new party.

The editorial board of *Iskra* was divided in terms of age. Plekhanov, Axelrod, and Vera Zasulich constituted the older generation and had been among the founders of the Emancipation of Labor group in Geneva in 1883. Lenin, Martov, and Alexander Nikolaevich Potresov were the younger generation, although they regarded themselves as "old men" compared to the "immature" and "infantile" advocates of Economism. Of the six, Axelrod, the son of a poor Jewish tavern keeper in the Chernigov province, was the only one who could legitimately claim a social background which justified his participation in a proletarian movement. Lenin, Plekhanov, and Zasulich came from the nobility, while Potresov (who was also called Starover) was the son and grandson of army officers. Nor was L. Martov (Julius Osipovich Tsederbaum)* qualified in terms of social background to be a member of this journalistic venture: he was born in Constantinople in 1873, where his father represented a Russian maritime shipping firm until the Russo-Turkish War caused the family to return to Russia; in his memoirs, published in Berlin in 1922 (a year before his death), Martov wrote of the "governesses, nurses, and cooks" who were employed by the family during his childhood.[31] In 1900, when Lenin organized *Iskra* and the journal *Zarya,* Martov was still in Russia, where he had completed three years of exile in the Turukhansk region in Siberia and was organizing local groups in support of Lenin's publishing plans. He did not join the *Iskra* staff in Munich until March, 1901.

In the latter part of August, 1900, Lenin, Axelrod, Potresov, and Zasulich had met with Plekhanov to lay plans for the new publishing venture and to set up the editorial board. In a remarkable memoir, "How the Spark Was Almost Extinguished" —written shortly after the Geneva negotiations, but not published until 1924—Lenin noted that Plekhanov was "suspicious, distrustful, and regards himself as being right to the point of the impossible."[32] At times during the Geneva meetings, Plekhanov would sulk in silence for hours; according to Lenin,

---

* The frequent use of pseudonyms—a result of the Party's conspiratorial nature—makes necessary their inclusion in this survey. In the case of persons who acquired prominence under assumed names, the original family name is usually given in parentheses; in other instances, the Party name is given in parentheses.

the whole atmosphere would change during his absence. The "old man" (*starik*) was opposed to Lenin's conciliationist tactics with Struve and to the idea of opening the pages of the new publications to the Economists and doing battle with them there; he manifested a great intolerance toward the Jewish Bund, holding that the latter was not a Social Democratic organization. In an effort to end a growing impasse within the group, Lenin, Potresov, Zasulich, and Axelrod went to Plekhanov's country home. When he declared that, as a result of the differences which had arisen, he would be simply a collaborator and not a member of the editorial board, they all objected. Then Plekhanov raised the problem of six votes being an "inconvenient" number. Zasulich, always more emotional than practical, proposed that Plekhanov have two votes in questions of tactics. All appeared to agree, but Lenin noted that "G. V. [i.e., Plekhanov] takes the reins and in the tone of the editor commences to assign departments and articles . . . a tone not permitting objections." Lenin was bitter and realized that his relations with his old teacher had reached a turning point. He and Potresov concluded that Plekhanov's offer to withdraw from the editorial board and merely collaborate had been "a simple trap, a calculated chess move, a snare," and that, in order to avoid "frightful delays" caused by Plekhanov, Germany and not Switzerland would have to be the place of publication.[33]

The suspicious Plekhanov, for his part, regarded Lenin and Potresov as careerists. Lenin reciprocated by making the "discovery" that Plekhanov was a "bad person . . . because in him [there] are strong motives of personal, petty self-esteem and vanity . . . an insincere person." Lenin, "greatly indignant" following his "infatuation" with Plekhanov and refusing to be one of the "pawns in the hands of this person . . . who does not permit and does not understand comradely relations," noted that henceforth it would be "necessary to regard all persons 'without sentiment,' to keep a stone behind one's back."[34] Some compromise obviously had to be found if *The Spark* was not to be extinguished. A final meeting was arranged, and prior to the meeting Lenin and Potresov wired to Germany that preparations should be made for publication there. Plekhanov—after employing, in Lenin's words, ineffective "threats" followed by no more effective "blandishments"—agreed that the editors should publish jointly a symposium, and that this was to prepare the ground for future collaboration on the newspaper and journal. Differences remained in the final meeting when Plekhanov declared that fundamental questions could not be put to a vote of the editors. Lenin confined himself to noting that it was necessary to permit polemical writings and that "the delineation of fundamental and particular questions will not always be easy." Lenin left Geneva convinced that Plekhanov would issue ultimatums and that his "disorganizing qualities" would assert themselves. However, the profound differences between the would-be editors were kept secret: "We decided to preserve appearances, so as not to permit enemies to feel victorious." On the surface, it was to appear that all was well and that the machine was functioning smoothly, but—as Lenin noted— "inside, a certain string broke, and in place of beautiful personal relations, there set in dry, business-like relations with constant calculation, according to the formula *Si vis pacem, para bellum* [if you wish peace, prepare for war]."[35] On the train from Geneva to Munich, Lenin drew up a plan under which he, Potresov, and Martov would be the editors, and Plekhanov and Axelrod would merely be collaborators. Plekhanov could divert himself with the publication of the theoretical journal *Zarya* ("The Dawn"), but the newspaper would be Lenin's.

The two older men remained in Switzerland and continued their efforts to have *Iskra* published in that country. Lenin was joined in Munich by Potresov, Martov, and Zasulich. The irregular little newspaper was printed in Leipzig, in Munich, and finally in Stuttgart on the presses of the German Social Democrats, many of whom Lenin was later to denounce and vilify as "opportunists" when they remained loyal to their country in World War I. Thus Plekhanov could exercise his influence only through correspondence. When Krupskaya joined Lenin in Munich in March, 1901, following the expiration of her exile, they obtained a Bulgarian passport, changing their name from Meyer (under which he had been living) to Jordanov. Krupskaya became the secretary of *Iskra* and provided Lenin with

strategic control over all communication between the newspaper
and its agents in Russia.

Iskra, with its motto "From the spark the flame will spring"
(taken from the reply of the Decembrists to Pushkin), was to
spearhead the drive for a new congress to reconstitute the Party
in 1903. In the period between the newspaper's founding in
1900 and the Second Congress in 1903, during which forty-five
issues were published, Lenin made maximum use of his position
on the editorial board in further developing and propagating
his views on how the Party should be organized. In an article
entitled "Where to Begin?" published in the fourth issue of
Iskra in May, 1901, Lenin described the newspaper as a "collective organizer" as well as a "collective agitator" and called
for a carefully drawn long-range plan for laying siege to the
enemy fortress. He counseled constant readiness to support every
protest and outbreak, "utilizing them to increase and strengthen
the armed forces available for the decisive battle."[36] Lenin took
issue with those who were "captivated by terror . . . as the principal and basic means of struggle" and declared: "In principle,
we have never renounced and cannot renounce terror. It is one
of the military operations which can be entirely suitable and even
necessary in a certain moment of battle, given a certain status
of the troops and under certain conditions." He warned that
terror could not be viewed as a "means of solitary attack independent of any army," but, rather, should be regarded as "one
of the operations of an active army closely related to and con-
forming with the whole system of struggle."[37]

The most important and fully developed exposition of Lenin's
views as they emerged prior to the Second Congress is found in
his work *What Is to Be Done?,* published in 1902. This pamphlet contains the usual denunciation of Bernsteinian revisionism
and of Economism—in which Lenin relegates to the "swamp"
those who disagree with him—but its primary importance derives
from the notion of revolution as a "profession" to which one's
whole life and not merely a "free evening" or two is to be
devoted. These professionals are to receive "training in the art
of struggling against the political police."[38] The narrower such
an organization of professionals, the more difficult it will be for

the police in an autocracy to draw it out. Since the end of his Siberian exile, Lenin had been combating what he termed *kustarnichestvo* (domestic handicrafts) in the movement. This term, used to refer to any inefficiently organized work, expressed his opposition to the system of primitive, loosely organized, or improperly coordinated local Social Democratic committees. Such groups could easily fall prey to deviationist tendencies, and, Lenin noted, "what at first sight appears to be an unimportant mistake may give rise to deplorable consequences, and only the shortsighted would consider factional disputes and a strict distinction of shades to be inopportune and superfluous."[39]

The campaign against Economism had to be intensive because, according to Lenin, in concentrating on improving the workers' lot by means of strikes, trade unions, picketing, cooperatives, and child-labor laws, Economism would inevitably lead to neglect of the political struggle—and revolution would degenerate into mere "social reform." The economic struggle did not interest Lenin, who declared that the "Social Democrat's ideal should not be a trade-union secretary, but a *tribune of the people* . . . able to take advantage of every petty event in order to explain his Socialistic convictions and his Social Democratic demands *to all* [Lenin's italics] . . ."[40] This emphasis on propaganda and agitation among *all* strata of the population contrasted sharply with the abstract Marxist preoccupation with the industrial proletariat: it symptomized the dependence of the Social Democratic movement upon the intelligentsia, as well as Lenin's apparent conviction that the industrial workers, if left to their own devices, would take the line of least resistance and prefer a wage increase to the political struggle. Hence Lenin's accusation against the Economists for their "bowing before spontaneity [*preklonenie pred stikhiinostyu*]," and his own advocacy of the "vanguard" thesis which required the Party to adopt an "activist" course on the basis of an "organized, many-sided political struggle" and not merely to rely passively on the tide of events. The Social Democratic organization, according to Lenin, must be composed of "professional revolutionaries"; all distinctions between workers and intellectuals would be wiped out, and the Party was to be a narrow one, with a limited membership, and "as conspiratorial as possible."[41] "Broad democratism" in the organization, as advocated by the Economists, was termed by Lenin "*an empty and harmful plaything*" and contrary to the basic tenets of any revolutionary organization.

Concluding this basic—if somewhat verbose—work, Lenin divided the development of Marxism in Russia (and among the *émigrés* in Western Europe) into three periods: the "emergence and strengthening" of the theory (1884-94); the period of "childhood and adolescence" (1894-98), in which certain successes were registered, the line dividing the Social Democrats from the followers of *Narodnaya volya* became very clear, and the genuine revolutionary had to consider "breaking with persons" who wished to remain faithful to the "heroic tradition" of the terrorists; and the time since 1898 (during which he wrote this work), characterized by Lenin as one of "dispersion, disintegration, tottering." He singled out for attack Struve, Prokopovich, and Berdyaev—as well as Alexander S. Martynov (Pikker), one of the editors of the Economist *Rabocheye delo,* who flirted with Menshevism following the Second Congress, but joined the Bolsheviks in 1923 and spent the last ten years of his life in the service of the Comintern. Lenin's answer to the question posed by his title was simple: "Liquidate the third period." He predicted a fourth period which would lead to the "strengthening of militant Marxism" and to the replacement of the "rear guard of opportunists" by the "genuine vanguard of the most revolutionary class."[42]

It is significant that on the title page of his most important work on the Party, Lenin should have quoted from Ferdinand Lassalle's letter to Marx of June 24, 1852: "Party struggles give to the Party strength and vitality. A great sign of weakness in a party is its diffuseness and the blurring of sharply defined boundaries. A party becomes stronger by purging itself." Indeed, this was the text upon which *What Is to Be Done?* was based, and it presaged both Lenin's and Stalin's preoccupation with the excommunication of Marxist heretics.

Soon after the completion of *What Is to Be Done?* in February, 1902, it became clear that the continued publication of *Iskra* in Germany involved too great a risk. The German police, aided by agents of the Czarist *Okhrana,* had picked up Lenin's trail, and a move became imperative. Plekhanov and Axelrod again advocated moving to Switzerland, but the majority favored England, so *Iskra*'s base of operations was transferred to London in April, 1902, remaining there for exactly one year.

Lenin spent half his time in the British Museum. Life was good in England: one's documents were not examined, and Lenin and Krupskaya, using the name Richter, were able to convince their landlady that they were Germans. During the summer of 1902, Lenin settled his differences with Plekhanov on the Russian agrarian problem. Relations between them had reached the point of severance in mid-May. As a result, *Iskra* had almost gone out of existence at that time, and it was only because of the intercession of the other members of the editorial board that the conflict was resolved. Lenin had written an article on "The Agrarian Program of Russian Social Democracy" and had expressed himself willing to incorporate suggestions offered by the other editors before publishing the article in *Iskra*. But Plekhanov had raised a number of objections which Lenin considered personal, and this had precipitated the crisis. In all likelihood, Plekhanov was motivated primarily by resentment over his unimportant role in the publication of *Iskra*. Earlier in 1902, in an exchange which lasted from January until April, Lenin had severely criticized two drafts of a program prepared by Plekhanov—to the extent of judging Plekhanov's second draft to be a "program *for pupils*" in the first class, a "textbook" commentary on capitalism in general rather than the "program of a fighting party in practice."[43] The memory of this earlier exchange had not helped matters.

Lenin's controversies with Plekhanov, as well as several trips to the Continent, made the year in England pass rapidly. In June and July of 1902, he spent several weeks at the shore in Brittany with his mother and his sister, Anna Ilyinichna Yelizarova. In October, Trotsky arrived in London after escaping from Siberian exile, and Lenin was pleased when the young revolutionary declared himself to be an "ardent *Iskra*-ite." In February and March of 1903, Lenin lectured to Russian *émigrés* in Paris. At this time, he also proposed that Trotsky be appointed to the editorial board of *Iskra*. Plekhanov, who could not stomach the young man (Trotsky was seven years younger than Lenin), categorically rejected the proposal. On the eve of the Party's Second Congress in the summer of 1903, when Plekhanov rejected Trotsky's candidacy a second time, Lenin was angered that "no one has sufficient courage to take exception with Plekhanov."[44]

At the time of Plekhanov's first veto, the Emancipation of Labor group again proposed that the publication of *Iskra* be transferred to Geneva. With only Lenin voting against the proposal, the transfer was effected in April, 1903. Significantly, as the time for the journey aproached, Lenin—according to Krupskaya's account—fell ill with a nervous ailment which included a body rash. We also know from the same source that Lenin's extreme nervousness manifested itself again during the Second Congress, which met from July 30 to August 23. While the Congress was convening in Brussels, Lenin could not eat his breakfast—much to the Belgian landlady's displeasure—and when it reconvened in London, he "reached the point where he absolutely ceased to sleep and was terribly agitated."[45] There was good reason for Lenin's disturbed state: the Second Congress represented to him a great turning point which would determine whether or not Russian Social Democracy would follow him or consign itself to the swamp to which he relegated those who disagreed with him.

The Second Congress came much closer to being the Party's constituent congress than did the first conference of nine delegates at Minsk in 1898. It consisted of thirty-seven sessions, many of them stormy ones. After holding fifteen sessions in a Brussels warehouse, the delegates were so harassed by Belgian police and detectives, as well as by fleas, that temporary adjournment became necessary. Reassembled in London, the delegates resumed their deliberations in a church hall free from interference by the police. There were forty-three voting delegates, as well as fourteen who had a "consultative vote" and could only participate in discussions. Lenin's successor, then obscure, did not attend: J. V. Stalin was in a Czarist prison in his native Georgia at the time.

The preparatory work for the Congress, including the drafting of a program, was undertaken by the *Iskra* editorial board. The Congress adopted maximum and minimum programs; the former provided for the dictatorship of the proletariat and the establishment of a socialist order; the latter called for a democratic republic, an eight-hour working day, and the liquidation of the last remnants of serfdom. In dealing with the agrarian question, the Party demanded for the peasants only the plots of land (*otrezki*) they had lost as a result of the 1861 Emancipation. It was not until the Third Congress in 1905 that, as a result of Lenin's prodding, the demand was made that all land be given to the peasants. Significantly, the adoption of the 1903 program did not stir undue controversy, because both the future Bolsheviks and Mensheviks accepted the idea of the dictatorship of the proletariat. Only one delegate, Akimov (Vladimir Petrovich Makhnovets), of the Economist newspaper *Rabocheye delo,* voted against it. Plekhanov accused Akimov of attempting to drive a wedge between him and Lenin, and he made an ironic, if incorrect, prophecy. The "father of Russian Marxism" noted that Napoleon had a "passion for separating his marshals from their wives" and that "some marshals deferred to him even though they loved their wives. Comrade Akimov," declared Plekhanov, "is in this respect similar to Napoleon—he wishes at any cost to divorce me from Lenin. But I shall manifest more character than Napoleon's marshals; I shall not be divorced from Lenin and trust that he does not intend to be divorced from me."[46] Krupskaya tells us that Lenin responded by shaking his head and smiling.

Yet, despite this banter, there was to be a divorce, and it was to have its beginnings in the conflict over the Party's Statutes. While there was general agreement on the long-range aims of the Social Democratic Party as incorporated in the program, the controversy over the Statutes reflected different views regarding organization and methods. Lenin—in keeping with the position he had outlined in *What Is to Be Done?*—proposed for the first paragraph of the Statutes a definition of membership which embraced "everyone who accepts the Party's program and supports the Party with material means as well as

by personal participation in one of the Party's organizations."
Lenin lost when his formula of "personal participation" was
rejected and that of Martov, providing for "regular personal
cooperation [*sodeistvie*] under the direction of one of the Party's
organizations,"[47] was adopted. Lenin argued that Martov's
imprecise formulation would admit every striker to membership
in the Party, though all strikers could no more be characterized
as revolutionaries than could all members of a cooperative or
trade union. To admit such elements under Martov's elastic
definition would lead to "dispersion, tottering, and opportunism"
—to settling for mere reform and seeking agreement with the
bourgeoisie. Axelrod, on the other hand, wished to broaden the
Party's membership to include such bourgeois intellectuals as
professors, students, and writers, who would accept the Party
program and contribute money without binding themselves
entirely to the organization. Lenin was not opposed to the Party's
making use of such persons, but they could not, in his opinion,
be admitted as members until they divested themselves of their
fears of discipline and permanent obligation.

When Trotsky (whose vigorous support of Lenin had earned
him the title "Lenin's cudgel") observed that the Party was not
a conspiratorial organization, Lenin took objection and contended that Trotsky had "incorrectly understood the principal
thought" of *What Is to Be Done?* Lenin restated his position
and noted that he was proposing "a whole series of various
types of organizations, beginning with the most conspiratorial
and narrow and ending with the relatively broad and 'free' . . ."
He charged Trotsky with having forgotten that the "Party must
be only the vanguard, the leader of the great mass of the working
class which entirely (or almost entirely) works 'under the control and guidance' of Party organizations, but which does not
and must not in its entirety enter the Party."[48] Lenin contended
that he had to oppose Martov's formulation because "it is better
that ten workers not call themselves Party members (genuine
workers do not seek rank!) than for one chatterbox to have
the right or possibility to become a Party member."[49] He declared that "every member of the Party is responsible for the
Party and *the Party is responsible for every member*" and called

for the guarding of the "firmness, steadfastness, and purity of our Party."

Yet, when the vote was taken on Paragraph One of the Statutes, it was Martov's formulation that was adopted by a count of twenty-eight to twenty-two.* Essential to Martov's victory was the support of the vacillating center group of four delegates with six votes, the group referred to by Lenin as the "swamp" (*boloto*). Although Lenin's rejected membership scheme did not gain acceptance until the Bolshevik-dominated Third Congress in 1905, he did register a victory of sorts at the Second Congress when his organizational views were adopted in large part. The Congress provided for two coequal Party centers: the Central Committee (Ts.K.) and the Central Organ (Ts.O.). The former was to unite and direct Party activities and confirm local committees, while the latter was to provide ideological leadership. Lenin regarded the Central Organ, *Iskra*, as having greater importance since it functioned abroad, beyond the reach of the Russian police, while much of the Central Committee membership operated within Russia. A third body, the Council (*Soviet*), was established with five members; two were to represent the Central Committee, two the Party's newspaper, and the fifth (Plekhanov) was to be elected by the Congress. The Council was to "conciliate and unite the activities of the Central Committee and of the editorial board of the Central Organ and represent the Party in relations with other parties." In the event that all the members of either body were arrested, the Council could co-opt by unanimous vote a new Central Committee or a new board of editors for *Iskra*. No member could serve on both the Central Committee and the *Iskra* editorial board.

Lenin's centralist views triumphed in Paragraph Nine of the 1903 Statutes which not only provided for confirmation by the Central Committee of all Party organizations other than those elected or confirmed by the Congress, but also declared that "all decisions of the Central Committee are obligatory for

---

* Nine delegates, among them Lenin and Martov, had mandates entitling them to cast two votes. This explains the fact that the number of votes cast exceeded the number of delegates at the Congress.

all Party organizations which are also required to provide means for the central Party treasury as designated by the Central Committee."[50] Lenin was also successful in having *Iskra* recognized as the Party's Central Organ and in having the number of editors reduced from six to three, with Zasulich, Potresov, and Axelrod as the ousted victims. Lenin and Plekhanov were to represent the "majority" of the Congress (the Bolsheviks), and Martov was to represent the "minority" (the Menshevik group formed as a result of the debate on the organizational question). Martov's views regarding the rights of local Party groups or circles had been rejected by the Congress as a result of the victory of Lenin's Bolsheviks on the issue of centralism and the complete subservience of local Party bodies.

At the time of the Second Congress, none of the delegates in London thought that the disagreements between the Bolsheviks and the Mensheviks were more than temporary. Plekhanov, who was shortly to become a fellow traveler of the Mensheviks, had voted with Lenin on the vital issues of the Bund, the definition of membership, and organizational centralism. He believed that Lenin's narrow formulation of membership would make it more easy to combat opportunists and would deter only the intellectuals ("imbued throughout with bourgeois individualism"[51]) from joining, since workers would not fear the Party's discipline.

The fact that Lenin obtained a majority in support of his ultracentralist views on Party organization was due to pure but immensely significant accident. His minority won out at the Second Congress only because five Bundists—representatives of the Jewish Workers' Union (Bund) of Poland, Lithuania, and Russia—and two Economists (Martynov and Akimov), who were supporters of *Rabocheye delo*, walked out of the Congress and thus weakened the opposition to Lenin's views. With the anti-Leninist group, headed by Martov, reduced from twenty-seven to twenty votes, Lenin's group now became the "majority" with 24 votes.[52] The issue of the Jewish Bund's status within the Party found Lenin and Plekhanov in agreement when it was taken up by the Congress on August 2 in Brussels. The Bund, at its Fourth Congress in April, 1901, had decided in favor of a federalist relationship with the Russian Social Democratic Labor Party (RSDLP) and instructed its Central Committee to abandon the autonomous status agreed upon at the Minsk Congress in 1898. Lenin and Plekhanov objected in the name of the "international solidarity of the working class," and Plekhanov declared that the good of the revolution was the supreme law: national particularities were not to hinder Party unity. Lenin asserted that "federalism is harmful because it legitimizes singularity and aloofness, elevates them to a principle, to a law"; he urged that the "complete estrangement actually existing among us" must not be covered with a "fig leaf" but must be resolutely opposed in the name of the "most intimate unity."[53] Lenin's insistence upon unmitigated centralism and his categorical opposition to federalism within the Party were related to his view that deviation in minor matters would lead ultimately to complete rejection of Marxist (Bolshevik) orthodoxy. Organizational opportunism could only invite total opportunism.

Lenin's all-or-none approach, his unwillingness to compromise, added to the general tension at the Congress in its final stages. Krupskaya has recounted how the "clouds began to gather" as the election of the three-man Central Committee and the editorial board of *Iskra* approached. The delegates could not forget the charges made by the Bund's representatives and by the Economists regarding a "desire to command" and to impose from abroad directives upon the Party in Russia. As the Congress neared adjournment, the evident fear was not that Zasulich, Axelrod, Martov, and Potresov wished to command, but that Plekhanov and Lenin would rule the Party. The rancor and the differences which had marked the debates convinced Lenin that it would be necessary to rid the *Iskra* editorial board of Zasulich, Potresov, and Axelrod. Finally, Lenin, Plekhanov, and Martov (representing the minority) were elected to the new board. During the debate on August 20, prior to the vote, Zasulich, Martov, and Trotsky interrupted Lenin with cries of "It is not true" when he denied Martov's assertion that the vote would leave a blot on his political reputation. Lenin asked that the secretaries note in the minutes the number of times he was interrupted.[54] When Martov made it clear that he would not participate on the new editorial board, the Congress authorized Lenin and Plekhanov, who appeared to be working hand in hand, to seek a third member.

The election of the Central Committee was marked by tension, noise, and disorder. It resulted in another victory for Lenin's majority. Elected were Gleb M. Krzhizhanovsky (Kler), Fridrikh Vil'gel'movich Lengnik (Kurts), and V. A. Noskov (Glebov). Two of these, Krzhizhanovsky and Lengnik, had been associated with Lenin in the St. Petersburg Union for the Struggle for the Emancipation of the Working Class. Although in Siberian exile at the time of the Second Congress, they were elected in absentia as loyal *Iskra*-ites. Krzhizhanovsky, who had signed Lenin's "Protest" against Mme. Kuskova's "Credo" while in exile in 1899, later served as Chairman of the Supreme Council of National Economy in the twenties, and in the thirties was Chairman of the Committee on Higher Education and a Vice-President of the U.S.S.R. Academy of Sciences.* Noskov, who had only a consultative vote at the Second Congress, was a less fortunate choice from Lenin's point of view: he broke with the Bolsheviks in 1904, and committed suicide in 1913.

The election of a "noncontroversial" Central Committee— two members of which were not even at the Congress—did not bridge the Bolshevik-Menshevik split. Martov accused Lenin of intending to use the new three-man editorial board as a wedge for gaining influence over the Central Committee in Russia. Other offended delegates charged him with placing the Party in a "state of siege" (*osadnoye polozhenie*) and with enacting "exclusive [*isklyuchitel'nye*] laws against individual persons and groups." Lenin responded by declaring that "in relation to unstable and faltering elements, we not only may, but we are obligated to establish a 'state of siege,' and the whole of our Party Statutes and all of our centralism approved henceforward

---

* Krzhizhanovsky, one of the longest-lived of the old Bolsheviks, died in March, 1959, at the age of eighty-seven. Having withdrawn into a technical career in electrical engineering, he managed to escape the Stalin purges.

by the Congress is nothing more than a state of siege of the so numerous sources of political diffuseness [*rasplyvchatost'*]."⁵⁵

This attitude, together with Martov's refusal to join the new editorial board, prompted the former editors of *Iskra* to boycott the editorial board shortly after the end of the Second Congress. Lenin, greatly disturbed, wanted to persuade his former collaborators to return to the fold. In a letter to Potresov written on September 13, 1903, he explained his actions at the Second Congress in the following terms:

> I am sifting all the events and impressions of the Congress, and I recognize that I often conducted myself and acted in terrible irritation, "furiously." I am willingly prepared to admit *before anyone* this fault of mine—if what was naturally called forth by the atmosphere, reaction, replies, struggle, etc., can be termed guilt. However, in viewing now, without any rage, the achieved results—what was achieved by means of furious struggle—I absolutely can see nothing whatsoever harmful for the Party and absolutely nothing offensive or insulting to the minority.⁵⁶

Lenin complained to Potresov that the work of the old six-member board had been characterized by "acutely painful, protracted, hopeless fights" and that it was necessary to have a "responsible [*dolzhnostnoe*] institution and not a collegium based on family relations and remissness [*khalatnost'*]." Yet, within a few weeks, it became clear that Lenin had erred in his conviction that the new three-member editorial board would correct the shortcomings which had "*for months* deprived us of efficiency."

In the face of the boycott by Martov and the former editors—as well as by Trotsky—Lenin and Plekhanov had no choice but to publish *Iskra* alone, and they collaborated on six issues (Nos. 46-51). Plekhanov began to discuss a compromise with Martov and his followers, but it was one that was not to Lenin's liking since it would give the dissidents a majority on the editorial board. Lenin foresaw the possibility of the Party Council's falling under the control of Martov; the editorial board of *Iskra* would appoint two of the five members of the Party Council and, with Plekhanov's fifth vote in that body, would be able to appoint new members to the Central Committee in the event of vacancies. Disagreement over this issue led to Lenin's resignation from the editorial board on November 1, 1903. Plekhanov took the matter in stride, issued No. 52 of *Iskra* alone, and, acting as the editorial board, returned Zasulich, Axelrod, Potresov, and Martov to that body by co-optation. Thus *Iskra*, beginning with No. 53, had the same editorial board which had functioned from December, 1900, until the Second Congress—with the notable exception of Lenin.

His alliance with Plekhanov dissolved, Lenin was beside himself with rage. His majority at the Second Congress had been reduced to a minority at the Congress of the League of Russian Social Democracy Abroad, which met in Geneva from October 26 to 31, 1903, and declared itself to be autonomous of the Central Committee and its statutes not subject to confirmation by any other body. Lenin had represented the League at the Second Congress and had obtained for it, in Paragraph Thirteen of the Party Statutes, recognition as the Party's "sole foreign organization." Now, as a result of Plekhanov's desire to please the opposition, Lenin had not only lost control of *Iskra* but was in danger of losing the Central Committee to the Mensheviks. On November 3, he informed Plekhanov of his desire to be appointed to the Central Committee now that he had resigned from the editorial board of *Iskra* and from the Party Council. The co-optation took place on November 25. Lenin was also named foreign representative of the Central Committee, and he rejoined the Party Council—this time as representative of the Central Committee. Following this turn at "musical chairs," the struggle to determine who would control the Party was to continue, and Lenin was to apply in practice what he had told the Congress of the League in October regarding the need for the "rule of the iron rod."[57]

CHAPTER II

THE WIDENING RIFT

An uprising is a fine thing when the progressive elements are rising against the reactionary. When the revolutionary wing rises against the opportunist, that is good. When the opportunist wing rises against the revolutionary, that is bad.

—Lenin, *One Step Forward, Two Steps Back.*

A group of comrades proposed the candidacy of Zemlyachka and myself [at the Third Congress]. I determinedly spoke out against the both of us. I said: "We can be good agents, but we are not suited to be leaders." Ilyich [Lenin] declared in jest to me: "Yes, truly, there is nothing of the general about you, but that is indispensable for a member of the Central Committee."

—M. Lyadov, *Iz zhizni partii v 1903-1907 gg. (vospominaniya).*

The schism between Lenin's Bolsheviks and the Mensheviks, although initially one of degree, could only widen as a result of maneuvers within the Party during the autumn of 1903. The Second Congress had elected a three-member Central Committee. In October, 1903, however, four more members were co-opted to that body, among them Leonid Krasin, who later played a prominent role as a Soviet diplomat in London and Paris and as Commissar of Foreign Trade. And in November, Lenin joined the Central Committee by co-optation following his resignation from the editorial board of *Iskra*; with him came a sixth new member, L. E. Gal'perin. Thus, within three months, the membership of the Central Committee had increased from three to nine. Lenin realized that his victory at the Second Congress had been a Pyrrhic one. He was anxious to consolidate his position and to keep the Central Committee out of Menshevik hands. For these reasons, he pressed the Committee to call a new Party congress. When the Central Committee took up the question in February, 1904, Lenin lost by a five-to-four vote. Two of the original three-member Central Committee—Krzhizhanovsky and Noskov—voted against Lenin, as did Krasin, Dr. F. V. Gusarov (who had joined the Committee in October), and Gal'perin. Lenin was supported only by Lengnik and by the two female members of the Committee, Maria Moiseevna Essen (Zverev) and Zemlyachka (Rozalia Samoilovna Zalkind; also known as Rosa Zalkind and Osipov), the latter voting by proxy.[1]

The position of the majority, which sought a compromise with the Mensheviks, so incensed Lenin that he spent the next three months writing *One Step Forward, Two Steps Back* (published in May, 1904). It was during this period that the schism in the Party reached dangerous dimensions.

Plekhanov had attempted to heal the breach; with this purpose in mind, he had insisted, in October, 1903, that Martov and his followers be reinstated on the editorial board of *Iskra*. Following Lenin's resignation, Plekhanov had published his signed article "What Is Not to Be Done" in the November 7, 1903, issue of *Iskra* (No. 52). The article was an obvious reference to Lenin's *What Is to Be Done?* In it, Plekhanov warned:

> Among us, many have become accustomed to thinking that a Social Democrat must be unyielding if he does not wish to commit the sin of opportunism. However, there are various kinds of unyieldingness [*neustupchivost'*], and there is a kind of unyieldingness which *in its practical results* is equivalent to the most undesirable kind of *compliance*. Unyieldingness toward those who would become our comrades makes us less strong in the struggle against those opponents who will never become our comrades.

At a meeting of the Party Council on January 28, 1904, Plekhanov declared, "I belong neither to the majority nor to the minority," but Lenin noted that no one else in the Council (Lengnik, Martov, and Axelrod) could make such a claim.[2] Further, Lenin said that "the present situation is too abnormal and requires correctives," and Axelrod observed that "we are all in agreement on this."

For Lenin, however, "agreement" meant the convocation of a third congress. He warned: "We are on the eve of a formal schism if the minority continues, without distinguishing between means, to strive to transform itself into a majority."[3] Lenin's success in monopolizing the position of leader and spokesman for the majority of the Party bespoke not only his great skill as a propagandist but also the incredible obtuseness of the Mensheviks. He suffered defeat in the Party Council on January 30, 1904, when he proposed the convening of a third congress; instead, the Council proceeded to approve the work of the new (Menshevik) *Iskra* and to appoint Mensheviks to the Central Committee. On January 31, Lenin addressed a letter to the Central Committee in an effort to win it to his side on the issue of a new Party congress. When, in February, 1904, the Central Committee refused to follow him, he decided to state his case as "majority" spokesman in his *One Step Forward, Two Steps Back*, which was significantly subtitled *The Crisis in Our Party*.

This lengthy diatribe, documenting the turning point in Lenin's attitude toward the Mensheviks, was prompted in no small part by an article which appeared in the January 15, 1904, issue of *Iskra* and was signed by Praktik (practical worker). This was the *nom de plume* of M. S. Makadzyub (Panin), who had been an *Iskra*-ite at the Second Congress and a member of Lenin's majority, but had joined the Mensheviks shortly afterward. Lenin was particularly irritated by the following observation in Praktik's article:

> The Congress as the [body of] highest instance of the Party is presented to us in the form of a "sovereign" divinity whose every wish must be accepted as sacred, on faith, without intelligent and obligatory criticism. The protracted dispersion in Party activity has elicited in our minds the image of the Central Committee toward which "uncontradicted obedience and subordination" are compulsory. Organizational discipline is depicted to us as "military" and automatic, that of the soldier, while at the same time it is a discipline from which we exempt our officers, generals, and field commanders . . . We even clothe our organizational ideas in a jargon borrowed by us from the military barracks of the capitalist autocratic order.[4]

Praktik also alluded to the "pointed and dangerous means of centralist organization." Replying to this charge, Lenin gave a lengthy analysis in *One Step Forward* of the various issues which had confronted the Second Congress and offered his own version of what had transpired at that conclave.

Lenin denounced as "opportunists" those who disagreed with him, and he leveled new charges against his opponents. Some of them had branded his behavior as Jacobinist; taking this cue, Lenin declared that the "division into the majority and minority is a direct and inevitable continuation of that division of Social Democracy into revolutionary and opportunist, into the mountain and the Gironde, which did not appear just yesterday or in the Russian Labor Party alone, and which will most likely not disappear tomorrow."[5] Lenin obviously did not chafe under the Jacobin label; he defined a Jacobin as one "indissolubly tied to the *organization* of the proletariat, recognizing his class interests—that is, a revolutionary Social Democrat." The Girondist, Lenin claimed, was the "yearning of professors and gymnasium students, afraid of the dictatorship of the proletariat, sighing for the absolute value of democratic demands—that is, an opportunist."[6] Lenin also accused his opponents of "tailism" in organizational matters, of adhering to the circle or local-group type of organization, of stressing the Party's program but being unable to see the need for a disciplined organization to fulfill it. Other sins of the Mensheviks were their "seignorial anarchism" (opposition to discipline and the subordination of the minority to the majority) and their "autonomism" (defense of the local Party units against the center). Lenin described seignorial anarchism (*Edelanarchismus*) as a "characteristic of the Russian nihilist . . . [for whom] the Party organization is a monstrous 'factory' and the subordination of the parts to the whole, the minority to the majority, appears [to be] . . . serfdom . . ."[7] The reference to the "factory" was in answer to an invidious analogy developed by Praktik in his article. Axelrod, in an issue of *Iskra* (No. 55), had also invoked the "factory" analogy when he complained of "members of the Party [being] transformed into small screws, into small wheels, with which the omniscient center disposes at its personal discretion."

In *One Step Forward*, Lenin restated his views on Party membership and declared that Axelrod, in seeking as wide a membership as possible (to include every striker), was "*reducing* social democratism [*sic*] to strike-ism."[8] Lenin reaffirmed his elitist, vanguard concept of the Party in unmistakable terms:

> We are the party of a class, and therefore *almost the entire class* (and in wartime, in the epoch of civil war, absolutely the whole class) must act under the leadership of our Party, must border upon our Party as closely as possible. But it would be Manilovism [smug complacency and futile daydreaming, derived from the character of Manilov in Gogol's *Dead Souls*] and "tailism" to think that at any time under capitalism the entire class or almost the entire class is able to rise to the level of consciousness and activity of its vanguard [*peredovoi otryad*], of its Social Democratic Party. No sensible Social Democrat [Communist] has ever yet doubted that under capitalism even the trade union organizations . . . are unable to embrace the entire or almost the entire working class. To forget the distinction between the vanguard and the whole of the masses which gravitates toward it, to forget the constant duty of the vanguard *to raise* ever-broader strata to this advanced level would mean to deceive oneself, to shut one's eyes to the immensity of our tasks, and to narrow these tasks.[9]

The Mensheviks, while agreeing that the Party should act as a vanguard of revolution, were not prepared to accept Lenin's narrow definition of its role and membership. In *One Step Forward,* Lenin accused them of "disorganizing" Party work, of acting hysterically, and of engaging in petty scandals and creating "scenes." He countered the charge that his majority at the Second Congress had been accidental—because of the walkout of the five Bundists and two Economists—by asking: "Was it accidental that the most ardent representatives of the *right* and not of the *left* wing of our Party walked out? Was it accidental that the *opportunists* and not the consistently *revolutionary Social Democrats* walked out?"[10] In answering a question by raising another question, in claiming a monopoly on being revolutionary, and in branding as "opportunists" all who disagreed with him, Lenin employed the characteristic tactics which later came to be identified with his name.

This important work, which signaled the adoption by Lenin of a more hostile and uncompromising attitude toward the Mensheviks, was permeated with derogatory charges and abusive language. Plekhanov, who drew Lenin's venom because of his article "What Is Not to Be Done," was charged with pursuing a "kill with kindness" policy toward Martov and the Mensheviks in insisting upon their return to the *Iskra* editorial board. Lenin derisively accused his old teacher of having "violated the fundamental principle . . . of dialectics: abstract truth does not exist; truth is always concrete."[11] He said further that the "supposedly new thought of Comrade Plekhanov comes to the not-very-new worldly wisdom: a little unpleasantness should not serve to hinder great satisfaction; a little opportunist foolishness and a few empty words are better than a great schism in the Party."[12]

Once he found himself in a minority both on the *Iskra* editorial board and in the Central Committee, Lenin did not hesitate to flaunt the majority; nor did the risk of creating a permanent split in the Party deter him from pressing for a resolution of the conflict and for the triumph of his own views at a new, third Party congress. By his definition, the victory which chance had given him at the Second Congress represented a "step forward," and his withdrawal from *Iskra* and failure to obtain the support of the Party Council and the Central Committee were "two steps back." Yet, Lenin, refused to be daunted by this turn of events. He concluded his book with the view that such temporary setbacks "occur in the life of individuals, in the history of nations, and in the development of parties" and that "it would be criminal cowardice to doubt even for a minute the inevitable complete triumph of the principles of revolutionary Social Democracy, proletarian organization, and Party discipline." He would triumph "in spite of the tinsel and the hue and cry of the *intelligentsia's* anarchism."[13]

True to this battle cry, Lenin launched an all-out campaign for the convocation of a third congress. In a letter of May 26, 1904, he warned all members of the Central Committee that "the agitation for a congress cannot now be halted by anything . . . [and] it is useless to chafe and storm against this agitation."[14] The first result of this drive was a meeting in

Geneva during August, 1904, at which Lenin gathered eighteen of his followers, including his wife and sister.[15] This group was the hard core of Lenin's faction and included such prominent future Bolsheviks as Anatole Lunacharsky, the historian Vladimir Bonch-Bruevich, and Vatslav Vorovsky (who was assassinated in Switzerland nineteen years later, on May 10, 1923, while attending the Lausanne Conference as a Soviet diplomat). Three more persons later joined in signing an appeal "To the Party," and this meeting of Leninists came to be known, impressively, as the Conference of the Twenty-Two.

The Russo-Japanese War had broken out in February, 1904, but the Menshevik-managed *Iskra* gave it scant attention. Its pages were filled, instead, with attacks on Lenin. Lenin, too, in all his writings during 1904, evinced little concern with or interest in the war. However, the manifesto of the Conference of the Twenty-Two, which he drafted, declared that "the shameful end of a shameful war is not so far off, and it will inevitably increase revolutionary excitement tenfold . . ."[16] It depicted the Party as suffering from an ailment produced by the conflict between the concept of local Party circles (*kruzhkovshchina*) allegedly favored by the Mensheviks and the vague and arbitrary concept of *partiinost'* ("partyness"—adherence to the Party line) advocated by Lenin (and constantly alluded to in Party literature to this day). The manifesto was intended to serve as an appeal to the Party for support in calling for the immediate convocation of a third congress.

This band of twenty-two demanded in their manifesto that the editorial board of *Iskra* be placed "in the hands of supporters of the Party majority,"[17] despite the fact that Lenin, in a letter of May 26, 1904, to the Central Committee, had expressed his "*unconditional* willingness" to publish "without changes and commentary" everything written by the former editors and, if necessary, "to make *Iskra* neutral, eliminating from it mutual polemics . . ."[18] This was neither the first nor the last time that Lenin was to mislead his opponents by offering promises which he had no intention of keeping. Speaking through the "twenty-two," he also demanded "precise regularization of relations" between the League of Russian Revolutionary Social Democracy

Abroad and the "all-Russian center, the Central Committee."
He proposed that the Party Council be elected in its entirety by
the Congress—that it unite the activity of the two Party centers
and exercise control over them. Paragraph One of the Statutes,
which had created so much ill will at the Second Congress, was
to be reviewed in the interests of a "more precise formulation
of the Party's bounds."

Thus, the campaign for a new congress, which was to serve
as the stage for Lenin's attempt to establish his control over the
entire Party, came into the open. However, in July, prior to
the Conference of the Twenty-Two, Lenin had suffered a set-
back in the Central Committee itself when several of its remaining members in Russia (V. A. Noskov, Leonid Krasin, and
L. E. Gal'perin) co-opted three new members who were not
Leninists. On August 18, 1904, Lenin, branded their action
"illegal" on the grounds that neither he nor Zemlyachka had
been informed of the meeting or invited to attend it.[19] Lenin
was in Switzerland at the time, but continued to regard himself
as a member of the Central Committee as well as leader of the
majority. Affairs in the Central Committee at that time had
become somewhat confused; Krzhizhanovsky and Dr. F. V.
Gusarov had withdrawn from its activities in the early summer
of 1904; Mme. Essen and Lengnik were under arrest, and
Zemlyachka had joined Lenin in agitating for a third congress.
It is clear, in any case, that in the summer of 1904 Lenin and
Zemlyachka were in a minority in what remained of the nine-
member Central Committee which had come into existence late
in 1903.

This did not dismay Lenin. For a brief period, he continued
to sign all his Party correspondence as "Member of the Central
Committee, Lenin." Since his position as member availed him
little, however, he moved in early October, 1904, to establish
an organizing committee for the convocation of the Third Congress. The membership of this so-called Bureau of the Committees of the Majority included—in addition to Lenin and his
Central Committee cohort, Zemlyachka—such future Soviet luminaries as Maxim Litvinov (Meyer Wallach) and Alexei Rykov.
However, Lenin's closest collaborator in this venture was A. A.

Bogdanov (Alexander A. Malinovsky; also known as Maximov), a physician who, two years before completing his medical training, had published a *Short Course in Economic Science* (1897)— a work which Lenin had reviewed warmly. The relationship between Bogdanov the philosopher and Lenin the practitioner of revolutionary politics was a curious one. Ultimately, Bogdanov's predilection for abstract philosophy and Lenin's abiding distaste for this discipline were to impose an insurmountable barrier between the two men and terminate their association. However, this did not occur until 1908-09, after Lenin had made full use of Bogdanov and then made him a whipping boy in his own pseudo-philosophical work, *Materialism and Empiriocriticism.*

In late 1904, Bogdanov was indispensable to Lenin in a new journalistic venture—the publication of the newspaper *Vperyod* ("Forward"), which was to be Lenin's voice against the Menshevik-dominated *Iskra. Vperyod*, the first issue of which appeared on January 4, 1905, had the task of campaigning for a new congress. Thus, the one Party was divided into two factions, each of which had sent a separate delegation to the Amsterdam Congress of the Second International in August, 1904, and each of which now published an organ that claimed to speak for the whole Party. The task of sustaining *Vperyod* was not an easy one. Shortly after the newspaper got under way, Lenin complained of the lack of collaborators in a letter addressed to Bogdanov and S. I. Gusev on February 11, 1905:

> Young forces are needed. I would advise you straightway to shoot on sight those who permit themselves to say that there is a lack of people. Russia is dark with people; it is necessary only more widely and boldly, more boldly and widely, and once again more widely and once again more boldly to recruit the youth, *without fearing it.*[20]

In January, 1905, events in Russia eclipsed Lenin's group and its plans: a priest of the Orthodox Church—and not Lenin's Party—had emerged as the spokesman for the proletariat of the Russian capital. Father George Gapon, the son of Ukrainian peasants, had studied at the St. Petersburg Theological Academy. In 1902, at the age of thirty-two, he became involved in workers' activities; and in February, 1904, he received permission to establish an Assembly of Russian Factory Workers of St. Petersburg. Undoubtedly, police agents had a voice in the Assembly, and Gapon, as a priest, embarked upon this venture only with the approval of his religious superiors and of the secular authorities. However, this in itself does not render the priest's motives entirely suspect, nor does it detract from the significance of the forces he was attempting to lead. If Father Gapon's movement is sometimes dismissed as "police socialism," it cannot be equated entirely with the Zubatov police-sponsored trade union movement, since that earlier effort was far less consequential.* The popularity of Father Gapon's Assembly, with its 9,000 members, helped precipitate the 1905 Revolution and the granting of concessions by the autocracy in October of that year.

The event which shook Russia and for which the priest was partly responsible was the march of tens of thousands of Russian workers and their wives and children to the Winter Palace in St. Petersburg on the Sunday afternoon of January 9 (22), 1905. The unarmed and orderly mob, led by the priest in his cassock, sang "God Save the Czar" and "Lord, Save Thy People." Its purpose was peaceful petition for an eight-hour working day, a minimum wage, improved and safer working conditions in the shops, and a constituent assembly elected on the basis of universal, equal, and secret suffrage. Father Gapon, prior to the demonstration, had naïvely requested that Nicholas II appear before the multitude to accept its petition and had somewhat presumptuously declared that he and his comrades would guarantee the Czar's safety. When the demonstrators were greeted not by the Czar but by troops and a fusillade which caused hundreds of deaths and casualties, the event of "Bloody

---

* The Zubatov movement, which began in 1901, took its name from Sergei Vasil'evich Zubatov, the chief of the Czarist secret police (*Okhrana*) in Moscow prior to 1903. It was a form of police-sponsored and controlled trade unionism designed to prevent the industrial workers from succumbing to the influence of revolutionaries and to improve working conditions. When this technique began to get out of control, it was abandoned by the autocracy.

Sunday" became a turning point in the history of the ruling House of Romanov. Father Gapon fled across the frontier and headed for Geneva, where he declared himself to be in sympathy with the Social Democrats.

Plekhanov was suspicious of the priest, but Lenin viewed him with some sympathy. In the January 31, 1905, issue of *Vperyod* (No. 4), Lenin hailed the rising of the proletariat against Czarism, referring to the "thousands of killed and wounded," and acknowledged Father Gapon as the "leader of the Petersburg workers." He was particularly impressed by Gapon's declaration: "We no longer have a Czar. A river of blood separates the Czar from the people. Long live the struggle for freedom."[21] In the same issue, but in another article, Lenin suggested that the priest, although a "participant and ringleader in the Zubatov [sic] society," might have been an "*unconscious* tool" in a deliberate plot hatched in certain governmental circles for an organized blood-letting as a warning to all liberals and revolutionaries in Russia. It is significant that Lenin felt called upon to defend Gapon and to argue that the priest's "We no longer have a Czar" declaration testified to his "honesty and sincerity" and indicated that he was no provocateur. It cannot be excluded, wrote Lenin, that "Gapon may be a sincere Christian socialist."[22] At the Third Congress, on May 6, 1905, Lenin consistently referred to him as "Comrade Gapon."

Lenin was later to find it expedient to refer to the priest as "provocateur Gapon,"[23] and Stalin's *Short Course* history was to declare (Chapter 3) that "the agent-provocateur . . . Gapon undertook to assist the Czarist *Okhrana* by providing a pretext for firing on the workers and drowning the working-class movement in blood." Yet, unaware of the bitterness and enmity in which Russian *émigré* life was steeped, Gapon had attempted in vain to coordinate the activities of eighteen revolutionary organizations and groupings in a conference held in Geneva on April 2, 1905. The parties invited included the Bolsheviks, the Mensheviks, the Bund, the Socialist Revolutionaries, the Party of Polish Socialists, the Lithuanian Social Democrats, the Armenian Revolutionary Federation, the Belorussian Socialist *Hromada*, the Revolutionary Ukrainian Party (RUP), the

Ukrainian Socialist Party, and the Finnish Workers' Party. Lenin and others withdrew from the conference on the grounds that it was dominated by the Socialist Revolutionaries. In the autumn of 1905, Father Gapon took advantage of the amnesty which had been granted by the Czarist Government and returned to Russia. In April of the following year, his body was found in the town of Ozerki on the Gulf of Finland. The murder was the work of a group of Socialist Revolutionaries, including the future Zionist Pincus Rutenberg, who had been led to believe that the priest was working closely with the police and that his execution was necessary for the good of the revolutionary cause.

The tragic fate of Father Gapon was soon forgotten amid other events which are generally referred to as the 1905 Revolution. Among these were the mutiny on the battleship *Potemkin* in June and peasant disturbances, particularly in Ukraine. The decisive general strike came in October; more than a million and a half workers took part; railroad traffic, the mails, and the telegraph came to a complete halt; banks and schools closed as the demand for constitutional government became a popular storm.

The Russian political *émigrés* in Geneva were hard put to keep up with this avalanche of events, but they made no effort to return to Russia quickly. Plekhanov remained in Switzerland, and Lenin did not arrive in St. Petersburg until after the end of the October general strike. The one exception was Trotsky, who was destined to play a leading role in the ill-fated St. Petersburg Soviet. Trotsky, spurred on by "Bloody Sunday," had returned to Russia in February, 1905. En route, he stopped off in Munich to visit the fabulous Parvus (Alexander L. Gel'-fand; also used the pseudonym Molotov in his writings prior to 1903), a Russian-born German socialist who had plans for acquiring great wealth and publishing a tri-lingual socialist newspaper. From Parvus, Trotsky appropriated the theory of "permanent revolution."

Arriving in Kiev in February, Trotsky took refuge in various places, including an ophthalmic hospital where, with the aid of a physician, he masqueraded as an eye patient while writing proclamations and exhortations for the underground press. In

Kiev, Trotsky met Leonid Krasin, who was busy operating a printing press and procuring arms and explosives. During the summer of 1905, Trotsky went to St. Petersburg, but soon had to flee to the relative security of autonomous Finland pending his return with the outbreak of the general strike.

Although Trotsky had broken with Lenin over the issue of centralism at the Second Congress in 1903, his flirtation with the Geneva Mensheviks did not extend beyond 1904. Yet, Trotsky's decision to return to Russia in February, 1905, did not raise Lenin's estimate of his former protégé whom he had wanted to bring into the editorial board of *Iskra* scarcely two years earlier. In the April 5 and 12 issues of *Vperyod* (Nos. 13 and 14), Lenin went so far as to refer to the pro-Menshevik (who was to become his comrade-in-arms in 1917) as "windbag [*pustozvon*] Trotsky." By way of contrast, Stalin (who was to become Trotsky's archrival) was already acquiring a reputation of sorts in 1905 as a "hard" Leninist by faithfully and briefly paraphrasing in the most elementary language what he had read of Lenin's writings on Party organization. In an unsigned article entitled "The Class of the Proletariat and the Party of the Proletariat," published in the illegal Georgian Party newspaper *Proletariatis Brdzola* ("The Struggle of the Proletariat") on January 1, 1905, Stalin denounced Martov's "dubious formulation" of Paragraph One and demanded that the Third Congress, which was to meet in April, adopt Lenin's "wonderful formulation." In condemning the notion that mere acceptance of the Party's program was sufficient to qualify for membership, Stalin declared that "it would be profanation of the holy of holies of the Party [*oskvernenie svyataya svyatykh partii*] to call such a chatterbox a Party member." "For Martov," he declared, "the Party is not a fortress but a banquet, admission to which is granted to every sympathizer."[24]

Stalin was not a delegate to the Third Congress because Bolshevism was pitifully weak in the Caucasus. His contribution to the Congress was a pamphlet entitled *Party Differences in Brief*, published in the Georgian language in May, 1905. This work, a plodding and tendentious analysis of developments since the organization of *Iskra* in 1900, contained numerous quota-

tions from Lenin's *What Is to Be Done?* and *One Step Forward.*
Its significance lies in the fact that Stalin thus chose to cast his
lot with Lenin, and the kindred nature of these two spirits was
demonstrated when Stalin felt called upon to defend Lenin
against Plekhanov's "idle talk." The two power-seekers were
not to meet until December, 1905, at the Party Conference in
Tammerfors (Tampere), Finland. On that occasion, they disagreed temporarily over tactics, but both men were one in their
determination to read the Mensheviks out of the movement and
to take over the Party.

Lenin expressed his refusal to seek a reconciliation and his
determination to pursue a "go-it-alone" policy through a new
Party congress in a letter to S. I. Gusev written on January 29,
1905: "How important it is to make haste with the announcement regarding the Bureau [of the Committees of the Majority]
and with the convocation of the Congress. For God's sake, do
not trust the Mensheviks and the Central Committee, but carry
out unconditionally everywhere and in the most decisive form
a schism, a schism, and a schism."[25] Within a matter of days,
an event in Moscow was to come to Lenin's aid. At a meeting
of the Central Committee in the apartment of the writer Leonid
Andreyev, six members were arrested; Krasin and A. I. Lyubi-
mov were not present and thus avoided arrest. Although these
two members had been denounced as "conciliators" because of
their desire to help bridge the rift in the Party, they modified
their position and, in agreement with Lenin's Bureau, approved
of the convocation of a new congress. Time was also on Lenin's
side: the Statutes adopted at the Second Congress in August,
1903, provided that Party congresses be held "not less frequently
than once in two years."

The controversial Third Congress met in London from April
25 to May 10, 1905. It was a purely Bolshevik affair, with
twenty-four voting delegates and fourteen more having a consultative vote which permitted them to participate in the debates.
Lenin attended as a representative of the Party Committee in
Odessa—a city which he had never visited—and Krupskaya,
Lunacharsky, and Lyadov were among the consultative delegates. Krasin was there as a voting delegate, along with Bogda-

nov, Litvinov, Vorovsky, and Zemlyachka. Two other voting delegates, Lev Kamenev (Rozenfeld) and Alexei Rykov, made their political debuts at this Leninist Congress; ironically, they were to pay with their lives in the 1930's for the alleged "impurity" of their Leninism. Other consultative delegates included the Ukrainian Mykola Skrypnyk, whom Lenin's successor was to drive to suicide twenty-eight years later, and M. S. Leshchinsky, who turned out to be a police spy. Plekhanov and the Mensheviks boycotted Lenin's Congress and held a conference of their own in Geneva. Trotsky, meanwhile, was learning the revolutionary art in Russia.

While the Third Congress was overshadowed by the events in Russia during the turbulent summer and autumn of 1905, a number of its decisions were of more than passing significance. The experience of the preceding two years had convinced Lenin that an organizational overhaul was necessary. Consequently, the Congress rejected the system of dual centers (*dvoetsentrie*) —that is, two central bodies in the form of a Central Committee and a Central Organ (the editorial board), balanced in the five-member Party Council where each had two members, and the fifth (Plekhanov) had been elected at the Second Congress. The Central Committee was now made the sole directing center of the Party and was empowered to appoint the responsible editor of the Central Organ from among its members. The Party Council was abolished. It came as no surprise that Lenin was elected both a member of the Central Committee and editor of the new Party organ, *Proletarii*, which replaced Lenin's *Vperyod*. In addition to Lenin, the Central Committee had four members: Krasin, Bogdanov, Rykov, and D. S. Postolovsky (who soon drifted away from the Party).

The Third Congress also concerned itself with the tactics the Party should adopt in the new revolutionary situation which had arisen in Russia. The concept of armed uprising was taken for granted, and the Party was directed not only to engage in propaganda and agitation, but also to stress the "practical organizational side" and to explain the significance of mass political strikes. On the question of participating in a provisional government, the Congress took the position that such participation was "permissible . . . for the purpose of a relentless struggle against all counterrevolutionary attempts and for the defense of the independent interests of the working class." Yet, this would depend upon the "relationship of forces [*sootnoshenie sil*] and other factors not subject to a precise preliminary determination." Regardless of whether or not participation in a provisional government would be possible, "permanent pressure on the provisional government would have to be exercised by the Party-led armed proletariat."[26]

The Third Congress's position on the agrarian question differed from that taken by the Second Congress, largely because of Lenin's growing appreciation of the peasantry as a potentially important factor on the Russian political scene—though he continued to regard the peasant class as a "spontaneous and politically unconscious force." While the Second Congress had been content to advocate no more than the return to the peasants of the *otrezki* (parcels of land lost in the reform of 1861), the Third Congress committed the Party to support "confiscation of landowner, Crown, Church, monastic, and appanage lands."[27] Significantly, Lenin insisted upon the narrower concept of "confiscation" rather than "expropriation" in order to avoid any implication of monetary compensation. Peasants were to be encouraged to refuse to pay taxes, perform military service, or carry out orders of the government. However, Lenin, adept as always in concealing his real aims, did not introduce the proposal to nationalize all land until the Fourth Congress. His hesitation regarding nationalization was prompted by considerations of expediency. As early as August, 1902, in the Party's theoretical journal *Zarya*, Lenin had published an article on "The Agrarian Program of Russian Social Democracy," in which he declared that "the demand to nationalize the land, being fully correct from the point of view of principle and fully suitable in certain instances, is politically inexpedient at this time." Lenin feared that to demand the nationalization of land under the conditions of an autocracy or even under a semiconstitutional monarchy "will far more quickly divert thoughts toward absurd experiments in state socialism rather than giving a push to the 'free development of the class struggle in the village.' "[28]

Marxist doctrine also colored this attitude: Lenin undoubtedly remembered the statement in the *Communist Manifesto* on the "idiocy of rural life." Plekhanov, it may be recalled, was opposed to *any* alliance with the peasantry. As early as 1884, in *Our Divergencies*, he had been content to leave the peasantry to the Populists and their successors. Lenin recognized that a rigid policy of the kind proposed by Plekhanov was not profitable; it was inadvisable to allow the Socialist Revolutionaries to monopolize the peasantry for themselves. Hence, the Third Congress, although condemning the Socialist Revolutionaries as a pseudo-socialist party, declared that "temporary combat agreements" with them, aimed at fighting the autocracy, "can be useful in certain instances" if they do not "violate the integrity and purity of its [Lenin's Party's] proletarian tactics and principles."

On the problem of healing the breach within the Party, Lenin's Third Congress combined conciliation with the threat of anathema. On the one hand, a resolution was adopted (but not published) authorizing the Central Committee to outline the conditions for a fusion with the Mensheviks (subject to the approval of the next congress). On the other hand, another secret resolution empowered the Central Committee to dissolve local Party committees which failed to accept the decisions of the Congress, and to create parallel Bolshevik local committees in such instances. The temper of the Congress was nevertheless unmistakable: in adopting Lenin's formulation of Paragraph One regarding Party membership, and in rejecting the broader definition adopted at the Second Congress, the participants hardly enhanced the prospects for a fusion of the two factions.

Yet, the events of 1905 were to contribute greatly to the temporary blurring of the distinction between Bolsheviks and Mensheviks. Lenin and Trotsky both preached the doctrine of permanent revolution. Trotsky wrote of it in the first issue of *Nachalo* as the "uninterrupted [*nepreryvnaya*] revolution." Lenin expressed this concept in an article on "The Attitude of Social Democracy Toward the Peasant Movement" published in *Proletarii* on September 1 (14), 1905, describing the goal of a socialist revolution in the following terms: "We stand for uninterrupted revolution. We will not halt halfway."[29] Two months earlier, in his pamphlet *Two Tactics of Social Democracy in the Democratic Revolution*, Lenin wrote of a nonsocialist "democratic dictatorship"—an obvious contradiction in terms—which would only later destroy the bases of capitalism, but which would initially effect a "radical redistribution" of land ownership, establish a republic, "uproot all the Asiatic, enslaving characteristics not only from the village but from the factory way of life . . . [create] an improvement in the status of the workers and raise their standard of living, and, last but not least, carry the revolutionary conflagration into Europe."[30] This was brave and explicit language, but quite remote from the immediate realities of Russia in the throes of the 1905 Revolution.

As the October General Strike approached, a Soviet of Workers' Deputies, with a representation of one deputy for each 500 workmen, acquired considerable strength in St. Petersburg. The outbreak of the general strike which the Party was planning for January, 1906, on the first anniversary of Bloody Sunday prompted Trotsky to cut short his stay in Finland and return to the capital, where he was now in less danger of being arrested. However, the Czarist Government had regained the upper hand and managed to blunt the force of the rebellion by appealing to moderate elements with the October 17 (30) Manifesto. This document provided for the convocation of a Russian parliament, the Duma, which was to exercise a veto power on all Czarist legislation, but this right was soon to be restricted by the regime. On the following day, October 18 (31), Trotsky ceremoniously tore up a copy of the Manifesto on a balcony of the University of St. Petersburg in the presence of a mob. It was the arrest of the St. Petersburg Soviet's nominal head, the lawyer Peter Alexeyevich Khrustalev (pseudonym of Georgii Stepanovich Nosar'), on November 26 (December 9), 1905, that brought Trotsky fully to the fore as the Chairman of that illicit body. On December 3 (16), Trotsky was arrested along with the other leaders of the Soviet and, after a sensational public trial, was sentenced to enforced settlement in exile within the Arctic Circle for an indefinite period. However, by simulating sciatica, he managed to obtain a delay while en route, escaped, and fled abroad.

The arrests of the members of the St. Petersburg Soviet followed the issuance, by the Soviet, of a "financial" manifesto which called upon the public to "cease paying redemption dues [for land] and all other Crown payments," to demand payment of wages and all transactions in gold, and to withdraw deposits from state and savings banks and insist upon payment in gold. This manifesto led to a bank run during December, 1905, in which withdrawals exceeded deposits by 89 million rubles. The Soviet also challenged the authority of the Czarist Government by declaring its refusal to honor the regime's debts contracted while it was "openly waging war upon the whole people."[31]

Although the October General Strike had quickly spent its force, the ashes of revolt were kept smoldering by the Moscow uprising of December 9-11 (22-24), 1905. This action, concentrated primarily in the barricaded Presnya District, was quickly suppressed within a week by the Semyonovski Regiment, which was able to reach Moscow in the absence of any effective strike or sabotage actions on the St. Petersburg–Moscow rail line. While the battle raged in Moscow, all was quiet in St. Petersburg. The stores in the capital were open—in contrast with the Bolshevik legal newspaper *Novaya zhizn'* (financed on a relatively lavish scale by Maxim Gorky), which had been closed on December 3 for having printed the Soviet's financial manifesto.

It was precisely during the suppression of the Moscow uprising that the Party Conference met in Tammerfors, Finland. This meeting was planned as the Fourth Congress by Lenin's Central Committee, which the Bolshevik Third Congress had elected in London in May, 1905. However, few members of the Party were able or willing to attend; this was particularly true of the Mensheviks, who had been holding a meeting of their own in St. Petersburg. When only forty-one delegates appeared, it was decided to turn the meeting into a conference of the "majority" rather than a Party congress. Among the small gathering at Tammerfors were Krupskaya, Stalin, Emilian Yaroslavsky, and Michael Markovich Borodin (Gruzenberg), who achieved notoriety in the 1920's as Communist High Adviser to the Chinese Kuomintang during the period of uneasy alliance between Chiang Kai-shek and the Communists.

The Tammerfors Conference called for a "unity" congress

and for the "immediate fusion of parallel [Bolshevik and Menshevik] organizations in the locales." It adopted a resolution condemning the forthcoming elections to the "police Duma" and calling for an "immediate armed uprising" (at a time when the Moscow uprising was being mercilessly crushed) as the only guarantee of a constituent assembly elected on the basis of general, direct, equal, and secret suffrage. This last resolution is said to have been drafted by a collegium of five which included Lenin and Stalin (known as Ivanovich at the time). It is known, however, that Lenin—at least at the time—opposed the policy of boycotting the Duma. Stalin, on the occasion of Lenin's fiftieth birthday on April 23, 1920, took it upon himself to note, with a presumptuousness that bordered on impudence, that one of Lenin's characteristics was "humility, [his] admitting his errors." As one of two examples, Stalin recalled how Lenin at Tammerfors had in his own mind favored participation in the elections to the First Duma, but then recognized his "blunder" (*promakh*) after an "attack by the provincials, Siberians, and Caucasians," and "sided with the [Bolshevik] faction."[32] Lenin, in any event, went along with the majority and denounced the Duma in articles written during January, 1906. However, within five months (in June, 1906), he again changed his mind and advocated participation. He obviously realized, though he did not admit it, that by boycotting the Parliament he was abdicating to the Mensheviks and the Trudovik faction of the Socialist Revolutionaries the use of an effective political instrument.[33]

The issue of whether or not to boycott the Duma hardened the Bolshevik-Menshevik split, despite the decision by the Tammerfors Conference to terminate the break. Some Social Democratic organizations had participated in the Duma elections, and 17 Social Democrats had been elected, along with 94 Trudovik Socialist Revolutionaries* and 179 Kadets (Constitutional Democrats)—out of a total Duma membership of 478. The Mensheviks took the position that since the 1905 Revolution had been a bourgeois movement directed against the remnants of

---

* The Trudoviki (Group of Toil) arose as a result of the decision of the Socialist Revolutionaries to boycott the First Duma; it was a rather inarticulate and programmatically weak party.

feudalism in Russia, the bourgeoisie should not be denied its due. Parvus editorialized in the first issue of Trotsky's newspaper, *Nachalo* ("The Beginning"), on November 13 (26), 1905: "We do not fear the successes of liberalism; on the contrary, they are the condition of our further successes."[34] Lenin, in contrast to Parvus, feared the successes of the bourgeoisie. While the Mensheviks were disposed to sit out each Marxian historical stage and to give the bourgeoisie its day, Lenin, champing at the bit, wished frantically to telescope this particular stage. The Mensheviks, in viewing a Russian bourgeois government as laying the groundwork for a future Russian proletarian regime, were opposed to any alliance with the peasantry, while Lenin was in favor of such an alliance.

Both the Bolsheviks and the Mensheviks were Marxists, and they agreed on ultimate goals—on the desirability and inevitability (for doctrinaire Marxists, the two terms are synonymous) of the dictatorship of the proletariat, and on the role of the Party as vanguard. Their disagreement was primarily over tactics, methods, and short-range goals. The cautious Mensheviks were perfectly willing to come to power, but only after the bourgeois revolution had run its course. However, they were willing to attempt to split off the liberal bourgeoisie and ally themselves with it in pursuit of common aims. Trotsky represented another point of view—one quite close to that of Lenin. Having broken with the Mensheviks, he advocated the self-reliance of the Russian proletariat, arguing that it should rely neither on the Russian bourgeoisie nor on the peasantry (after all, it was peasant troops who had fired the shots heard on Bloody Sunday that killed striking workers). The only allies which the Russian proletariat could have, according to Trotsky's version of permanent revolution, were the foreign proletariat, particularly that of Germany. Implicit in this view was the assumption that the Russian proletariat could not be successful in Russia if it acted alone; its staying power would depend upon the spread of revolution to Western Europe.

Any attempt to distinguish between Bolsheviks and Mensheviks in late 1905 and 1906 courts the danger of oversimplifying and of reading into evidence differences which had caused great animosity in 1903-04, but which had temporarily become less important following the issuance of the October Manifesto. One of these issues which faded in importance for a time was the question of Party organization. The relaxation of autocratic controls in Russia after October, 1905, made illicit underground activity less necessary; however, this issue was to rear its head again within a few years and lead to bitter controversy over the so-called "Liquidationist" deviation. Another aspect of the organizational problem became more acute in 1905-06. In three articles written following his return to St. Petersburg in November, 1905, Lenin had expressed some doubt regarding the advisability of broadening Party membership. These were published in *Novaya zhizn'* between November 10 and 16 (23 and 29) under the title "Concerning the Reorganization of the Party." Lenin warned that developing a new, open, and legal Party apparatus (without disbanding the conspiratorial underground) could invite the risk that "the Party will become dissolved in the mass, the Party will cease to be the conscious vanguard of the class, the Party will demean itself to the role of a tail."[35] While Lenin was confident that new, youthful elements could be absorbed and controlled by the regular Party organization, he was soon confronted with the Menshevik demand, spearheaded by Axelrod and Plekhanov, that the Party go to the masses and call a workers' congress. The Mensheviks, according to Martov, wanted to abandon Blanquist and underground forms of Party organization.[36]

Thus, the convocation of the Fourth "Unity" Congress in Stockholm from April 23 to May 8, 1906, did not in itself guarantee that the differences between the two factions would be resolved. Lenin suffered a very unpleasant defeat at this Congress when the Mensheviks succeeded in electing a majority of the more than 100 delegates and in obtaining adoption of their proposals, usually with a dozen or more votes to spare. At that time, the Mensheviks were stronger in St. Petersburg, in the south, and in the Caucasus, while the Bolsheviks were dominant within the Party in Central Russia and in the Urals.[37] The victory of the Mensheviks was significant because delegates had been elected by the Party membership at the ratio of 1 to 300, making this a more representative congress. The ten-member Central Committee elected by the Fourth Congress contained seven Mensheviks and only three Bolsheviks: Rykov, Krasin, and Vasilii Alexeyevich Desnitsky (Stroev). Nor was Lenin elected to the editorial board of the Party organ; there, too, the Mensheviks were in command with Martov, Martynov (against whom Lenin had vented his spleen so often), Potresov, Fedor Dan, and Peter Maslov (John or "Dzhon").

The issues that divided the Bolsheviks and Mensheviks at the "Unity" Congress—it was to be called the "Fourth" only later by Bolshevik historians—included municipalization of the land, advocated by Maslov and Plekhanov, and land national- ization, advocated by Lenin. By "municipalization," the Menshe- viks meant placing the confiscated lands at the disposal of local organs of self-government; with their majority, they succeeded in defeating Lenin's proposal. Lenin had argued in vain that municipalization or any solution other than his nationalization policy would inevitably lead to a restoration of the old regime. At the same time, Lenin contended that "the Russian revolution can conquer by its own forces, but it cannot in any case retain and strengthen its conquests with its own hands." This could be done, he said, only if there is a "socialist cataclysm" in the West, and "without that condition, a restoration is inevitable under municipalization, under nationalization, and under divi- sion [of the land] . . ."[38] Trotsky was in a Czarist prison at the time, but his doctrine of permanent revolution was ably expounded in Stockholm by Lenin.

On the issue of participating in the Duma, Lenin argued at Stockholm that the Kadets were correct in stating that voting for another, non-Kadet party would simply weaken the anti- reactionary front and would lead to a victory for the Black Hundreds (*Chernosotentsy*). Lenin noted that the elections were really between the Kadets and Black Hundreds, and that the participation of a third party would only syphon votes away from the former and enable the candidates of the latter to win by pluralities. Yet, Lenin spoke out against any alliance with the Kadets—a party which, according to him, wished to extinguish the revolution. He told the Mensheviks: "You view the Duma exclusively from the point of view of governmental pressure upon us, of governmental oppression again the revolution. We [Bolsheviks] view the State Duma as the representation of a given class, as an institution with a given party make-up. Your reasoning is absolutely incorrect, incomplete, and is constructed in an un-Marxist way."[39] The Menshevik resolution adopted at the Fourth Congress provided for utilization of the Duma and for creating conflicts between it and the Czarist Government, but it did not permit the Party to enter into a bloc with other parties in the election campaign.

In the end, Lenin voted at Stockholm, along with sixteen other Bolsheviks, for the Party's participation in the Duma elections which were yet to be held in certain of the non-Russian borderlands, particularly in Georgia. Lenin and his followers who voted for this resolution later issued a declaration explaining their vote: "We regard it as useful and important to condemn on behalf of the Party blocs with other parties, [while] to the question of Duma elections which have not taken place, we attach no practical significance and are not in the least sympathetic toward such elections."[40] Yet, the record stands that Lenin voted for participation in the Duma elections. It is also clear that Stalin, along with fifteen other Bolsheviks, abstained from voting on this resolution despite his previous outspoken opposition at the Tammerfors Conference to such participation.[41]

An important issue upon which Lenin was defeated, and one that served to give the new unity at Stockholm a hollow nature, was the question of expropriatory raids for the purpose of replenishing the Party's coffers. In the tactical platform drafted by Lenin in March, in preparation for the Fourth Congress, a provision was included declaring as "permissible . . . fighting operations for the seizure of financial means belonging to the enemy, i.e., to the autocratic government, and for the use of these means for the needs of the uprising . . ."[42] The Menshevik majority at the Fourth Congress adopted a resolution regarding the necessity of "combatting the operations of individuals or groups with the purpose of seizing money in the name of or under the device of the Social Democratic Party."[43]

The Party's participation in a provisional revolutionary government was another bone of contention between Bolsheviks and Mensheviks. While regarding their combat agreements—even with those parties which accepted the idea of armed uprising—as purely temporary, the Bolsheviks declared that their participation in such a government "along with revolutionary bourgeois democracy is permissible, depending upon the relationship [*sootnoshenie*] of forces, and must be conditioned formally upon control by the Party over its plenipotentiaries" serving in the government.[44] This was hardly a clear commitment to participate in a provisional government. Nevertheless, it served to create the effect of action at a time when the confused Mensheviks were silent on this matter. Actually, in 1905-06, the Mensheviks were opposed to collaboration with bourgeois elements in a provisional government, and Lenin was later to deride them for viewing "the establishment of a provisional revolutionary government . . . [as] Blanquism, as Jacobinism and all other mortal sins."[45] Whatever their position, the Mensheviks were afraid to commit themselves on this question; they played an obvious waiting game in the hope that events would make a decision for them.

Regarding the question of single or dual control in Party organization, whereas at the Third Congress Lenin had succeeded in explicitly making the Central Organ subordinate to the Central Committee, at Stockholm the principle of dual centers was restored by the Mensheviks. The 1906 Statutes empowered the editorial board of the Central Organ to participate in Central Committee meetings at which "questions of a political character were discussed."[46] Yet, both the Bolsheviks and the Mensheviks were agreed upon democratic centralism, and this concept was included for the first time in Paragraph Two of the Party's Statutes adopted by the Stockholm Congress. However, the meaning of this term was not defined until Lenin, who was to invoke it against any and all factionalism except his own, blithely proceeded to challenge the decisions taken by the majority at Stockholm.

This he did in a relatively subtle manner. Immediately after the conclusion of the Congress, Lenin drafted an appeal to the Party on behalf of the "delegates to the Unity Congress belonging to the former faction of 'Bolsheviks.' " He declared: "There is no longer any schism . . . We are against every schism [*raskol*]." Yet, he also accused the Congress—actually, the Mensheviks—of having "embarked upon the path of parliamentarism" without providing appropriate guarantees against the Party's becoming ensnared and diverted by this tactic, of having erred in adopting municipalization of land, and of having taken an unclear position regarding the errors of the abortive Moscow December uprising and settling for "certain timid evasions of armed uprising." In a statement which was a masterpiece of contradiction, Lenin promised: "We must and we shall ideologically oppose those decisions of the Congress which we regard as being in error. But, at the same time, we declare before the entire Party that we are against every schism. We stand for subordination to the decisions of the Congress."[47] In signing this ominous document, Lenin was joined by twenty-five comrades, including Emilian Yaroslavsky, G. Alexinsky, Andrei Sergeyevich Bubnov, Kliment Efremovich Voroshilov, Rykov, and Krasin.

Thus, the threat of schism remained. Indeed, the break had come close to reasserting itself at the Stockholm Congress when the Mensheviks attempted to increase the requirement for convoking a new congress from approval by one-half of the membership to approval by two-thirds of the membership. Lenin knew that he could never muster on his side the representatives of two-thirds of the Party's membership to undo the Menshevik victory at Stockholm. He delivered an ultimatum in which he declared that "the smallest attempt to reduce that minimum of autonomy and rights of the opposition which the factional Third Congress recognized will mean an inevitable schism."[48] The Mensheviks backed down on this issue, and for the moment, unity was preserved.

No doubt, the Stockholm Congress would have ended quite differently had the steamer between Finland and Sweden, on which most of the Menshevik delegates were traveling, gone down—as it almost did when it went aground in the dead of night. The Russian passengers were returned to the Finnish port of Hango, from which they had departed less than twenty-four hours earlier, without the necessary Russian passports, but aided by Finnish Social Democrats. Though Lenin was not on this steamer, Mikhail Vasil'evich Frunze, Voroshilov, and Bubnov were among the passengers who returned to Hango and then embarked for Stockholm a second time. The joke among the Bolsheviks at the time was that going down with the ship would have been in the Party's interests since two Mensheviks would have drowned with every Bolshevik.[49]

For Lenin, however, the defeat at Stockholm was no joking matter; his sole success was with Paragraph One, wherein his formulation of Party membership was retained. He attempted to make the best of the situation by appearing to exercise moderation and by paying lip service to Party unity. At the same time, he never abandoned the we-they dichotomy when he wrote about the Mensheviks in the months following the Fourth Congress, and he continued to denounce them for their passivity.

Relations between the two factions became noticeably strained again on August 27 (September 9), 1906, when Lenin presided over a Bolshevik meeting in the Russo-Finnish frontier village of Terioki; at this time, it was unanimously decided to insist upon the convocation of a new congress. Plekhanov responded to this renewed agitation—a repetition of Lenin's 1904 activities for the Third Congress—with an article published in the September 17, 1906, issue of *Sotsial-Demokrat* (No. 1) in which he observed:

> It is known that at our last Party Congress, the former "Bolsheviks" [i.e., the members of the majority] found themselves in the *minority*. This they did not like. And here they are attempting to obtain a new congress on the calculation that the majority of votes there may in some way come to be on their side. If this calculation does not prove to be correct, they lose nothing; and if it proves to be correct, they win in the sense that they find themselves "in power."

Plekhanov warned that the internal struggle was paralyzing the Party's forces and expressed grave doubt as to the Party's future. He accused the Bolsheviks of being "prepared to sacrifice the over-all interests of the Party in the interests of their faction."[50] He recalled how, on an earlier occasion, Lenin had professed to him his desire ("with all my soul") to unite with the Mensheviks. The "father of Russian Marxism" had replied to his former pupil: "I believe it, but you aspire to unite with them [the Mensheviks] in the same way that a hungry person yearns to unite with a piece of bread: you want to eat them."[51]

In defiance of the Party's Central Committee, which he no longer ruled, Lenin published broadsides against the Mensheviks and Plekhanov in no fewer than three Bolshevik legal newspapers which appeared in St. Petersburg following the Stockholm Congress. The first of these, *Volna* ("The Wave"), appeared as a daily from April 26 (May 9) to May 24 (June 6), 1906; seven of its twenty-five issues were confiscated, and the "responsible editor" was prosecuted. Two days after *Volna* was closed, it was replaced by *Vperyod* ("Forward"), which lasted until June 14 (27). A third newspaper, *Ekho* ("The Echo"), made its appearance within eight days, but ten of its fourteen issues were confiscated by the government, and it was closed on July 7 (20), 1906, on the eve of the dissolution of the First Duma.

This last event prompted Lenin to write a pamphlet, *The Dissolution of the Duma and the Tasks of the Proletariat,* in which he interpreted the measure as a "return to autocracy." His answer to this move by the government was an appeal for an "all-Russian uprising . . . not a 'rebellion' [*bunt*], not a 'demonstration,' not a strike . . . but a struggle for power, a struggle for the purpose of the overthrow of the government."[52] This uprising would overthrow the autocracy and create a truly popular representative body—a constituent assembly. Ironically, when such a body was ultimately elected eleven years later, Lenin was to disperse it by force of arms on January 18, 1918, at its first meeting. Lenin's 1906 appeal for an armed rising was without effect; even the short-lived mutinies—in the fleet at Sveaborg (Suomenlinna, in the Gulf of Finland near Helsinki) and at Kronstadt in late July and early August, 1906—could hardly be attributed to Lenin's pamphlet.

The Czarist regime, in dissolving the First Duma, noted that the law concerning the Duma remained unchanged and promised the convocation of a new Duma by February 20 (March 5), 1907. This move and the ineffectiveness of the so-called "Viborg

Manifesto" signed by members of the First Duma (calling on the populace to give the government neither money nor soldiers) raised anew the question of whether or not to boycott the Duma. Lenin, writing on August 21 (September 3), 1906, in his latest newspaper, *Proletarii* (printed in Viborg and smuggled into St. Petersburg), declared that "the time has now arrived when revolutionary Social Democrats must cease being boycottists." He noted that "we shall not refuse to utilize this arena of struggle, by no means exaggerating its modest significance, but, on the contrary, completely subordinating it to another kind of struggle—by means of strikes, uprisings, and the like."[53] In promising a fifth congress, Lenin also declared that it would provide for "an electoral alliance for several weeks [*sic*] with the Trudoviki"—the predominant peasant party of the day— in the event of elections to a new Duma. Because the Stockholm Congress had forbidden all blocs with other parties, Lenin argued, a new congress was necessary in order to approve such a temporary alliance. An electoral alliance would defeat the Kadets, the largest party in the First Duma.

Yet, at the Second Tammerfors Party Conference in November, 1906, Lenin was defeated by the Mensheviks and the Bund on this issue when they adopted by a vote of eighteen to fourteen a resolution permitting electoral alliances even with the bourgeois Kadets—although not in the labor *curiae*. The Mensheviks' resolution allowed "local agreements with revolutionary and oppositional-democratic parties" in the rural and in the other urban electoral *curiae* if it became clear in the course of the campaign that a right-wing victory would otherwise result.[54] This meant that, from the Menshevik viewpoint, an alliance with the Kadets was permissible under the general control of the Central Committee if it led to the defeat of the Duma candidate of the monarchist Octobrist Party or of the reactionary Black Hundreds. From Lenin's opposing point of view, the Kadets were to be combatted and not sought after as electoral allies.

Thus, the Bolshevik-Menshevik disagreement continued to revolve around tactics. Both factions agreed on the need to foster the idea of the class struggle, to "explain to the masses the illusory nature of all hopes for a peaceful way out of the struggle

for power between the people and the autocracy," and to utilize
the Duma for the convocation of a fully empowered constituent
assembly by revealing the Duma's impotence as a legislative
body under an autocratic monarchy.[55] While both the Bolsheviks
and the Mensheviks agreed on long-range goals, the disagreement over means relentlessly deepened the division between the
two factions, ultimately leading to the emergence of two similar
but bitterly antagonistic parties.

The elections to the Second Duma, held in February, 1907,
resulted in a victory for the Menshevik position: thirty-six Mensheviks were elected, as compared with eighteen Bolsheviks and
eleven centrists (who usually voted with the Mensheviks); the
Kadets lost nearly half the seats they had held in the First Duma.
Tensions between the Bolsheviks and the Mensheviks became
aggravated during the electoral campaign in St. Petersburg,
where the former controlled the local Party committee while the
latter controlled the Central Committee elected at Stockholm.
A provincial and city conference of seventy-one voting representatives (forty Bolsheviks and thirty-one Mensheviks) met in
St. Petersburg on January 6 (19), 1907. The Bolsheviks expressed opposition to an electoral fusion with the Kadets. However, the "pure" Bolsheviks—of whom Lenin was *not* one at
that conference—were opposed to an electoral bloc with anyone.
Lenin; who led the so-called Bolshevik "dissidents," favored a
temporary bloc with the Trudoviki. The Menshevik Central
Committee disapproved of the conference and declared that its
decisions were not binding; the Central Committee had favored
two conferences—one for the city itself, where the Mensheviks
were stronger, and another for the province, where the Bolsheviks
enjoyed greater strength. When the Bolshevik majority refused
to accept the advice of the Central Committee, the thirty-one
Mensheviks walked out of the conference. The Bolsheviks, in-
voking the usual double-standard argument, contended that the
Central Committee had no right to interfere with the autonomy
of local Party organizations—a line which they quickly abandoned, of course, when the Central Committee became purely
Bolshevik.[56]

In his arguments with the Mensheviks, Lenin employed the

old trick of oversimplifying his adversaries' position. He emphasized their supposed willingness to enter into a bloc with the Kadets, while, in fact, they were also prepared to enter into an electoral alliance with the peasant-socialist–oriented Trudoviki and with the Popular Socialists. The latter group was composed of intellectuals who had broken off from the Socialist Revolutionaries and had taken a more moderate stand under the leadership of Nikolai Fedorovich Annensky, V. A. Myakotin, and A. V. Peshekhonov. A week after the St. Petersburg conference, where the Mensheviks had staged their walkout, Lenin accused them of being "the petty-bourgeois part of the workers' party."[57] Yet, Lenin admitted that he did not know of actual negotiations between the Mensheviks and the Kadets over the division of seats in the event of a bloc, and he even conceded that his old enemies might have merely hinted at a bloc.[58] In an article written on January 15 (28), 1907, he accused the Mensheviks of pursuing "the Oblomov idea of a bloc of all left parties"—again employing a favorite figure of speech, based on the ineffective character in Ivan Alexandrovich Goncharov's novel. In this article, Lenin openly declared war on the Mensheviks and asked: "Who is with us?"[59]

Basic to this issue was the question of whether the Social Democrats could register any respectable electoral showing alone. Lenin was convinced that, united, they could defeat the Kadets in St. Petersburg. Acting on this assumption, and with much self-righteous indignation, on January 20 (February 2), 1907, he published a pamphlet entitled *The Elections in Petersburg and the Hypocrisy of the 31 Mensheviks*. In intemperate language, Lenin accused the Mensheviks of having sold the votes of the workers and of having "gotten into an opportunistic, petty-bourgeois bloc."[60] In actuality, the Mensheviks were motivated by the fear that failure to form a bloc with the Kadets would lead to a victory for the united, reactionary Black Hundreds. Lenin denied the existence of such a danger and bluntly declared that the Mensheviks, if they really feared a victory of the right, would reach an agreement with the Kadets at any price—something which they were actually unprepared to do.

The incensed Menshevik Central Committee ordered Lenin

to stand trial before an *ad hoc* Party court composed of three
members from Lenin's side, three from the Committee's side,
and a presidium of three representatives appointed by the Central Committees of the Latvian and Polish Social Democratic
Parties and by the Bund. The charge was that Lenin had written
and published in a manner "impermissible for Party members."
This Party tribunal met only twice, as its status was to be
determined by the impending Fifth Congress. At the first session,
held late in March, 1907, Lenin defended himself by turning
prosecutor and accusing his own judges. He contended that he
had accused the Mensheviks of "selling" workers' votes not for
money but rather for seats in the Duma. He conceded that his
language would have been "impermissible for members of a
single [*edinoi*] party," but the Menshevik-controlled Central
Committee remained silent regarding the absence of a united,
single Party at the time the offensive pamphlet was written.
Lenin thus denied that the Mensheviks were still his Party comrades; he justified his choice of abusive language "because a
schism obliges one to wrench the masses out from under the
leadership of the secessionists."[61]

Indeed, Lenin expressed regret that he had not gone far
enough in the direction of wrenching away the masses in St.
Petersburg, since the Kadets had won an overwhelming victory
there in the elections to the Second Duma. He accused the
Central Committee of having initiated the schism among the
Social Democrats in St. Petersburg and singled out for particular
attack the Menshevik F. I. Dan, whom he was to accuse at the
Fifth Congress of having "'drunk tea' *in private*" with the
Kadet leaders Paul Miliukov and Vladimir D. Nabokov in
November, 1906.[62] Concluding his statement before the Party
tribunal, Lenin branded the conduct of Dan and the thirty-one
Mensheviks as "dishonest" (*nechestnoe*) and threatened that
the verdict of the Party court would determine whether the
St. Petersburg schism would be the last ". . . or [whether] it will
be the beginning of a new schism and . . . a new general struggle
with poisoned weapons."[63] The tribunal avoided handing down
a verdict by leaving the matter to the approaching Party
Congress.

CHAPTER III

FROM FACTION TO PARTY

Certainly, it is the sacred right of every citizen and, particularly, of every intellectual to follow whichever ideological reactionary they wish. But if people, having broken completely with the very *bases of Marxism* in philosophy, then commence to revolve, confuse, equivocate, to affirm that they are "also" Marxists in philosophy, that they are "almost" in agreement with Marx and only "complement" him a wee bit—that is an altogether unpleasant spectacle.

—Lenin, *Materialism and Empirio-Criticism* (Part I, Chapter IV).

The dialectic of history is such that the theoretical victory of Marxism compels its enemies to disguise themselves as Marxists. Internally rotten liberalism attempts to enliven itself in the form of socialist opportunism.

—Lenin, "The Historical Fate of the Teachings of Karl Marx," in *Pravda*, March 1, 1913.

A headless person or, more precisely, a person with a turnip on his shoulders instead of a head—that is nonpartisanship.

—J. V. Stalin, in *Zvezda*, April 15, 1912.

The Fifth Congress of the Party, which met in a London church from May 13 to June 1, 1907, was to be the last one held for more than a decade to come. It met only after considerable difficulty. Originally, the conclave was to have been held in Copenhagen, and more than 200 delegates had gathered in that city. They attracted considerable attention—so much attention, in fact, that the Danish authorities gave them twelve hours in which to leave the country. The time limit and the large number of delegates left the Congress no choice but to take to the sea. The alternative for the delegates was arrest and deportation to Russia.

Arrangements were quickly made to go to the Swedish port of Malmö, where the delegates arrived in full force in the dead of night. With the aid of Swedish Social Democrats and some men in bowler hats, they found quarters—only to be barred from them by the police. The men in bowler hats had turned out to be detectives. The delegates sat on their suitcases in a public square at 2 A.M. cursing everyone—the Central Committee, the Swedes, and the world bourgeoisie.[1] The Swedish Government forbade all meetings and gave the Russians three days in which to leave the country, but the police mercifully arranged for the delegates to be divided into small groups and housed at various hotels by daybreak.

Again, London was to receive the peripatetic delegates as it had in 1903, and a parliamentary democracy would once more provide a haven for the deliberations of several hundred men who were bent upon destroying it. To reach London, it was necessary to cross Denmark, and the Danish Social Democrats managed to obtain permission for the Russians to make the crossing. There was, however, one unpleasant incident at Esbjerg where the Russians went to hotels operated by Social Democrats and, thinking that everything was at the owners' expense, ate and drank their fill—only to be presented with a most unsocialist bill the next morning. After heaping abuse upon these "roguish innkeepers," the Russians grudgingly paid and embarked for England, landing at Harwich.[2]

The British, living in a free country and accustomed to seeing all kinds of visitors from their far-flung empire, paid little attention to this group attired mostly in Russian *kosovorotki*. The delegates were impressed by the two-storied trolleys, the crowds, the large shopwindows, and the "underground" (one with which the Bolsheviks, despite all their experience in subterranean activities, were not familiar). The delegates gathered in London's Russian-Jewish quarter in Whitechapel, where they took rooms. K. D. Gandurin, a delegate from Ivanovo-Voznesensk and the secretary of its purely Bolshevik city Party committee, recalled in his memoirs his stay with the family of an immigrant tailor, noting that a "qualified worker in England has a piano and has his child taught music" and "how unlike our dirty and dusty Ivanovo-Voznesensk life this was."[3]

On May 13, 1907, Plekhanov opened the Fifth Congress in London, just as he had opened the Second Congress less than four years earlier in Brussels. This Congress was a far larger and more impressive gathering than any which had preceded it—the assemblage of more than 300 delegates was certainly a far cry from the First Congress held in Minsk only nine years earlier, attended by only nine delegates. As a result of the 1905 Revolution, the Party's membership was said to have increased to nearly 150,000—though this was probably an inflated figure.[*] There were 279 voting delegates and 42 with a consultative vote; among the latter was Stalin, who had been a voting delegate at the Stockholm "Unity" Congress a year earlier.

The Fifth Congress was unique not only because of its size, but also because of the presence of ten of the Social Democratic deputies to the Second Duma. The Bolshevik strength among the 279 voting delegates was limited to between 81 and 90 votes, while the Mensheviks controlled from 80 to 85. This meant that the balance was held by the delegates representing the non-Russian parties; of these, the Poles had between 39 and 45 votes, the Bund between 54 and 56, and the Latvians 25 or 26 votes.[4] Since the Bundists usually voted with the Mensheviks, the Bolsheviks were able to muster a majority of two or three votes only with the aid of the Poles and the Latvians.[5] It now became clear why Lenin had attached so much importance to the admission of these two non-Russian parties into the All-Russian Social Democratic Labor Party at the Stockholm Congress in April, 1906. It must be recognized that, in the delicate voting balance which prevailed at the Fifth Congress, Lenin demonstrated no mean ability as a tactician and master of the art of parliamentary maneuver. For example, he mentioned at the Congress that Trotsky was "drawing closer to our

---

[*] Of this number, less than one-third (46,000) were Bolsheviks, and there were 38,000 Mensheviks; the Bundists and Polish Social Democrats each numbered 25,000, and there were 13,000 Latvians.—*V.K.P.(b) v rezolyutsiyakh* . . . (6th ed.; Moscow: Partizdat, 1940), Part I, p. 97.

views" in advocating a left bloc of peasantry and proletariat against the liberal bourgeoisie. In deliberately muting his difference with Trotsky, Lenin was seeking to avoid antagonizing Trotsky's centrist group, which contributed to the balance of voting power.[6]

The target of Lenin's maneuvering was again the Menshevik wing of the supposedly unified Party. The tensions which had led to the walkout of the thirty-one Mensheviks from the St. Petersburg conference were still in evidence.[7] Thus, when a Presidium that included Lenin and the Menshevik F. I. Dan was elected at the first session of the Fifth Congress, Dan read an announcement from the St. Petersburg Mensheviks vainly protesting Lenin's election. The Bolsheviks interrupted the reading with hoots and the scuffling of shoes. Lenin denounced the Mensheviks for their alleged flirtation with the Kadets and accused them of having been opposed to participation in a provisional revolutionary government in 1905 because they believed it was the privilege of the bourgeoisie to be the "principal mover or leader" of the bourgeois revolution. The Bolsheviks, Lenin held, took the position that the bourgeoisie can only vacillate between revolution and reaction, and is incapable of leading its own revolution. Therefore, the proletariat must lead the bourgeois revolution, but can do so only with the support of the peasantry.

Despite all this bombast, Lenin's Bolsheviks did not gain a clear-cut victory at the inconclusive Fifth Congress. However, with the aid of the center (the "swamp"), the Bolshevik position regarding the Duma was adopted. The resolution stressed the need to explain to the people the complete uselessness of the Duma as a means of realizing the demands of the proletariat, the revolutionary petty bourgeoisie, and especially the peasantry.[8] However, the resolution on the activities of the Social Democratic deputies did not contain the Bolsheviks' specific criticism of the deputies' actions, such as their having voted for a Kadet as presiding officer of the Duma. Nor did it include their charge that the deputies "unfortunately did not always develop with full consistency the point of view of the proletarian class struggle."[9] Instead, it declared that the Social Democratic faction in the Duma "stood guard over the interests of the proletariat and the revolution."[10] As a result, it was said that the Bolshevik "barrel of honey" had been spoiled by a Menshevik "spoonful of tar."

With the aid of the center, the Bolsheviks did gain a majority for their resolution on nonproletarian parties—a motion that was strongly critical of the Kadets. While acknowledging the Socialist Revolutionaries, the Trudoviki, and the so-called Popular Socialists as the representatives of "broad masses of the village and urban petty bourgeoisie," the resolution criticized their "nebulous socialist ideology" and called for the Party to unmask their "pseudosocialist" character and to compel them to choose between the Social Democrats and the Kadets.[11] Lenin's Bolsheviks also scored a victory on the issue of the convocation of a broad, nonpartisan workers' congress, which some Mensheviks desired. The resolution adopted by the Fifth Congress denounced this idea as one inevitably leading toward the disorganization of the Party and the subordination of the masses to the influence of bourgeois democracy.

The Congress condemned the Bolshevik expropriatory raids in no uncertain terms, declaring them to be "anarchist methods of struggle [which] introduce disorganization into the ranks of the proletariat." It also ordered the "fighting units" to be disbanded, although it did "not predetermine the question of the forms of organizing the arming of the masses in the period of open attack."[12] Two of the most notorious raids had occurred in March, 1906: one in Tbilisi (Tiflis) province, executed by six armed persons disguised as soldiers, provided 315,000 rubles; another one in Moscow, supposedly carried out by twenty factional Socialist Revolutionaries, relieved a merchants' bank of 875,000 rubles.[13] This resolution by the Fifth Congress notwithstanding, a large raid was carried out in Tbilisi on June 13 (26), 1907, providing the Bolsheviks with 250,000 rubles.[14]

The results of the noisy Fifth Congress were not nearly as impressive as its size; if anything, they merely served to indicate how divided the Party was. In an effort to forestall an open schism, the "appraisal of the current moment" was removed from the agenda by a vote of 137 to 89. But the Congress was also badgered by more practical problems. For one thing, the Party was running short of funds.

The delegates were being paid a per diem of two to two and a half shillings, but since they were so numerous, even this modest obligation could not be met. It became clear that the Party would require a very substantial loan from some individual. The only Russians who were sufficiently prominent to vouch for such a loan were Plekhanov and Maxim Gorky (who was attending the Congress, but not as a delegate); the former is said to have declined the honor. Funds were finally obtained from the soap manufacturer Joseph Fels, who granted the Party an interest-free loan of 1,700 pounds sterling, but demanded in return a promissory note signed by all the delegates. They complied with this condition on May 30, 1907, since the note and their signatures had "no practical significance"[15] in their eyes. The note was payable on January 1, 1908, but the Party did not redeem it then. The loan was supposedly repaid by the Soviet Government ten or more years later. If such repayment actually occurred, the Bolsheviks magnanimously paid the hotel bills and living expenses of their mortal enemies, the Mensheviks and the Bundists.

Another difficulty arose when the Congress was told to vacate the Brotherhood Church no later than June 1. This made it impossible for a Central Committee to be elected by the entire Congress. It was decided to convene a committee composed of one member for every four delegates. The Congress empowered this seventy-five–member committee, presided over by Lenin, to elect twelve members to the Central Committee: five Bolsheviks, four Mensheviks, and three from the non-Russian nationalities. The Bolsheviks had twenty-two of the seventy-five seats in the electoral committee, the Mensheviks twenty-one, the Bundists fourteen, the Poles eleven, and the Latvians seven. The new Central Committee included no one of prominence from the Bolsheviks, with the possible exception of Victor P. Nogin, an old *Iskra* agent who was to head a Soviet textile syndicate prior to his death in 1924. It is significant that Lenin, Zinoviev, Krasin, Bogdanov, Rykov, Taratuta, and four others were elected not as full members but as alternates to replace members in the event of arrests. Of the four Mensheviks in the Central Committee, Martynov and Noi Nikolaevich Zhordania were the most prominent, while Martov and six others were elected alternates. The two Polish members elected were Felix Dzierzynski and Adolf Warski. In addition to the twelve Central Committee members chosen by the Congress committee, three were added later—two from the Bund and one Latvian representative.

Thus, Lenin did not win a real victory at the Fifth Congress. He did succeed in discrediting the Menshevik Central Committee elected at Stockholm the year before, and he managed to obliterate the Party tribunal which was to try him. More important, he was able to re-establish, in Paragraph Seven of the Party Statutes, his principle of unitary control which explicitly provided that the Central Committee appoint the editors of the Party's Central Organ and control their activities. This constituted rejection of the principle of dual centers, which had been reasserted in the 1906 Statutes at Stockholm. Thus, Lenin succeeded in imposing upon the whole Party his principle of a single center, which had first been adopted at his purely Bolshevik Third Congress in London.

These were, indeed, symptoms that the Party was gradually assuming more of the characteristics which were to be described as Leninist and which have governed the Soviet Party to this day. Yet, Lenin was not to have entirely smooth sailing. The defeat of the Mensheviks left them even more chagrined than usual. Nor were matters helped by Lenin's abundant sarcasm, as when he told the Congress derisively: "Poor Mensheviks! Again, they are in a state of siege. They are 'besieged' not only when they are in the minority, but also when they are in the majority!"[16]

But Lenin was soon to have occasion to wonder whether he was still the leader of the Bolsheviks. Dissension arose in the Bolshevik camp soon after the Fifth Congress adjourned, when the Second Duma was dissolved on June 3 (16), 1907, and its Social Democratic deputies were arrested. Lenin, Krupskaya tells us, was "overwrought and could not eat" following his return to Finland after the Fifth Congress. He rested at Stirsudden and wrote a preface to the second edition of his *The*

Development of Capitalism in Russia. On August 3-5, 1907, Lenin attended a Party conference at Kotka,* Finland, at which the principal topic of discussion was the attitude to be adopted by the Party on the elections to the Third Duma scheduled for September 1.

Dissolution of the Second Duma had come in the wake of the discovery by Czarist authorities of a plot against the government. The government used this plot to demand the expulsion of all the fifty-five Social Democratic deputies in the Duma. Conceivably, dissolution could have been avoided, or at least postponed, had the Duma acquiesced in this expulsion of the Social Democrats. The parliament, however, was unwilling to do the government's bidding. The government's move was obviously prompted in part by growing chagrin at the Duma's embarrassing interpellations, its concern with the agrarian question, its criticism of the budget and government excesses, as well as its demand for a responsible executive. The plot in question, which linked the Social Democratic deputies to a group of Party members interested in promoting unrest in the St. Petersburg garrison, was uncovered in information provided by a female agent of the *Okhrana* who had infiltrated the organization.[17] The arrest of most of these deputies following the dissolution caused many Bolsheviks to doubt seriously the usefulness of participating in the Third Duma, which was to convene on November 1, 1907. The new electoral law, issued simultaneously with the dissolution of the Duma, sharply reduced the suffrage of the non-Russian peoples, the peasantry, and labor.

The Party conference at Kotka in early August, 1907, was attended by nine Bolsheviks, five Mensheviks, five Polish Social Democrats, five Bundists, and two Latvian Social Democrats. Lenin found himself in agreement with his Menshevik enemies on the need to participate in the Third Duma, despite the new restrictions upon suffrage. However, the other Bolsheviks at Kotka followed the lead of Bogdanov and advocated a boycott, although their resolution received only nine votes. Lenin's anti-boycott resolution was adopted in the end by a vote of fifteen

* Certain earlier Party sources state that this conference was held at nearby Viborg (Viipuri).

to eleven, but only after Bogdanov's followers had decided that his resolution was less dangerous than that of the Mensheviks. Lenin defended his position by asserting that he could support a boycott only if there were some possibility of a large-scale strike, which could grow into a general strike similar to the one which had occurred in October, 1905. However, since Lenin felt that there was no longer any revolutionary enthusiasm abroad in Russia, such a policy would transform the idea of a boycott into a fetish.[18]

The split in the Bolshevik ranks at the Kotka conference, although it seemed only transitory, was to have grave consequences by opening the door to a whole series of personal altercations based on disagreement over what constituted true Bolshevism. After the break between Lenin and Bogdanov—supposedly based only on philosophical differences, but in all likelihood related also to their continuing disagreements over the Duma question—there came a spate of new deviations which threatened Bolshevik unity.

When Lenin returned to Finland in late August, after attending the Stuttgart International Socialist Congress, it became increasingly clear that he would soon have to flee to Western Europe. The Bolsheviks had been publishing their *Proletarii* illegally in Finland since August, 1906, and smuggling it into St. Petersburg. Twenty issues of the newspaper were distributed in this manner. By the end of 1907, however, it became necessary to transfer publication to Western Europe, where it was resumed in February, 1908, and ended in December, 1909. The editorial board included Lenin, Bogdanov, and Iosif Fedorovich Dubrovinsky (Innokentii).

Lenin fled from Finland in December, 1907, under threat of arrest. More than nine years were to pass before he would return, in April, 1917—and then thanks only to the existence of a liberal Russian regime and to the cooperation of the Germans. The flight from Finland to Sweden had an element of fateful drama. Had Lenin boarded the steamer for Sweden at Turku (Åbbo) on the Finnish mainland, he probably would have been arrested by the Russian police. In order to avoid this risk, he was advised to proceed to the nearest island and board the steamer there, but this entailed a walk of three versts (two miles) across the ice. The ice was not very thick, and no guides were available for the trip. Lenin finally obtained the services of two not very sober Finnish farmers for whom—in accordance with the old Russian proverb concerning drunkards—the sea was only knee-deep. At one point during the crossing, the ice began to break, and Lenin barely escaped with his life; he later recalled thinking at the time, what a foolish way to die![19] Thus, the future of Bolshevism hung in the balance in December, 1907, on the thin ice off the coast of Finland.

After waiting two weeks for Krupskaya to rejoin him in Stockholm, Lenin proceeded with her to Berlin and then to Geneva. He immediately plunged into publication plans as a board member of *Proletarii,* and the first issue of the newspaper to be published abroad (No. 21) appeared on February 26, 1908. However, Lenin was soon to turn his attention to philosophy—an area which, as a practical revolutionary, he had shunned thus far. The principal reason for Lenin's trek into this new discipline was Bogdanov, his fellow editor of *Proletarii* and his former right-hand man, who had been so indispensable to him in organizing the purely Bolshevik Third Congress in 1905.

Bogdanov had become attracted by the views of the Austrian physicist-mathematician Ernst Mach and was attempting to reconcile Mach with Marxism. In writing to Gorky on February 25, 1908, Lenin expressed concern over Bogdanov's views and over the "differences between the Bolsheviks on philosophical questions." Yet, he also admitted to Gorky: "I do not regard myself as sufficiently competent regarding these questions to rush into print."[20] Lenin explained the origins of the controversy which was brewing. In the autumn of 1904, he and Bogdanov had "drawn closer as Bolsheviks." The two had concluded that tacit bloc which silently set aside philosophy as a neutral area, even though Plekhanov, an ardent anti-Machist, had criticized Bogdanov's philosophical views in 1902-03. In the heat of revolutionary activity in 1905-06, Lenin explained, there had been no time to devote to philosophical questions, but in the summer of 1906 he had become "unusually angry and maddened" by the publication of the third part of Bogdanov's *Empiriomonism.*[21]

By 1908, Lenin had become profoundly disturbed by various philosophical tendencies among the Bolshevik intellectuals. He accused Bogdanov, as well as V. Bazarov (Vladimir Alexandrovich Rudnev), of confusing Marxism and Kantianism; empiriomonism he equated with idealism, and empiriocriticism with preaching of the variety of agnosticism.

Lenin's letter had been prompted by an article of Gorky's, submitted to *Proletarii,* which contained certain passages of a pro-Bogdanov nature. Lenin was against printing the article without revision; he asked Gorky to remain neutral in philosophical matters and not to exacerbate the conflict within the Bolshevik camp. However, Lenin was not overly optimistic about resolving the controversy. He noted: "I regard a certain quarrel between the Bolsheviks on the question of philosophy as absolutely inevitable." Yet, he added that "to split" over that question "would be stupid," since Bazarov, a Machist, had after all been in agreement with him in opposing a boycott of the Duma.[22]

During the second half of April, 1908, Lenin visited Gorky on the isle of Capri. At that time, he declined to collaborate with Bogdanov, Lunacharsky, and Bazarov in the publication of a symposium to be entitled *Outlines of the Philosophy of Collectivism,* since he disagreed with them. They, in turn, refused to join Lenin in writing a history of the 1905 Revolution which was to be a rebuttal of an allegedly Liquidationist history being prepared by anti-Leninists who supposedly wished to liquidate the illegal underground Bolshevik Party organization. Lenin then determined to try his hand at philosophy and, during May and June of 1908, spent several weeks in the British Museum doing research for a volume which was hastily written and completed in October and imposingly called *Materialism and Empiriocriticism, Critical Notes Concerning One Reactionary Philosophy.* Two thousand copies of this tendentious and polemical work were published legally in Moscow in May, 1909, with the author identified as Vl. Ilyin.

Lenin's repetitious and denunciatory work, in which quotations abound *ad nauseum,* was characterized by Axelrod as containing "no new thoughts" and as possessing "neither the flexibility of philosophical thought, nor the exactness of philosophical definitions, nor a profound understanding of philosophical problems."[23] In attacking Bogdanov, Lenin criticized the empiriocriticism of Mach, which Bogdanov had allegedly deemed compatible with Marxism. Mach's philosophy of "critical experience" involved a psychology based upon physical phenomenalism, "economy of thought" (the notion that thought and science are based upon the conservation of effort and the satisfaction of needs), and the view that experience is based upon consciousness and sensation. The other target of Lenin's pen was Richard Avenarius, a professor at the University of Zurich and the founder of empiriocriticism. Lenin accused Avenarius of equating the external world with consciousness and of refusing to subordinate the psychical to the physical. The "crime" of these men was that they sought to reconcile materialism and idealism and, in doing so, "betrayed" the former.

Bogdanov, influenced by empiriocriticism, had preached his own empiriomonism, a philosophy based exclusively upon experience in which the consciousness of the individual was allegedly replaced by the collective consciousness. Lenin's belated criticism of Bogdanov was based on the contention that he had regarded nature as the product of consciousness, had equated social life with psychical activity, and had thus denied materialism. Empiriocriticism and empiriomonism were denounced by Lenin as being nothing more than a restatement of the anti-materialist "subjectivist-idealist" views of the Anglican Bishop George Berkeley, who regarded objects as collections of ideas and equated the object with sensation. Although Bogdanov's views received much attention in Lenin's *Materialism and Empiriocriticism,* the philosophical polemic was also directed against such Machists as Anatole V. Lunacharsky, N. Valentinov (Nikolai Vladislavovich Vol'sky), and Bazarov, as well as against the Menshevik empiriosymbolist Paul Solomonovich Yushkevich, who had adopted Henri Poincaré's views regarding natural laws as conditional symbols employed for the sake of convenience.

Of great significance was Lenin's appraisal of the consequences of the Machists' actions. Each of these men claimed to be a Marxist and denied vehemently that he was an idealist in philosophy. Yet, Lenin charged them with having, in fact, departed from the fundamentals of Marxism, notwithstanding their use of Marxist terminology. He declared Bogdanov's "development of Marx . . . [to be] *in no way different* in *substance* from the refutation of Marx by the idealist and gnosiological solipsist [Richard] Schubert-Soldern," a representative of the "immanent school" who argued that perception or cognition was based on the consciousness of the person who is perceiving. However, Lenin was not too harsh with the independent-minded Bogdanov; he conceded that his former lieutenant "is personally a mortal enemy of all reaction and, particularly, of bourgeois reaction," and yet he insisted that Bogdanov's "theory of the 'identity of social existence and social consciousness' *serves* this reaction." Lenin added: "It is a sad fact, but a fact."[24] The accusation that Bogdanov's views were permeated with an idealism "disguised in Marxist terms, falsified under Marxist words,"[25] found a latter-day counterpart in Stalin's famous assertion at the Central Committee plenary session on March 3, 1937. On that occasion, in the midst of the great Yezhov purges, Stalin declared: "The present-day wreckers and diversionists, the Trotskyites—these are for the most part Party people, with a Party card in their pocket . . ."[26] Thus, the Leninist charge of concealed heresy was to receive its ultimate refinement in Stalinism.

In his treatment of absolute and relative truth in *Materialism and Empiriocriticism,* the founder of Bolshevism gave his movement yet another basic tenet. Again Bogdanov served as the devil's advocate. He had asserted in his *Empiriomonism* (Part III, pp. iv-v) that truth is an ideological entity, an organized form of human experience based upon collective experience, and that "Marxism includes the negation of the unconditional objectivity of any truth, the negation of all eternal truths." This was interpreted by his antagonists as meaning that truth is that which is socially significant in a given historical epoch. Lenin and Plekhanov ridiculed this view, contending it implied that, if people once believed in hobgoblins and spirits, these phenomena must have existed objectively.[27] Thus, in Lenin's view, Bogdanov had denied the existence of objective truth and had

ceased to be a good materialist by having confused the physical
with the psychical.

Lenin raised the question of the existence of objective truth
independent of humanity, as well as the question of whether man
can express objective truth immediately, fully, unconditionally,
and absolutely, *or* only approximately and relatively.[28] Bogdanov's
famous detractor came down squarely on the side of absolute
truth, contending that it was being approached in the course
of a historical process and was composed of a limitless series of
relative truths. According to Lenin, the road to objective truth
lay exclusively in Marxist theory, while all other roads led to
"snarls and lies."[29] In the process of arriving at the conclusion
with which he had actually begun his work, Lenin denied the
value of relativism, although he recognized that relative truth
had its place as a means but not as an end in itself. He declared
that "to place relativism at the basis of the theory of perception
inevitably means to condemn one's self either to absolute skepti-
cism, agnosticism, and sophistry, or to subjectivism."[30] Thus,
Lenin adopted Friedrich Engels' position (developed in *Anti-
Dühring*) that relative truths inevitably lead to absolute truth.
He condemned Bogdanov as a relativist and praised Engels as
a dialectician.

Yet, a contradiction emerged in this work—one which Communists have been able to resolve only by fiat. Lenin recognized
that the dialectic supposedly contains relativism, and he chided
Bogdanov for emphasizing his opposition to eternal truth, dogmatism, and statics, since Marxism recognizes that the "world
is eternally moving and developing matter . . . reflected by
developing human consciousness." At the same time, he made
it clear that the Party alone—in the last analysis, Lenin himself—would decide how matter was to be reflected. Thus, we
find Lenin declaring that in philosophy there is no "unpartisan"
approach, and in political economy there is only "party science."[31]

The controversy that evoked Lenin's intemperate and unread-
able *Materialism and Empiriocriticism* was not merely an abstract philosophical dispute, but was related also to the rise of
"Recallism" (*Otzovism*) within the Bolshevik ranks. This movement, which challenged the correctness of Lenin's decision to

participate in the Third Duma, had developed during the spring of 1908 as a result of dissatisfaction with the conduct of the Social Democratic deputies, and it demanded that the Party recall them. The Party's eighteen deputies in the Third Duma were predominantly Menshevik; the Central Committee, in which the Bolsheviks were now the largest single faction, quickly became displeased when the deputies adopted a declaration, written by Potresov, which made no mention of land confiscation or of the need for a constituent assembly. The Menshevik deputies also had little desire to report to legal meetings of workers on their activities. In addition, when the Duma, at its third session, decided to send the Czar a telegram of greeting, the Social Democratic deputies absented themselves instead of exploiting the opportunity to "describe" conditions in the country.

Criticism of the Social Democratic Duma deputies by the Central Committee merely served to exacerbate tensions between the Bolshevik and Menshevik wings of the Party. At the same time, many Bolsheviks who had been "Boycottists" in the debate over participation in the Duma became "Ultimatists": they demanded that the Central Committee issue the Party's Duma deputies an ultimatum requiring them to obey the instructions of the Central Committee. Alexinsky, a prominent Ultimatist and leader of Bolshevik deputies in the Second Duma who later became an anti-Soviet *émigré*, agreed that the Bolshevik Duma faction was not sufficiently Party-oriented. Yet, he rejected Recallism because it would bring about an undesirable split in the Party. Instead, he advocated the issuance of two ultimatums—one calling for the unconditional subordination of the Social Democratic Duma faction to the Central Committee, and the other demanding the deputies' participation in Party activities outside the Duma.[32] The discussion among the Bolsheviks over the role of the Social Democratic faction continued while the Duma was in recess during the summer. The winter of 1908-09 witnessed an intensification of the internecine controversy, with Lenin compelled to speak out against both the Recallists and the Ultimatists.

Thus, beginning in 1908, Lenin was confronted with opposition from within his own Bolshevik camp, in addition to the continued criticism from the Mensheviks. The conflict with the latter had been intensified by the scandal growing from the Tbilisi expropriatory raid of June 13 (26), 1907. Since many of the notes stolen in that raid were in the denomination of 500 rubles, it became very difficult to exchange them. When a synchronized attempt was finally made in December, 1907, in a number of Western European countries, the perpetrators were arrested; among them was Maxim Litvinov, the future Soviet foreign commissar, who was seized in Paris but was not extradited to Russia. The attempt to exchange the bank notes was foiled by a Russian police spy in Berlin, Dr. Jacob Zhitomirsky, who enjoyed Lenin's confidence and had divulged the plan to the authorities. This unsavory affair and the attendant publicity prompted a Menshevik campaign to discredit Lenin's leadership.

The plenary session of the Bolshevik-dominated Central Committee, which met in Geneva on August 24-26, 1908, took up charges brought by Martov against Lenin's Bolshevik center. An investigatory commission was authorized. The Mensheviks, however, were unable to obtain any results in their campaign against the Bolshevik expropriatory raids because the Polish and Lithuanian Party representatives in the Central Committee tended to vote with the Bolsheviks.[33] In addition to the question of the raids, the Bolsheviks and the Mensheviks were in disagreement over the issue of Liquidationism.* Under the circumstances, the two issues were related.

The Mensheviks, wishing to reduce the influence of the Bolsheviks, refused to yield their control over the Party's Foreign Bureau. The August, 1908, meeting of the Central Committee was merely the beginning of a splintering process which reduced the fiction of Party unity to shambles. All of the various groupings within Russian Social Democracy, including the Bund, were represented at the All-Russian Conference of the Party which met in Paris on January 3-9, 1909, and comprised only sixteen voting delegates. The Bolsheviks were the strongest element pres-

---

* The charge of Liquidationism was based on the assumption that the Mensheviks wished to liquidate the illicit underground Party apparatus. Actually, they wanted to create a mass party, which they regarded as being more appropriate for the period.

ent, since the Mensheviks, with only three delegates, were attempting to sabotage the meeting and had held a congress of their own in Basle in December, 1908. The lines between the two factions became even more taut when the Bolsheviks demanded that the Menshevik-controlled Foreign Bureau admit to its ranks a Central Committee representative with a veto power; they demanded also that the primarily Menshevik *émigré* Party groups pay 85-90 per cent of their Party dues into the Central Committee's treasury.[34]

The January, 1909, Conference* generally followed the Bolshevik line, although the Bund, as usual, vacillated between the two wings of the Party—if it could, indeed, be termed a "party" in 1909. The Conference called upon the Mensheviks to submit to Party discipline and condemned the Recallists, whom Lenin had called "Liquidators of the left" because he considered their extremist anti-Duma attitude as dangerous as the Liquidationism of the Mensheviks.

On the Central Committee, Bogdanov's place as Lenin's right-hand man, after the so-called "philosophical controversy" of 1908, had been taken by Zinoviev. The period following the Conference witnessed a relentless deepening of the schism—not only within the Party as a whole, but also within the Bolshevik ranks. By the end of June, 1909, the break became complete when a meeting of the "broadened" editorial board of the Party organ, *Proletarii* (actually controlled by Lenin), was held in a Paris café on the Avenue d'Orléans. The broadening of the membership was to assure a victory for Lenin. This was actually a gathering of Lenin's Bolshevik center, and it included such future Soviet luminaries and "enemies of the people" as Zinoviev, Kamenev, Rykov, Mikhail Tomsky, and Mykola Skrypnyk. Kamenev, in particular, played an important role since he had written the first article against Bogdanov, published in *Proletarii* (No. 42) on February 25, 1909, and ominously entitled "Not by the Same Road." Prior to this salvo against Bogdanov, the Bolshevik official organ had maintained an uneasy silence on the philosophical controversy.

---

* Sometimes referred to as the December, 1908, Conference in accordance with the Julian calendar.

Bogdanov was the principal culprit in the eyes of the majority at this twelve-member meeting in June, 1909, and he was at last excluded from Lenin's Bolshevik center. He was read out of the fold and removed from the editorial board—not only for his "idealist philosophy," denounced by Lenin in *Materialism and Empiriocriticism*, but also for his opposition to the Party's participation in the Duma. Actually, Bogdanov would have been tolerated by Lenin and would not have been excommunicated had he "submitted to the discipline of the Bolshevik faction."* The practice of demanding contrite recantation was one which Lenin bequeathed to Stalin, although it should be noted that the pupil demonstrated far greater ability in compelling compliance than did the mentor.

The *Proletarii* meeting also condemned Recallists and Ultimatists for their refusal to recognize the usefulness of the Duma as a tribunal for agitation and propaganda. Earlier, in the April 17 issue of *Proletarii*, Lenin had strongly denounced these two closely related positions as a "caricature of Marxism" and had likened them to the Economists of the preceding decade, from whom they actually differed quite markedly.[35] The resolution of the *Proletarii* meeting condemned both the "Liquidators of the right"—the Mensheviks who emphasized exclusively legal means because of their affinity for "parliamentary cretinism"—and the "Liquidators of the left" who "turn the matter inside-out: for them legal means do not exist in Party activity, illegality is . . . everything."[36] Thus, Lenin firmly adhered to his earlier position—first developed in *What Is to Be Done?*—on the need to employ every effective means at the Party's disposal, both legal and illegal.

Advocacy of Liquidationism of the left was not the only aspect of Bogdanov's behavior to be censured by the *Proletarii* meeting. The so-called "God-building tendencies" in Russian Social Democracy were condemned, as was the closely related Party school on the island of Capri. God-building was viewed

---

* During World War I, Bogdanov served as a physician in the Russian Army. Having given up politics, he founded and directed the Moscow Blood Transfusion Institute; he died in March, 1928, as a result of an unsuccessful experiment which he performed upon himself.

by the meeting as an anti-Marxist attempt to "give to scientific socialism the character of religious belief."[37] The principal culprit in this deviation was Anatole Lunacharsky, but Gorky and Bazarov were also included. However, Lenin had made it clear in *Materialism and Empiriocriticism* that Bogdanov, although not himself a God-builder, was to blame. Lunacharsky had advocated the "idolization of the higher human potentials," and Lenin contended that such a view could only be based upon Bogdanov's philosophy.[38] God-building arose from Lunacharsky's somewhat romanticized notions regarding the need for socialism to have an emotional equivalent of religion. Thus, certain Russian Marxists believed that socialism, if it was to be successful, had to take on some of the attributes of religion, while at the same time firmly denying the existence of God. Among these Marxists, Lunacharsky began preaching the cult of the human collectivity. In 1908, in the symposium on *Outlines of the Philosophy of Marxism*, Lunacharsky drew Lenin's fire by asserting that "God as omniscience, felicity, omnipotence, as universal eternal life is truly all that is human in its highest potentiality."[39] In the same year, in another publication, Lunacharsky declared: "Socialism, as a doctrine, is the true religion of humanity, bared of the mystical shrouds in which the imperfect development of the mind and feeling of our fathers dressed it. The collaboration of humanity is to have the goal: *there must be* a living and omnipotent god. *We* shall create him."[40]

Ironically, the idolatry which Lenin castigated so vehemently was to become the psychological mainstay of Soviet totalitarianism; one of its refinements was the "cult of the person" as practiced under Stalin. The use to which Lenin's embalmed cadaver was put as a twentieth-century tribal totem—joined temporarily by Stalin's in 1953—epitomized the new secular faith based on the worship of matter. However, what Lenin objected to in 1909 was the very thought of an analogy between socialism and religion.

Lenin's campaign against the God-builders was to continue through 1913 and was to affect his relations with Gorky. The founding of the Capri Party School in 1909 marked the beginning of an estrangement, although the two men never permanently severed their relationship. The *Proletarii* meeting of June, 1909, declared that the Capri School was "a new center [which has] seceded from the faction of Bolsheviks" since it had established its own relations with local Russian Party committees, organized its own treasury, fund-raising efforts, and network of agents (*agentura*), without having informed either *Proletarii* or the common Party center. The resolution adopted at this meeting stated that the Bolshevik faction could bear no responsibility for this school since it was founded by the advocates of "Recallism, Ultimatism, and God-building."[41]

The Capri School, known as the First Higher Social Democratic Propagandist-Agitator School for Workers, had been organized by Bogdanov, G. A. Alexinsky, Lunacharsky, and Gorky—men who considered themselves good Bolsheviks, but who were not willing to follow Lenin in all things. Others who joined the faculty included M. N. Lyadov and Mikhail N. Pokrovsky, the Marxist historian of Russia. The school opened early in August, 1909, never had more than fifteen students (all of them workers sent from Russia), and barely lasted until the end of the calendar year. Yet, Lenin was much disturbed by this "threat" to his leadership and in August twice declined invitations to lecture there on the grounds that the school was a center of Recallism and God-building. On August 30, 1909, he wrote to a group of seven Capri students that the school had been "deliberately hidden from the Party" in order to remove it from Party control. In the same letter, Lenin noted that "even the nonfactional [i.e., neither Bolshevik nor Menshevik] Comrade Trotsky immediately understood . . . that to form a school on the isle of Capri means to conceal the school from the Party . . ."[42] After indicating to the students that they could expect to hear the best Party lecturers only in Paris—but not in such a backwater as Capri—Lenin invited them to the French capital and expressed his willingness to lecture to them there. By November, almost half the Capri student body had arrived in Paris to hear Lenin lecture, after they had been excluded from the school. The split in the Capri student body caused the Moscow Party Committee to withdraw its support of the school, but the Petersburg Committee, controlled by the Recallists, filled the breach. Nevertheless, the school went out of existence in December, 1909.

Lenin never ceased his attempts to win Maxim Gorky back to his brand of Bolshevism, as distinct from the "pure" Bolshevism of Bogdanov, Lunacharsky, and Alexinsky. Gorky's principal offense had been his flirtation with God-building as expressed in his *The Confession*, published in 1908. In that work, the protagonist—Matvei, a humble person of unknown parentage—seeks God and, after undergoing various kinds of religious experience, concludes that the people—omnipotent and immortal—are the creators of God. Lenin would have none of this notion of a religion of humanity, since the very idea of any kind of divinity was anathema to him.

The disagreement between Lenin and Gorky was marked by a further exchange of views as late as November and December, 1913. Gorky was understood by Lenin to have rejected God-seeking—a non-Marxist movement attributed to such thinkers as the novelist Dmitrii Sergeyevich Merezhkovsky, the philosopher N. A. Berdyaev, and the future theologian Sergei Nikolaevich Bulgakov—and to have declared: "If you do not sow, you will not reap. God is not with us, you have not yet created Him. Gods are not sought, *they are created*; life is not imagined, it is created."[43] In a letter of November 9, 1913, Lenin reprimanded Gorky in the following terms:

> God-seeking differs from God-building or from God-construction or from God-creation, etc., no more than the yellow devil differs from the blue devil. To speak of God-seeking not in order to speak out against *all* devils and gods, against all ideological acts of sexual deviation with a corpse [*trupolozhstvo*] (every little god is an act of sexual deviation with a corpse—even though it be the cleanest, most ideal, not sought-after but created little god, it makes no difference), but to express a preference for the blue devil instead of for the yellow one is a hundred times worse than to say nothing at all.[44]

Lenin was willing to concede that Gorky's intentions were good, but noted that once his position "went to the masses . . . its *meaning* is defined not by your good intentions, but by the rela-

tionship of social forces, by the objective relationship of classes."
He contended that autocracy and clericalism would employ
Gorky's notions to "keep the people in slavery."[45]

Gorky soon dropped his preoccupation with God-building
as it lost its novelty. The men with whom he was associated in
the Capri Party School established the so-called *Vperyod* Literary Group in December, 1909. (Significantly, this group was
named after the newspaper published by Lenin following his
break with Plekhanov and his resignation from *Iskra* in 1903
for the purpose of defending the pure Bolshevism allegedly
betrayed by Plekhanov.) The leading lights of this group were
Bogdanov, Lunacharsky, and Alexinsky. They acted on the conviction (not unlike Lenin's in 1903) that they were advocating
the most uncorrupted species of Bolshevism in the form of Recallism, Ultimatism, and God-building. In July, 1910, the group
began publication of a symposium on current questions entitled
Vperyod, of which three issues appeared prior to May, 1911.
In 1912, it was succeeded by *Na temy dnya* ("On Topics of the
Day"), and four issues were published—the last in January, 1914.
In late 1910 and early 1911, they founded a second factional
school in Bologna. Among the lecturers were Bogdanov, Lunacharsky, Pokrovsky, Lyadov, Mikhail Lazarevich Vel'tman (also
known as M. P. Pavlovich), and Alexinsky, as well as Trotsky
and Madame Alexandra Kollontai, both of whom were regarded
as Menshevik sympathizers at the time. Lenin refused to lecture
on the grounds that it was a "factional" enterprise, "harmful
for the Party, and non-Social Democratic."[46] Again, he invited
the students to Paris and offered to lecture to them there. Although the school soon moved from Bologna to Paris, its demand
for autonomy and the right to invite such lecturers as it pleased
produced a rift with the Central Committee and led to the
school's dissolution.

These various groupings, comprising what could only be
described euphemistically as a "party," came together again on
January 15, 1910, at a plenary session of the Central Committee which met in Paris until February 5. Bolsheviks, Mensheviks,
Bundists, Poles, Latvians, and *Vperyod*-ites were represented
among the fourteen voting members. Lenin, as a candidate-

member of the Central Committee, had no vote but represented the Party organ, *Sotsial-Demokrat*. Kamenev attended as a nonvoting representative of the Bolshevik organ, *Proletarii*, and Martov represented the Menshevik newspaper, *Golos Sotsial-Demokrata*. Trotsky had no vote either, but attended as representative of his "nonfactional faction" and its newspaper, the Vienna *Pravda*. This plenary session witnessed an attempt to reconcile the various warring factions, largely through Trotsky's moderating influence. Again, Lenin did not have complete control over his own Bolshevik faction. The Bolsheviks-Conciliators, led by Kamenev and V. P. Nogin, sided with Trotsky in attempting to dissolve all factions and restore Party unity. Then, too, the language of the resolutions was more subdued in reference to the Liquidationists than that proposed by Lenin.

This meeting of the Central Committee was revealing in another respect. Lenin was unable to control his own Bolshevik factions, but he did enjoy some support from the so-called "Mensheviks-Party men" who were followers of Plekhanov, although the "grand old man" of Russian Marxism was not present at the meeting. Thus, the Party was not only split into Bolshevik and Menshevik wings, but these, in turn, were split. To further complicate matters, Trotsky led a Centrist group. Plekhanov had been drawing closer to an alliance with Lenin as the meeting approached. He had participated in the Menshevik Liquidationist newspaper, *Golos Sotsial-Demokrata*, since its founding in February, 1908, when he was all for combatting "Bolshevik Bakuninism." In May, 1909, however, he broke with his followers and drifted toward a *rapprochement* with his old enemy, Lenin. It appears that Plekhanov was motivated largely by profound concern over the numerous fissures which had opened in the Party, but he was undoubtedly also pleased by Lenin's open declaration of war against Bogdanov and the other alleged Russian Machists whom he had been abusing for six years.

Lyadov, a member of the anti-Leninist *Vperyod* Group, described Plekhanov's relations with Lenin with bitter sarcasm:

> With the lightness of a ballerina, Plekhanov, for almost the fourth time since the Second Congress, leaps from the

Mensheviks into the embrace of Lenin, whom he was
anathematizing in all conclaves only a short time before.
And Lenin, who at the Third Congress still declared, in
response to Plekhanov's challenge, that Bogdanov's Machism
bore no relationship to his correct tactical position—that
same Lenin now joins Plekhanov in a defensive and offensive alliance in order to expel Bogdanov for his Machism.
Forgotten are all the profound differences over principles . . .[47]

Yet, the alliance between Lenin and Plekhanov was to be of
brief duration, thanks largely to the "disruptive" efforts of the
Bolsheviks-Conciliators, the followers of Bogdanov's *Vperyod,*
and the Mensheviks who published *Golos Sotsial-Demokrata.*

Nevertheless, this Central Committee session gave at least the
appearance of having effected a reconciliation of the various
warring factions. It was supposedly agreed that each group would
dissolve its organizational center and that both *Proletarii,* and
Golos Sotsial-Demokrata would be closed. The Party organ,
Sotsial Demokrat, was to continue publication under an editorial
board composed of Lenin and Zinoviev from the Bolsheviks,
and Martov and Dan from the Mensheviks, as well as a Polish
representative. The Central Committee granted recognition to
the *Vperyod* Literary Group, although it expressed the hope that
the group's separate existence could soon be terminated. Lenin,
who was on the defensive throughout the three-week plenary
session, agreed to destroy the remaining 500-ruble bank notes
from the 1907 Tbilisi expropriation. Part of the Bolshevik funds
was placed in the hands of three German trustees—Karl Kautsky, Franz Mehring, and Clara Zetkin—to be used only for
payment of general Party (nonfactional) expenses.* However,

---

* The funds in question had been obtained in 1906 from the estate
of Nikolai Pavlovich Schmidt, a Moscow furniture manufacturer who
had aided the December, 1905, uprising in the Presnya District and who
had bequeathed his wealth to the Party before he died in prison. Not
wishing to have this money fall into the hands of the Menshevik-controlled
Central Committee (this was after the Stockholm Congress), Lenin arranged to have his agents, one of whom was Victor Taratuta (whose real
name was Vasilii Fedorovich Lozinsky), marry Schmidt's two sisters who
were his legal heirs. Since the younger sister, Elizaveta Pavlovna Schmidt,

in the event of a recurrence of the schism, the funds were to be returned to the Bolshevik faction. The meeting also recognized Trotsky's Vienna newspaper, *Pravda*, and granted it a subsidy from Party funds; Kamenev was delegated to it as Bolshevik representative and as third editor. It was decided to establish a Party school outside Russia, but difficulties were soon encountered when Bogdanov and the organizers of the defunct Capri School reconstituted themselves as the Bologna School.

Thus, the underlying conflict and tension persisted. The Bolsheviks published a new factional organ, *Rabochaya gazeta*, in Paris on November 12, 1910, replacing *Proletarii*. Plekhanov, Kamenev, and Zinoviev aided Lenin in this venture, which was rationalized by the failure of the Mensheviks to terminate publication of *Golos Sotsial-Demokrata*. The latter did not cease to appear until December, 1911. Only nine issues of *Rabochaya gazeta* appeared between November, 1910, and August 12, 1912. This meager effort, as compared with that of the earlier *Iskra*, signifies the low state to which the Party had sunk since the initial outburst of revolutionary enthusiasm in 1905.

Despite these difficulties, Lenin succeeded in organizing a Party school in the Paris suburb of Longjumeau. The school, which only functioned during the summer of 1911, was attended by Party people who posed as Russian village schoolteachers. Lenin lectured on political economy, the agrarian question, and the theory and practice of socialism. Other lecturers dealt with Party history, Western European labor movements, law, finance, literature, and journalism. Since the students were to return to Russia, it was necessary to shroud the school in secrecy and to

---

was not of legal age, she could only obtain her legacy by marrying. Her fiancé turned out to be none other than Taratuta, who was also secretary of the Moscow Party Committee from 1905 to 1907. However, when Taratuta could not marry the girl because he was in trouble with the authorities, he arranged, instead, for his fiancée to contract a fictitious marriage with another Bolshevik, Ignatiev. This enabled her to obtain the legacy and turn it over to Lenin in 1908, to the chagrin of the less resourceful and more scrupulous Mensheviks. With these funds, he published *Proletarii.—See* Krupskaya, *Memories of Lenin, 1893–1917* (London: Lawrence and Wishart, 1942), p. 139.

limit contacts between the student body and the *émigrés* in Paris. These precautions, however, proved worthless because one of the diligent students was a police agent.

Two police spies were also among the delegates to the All-Russian Party Conference which met in Prague in January, 1912, and which marked Lenin's final break with the Mensheviks. One of them, Roman Vatslavovich Malinovsky, later rose high in the Party, became a deputy and the leader of its faction in the Fourth Duma, and deceived Lenin until the Russian Provisional Government opened the police archives in 1917.* (More will be said of him later.) In calling the Prague Conference, to which he gave the status of a congress, Lenin bypassed the Central Committee of the "united" Party as well as the Menshevik-dominated Foreign Bureau of the Central Committee. As in 1904, so now in 1911, Lenin organized his own splinter group around his factional newspaper (*Rabochaya gazeta* in 1911 and *Vperyod* in 1904) and launched an All-Russian Organizational Commission (ROK) which pressed for the convocation of the Prague Conference. The Conference met on January 18-30, 1912. Fourteen voting delegates were present, only one of whom, Zinoviev, enjoyed any prominence. Lenin and Kamenev were among the nonvoting delegates. Over Lenin's protests, half the voting delegates decided to extend invitations to Plekhanov, to Trotsky's Vienna *Pravda* Group, and to the *Vperyod* Literary Group. Actually, Lenin had nothing to fear because all of them declined to attend, and he was able to consummate his efforts to end, once and for all, the talk of uniting the various factions. The Social Democratic faction in the Duma sent two of its members, the Bolshevik Poletaev and the pro-Bolshevik Menshevik V. E. Shurkanov (who later turned out to be an *agent provocateur*), but they did not arrive in Prague until after the Conference had adjourned.

The convocation of the Prague Conference was rationalized on the grounds that the Central Committee had not functioned in Russia for more than two years; the Conference declared itself to be an "all-Party conclave" and the "supreme Party body."[48]

* The other police spy at the Prague Conference was A. S. Romanov, from the Tula Party organization.

Its resolution expressed dissatisfaction with the way in which the non-Russian Party organizations, particularly the Bund, were conducting their operations apart from the Russian Party organizations. It called for the restoration of the illicit Party organization, particularly as a means of influencing the strike policies of trade unions, as well as for broader use of every kind of legal means.[49] Liquidationism was condemned as harmful, and all Party members were called upon to combat it. The Prague Conference also withdrew recognition and financial support from Trotsky's Vienna *Pravda* and designated Lenin's *Rabochaya gazeta* as the Central Committee's official organ. A Central Committee of seven members was elected; it included Lenin, his right-hand man Zinoviev, Ordzhonikidze, and the police spy Malinovsky. Among the four candidate-members were A. S. Bubnov, M. I. Kalinin, and Elena Stasova.* Having obtained for the Central Committee the right of co-optation, Lenin quickly proceeded to appoint two of his followers, Stalin and Ivan Stepanovich Belostotsky, to that body.

However, the police, through their agent, Malinovsky, quickly got wind of Lenin's plans for the re-establishment of an underground in Russia. Numerous arrests of Party activists followed. Yet, in spite of these setbacks, Lenin had the advantage of being

---

* Stasova, at the age of eighty-two, was to reappear at the Twentieth Party Congress in February, 1956, after having been consigned to insignificance by Stalin for nearly two decades. Indeed, in Stalin's *Short Course* history, no mention was made of her having been elected to the Central Committee in 1912. The daughter of a Czarist government official, she learned French and English at home as a child and joined the Party in 1898. In 1905, she became secretary of the St. Petersburg Party Committee and held the post until the autumn of 1907, when she went to Tbilisi to serve as a propagandist and Central Committee representative. Arrested for the third time in 1912, she was exiled to the Yenisei province in Siberia and remained there until the autumn of 1916, when she was permitted to return to the capital to see her aged parents. Following the Bolshevik seizure of power, she served in the Party Secretariat, helped organize the First Congress of Peoples of the East in Baku, and was active in the Comintern from 1921 to 1926. Between 1927 and 1938, she served as President of the Central Committee of MOPR (International Aid Organization for Revolutionary Fighters); after 1938, she did French-language editorial work.

able to speak in the name of the Party and to excommunicate the Menshevik Liquidators, the *Vperyod* group of "pure" Bolsheviks (Recallists, God-builders, and Machist "idealists"), the Bundists, and Trotsky's own neutral faction. Most of these groups gathered in Vienna in August, 1912, in the name of Party unity and formed the so-called "August Bloc" which Lenin was to denounce as Liquidationist. Their sole aim was to remain in the Party from which Lenin had excommunicated them.

Early in July, Lenin had moved from Paris to Cracow in West Galicia, which was under Austrian rule at the time. The move was made with the approval of the Austrian authorities, who regarded the presence of an enemy of Russian Czarism as potentially useful. Lenin had complained about the high prices and the interminable Russian *émigré* squabbles in the French capital, but his real reason for moving was to be near the Russian frontier. Another convenience was that the Polish and Austrian police did not collaborate with the Russian police, as did the French, and Lenin's mail was not opened in Cracow as it had been in Paris. Since Cracow was close to Russian Poland, it was possible for Lenin to evade Russian censorship by having peasant market women carry mail across the Austro-Russian frontier. In Cracow, Krupskaya noted, exile was only semiexile, and Lenin received the St. Petersburg newspapers within three days after publication. He could thus be in closer contact with the renewed Party activity within Russia.

On April 22 (May 5), 1912, the Bolshevik legal daily newspaper, *Pravda* ("The Truth"), made its appearance. Its circulation was soon to reach 60,000, only to decline again to 23,000 within a few months. The Mensheviks (or Liquidators, as Lenin consistently called them) began to publish their own St. Petersburg newspaper, *Luch* ("The Ray"), in September. *Pravda*'s first appearance came shortly after the Lena Goldfields shooting of April 4 (17), in which at least 200 workers were killed and between 250 and 300 were wounded. The shooting had occurred when the laborers requested that their strike committee be released from jail. This tragic event was followed by an outbreak of sympathy strikes among factory workers in various Russian cities. Lenin was heartened by these events, which he regarded as proof of a new "revolutionary boom."[50]

When the elections to the Fourth Duma were held in the autumn of 1912, only six Bolsheviks and seven Mensheviks were elected. This meant that the Liquidators enjoyed a majority in the Social Democratic Duma faction, and they elected one of their number, the Georgian Nikolai Semenovich Chkheidze, chairman of the faction. The Bolshevik deputies—who, significantly, were elected from the workers' *curiae*—included Gregory Petrovsky, Alexei Egorovich Badaev, and the police spy Roman Malinovsky. The uneasy collaboration between Bolsheviks and Mensheviks in the Duma continued until October, 1913, when the Bolsheviks, under pressure from Lenin, demanded equality with the Menshevik majority. This led to the formation of a separate Bolshevik parliamentary faction which claimed to represent the entire Party.

Yet, Duma activities absorbed only a small part of Lenin's time in 1912 and 1913. Following the Fourth Duma elections, he became increasingly interested in the nationality problem of the Russian Empire—in the use to which the phenomenon of nationalism could be put and the risks involved in utilizing it. Lenin's move to Cracow had made him aware of the animosity of the Poles toward the Russians. The First Balkan War in the autumn of 1912 had underscored the importance of nationalism, which was the primary force behind the military campaign of the small Balkan states against Turkey. Lenin was plagued, also, with the demands of the Jewish Social Democratic Bund, which had adopted a position akin to that of some Austrian Socialists. The latter's solution to the nationality problem was national-cultural autonomy, a nonterritorial form of autonomy which gave to each nationality in a multinational state the right to form an extraterritorial national union. This union was to function in the cultural sphere as a representative body. Its appeal among Jewish Socialists lay in its nonterritorial aspect, which enabled a nationality composed of noncontiguous groups to preserve its cultural identity. Lenin had opposed the position of the Bundists as early as 1903 and had declared that "the idea of a separate Jewish people is reactionary in its political meaning," prevents assimilation (of the Jews by the Russians), and promotes the "mood of the 'ghetto.' "[51]

By 1912, the nationality issue had become more pressing.

In the Fourth Duma, the demand for Ukrainian schools and the teaching of Ukrainian history was raised.[52] Lenin was concerned lest the growing force of nationalism disrupt the centralized Party with which he wished to embrace all nationalities. At the same time, he recognized a powerful force in the struggle which the non-Russian peoples were waging for the preservation of their national identity in the face of Czarist nationality policy—one that could be used against the imperial regime. On at least three occasions during the summer and autumn of 1913, Lenin pointed out that the Russians constituted only 43 per cent of the population of the Russian Empire.[53] Thus, he found himself forced to recognize the right of the non-Russian peoples to self-determination and to secession—but only in principle, and not really in practice. He also expressed a willingness to let the non-Russian languages be employed, although he was convinced that the growth of capitalism would impel non-Russians to learn Russian as a matter of convenience, just as a great proportion of the Italian-speaking Swiss spoke French as well.[54] At the same time, Lenin could declare that "only clericals or bourgeois can speak of national culture," and that "only the unity and fusion of the workers of all nations in *all* workers' organizations in the struggle against capital can lead to the 'solution of the nationality question.' "[55]

Yet, it was somewhat embarrassing for Lenin, a member of the oppressor Russian nationality, to be preaching homilies to the non-Russians. It was understandable, therefore, that he should call upon his faithful Georgian follower, Stalin, and give him the task of expounding the Party's position on the nationality problem. Earlier, Stalin had proved his worth to Lenin as a behind-the-scenes organizer of the infamous expropriatory raids. As Central Committee member, he had also supervised the publication of the first issue of *Pravda* in April, 1912. Now his non-Russian nationality was to make him even more useful. Stalin had come to Cracow in January, 1913, to attend a meeting of Central Committee members and Party workers, and had then proceeded to Vienna. There, aided by Bukharin (since Stalin knew little German), he wrote a lengthy article on "Marxism and the National Question." Lenin was highly pleased. In

February, 1913, he wrote to Gorky: "With regard to nationalism, I am fully in agreement with you that we must concern
ourselves [with it] more seriously. We have a wonderful [*chu-
desnyi*] Georgian who has sat down and is writing for *Pros-
veshchenie* ["Enlightenment," the Party journal] a big article,
having gathered *all* the Austrian and other materials."[56]

Stalin, like Lenin, aimed his article at the idea of national-
cultural autonomy and defined the nation as a "historical category of a definite epoch, the epoch of rising capitalism."[57] He
contended that national barriers were being erased, and as proof
he quoted from the assertion in the *Communist Manifesto*:
"National differences are daily vanishing more and more, owing
to the development of the bourgeoisie, to freedom of commerce,
to the world market, to uniformity in the mode of production
and in the conditions of life corresponding thereto. The supremacy of the proletariat will cause them to vanish still faster."[58]
In the Leninist tradition, Stalin lashed out at the Bund, dismissed
the Jews as a "paper" nation, and declared that they "do not
understand each other (since they speak different languages),
live in different parts of the globe, will never see each other,
will never act together either in time of peace or in time of
war."[59] Yet, writing as he was at the time of the First Balkan
War, Stalin had little choice but to follow Lenin in recognizing
the principle of self-determination of nations, including the right
of secession. However, he qualified this—actually negating it—
by declaring that the right need not be granted in all instances.
The question of whether a nation would be given autonomy,
federal status, or the right to secede would, according to Stalin,
depend upon the "concrete historical conditions in which a given
nation finds itself." He warned that "conditions, like everything
else, change, and a decision which is correct at a given moment
may be entirely unacceptable at another moment."[60]

After completing "Marxism and the National Question,"
Stalin returned to St. Petersburg in February, 1913, but was
quickly arrested, thanks to Malinovsky, who had reported all
that had transpired at the January Cracow meeting. This was
Stalin's fifth arrest, and while he had escaped on previous occasions, he was now exiled to the remote tundra on the Lower

Yenisei in Northern Siberia. Lenin's attempts to help Stalin escape were doomed when he placed them in Malinovsky's hands, and Stalin remained in Siberia until the collapse of the Russian monarchy. When Lenin sent Jacob Sverdlov to St. Petersburg to assume the editorship in Stalin's place (Stalin had been too soft on the Mensheviks), he, too, was quickly arrested.

The meeting of Central Committee members and Party workers which took place at Poronin in Galicia from October 5 to 14, 1913, found Malinovsky among the twenty-two participants. Prior to this gathering, referred to as the "August meeting" (for conspiratorial purposes), Malinovsky had attempted to remove suspicion from himself by declaring that a spy was "close to the six" Bolshevik Duma deputies; he thus cast suspicion upon another police agent, Miron Chernomazov, who was later removed from the editorial board of *Pravda*.

Roman Malinovsky, a Russified Pole, had begun his career as a police spy on a regular basis* in November, 1909, when he was arrested at a Social Democratic meeting held in conjunction with an antialcoholic congress. He was released in January, 1910, and resumed his trade union work—as a fully paid *agent provocateur*. His contacts with the Menshevik Liquidators continued. It was they who first cast suspicion upon him but failed to show any real proof. On orders from police superiors, Malinovsky moved closer to the Bolsheviks in 1911 and was accepted by Lenin, who did not have many followers at the time. Thus, in January, 1912, Malinovsky attended the Prague Conference and was elected to membership in the Central Committee. In the autumn of the same year, he was elected to the Fourth Duma from the Moscow workers' *curia* with the aid of the police, who conveniently arrested his principal electoral opponent. Thus, representing both Lenin's Party and the police in the Duma, Malinovsky carried out many Party directives, and Lenin was pleased with his record as a parliamentarian.

---

* He was originally a tailor, metalworker, and common thief. It is not certain when he first became an informer for the police, but he was probably first attracted to this type of activity by the financial reward involved in it.

But as treasurer of *Pravda*, this spy provided the police with lists of the newspaper's donors; when he himself contributed money to *Pravda,* it was charged against his police expense account. Once *Pravda* was fined for publishing an article written by Malinovsky. Thanks to this Central Committee member, the police knew of Lenin's every move in Cracow.

Malinovsky's role in the Duma was not an easy one. His speeches were often prepared in Cracow, but his police employers, with whom he met in private rooms in the capital's best restaurants, exercised a censorship of sorts prior to delivery. Though a demagogic and brusque speaker, Malinovsky usually followed his notes rather closely when addressing the Duma. On occasion, he found it necessary to employ various devices to avoid speaking. His dual role often caused him to make statements in the Duma chamber which displeased the police officials, who were paying him 500 rubles a month for his valuable information—in addition to his Duma salary.[61]

This police sponsorship of a Bolshevik Duma member was a dangerous, bold game, and had it become public knowledge, it would have completely discredited the Duma. Thus, the new Deputy Interior Minister, Vladimir Fedorovich Dzhunkovsky, who feared a scandal, ordered Malinovsky's resignation and received it on May 8 (21), 1914. The spy had little choice but to comply, accept the pay-off of 6,000 rubles, and permit himself to be escorted across the frontier. He did so feigning dissatisfaction with parliamentary life and ill health. Malinovsky's resignation caused the earlier charges against him to be renewed, and he proceeded directly to Lenin in Cracow and boldly asked the Central Committee to investigate the accusations against him. A commission of three, headed by the Polish Social Democrat Jacob Haniecki (Fürstenberg) and including Lenin and Zinoviev, cleared Malinovsky of the charges. The spy was able to capitalize upon the fact that his leading accusers were the Mensheviks Martov and Dan, and for Lenin this was enough to cast doubt upon the veracity of the charges, since no Menshevik could possibly be telling the truth.[62] And after all, had not Malinovsky and Lenin visited Paris and Brussels together on Party business in January, 1914? Malinovsky had also told Lenin a convincing story of his having once been convicted on a charge of attempted rape and of this being used by the police to blackmail him into resigning his Duma seat. Of course, Lenin could not bear to think that the leader of the Bolshevik Duma faction—the man who had intensified the campaign against the Menshevik Liquidators and had effected the split with them in the Duma in 1913—could be a police agent.

Lenin's Party tribunal contented itself with finding Malinovsky guilty of having violated discipline and deserting his post in the Duma. At the outbreak of World War I, the spy enlisted in the Russian Army fighting on the French front; he was taken prisoner, interned in a German prison camp, and received mail and food parcels from Lenin and his wife. In November, 1918, he unexpectedly arrived in Petrograd and was soon arrested. Malinovsky's pleas that Lenin intercede on his behalf went unheeded, and he was executed by a firing squad. Thus ended the fabulous career of one of Russia's most prominent doubles, who served both sides only to serve neither side.

The summer of 1914 had been unpleasant for Lenin not only because of the Malinovsky case. The specter of world war became real—despite Lenin's conviction, expressed in a letter to Gorky in January, 1913, that "war between Austria and Russia would be a very useful thing for the revolution in all of Eastern Europe, but there is little likelihood that Franz Joseph and Nikolasha [Czar Nicholas II] will give us this satisfaction."[63] On August 7, 1914—the day after Austria declared war on Russia—Lenin was visited by a police official who searched his rented house in the Carpathian Mountain village of Poronin and seized his statistical notes on the agrarian question, having mistaken them for code. The next day, Lenin was taken to the town of Nowy Targ and imprisoned. Before leaving Poronin, he managed to contact Haniecki, who, in turn, telegraphed the Social Democratic deputy Marek. Krupskaya joined Haniecki in appealing to the Socialist deputy Victor Adler, a member of the International Socialist Bureau. Adler vouched before the Austrian Minister of Interior that Lenin was irreconcilably hostile to the Czarist regime and would do almost anything to weaken and destroy it. Released on August 19, Lenin then proceeded to Vienna. From there, he and Krupskaya decided to go to Berne in neutral Switzerland. Soon they were joined by Zinoviev and his wife, who had also been living in Austrian Poland.

Lenin and Zinoviev were almost all that remained of the active Bolshevik organization. Many were under arrest. Stalin was in exile inside the Arctic Circle, fishing and hunting in solitude. The Bolshevik Duma deputies (Petrovsky, Badaev, Nikolai Shagov, Matvei Muranov, and Fedor Nikitich Samoilov) were arrested in November, 1914, along with Kamenev, the Central Committee representative in Russia. *Pravda* had been closed by the Czarist regime on July 8 (21), 1914, and thus was temporarily terminated its somewhat trying existence of more than two years.*

Lenin was incensed by the failure of the International Socialist Bureau to prevent the outbreak of war. His fury knew no bounds when he learned that the French and German parliamentary Socialists had voted for war credits and that Plekhanov had become a Russian patriot and a "French chauvinist." As if to add insult to injury and make the fantastic real, the French Socialists Jules Guesde and Marcel Sembat became ministers—

---

* The editors of *Pravda* first encountered real difficulties on July 5 (18), 1913, when the newspaper was closed by the authorities after having appeared for more than fourteen months. Within eight days, it reappeared as *Rabochaya pravda* ("Workers' Truth"), but was closed on August 1 (14), 1913. It immediately reopened as *Severnaya pravda* ("Northern Truth"), which closed on September 7 (20), 1913. Four days later, it reappeared as *Pravda truda* ("Truth of Labor"), but was closed on October 9 (22), 1913. *Za pravdu* ("For Truth") replaced it, but was, in turn, closed on December 5 (18), 1913. It was followed by *Proletarskaya pravda* ("Proletarian Truth"), which lasted for thirty-four issues until January 21 (February 3), 1914. The last (and eighth) pre-Soviet *Pravda* was called *Trudovaya pravda* ("Labor Truth") and commenced its brief existence on May 21 (June 3), 1914. In each instance, the format and general line of the newspaper remained unchanged, despite the change in name and the arrest of the responsible editor (known also as the "sitting editor," since he was the one to go to jail whenever there was a scrape with the law). (*See* Whitman Bassow, "The Pre-Revolutionary *Pravda* and Tsarist Censorship," *American Slavic and East European Review,* February, 1954, pp. 47–65.)

the former without portfolio, the latter Minister of Public Works. They were joined by Albert Thomas, who later became Minister of Munitions. Within the Russian Social Democratic movement, too, strange things began to happen. Martov and Trotsky, whom Lenin had been denouncing as Liquidators, adopted an internationalist (antiwar) stand and, in mid-November, 1914, in Paris, began to publish their own newspaper, *Golos* ("The Voice"), the organ of the "international wing of the Mensheviks." War had made strange bedfellows.

It appeared, at the time, that World War I had brought to an end Lenin's efforts to create a Party in his own image. And yet, ironically, it was the outbreak of war that prevented the International Socialist Bureau from forcing unity upon the Russian Social Democratic Labor Party and effecting a merger of its various factions. To this end, the Bureau convened an All-Russian "Unity" Conference in Brussels in mid-July, 1914. Lenin would not deign to attend, but sent a Bolshevik delegation headed by his lieutenant and old friend, Inessa Armand. Lenin had given her explicit instructions, and she adhered to them scrupulously. The essence of his position was that unity was possible only if all groups within the Russian Social Democratic Labor Party accepted the decisions of the Prague Conference of January, 1912, and submitted to the dictates of his Central Committee. The advent of the war prevented the International Socialist Bureau from calling Lenin to account. It is ironic also that both Lenin and the Czarist *Okhrana* wished to see the Bolshevik-Menshevik schism perpetuated. Indeed, Lenin had planned to convene a Party—or, more correctly, a Leninist factional—congress in August.

Instead, the war made it necessary for Lenin and Krupskaya to live in Switzerland—and life was temporarily bearable at a frugal level, thanks to a small inheritance which Krupskaya's aged mother had received from a deceased sister. During this period, Lenin's energies and thoughts were devoted to a single task: the propagation of defeatism and the overthrow of the "war-making" ruling classes. In a letter written on October 17, 1914, to Alexander G. Shlyapnikov, wartime Party representative in Stockholm, Lenin noted: "In Russia, chauvinism hides behind words about 'belle France' and about unfortunate Belgium (but what about Ukraine, etc.?) or behind 'popular' hatred of the Germans (and of 'Kaiserism')." He contended that these sophisms had to be fought and replaced by the slogan "The *least* evil would be—the defeat of Czarism now and at this moment." The slogan of peace Lenin regarded as "incorrect" and as a "philistine, clerical slogan," while the proletariat, in his view, should be guided by the call to civil war.[64]

On November 1, 1914, Lenin renewed publication of *Sotsial-Demokrat* as the Party organ. In this issue (No. 33), he printed the appeal of the Central Committee under the title "War and Russian Social Democracy." He attempted to gather about him anyone—including former enemies—who would follow his internationalist, defeatist, and civil-war line. Thus, Madame Alexandra Kollontai, who had been with the Mensheviks and had lectured in the factional Bologna School, began to correspond with Lenin. He gave her many assignments to carry out in Scandinavia and in the United States for the purpose of rallying the left-wing Socialists in opposition to the war. During the summer of 1915, Lenin and Zinoviev published a pamphlet, *Socialism and the War*, in which they explained the Party's view on the war: the Party, they contended, opposed pacifism since it still believed in class war and in the warfare of colonies and of oppressed nationalities against the imperialist and oppressor country, even though the imperialist war was to be condemned.[65] It was in this pamphlet that Lenin defined imperialism as the "highest stage of capitalism." The first half of 1916 was devoted by Lenin, now in Zurich, to an attempt to document this thesis on imperialism in a work bearing the same title.

However, the Russian's extremist views did not attract much support during the years of World War I. At the Zimmerwald, Switzerland, international conference of Socialists (September 5-8, 1915), Lenin was not able to muster even one-third of the thirty-five delegates in support of his proposal that a third international be organized and that political strikes, fraternizing in the trenches, street fighting, and open civil war be fomented. Krupskaya later recounted how irritable Lenin was following his lack of success at Zimmerwald and how he required several days in the mountains to calm down. At the second international conference of Socialists, held in the Swiss village of Kienthal (April 24-30, 1916), Lenin's left wing gained a few votes, but failed to persuade the conference of the need to establish a new Socialist International and to break once and for all with any and all Socialists who were patriots.

The second half of 1916 found Lenin in serious financial difficulty, and Krupskaya had to find employment. Lenin invoked even sharper invective in his polemics with the leaders of the Second International and with "social chauvinists," "social pacifists," and "social patriots." Yet, this self-righteousness was to be tempered by a certain pessimism, a feeling of helplessness which, sooner or later, becomes the lot of all political *émigrés*. Thus, on the occasion of the twelfth anniversary of Bloody Sunday in January, 1917, Lenin, addressing a Swiss audience, noted that "it may be that we, the elders, will not live to see the decisive battles of this coming revolution."[66] Yet, unbeknown to Lenin, the events which would dissipate this ennui, to which he never readily succumbed, were in the making. His faction, which had constituted itself as the Party at Prague in January, 1912, would soon heed Marx's advice to the proletariat in the *Communist Manifesto* and attempt to "constitute itself *the* nation."

CHAPTER IV

THE SEIZURE OF POWER

It has long been noted by experienced and intelligent people that there is no greater moment of danger for a government in a revolutionary epoch than the beginning of concessions, the beginning of vacillation ...
—Lenin, in *Iskra*, March 1, 1903.

There is no country in the world *presently* enjoying such freedom as Russia.
—Lenin, "The Tasks of the Proletariat in Our Revolution" (April 23, 1917).

We are not pacifists. We are opponents of imperialist wars for the division of plunder among capitalists. But we have always declared it to be nonsense for the revolutionary proletariat to renounce revolutionary wars which *might* prove to be necessary *in the interests of socialism*.
—Lenin, "Farewell Letter to the Swiss Workers" (April 8, 1917).

The abdication, on March 2 (15), 1917, of Nicholas II, last Romanov emperor of Russia, produced great changes in the makeshift household of the Russian *émigré* W. Uljanoff (better known as Lenin), who was located at 14 Spiegelgasse in Zurich. The plan to edit a concise pedagogical dictionary in order to earn some badly needed money could now be abandoned. Lenin was unable to sleep, so great was his anxiety to return to Russia. But how? The British and French, he knew, would probably intern him if he passed through their countries. In a moment of fantasy, he even thought of attempting to arrange an airplane flight. However, on March 19, he wrote in the strictest confidence to Vyacheslav Karpinsky, the Bolshevik representative in Geneva. He told Karpinsky that he was considering returning to Russia via Holland and England, but would need papers made out in Karpinsky's name. Lenin proposed that he would attach to these papers a photograph of himself wearing a wig, and Karpinsky was to remain in hiding in Switzerland for three weeks until he had arrived safely in Russia.

This not very practical plan was abandoned as a result of a meeting of Russian *émigrés* held on the same day in Geneva; the Menshevik internationalist Martov suggested that those who wished to return to Russia should seek to do so via Germany, in exchange for the return of German civilians interned in Russia. Lenin was very pleased when Karpinsky wrote him of Martov's plan, and he suggested that "non-Party Russians and Russian patriots should appeal to Swiss ministers (and influential people like lawyers, etc., which could also be done in Geneva), with a request that they should *discuss* this with the envoy of the German Government in Berne." Lenin also warned that "we [Bolsheviks] cannot participate [in the talks] either directly or indirectly; our participation will *spoil* everything."[1] His concern was unwarranted, for when the negotiations proved fruitful, he and his Bolsheviks, whose defeatist position was well known to the Germans, were to be included in the group of repatriates that was to cross Germany.

During the period between the Czar's abdication and Lenin's return to Russia, he (Lenin) reformulated his views on the seizure of power. In the first of his five *Letters from Afar*, all of which were written during this period, he warned: "The first revolution, given birth to by the world imperialist war, has burst forth. This first revolution will certainly not be the last."[2] This first letter was written on March 20. Two days earlier, Lenin had lectured on the Paris Commune to a Swiss audience at Chaux-de-Fonds on the occasion of the forty-sixth anniversary of the unsuccessful Paris insurrection.

The Commune was no new topic for Lenin. He had given it his attention shortly after the Bloody Sunday of January, 1905, and had written of it in 1907, in 1908, and in 1911. He was acutely conscious of the Commune's errors and wished to make certain that they would not be repeated in Russia.*

---

* The Paris Commune, it may be remembered, had emerged from the chaos of defeat suffered in the Franco-Prussian War. The National

In attempting to analyze the underlying causes of the failure of the Commune, Lenin naturally quoted Marx's opinion that the Commune should not have confined itself to Paris but should have marched on Versailles. In 1908, Lenin had believed that the Commune erred in pursuing two aims—one national and anti-German, the other class or social: "In the uniting of contradictory goals—patriotism and socialism—lay the fateful error of the French socialists."[3] He was convinced that the Commune had been mistaken in going only "halfway," in not "expropriating the expropriators," and in failing to nationalize the Bank of France. Another error lay in the "unnecessary generosity of

---

Assembly, which had chosen a republican form of government, had named the historian Adolphe Thiers as chief executive, and decided to sue for peace. More than 600,000 German troops occupied part of the country pending payment of the indemnity imposed by the Treaty of Frankfurt. Paris, which had been under siege and had capitulated in January, 1871, was plagued by unemployment, and its disgruntled populace disliked the presence of so many royalists in the National Assembly sitting in Bordeaux. To complicate matters, the Assembly ceased paying the National Guard and ordered payment of all rents and debts. The Guard retained its arms, and when Thiers and his ministers entered Paris with troops, a clash ensued and two generals were killed by mutineers on March 18, 1871. Thiers decided to withdraw to Versailles, where the Assembly was now sitting, and to lay plans for retaking Paris and crushing the rebellion. The Communards—who were called such by their enemies, but who referred to themselves as Fédérés—elected a Municipal Council which was composed only partly of workers and included many bourgeois revolutionaries, who were motivated by the fear of so many royalists in the National Assembly and by the fact that the Assembly sat in Versailles, the symbol of the *ancien régime*. Thus, the myth that the Commune was a workers' regime has little foundation in fact. However, the Commune did adopt the red flag and the old revolutionary calendar, and declared war on the government of Thiers in Versailles. The government, for its part, amassed 100,000 troops around Paris, and on May 21, 1871, these troops entered the city by surprise. Eight days of fierce and bloody street fighting followed. Recognizing that defeat was at hand, certain partisans of the Commune set fire to the Tuileries, the Cour des Comptes, and the Hôtel de Ville. They shot approximately 150 hostages, including the Archbishop of Paris and the President of the Cour de Cassation, as well as priests. The government showed no mercy and executed almost 20,000 in reprisal; many were given prison sentences, and more than 7,000 were exiled to New Caledonia.

the proletariat: it was necessary to annihilate its enemies, but it attempted [instead] to exercise moral influence upon them, ignoring the significance of the purely military operations in civil war . . ."[4]

Despite these cardinal errors, Lenin noted certain achievements of the Commune: that it replaced the standing army ("that blind instrument in the hands of the ruling classes") with a "general arming of the people"; that it separated the church from the state; that it abolished state salaries paid to the clergy; and that it secularized public education and "in this way administered a powerful blow to the gendarmes in cassocks." He also approved of the Commune's adoption of such measures as the abolition of money penalties and of night work in bakeries, the transfer to workers' cooperatives of all abandoned or closed factories and workshops in order to resume production, and the payment to persons in government and administration of salaries no higher than the average worker's wage and in no case more than 6,000 francs per year.[5]

The Commune's defeat did not detract, in Lenin's eyes, from its greatness and glory as a lesson for the revolutionary cause. He likened the abortive Moscow uprising of December, 1905, to the Commune and saw an analogy—albeit a very dim and imperfect one—between the reign of Nicholas II and Napoleonic France, charging the Russian "autocratic clique [of having] brought the country to the horrors of economic ruin and national humiliation."[6] Ten years later, in January, 1918, Lenin was to refer to the Commune as the "embryo of the Soviet regime" and to characterize the Thiers government as the regime of the "French Kadets and Mensheviks and right Socialist Revolutionaries."[7] On the same occasion, he noted that the Commune had not built up its own apparatus and that France had failed to understand its mission.

In order to make certain, in March, 1917, that the errors of the Commune would not be repeated in Russia, it was imperative for Lenin to return to Russia. The Russian *émigrés* had entrusted to the Swiss Socialist, Fritz Platten, the negotiations with Baron Romberg, the German Minister in Berne. Prior to April 2, the negotiations with Romberg and with the Swiss Government were in the hands of Robert Grimm, secretary of the Swiss Socialists and editor of their official organ, *Berner Tagwacht*. He had presided over the Zimmerwald and Kienthal Conferences and was regarded by Lenin as a pacifist. Platten replaced him as negotiator at the request of the impatient Lenin who thought that Grimm had been delaying the talks. A series of conditions was drawn up by Platten and was accepted by the Germans almost without change. It provided that all Russian *émigrés* could cross Germany, irrespective of their views on the war. Thus, the Germans were willing to facilitate the return of Russian *émigré* "defensists" (supporters of the Russian war effort) so long as it could serve as a cover for the return of Lenin and his antiwar "internationalists." A second provision guaranteed that the railway car in which the *émigrés* were to cross Germany would enjoy extraterritorial status; no one was to be permitted to enter the car without obtaining permission from Platten, who accompanied the *émigrés* to Sweden but was refused permission to enter Russia. There was to be no control of passports or baggage. Another provision contained the only explicit obligation assumed by the Russian *émigrés*: they were to agitate in Russia for an exchange of Austro-German internees equal to the number of returning *émigrés*.[8] The Russians were to pay for their passage.

The first party of *émigrés* left Berne on April 9, 1917, and included seventeen Bolsheviks in addition to Lenin and Krupskaya, as well as several Bundists and followers of the internationalist Paris newspaper *Nashe slovo*. Lenin was accompanied by Zinoviev and his wife and by Inessa Armand. Karl Radek, who had been active in the Polish and German Social Democratic movements and had collaborated with Rosa Luxemburg, was also in the group, but the Russian Provisional Government refused entry to him and Platten at the border on the grounds that they were not Russian subjects. The *émigrés* traveled by sea from Sassnitz in Germany to Trälleborg in Sweden on April 13 and, after a brief stop in Stockholm, arrived in Petrograd's Finland Station late at night on April 16. There Lenin mounted an armored car (which is still exhibited in Leningrad today) and addressed a crowd. Later, he proceeded to the Bolshevik

Central Committee headquarters, housed in the residence of Kshesinskaya, the one-time royal mistress and ballerina.

Lenin's arrival in Petrograd not only resulted in a shock treatment for the Bolshevik organization. It also prompted the charge that he was a German agent, since he had received permission to cross Germany. The accusation that the Bolsheviks received money from the Germans assumed great importance in July, 1917, and, as will be shown, was not without validity. At a meeting of the Executive Committee of the Petrograd Soviet held on April 17, Lenin declared that some non-Russian international socialists in Switzerland had told him: "If Karl Liebknecht were now in Russia, Miliukov [the Russian Foreign Minister] would let him go to Germany; the Bethmann-Hollwegs are letting you, Russian internationalists, go to Russia. Your task is to go to Russia and combat both German and Russian imperialism."[9] On this occasion, Lenin expressed agreement with this formulation of the question. Yet, one can ask: how was German imperialism to be combatted on Russian soil except by bearing arms on behalf of the Provisional Government of Russia? This Lenin, as a defeatist and a man who had never borne arms, was unwilling to do himself, nor would he urge others to do it.

Thus, in a sense, Lenin was doing the bidding of the Germans in advocating defeatism within Russia, although he was acting from entirely different motives than those which prompted the Germans to grant the Bolsheviks right of passage. It is clear that the Germans miscalculated badly: their thinking was comparable to that of the military strategist who plots to use bacteriological warfare against the enemy in the belief that his own troops enjoy immunity. At the same time, it is difficult to picture the independent and strong-willed Lenin consciously acting as someone else's tool.

Lenin made it clear from the moment of his arrival in Petrograd that he would continue to oppose the Provisional Government of Russia. In a telegram to certain Bolsheviks who were departing for Russia from Scandinavia, he had defined the Bolshevik tactic as "complete mistrust, no support of the new [Provisional] Government, Kerensky is particularly suspect, the

arming of the proletariat is the sole guarantee; immediate election
of the Petrograd Duma [municipal council]; no *rapprochement*
with other parties."[10] In the third of the *Letters from Afar,* written on March 24, Lenin urged that there be a fusion of the
"police, army, and bureaucracy with the people armed to a
man," and he added that this should be done along the lines
indicated by the lessons of the Paris Commune and the Russian
Revolution of 1905.[11]

Before Lenin's arrival, Petrograd was under a tenuous dual
authority: the Provisional Government, which had emerged
from the expired Fourth Duma, and the Soviet of Workers' and
Soldiers' Deputies. The latter had assumed certain functions of
government in the capital with the collapse of the Czarist regime,
which had been precipitated by the Czar's abdication in the wake
of a wave of strikes and bread riots. These functions of the
Soviet included the organization of a workers' militia to replace
the hated Czarist police. In addition, the government's control
of the armed forces was challenged when the Soviet issued its
Order Number One on March 14, one day before the Czar's
abdication. This order called for soldiers' committees in all military units and urged all military companies to send representatives to the Soviet of Workers' Deputies. Orders of the Military
Commission of the State Duma (of the Provisional Government)
were to be carried out only if they did not contradict orders and
decisions of the Soviet. All weapons and armored cars were to
be under the control of the company and battalion soldiers' committees and were not to be given to officers under any circumstances. Although calling for the "strictest military discipline"
on the part of the soldier while on duty, this order provided that
soldiers off duty were to enjoy all the rights of citizens. Saluting
while off duty was abolished, and officers were forbidden to
address troops in the familiar form.[12]

The Petrograd Soviet enjoyed a distinct advantage over the
Provisional Government. The latter was composed of relatively
conservative Kadets and Octobrists (former constitutional mon-
archists) and included only one member of the Soviet—the
Socialist Revolutionary Alexander Kerensky, who became Minister of Justice in violation of the decision of the Soviet Executive

Committee not to participate in the Cabinet. While it failed to support the Provisional Government, the Soviet did not initially adopt Lenin's position of categorical defiance of the regime.

Lenin first expressed this defiance publicly in his ten *April Theses,* which were delivered on April 17 at a meeting of Bolshevik members of the All-Russian Conference of Soviets and were published in the April 20 issue of *Pravda.* He spoke openly of the Provisional Government as "capitalistic [in] character," of the "complete mendacity of all its promises," and of the need for a "transfer of power to the proletariat." He denounced the government's policy of continuing the war and of seeking territorial acquisitions, and he advocated the propagation of his views within the army, as well as fraternization between the troops of Russia and those of the Central Powers. Recognizing that the Party had only a "weak minority" in the Soviets of Workers' Deputies, Lenin contended that it was necessary to explain the "errors" of the "petty-bourgeois opportunist" majority in a "patient, systematic, and persistent" manner. "So long as we are in the minority," Lenin declared, "we are carrying on the work of criticism and the explanation of errors, preaching at the same time the transfer of all state authority to the Soviets of Workers' Deputies so that the masses may by experience deliver themselves of their errors."[13] He warned that the establishment of a parliamentary republic would be a step backward. As an agrarian program, Lenin again proposed confiscation of all landowners' property and the nationalization of all land, to be placed at the disposal of local Soviets of Agricultural Laborers' and Peasants' Deputies, composed of the poor. All banks were to be merged into a single national bank controlled by the Soviets, which would also control production and distribution. Lenin also called for an immediate congress of the Party and changes in the program regarding the imperialist war and the demand for a state commune on the Parisian model. The International was to be revived, and the Party was to change its name.

Several days later, Lenin explained, in a pamphlet entitled *The Tasks of the Proletariat in Our Revolution,* why it was desirable that the Party abandon the Social Democratic label and call itself Communist. First of all, Marx and Engels had called themselves Communists and had written the *Communist Manifesto* precisely because socialism would replace capitalism, only "to grow gradually into" Communism. A second reason offered by Lenin was that the latter part of the term "social democracy" is "scientifically incorrect," since democracy is a state form and "Marxists are opponents of *every* state." As a third reason, Lenin asserted that the new type of state, comparable to the Paris Commune and necessary for the "transition to socialism," had already been brought into being in Russia, if only in a "weak, embryonic form." Although this new state was only being born in Russia in April, 1917, a fourth reason was also advanced by Lenin: he contended that the position of international socialism had changed radically from what it had been in the period between 1871 and 1914, when it was necessary to employ the "false, opportunist term, 'social democracy.' " Lenin believed that a "new epoch" had opened as a result of the "imperialist war" and that the majority of Social Democratic leaders, parliamentarians, and newspapers had "betrayed" socialism and had "gone over" to the side of their own national bourgeoisie.[14] He called upon his followers "not to imitate the woebegone Marxists of whom Marx said: 'I sowed dragons, and I reaped a harvest of fleas.' "[15] Declaring that "we wish to reconstruct the world," Lenin called for a proletarian revolution as the sole means of ending the war. To this end, he summoned his partisans to cast off the "dirty shirt" and don "clean underclothing."

All Bolsheviks, however, had not been willing to heed Lenin's advice. On March 28, Kamenev published in *Pravda* an article entitled "Without Secret Diplomacy," in which he disputed Lenin's position on the war and spoke out against disorganizing the army by having the troops evacuate the trenches. Instead, he predicted that the soldier would not lay down his arms but would "answer bullet with bullet." The Party, according to Kamenev, was not to overthrow the Provisional Government but was to exert pressure upon it in order to obtain a general peace settlement without annexations and indemnities. He wrote of revolutionary Russia's appealing to its allies, and he appeared to rule out the idea of a separate peace. Significantly, Stalin, as a member of the editorial board, did not object to the publication of anti-Leninist views. Even after Lenin returned to Russia, Kamenev continued to disagree with him. When the *April Theses* appeared in *Pravda*, Kamenev responded with an article published on the following day (April 21) under the title "Our Differences." Kamenev referred to the *Theses* as representing Lenin's "*personal* opinion" and warned against the Party's being transformed into a "group of propagandist Communists." He defended *Pravda*'s position, adopted prior to Lenin's return, which had regarded the "bourgeois-democratic revolution" as incomplete and which was somewhat tolerant of the Provisional Government. In no uncertain terms, he rejected Lenin's views as "unsuitable." Only new decisions of the Central Committee or of an all-Russian Party conference, said Kamenev, could modify or reject the position taken by the Party's Central Organ.

Such a gathering, the so-called April Conference, met in Petrograd from May 7 to 12 and had 133 voting delegates, representing more than 70,000 Party members. Lenin dominated the proceedings and succeeded in obtaining sufficient support for his uncompromising position on the need to accelerate the revolution. In his opening speech, he expressed the view that the Russian revolution was only a part of the world revolutionary proletarian movement which was "growing stronger day by day."[16] Lenin criticized Rykov's belief that socialism must come from other, more industrialized countries rather than from Russia. The movement had to be carried forward in Russia with the slogan "All power to the Soviets," so that the bourgeois Provisional Government could be replaced by the Soviets, which had yet to fall under the domination of the Bolsheviks. But Lenin warned that the Provisional Government, even though it was one of capitalists and landowners, could not be overthrown immediately.

The April Conference, in addition to criticizing the Provisional Government, adopted a number of resolutions. While advocating fraternization among the troops, it cautioned that the war would not be ended by unilateral action. Although it branded as base slander the assertion that the Party favored a separate peace with Germany, it also condemned "revolutionary defensism" as advocated by the Mensheviks. On the agrarian question, the Conference proposed confiscation of the property of landowners and of the Church, the placing of all land at the disposal of local peasant committees, and acceptance of the principle of nationalization (which few understood as meaning the abolition of private landholding).

The nationality problem plagued the Party at the April Conference. Although Stalin had initially favored *Pravda*'s soft line toward the Provisional Government, he supported Lenin after the latter's arrival in Russia and was given the task of presenting the Central Committee's report on the nationality question. Lenin's position was one of recognition of the right of national self-determination, and he advocated that Finland be accorded the autonomy which it was demanding of the Provisional Government. In recognizing the right of Finland, Poland, and Ukraine to secede from Russia, Lenin asserted to his opponents that "one would have to be insane to continue the policy of Czar Nicholas."[17] Opposition to any recognition of the right of national self-determination came from such Bolsheviks as Bukharin, Georgii Pyatakov, and Felix Dzierzynski, who argued that nationalism was a reactionary remnant of feudalism and should be given no quarter. In desperation, Lenin called his opponents "chauvinists" and told them to go wherever they wished. Stalin answered them by asking if they really thought that the anti-British national movement of the Irish was reactionary.[18] Actually, Lenin's opponents were splitting hairs; they had apparently forgotten that Lenin never regarded national self-determination as anything more than a tactical concession. In 1917, it was a particularly useful club with which to beat the Provisional Government because of its hesitancy in granting concessions to the Ukrainians, who had established their own anti-Communist council (*rada* in Ukrainian), the All-Ukrainian Central Rada.

Indeed, by June, 1917, there was no more ardent advocate than Lenin of the correctness of the Ukrainian demands and of their right to secede from Russia.[19] Yet—ironically, but not surprisingly—when the Ukrainians finally exercised that right following the Bolshevik seizure of power in Petrograd, Lenin ordered his army to invade the territory of the independent Ukrainian People's Republic. In the spring of 1917, however, the Russian Provisional Government had to be reckoned with. Lenin could not seize power at that time. It was first necessary to bolster Bolshevik influence in the industrial establishments of the capital and in the Petrograd Soviet. To this end, Party paramilitary detachments, the workers' guard, had been formed in the Viborg district of Petrograd in accordance with a decision by the local Soviet on May 11. Later that month, the Bolshevik ranks were strengthened when the so-called Inter-Borough Party organization (the *Mezhraiontsy*), composed of Trotsky and his followers, moved closer to Lenin.

Meanwhile, the Provisional Government was grappling with certain nettling issues. Its Foreign Minister, the historian Paul Miliukov, had sent a note to the Western Allies pledging Russia's continued participation in the war. The publication of this note on May 2 caused a storm which led to Miliukov's resignation on May 15, two days after the War Minister, Guchkov, had also resigned. During this crisis, the government announced the need for broadening the Cabinet and creating a coalition. The new Cabinet announced on May 18 included three Socialist Revolutionaries: Kerensky as War Minister, Victor M. Chernov as Minister of Agriculture, and Paul N. Pereverzev as Minister of Justice. Two Mensheviks, Irakli G. Tseretelli and M. I. Skobelev, joined the coalition as Minister of Posts and Telegraphs and Minister of Labor, respectively. Although the Cabinet was headed by Prince Georgii Evgen'evich L'vov, Kerensky enjoyed the greater prominence, especially after he ordered the army to prepare for a new military offensive.

In this situation, Lenin's Bolsheviks exploited the unpopularity of the war and stepped up their antiwar campaign. On May 28, the first issue of *Okopnaya pravda* ("Trench Truth") began to appear on the northern front and continued to be distributed until its Bolshevik editor was arrested on June 17. At the First All-Russian Congress of Soviets on June 22, Lenin delivered a lengthy address on the war, in which he defined the conflict as the "continuation of bourgeois politics and nothing more." He charged that despite the presence of a few ministers bearing the socialist label, the bankers were in control of the Provisional Government. In simple language, Lenin paraphrased the thesis of his recent work, *Imperialism, The Highest Stage of Capitalism,* and asserted that the Provisional Government was pursuing an imperialist policy. He declared that the Bolsheviks rejected a separate peace "like every other agreement with the capitalists" and referred to it as an "agreement with German bandits." Lenin also noted that there existed another kind of separate peace—one with the Russian capitalists and bankers in the Provisional Government—which he also condemned.

While Kerensky was making final preparations for the ill-fated July offensive, Lenin used the First Congress of Soviets as a sounding board with which to embarrass the Provisional Government by asking why the secret treaties with the Allies were not being published. In this way, he was able to substantiate his denunciation of the Provisional Government as imperialist, since it desired to acquire non-Russian territories as well as the Dardanelles. In view of the fact that the Bolsheviks had only 13 per cent of the votes (103 out of 790) at the First Congress of Soviets and were also in the minority in the Petrograd Soviet, Lenin had little reason to be gentle with that body. He took the Soviet to task for having decided to participate in the Provisional Government, and he declared that its members should not blame the "German social chauvinists" when they themselves were equally guilty and had supported the Russian "liberty loan." He accused them of paying lip service to "peace without annexations and without indemnities," while they actually pursued just the opposite policy and were also unwilling to grant Finland and Ukraine the right of self-determination. Lenin also criticized the Mensheviks and Socialist Revolutionaries for projecting such a peace on the basis of a *status quo ante bellum.* He asked how England could be compelled to return the colonies which she had seized from Germany, or how Japan could be induced to return Kiaochow and the islands seized from Germany in the Pacific. Lenin proposed instead that the secret treaties be published and war declared on the German capitalists, and that the alliance with the Anglo-French capitalists be severed. Yet, ironically, within nine months Lenin himself was to sign a separate peace—or at least a truce—with the German capitalists. But at the Congress of Soviets, he warned frankly that "we [Bolsheviks] are not Tolstoyans" (i.e., pacifists) and declared that "under certain circumstances a revolutionary war cannot be avoided."

While revolutionary war could not be avoided, however, it certainly could be postponed. The relatively weak, though growing, position of the Bolsheviks in the summer of 1917 prompted the Bolshevik leadership to exercise caution. Thus, when the Congress of Soviets forbade a Bolshevik demonstration planned for June 23 and placed a three-day ban on all demonstrations, the Bolshevik Central Committee decided to acquiesce and comply with the order. Then, on June 25, the Congress announced its own demonstration to be held on July 1; though the Bolsheviks protested, they decided to take advantage of the rally with its 400,000 participants in order to propagate their antiwar and anti-Provisional Government slogans and demands for "all power to the Soviets."

As it became clear that Kerensky's July military offensive against the Central Powers was failing, opposition to the Provisional Government in the capital gathered strength. The "white night" of summertime in the capital, with its interminable sunset, was also conducive to political agitation and demonstrations. On July 11, Lenin went to a village near Mustamyaki, outside Petrograd, to visit the historian Bonch-Bruevich. On July 17, he was summoned back to Petrograd after demonstrations by mutinous troops and Bolshevik-led workers had become violent and begun to assume the earmarks of an outright attempt to overthrow the Provisional Government. Lenin addressed a mob from the balcony of the Kshesinskaya residence and then participated in a Central Committee night session which adopted a resolution advocating an end to the demonstrations.

The Provisional Government was able to bring in loyal troops and began to restore order. On July 19, Lenin—sensing that the Party and the mobs were not yet strong enough—argued against the proposal by certain Bolsheviks to call a general strike. The Provisional Government raided the editorial offices and printing plant of *Pravda* on July 18 and occupied the Central Committee headquarters on the following day. Lenin's arrest, along with that of Kamenev and Zinoviev, was ordered on July 19. On the following day, Lenin's quarters were searched, but he had already gone into hiding. On August 5, he was indicted for treason and for having organized an armed uprising—the so-called "July days."

The demonstrations of July 16-17 had coincided with the publication of a statement in the not very reputable newspaper *Zhivoe slovo* under the signatures of Grigorii Alexeyevich Alexinsky and Vasilii S. Pankratov (the former was a one-time Bolshevik and leader of the Party's faction in the Second Duma, the latter a Socialist Revolutionary who had spent fourteen years in prison for political activity). The statement accused Lenin and the Bolsheviks of having received funds from the Germans and of having acted as their spies. It was based on information supplied by a Russian officer, an Ensign Yermolenko, who had been a prisoner of war in Germany and had turned up at Russian Staff Headquarters on the Eastern Front in the spring of 1917. The Ensign asserted that he had been given safe conduct to the Russian lines by the Germans in order to agitate for a separate peace, and that he had been told that Lenin was also working for the Germans under the same orders.

The accusation published by Alexinsky and Pankratov undoubtedly served to reduce Bolshevik influence following the violent demonstrations of July 16-17. Yet, the charge was not proved, and many opponents of the Bolsheviks refused to believe that Lenin had taken money from the Germans. The President of the Petrograd Soviet, Chkheidze, for one, had attempted to prevent publication of the accusations. Within a few days, Lenin had coined the term "Russian Dreyfusiade" in referring to this campaign of calumny against him, likening the Bolsheviks to Captain Dreyfus, who had to be convicted of espionage at any cost.

Evidence that the Bolsheviks received money from the Germans is both circumstantial and indirectly documentary. In the former category is the fact that large sums of money were transferred to Petrograd from Stockholm in 1917 to a Madame Eugenia Mavrikievna Sumenson. The funds were sent by Lenin's old friend, the Polish Social Democrat Jacob Haniecki, under the guise of commercial transactions. French counterintelligence agents had uncovered telegraphic communications of a semicryptic nature regarding these "commercial" transactions and made them available to the Provisional Government. Madame Sumenson was arrested along with the lawyer Mechislav Yulievich Kozlovsky, a former Polish Social Democrat who had also been handling unusually large sums. At the time, the Bolsheviks conveniently claimed that they had no knowledge of any Madame Sumenson and that Haniecki and Kozlovsky were not Bolsheviks.[20]

It is more than doubtful that the funds which Haniecki transmitted to Russia from Stockholm were, indeed, sent for commercial purposes. Haniecki was more of a Bolshevik than a Polish Social Democrat and had become a member of the All-Russian Central Committee in 1907 following the Fifth Congress. After the February Revolution of 1917, he supposedly stationed himself in Stockholm for the purpose of "maintaining ties between the Russian Bolsheviks and foreign revolutionary Social Democrats."[21] Haniecki had been in close touch with Lenin while the latter was in Cracow, and the record of Lenin's correspondence during World War I reveals many letters sent to him. Krupskaya recalled that it was to Haniecki that Lenin first turned for aid in crossing Germany when the possibility of returning to Russia arose in March, 1917.

It is significant that Haniecki had retained his connections with Parvus (Gel'fand),* one of Trotsky's former associates in

---

* Referred to as Helphand and Parvus in the German documents. Parvus approached the German Ambassador in Constantinople in the latter part of 1914 with a plan to destroy the Czarist regime by granting financial aid to Russian and non-Russian revolutionaries. It was his intention to bring about the establishment of socialism in Russia in this way. Parvus presented his views in a memorandum entitled "Preparations for a Political Mass Strike in Russia," dated March 9, 1915. (The text of this memorandum may be found in Zeman, *op. cit.*, pp. 140–152). In many ways an astute observer of the Russian scene, he acquired German citizenship and was supplied with millions of marks for propaganda and intelligence operations within Russia, which he conducted from Copenhagen under the sympathetic eye of the German Minister to Denmark, Count Ulrich von Brockdorff-Rantzau.

the 1905 Petrograd Soviet, with whom Lenin had broken earlier. Parvus had great abilities as a businessman and had amassed a small fortune. His reputation as an "extreme [German] social chauvinist" and as a "direct agent of German imperialism"[22] did not deter Haniecki from working for him. Significantly, this continued relationship with an enemy of Lenin's did not cause Lenin to break with Haniecki. The two remained on good terms, and Lenin defended both Haniecki and Kozlovsky in an article published in the *Pravda Bulletin* on July 19. The continued existence of this incongruous Lenin-Haniecki-Parvus triangle could be explained by the usefulness of Haniecki as a source of funds.

The fact is that the Party's expenditures increased tremendously during 1917. The resumed publication of *Pravda* and the publication of newspapers for soldiers, including *Soldatskaya pravda,* required substantial sums of money. The question of how all these activities were financed cannot be answered satisfactorily in terms of payment of Party dues, even though the membership is reported to have increased from about 20,000 to 200,000 between March and October of 1917. The mere fact that, as Krupskaya recounted in her memoirs, there was no real Party secretariat at that time (it was actually a one-man operation carried out by Jacob Sverdlov) indicates the limited means available for collecting large sums of money from a somewhat dispersed membership during the hectic months of 1917.

It seems clear that other sources of funds had to be tapped in order to carry on this broad kind of agitational and subversive operation. German documentary evidence unearthed by British authorities after World War II makes it clear that the German Government was financing Lenin's Bolshevik movement in an effort to weaken the Czarist regime and, later, the Provisional Government. The text of a communication of December 3, 1917, sent by the Minister of Foreign Affairs, Baron Richard von Kühlmann, to an official for transmission orally to the Kaiser contains the following statement: "It was not until the Bolsheviki had received from us a steady flow of funds that they were in a position to be able to build up their main organ, *Pravda,* to conduct energetic propaganda and to extend appreciably the originally narrow basis of their party."[23] The Germans apparently conveyed funds to the Bolsheviks through various channels, but there seems to be no direct documentary evidence to prove that Lenin was aware of how significant this source of support actually was.

If Lenin had, indeed, been aware of large-scale German financial support, would he have been any the less indignant in branding the charges as a "crude lie," "slanders," "calumnies," and "vulgar machinations"? The answer is probably no: appearance of righteous indignation would have had to be maintained in any case. A much more significant clue is the fact that Lenin, as shown in his writings and practices prior to 1917, never had scruples regarding the means used in a given situation. If one accepts the right of passage across Germany as a gift from the German Government—as Lenin did in April—why draw a line in the matter of a grant-in-aid from the same source or from various ill-defined sources when the cause is just and truth is on your side? It must be borne in mind, however, that the interests of the Bolsheviks and of the Germans coincided only temporarily. The Bolsheviks obtained power in the end and defeated Kerensky's Provisional Government, not because they received German money, but for far more significant reasons. The Provisional Government's dilatory approach to the question of a peace treaty and to the nationality and agrarian problems was one of these reasons. More important, however, were the perseverance of the Bolsheviks, their alertness in recognizing the significance of certain issues, and Lenin's leadership.

The Party was in an uncomfortable position in August, 1917. It was accused of being in the service of the Germans. Lenin and Zinoviev were in hiding, defying the judicial organs of the Provisional Government rather than attempting to refute the charges of treason in open court. The Provisional Government appeared to have the upper hand. It had arrested such other prominent Bolsheviks as Kamenev, Lunacharsky, Trotsky, and Madame Kollontai. Lenin and Zinoviev, in a letter published on July 28, declared: "After all that occurred on July 6-8 [19-21], not a single Russian revolutionist can nourish constitutional illusions any longer. A decisive encounter between the revolution and the counterrevolution is taking place."[24] The Petrograd Soviet, with its Socialist Revolutionary–Menshevik majority, was now attacked by Lenin for not having condemned the Provisional Government's order to arrest the Bolshevik leadership. He thus identified the Soviet with the counterrevolution and equated the Bolsheviks exclusively with the revolution. The earlier slogan of "All power to the Soviets" was abandoned after July 17 in keeping with Lenin's assertion regarding "slogans which were correct yesterday, but which have lost all meaning today."[25] The Soviets, said Lenin, can and must play a role in the new revolution, but the present Soviets were compromised by their Socialist Revolutionary and Menshevik membership and were "impotent and helpless" before the forces of the counterrevolution. He likened them to "rams who have been brought to slaughter, placed under the ax, and are plaintively bleating."[26] According to Lenin, new Bolshevik-dominated Soviets were the solution. His article "On Slogans" contained an ominous warning: "The essence of the matter is that, at present, power can no longer be seized peacefully."[27]

It was at this turning point in the Bolshevik relations with the Soviets that the Party convened its Sixth Congress, which met semilegally in Petrograd between August 8 and 16, 1917. Many prominent Party leaders were absent, including Lenin, Trotsky, Kamenev, Zinoviev, Lunacharsky, and Madame Kollontai. The report of the Central Committee was delivered by Stalin, and Bukharin reported on how the war with the Central Powers might be terminated. The Congress was attended by 157 voting delegates and 107 with a consultative vote. Of these, only 171 completed a questionnaire given to them. These 171 delegates were distributed among the various nationalities as follows: 92 Russians, 29 Jews, 17 Latvians, 8 Poles, 6 Ukrainians, 6 Georgians, 4 Lithuanians, 3 Estonians, 2 Finns, 2 Moldavians, 1 Armenian, and 1 Persian. Also significant was the age distribution of the 171 delegates: 98 were between the ages of twenty-five and thirty-four, and 30 were between thirty-five and thirty-nine.[28]

The youthful delegates first probed the meaning of the abortive "July days"—the demonstrations which had driven the

Party underground—and attempted to chart a new strategy. The fact that the July demonstrations had gotten out of hand was criticized by some delegates, particularly Dmitrii Z. Manuilsky, who was to become a leader in the Comintern and ultimately Foreign Minister and United Nations representative of the Ukrainian Soviet Republic. Manuilsky (who used the pseudonym Bezrabotnyi, meaning "unemployed") conceded that the Party had acted correctly in "taking the movement in hand," but criticized the Central Committee representatives for not having "explained to the masses the distinction between an organized demonstration and an armed uprising."[29] Yet, a statement made at the Sixth Congress by N. I. Podvoisky, the representative of the Petrograd Military Organization, cast doubt upon the spontaneity of the demonstrations. Podvoisky noted that the Military Organization had begun its work among the troops in the capital on the second day following the collapse of the autocracy. He explained that once his organization realized that the demonstration could not be prevented, it attempted at least to have it conducted in an organized manner.[30]

In answer to the criticism that the Central Committee had become the Petersburg Party committee and had cut itself off from the provinces, Stalin conceded that this was partially correct. He explained, however, that "the leading forces of the revolution" were in the capital.[31] Yet, the fact that Lenin had denounced the Soviets and had declared all power to be in the hands of the counterrevolution prompted some delegates to question the wisdom of dropping the slogan "All power to the Soviets." They argued that abandoning this battle cry would only aid the counterrevolution. Stalin attempted to mediate by suggesting that to mute the slogan did not transform its meaning into "Down with the Soviets."[32] He proposed that the Party continue to participate in the Central Executive Committee of the Soviets and reminded the delegates that the Bolsheviks were working satisfactorily with those Soviets in which they held a majority. At the same time, Stalin announced: "The peaceful period of the revolution has come to an end. The period of conflicts and explosions has commenced."[33] In other words, the Provisional Government may have won a round, but the fight was not yet over.

Another prominent issue at the Sixth Congress concerned Lenin's and Zinoviev's decision to go into hiding in order to escape being arrested and tried by the Provisional Government at a time when the Party was accused of having ties with Germany. Some delegates judged Lenin's action to be harmful to the Party, and a resolution by Volodarsky expressed this view. Manuilsky supported this resolution on the grounds that refusal to face trial was "providing the bourgeoisie with a trump card." He suggested that the trial be turned into a "Dreyfus affair" in the "interests of the revolution and the prestige of our Party."[34] The trial of Lenin, in Manuilsky's opinion, would be the trial of the entire International. However, such Party stalwarts as Dzierzynski, Bukharin, and Ordzhonikidze came to Lenin's support. Lenin and Zinoviev dispatched a letter to the Congress in which they declared that they would submit themselves for trial only to the Constituent Assembly because "at present there are no guarantees of justice in Russia."[35] Not only Bolsheviks defended Lenin and Zinoviev against the charge that they were German agents. Even Lenin's old enemy Martov sent a letter of greeting to the Sixth Congress in which he expressed confidence in Lenin. After a brief debate, the Congress adopted a resolution approving Lenin's action.

The Congress also approved a new set of Party Statutes which strengthened membership requirements by establishing an initiation fee of 50 kopecks and specifying that dues of not less than 1 per cent of a member's wages be paid regularly, in place of the earlier and less specific provision for "supporting the Party with material means." The Statutes also provided for "subordination [of the members] to all decisions of the Party" and required that candidates for membership be recommended by two members and approved by the local Party organization. Paragraph 12 defined for the first time the functions of the Party Congress in a fourfold form which was to be retained in successive statutes even in the post-Stalin period. A beginning was made toward defining "democratic centralism" in a resolution which declared: "Party factions in state, municipal, soviet, and other institutions in the capacity of Party organizations subordinate themselves to all decisions of the Party and to the respective leading Party centers."[36]

The growth of Party membership during 1917 reflected new interest in the perennial question of Russia's role in showing a benighted world the way to a better future. Lenin had expressed his view on this question in his "Farewell Letter to the Swiss Workers" (written on April 8, 1917), asserting that the Russian proletariat had the "great honor to *initiate* a series of revolutions generated by the objective nature of the imperialist war." However, he noted that the view which regarded the Russian proletariat as the revolutionary-proletariat—elect among the workers of other countries was alien to the Russian Social Democrats. He observed that the "proletariat of Russia is *less* organized, prepared, and conscious than the workers of other countries" and that it was not particular qualities but only circumstances which had placed the Russians in the lead "*for a certain, possibly very short, time* [Lenin's italics]."[37]

Thus, Lenin believed that the events in Russia would be followed by revolutions in Western Europe. Yet, this did not lessen his impatience with the Provisional Government, now headed by Kerensky following the "July days" and the resignation of Prince G. E. L'vov. Lenin even suggested that the Bolsheviks "had every opportunity to commence the unseating and arrest of hundreds of officials, to occupy dozens of state and governmental buildings and institutions."[38] However, he denied that the Bolsheviks had attempted to do this in the July demonstrations, even though the opportunity had supposedly been there.* In addition to defending himself against the charge of being a German agent, Lenin denounced Kerensky as a Bonapartist, suggesting that he relied more and more on the military. Ironically, it was precisely the military which presented the next challenge to Kerensky's regime—in the form of an attempted coup by General Lavr G. Kornilov, who had become the supreme commander of the Russian Army following the "July days."

Thus, the Bonapartist turned out to be not Kerensky but Kornilov, who had begun to move troops on Petrograd on

---

* The former Socialist Revolutionary and Menshevik, N. N. Sukhanov (Nikolai Nikolaevich Himmer), author of the most detailed eyewitness account of the events of 1917 (*see* n. 49, this chapter), has asserted that Lunacharsky informed him that Lenin was planning a coup on July 17.

September 7. The attempt failed when Kornilov's forces dissolved within four days under the pressure of sabotage by railroad workers and telegraphers and agitation conducted among the troops. On September 12, Kerensky replaced Kornilov as supreme commander. By appointing himself generalissimo, Kerensky forfeited whatever support he may have enjoyed among the officers' corps. Moreover, he was unable to prevent the rapid loss of support for the Provisional Government among the troops and peasants. Kerensky broke with his Minister of Agriculture, the Socialist Revolutionary Victor Chernov, who resigned from the Provisional Government in September because of Kerensky's hesitancy in dealing with the agrarian question.

It was with the suppression of the Kornilov coup that the Bolsheviks began to gain influence again in Petrograd at the same time that Lenin, disguised as a railway fireman, had to flee to Finland from his place of hiding outside the Russian capital. Kerensky's dependence upon the Soviet in his struggle against Kornilov could only reveal the pathetic impotence of the Provisional Government. Lenin expressed it in this way, in a letter to the Central Committee dated September 12: "We will fight, we are fighting against Kornilov, even *as Kerensky's troops do,* but we do not support Kerensky; we expose his weakness."[39] As a result, in late September, Lenin was able to resurrect the slogan "All power to the Soviets," which he had abandoned after the July disorders. In letters to the Central Committee, written between September 25 and 27, Lenin declared: "Having obtained a majority in the Soviets of Workers' and Soldiers' Deputies of both capitals [Moscow and Petrograd], the Bolsheviks can and must seize state power."[40] As further proof of Bolshevik strength, Lenin cited the vacillation of the Socialist Revolutionaries and Mensheviks and promised that "the Bolshevik government *alone* will satisfy the peasantry." He cited Marx's view that uprising must be treated as an art, but proceeded to make some contradictory statements. In one letter, he declared that "it would be naïve to wait for a 'formal' majority on the side of the Bolsheviks." In another, he asserted that "we have back of us a *majority* of the people because Chernov's resignation is . . . the most graphic sign that the peasantry *will not receive land* from a bloc of the Socialist Revolutionaries or from the SR's themselves."[41]

When the Central Committee met without Lenin on September 28, the majority of the members refused to take seriously his flat prediction that the rest of the country would follow the Bolsheviks once they seized power in Petrograd and in Moscow. Instead, the Central Committee decided to participate in the Democratic Conference convoked by the Central Executive Committee of Soviets; this decision was contrary to Lenin's advice to boycott the Conference on the grounds that the "decision lies *outside* of it in the workers' sections of Petrograd and Moscow." In one of the letters to the Central Committee, Lenin demanded that the Party have its forces surround the Alexander Theater in which the Democratic Conference was meeting. The Conference sat from September 27 to October 5; its delegates represented organs of local self-government, cooperatives, Soviets, factory committees, army units, and trade unions. A provisional Council of the Republic, the so-called Pre-Parliament, was formed from the Conference membership to serve as an interim representative body prior to the oft-postponed convocation of the Constituent Assembly. Lenin, writing on October 7, criticized the Bolsheviks for not having quit the Democratic Conference entirely, although they did walk out of the first day's session of the Pre-Parliament, punctuating it with a denunciation of the "government of betrayal of the people" and a declaration that the Pre-Parliament was counter-revolutionary.

Lenin had been upset by the Central Committee's cold shoulder toward his demand that it prepare for the seizure of power. In a letter of October 10 to Ivar T. Smilga, a Latvian who had been elected to the Bolshevik Central Committee in April, Lenin expressed impatience with the dilatory tactics of the Party leaders in Petrograd at a time when, in his view, Kerensky was arranging with the army for the use of troops to suppress the Bolsheviks. Lenin complained: "And what do we do? We only pass resolutions. We lose time. We set 'dates' (October 20 [November 2], the Congress of Soviets—is it not ridiculous to delay? Is it not ridiculous to rely on that?). The

Bolsheviks do *not* conduct systematic work in order to prepare *their own* military forces for the overthrow of Kerensky."[42] Lenin rejected the naïve hope that "the wave will sweep Kerensky away" and declared it to be "the same as relying on chance." He instructed Smilga to organize and propagandize Russian troops stationed in Finland in preparation for the Bolshevik armed uprising. In this letter, Lenin also proposed a bloc with the Left Socialist Revolutionaries in the hope of obtaining in this way a majority in the still-to-be-elected Constituent Assembly.

On October 12, two days after writing to Smilga, Lenin dispatched a missive to the Central Committee in which he declared for an immediate armed uprising instead of the "absolute idiocy" of awaiting the Congress of Soviets. In order to shock the Central Committee out of its lethargy and prevent the ruin of the revolution, Lenin tendered his resignation, "leaving myself the freedom to agitate *in the lower ranks* of the Party and at the Party Congress."[43] The Central Committee ignored the offer to resign, and Lenin continued to bombard it, as well as the Moscow and Petrograd Party committees, with demands for action. Within a few days, he wrote the leading Party committees: "Victory is assured, and there are nine chances out of ten that it will be bloodless. To wait is a crime against the revolution." He proposed the slogan: "Power to the Soviets, land to the peasants, peace to the peoples, bread to the hungry."[44]

Convinced that the other members of the Central Committee had forgotten five principal rules of the art of uprising, as expounded by Marx, Lenin paraphrased them as follows in a letter of October 21: (1) "Never *play* at uprising, but once it is begun, know firmly that you have to go to the very end"; (2) "it is necessary to gather a *great preponderance of forces* in a decisive place at a decisive moment, lest the enemy, being better prepared and organized, destroys the insurgents"; (3) "once the uprising has been begun, it is necessary to act with the greatest decisiveness, to take the *offensive* unfailingly and unconditionally"; (4) "it is necessary to strive to take the enemy by surprise, to take advantage of the moment while his troops are scattered"; (5) "it is necessary to strive *daily* for even small successes (one may even say hourly in the case of an individual city), maintaining under all circumstances a '*moral superiority.*' "[45] Calling for audacity, Lenin advised the Central Committee to marshal its forces among the sailors, workers, and soldiers for the purpose of seizing the telephone exchange, the main telegraph office, the railroad stations, the bridges, and the military schools.

In another letter, written on the same day to Bolsheviks who were attending the Northern Regional Congress of Soviets, Lenin termed the chances of winning as ninety-nine out of a hundred and accused Kerensky and the Kornilovites of wanting to deliver Petrograd to the Germans in order to save the Provisional Government. He warned that "delay means death."

On October 16, the Central Committee had agreed that Lenin should come to Petrograd from Viborg. On October 23, he attended a Central Committee meeting for the first time since the "July days" and attempted to galvanize his comrades with the warning that it would be "senseless" to wait for the Constituent Assembly, "which obviously will not be with us."[46] Lenin won a victory when the Central Committee, by a vote of ten to two, adopted a resolution which declared an armed uprising to be inevitable and the time "fully ripe." The two dissenters were Kamenev and Zinoviev. Upon the suggestion of Dzierzynski, a political bureau was established within the Central Committee; its seven members were Lenin, Trotsky, Stalin, Kamenev, Zinoviev, Grigorii Ya. Sokol'nikov (Brilliant), and A. S. Bubnov.

On October 24, Kamenev and Zinoviev prepared a statement which they appended to the Central Committee's minutes in order to clarify their position. It was their opinion that an armed uprising would mean staking the Party's fate on a single card—an unwise strategy at a time when the Party's strength was growing. They denied Lenin's assertion that a majority of the country was behind the Bolsheviks and warned of the dangers of overestimating the Party's strength and underestimating the enemy. They were convinced that a defensive policy on the part of the Bolsheviks would contribute to the collapse of the Provisional Government—a collapse that was inevitable and would be facilitated by Bolshevik participation in the Constituent Assembly. In criticism of Lenin, they declared that it was incorrect to formulate the question in terms of "either now or never" and referred to armed uprising as a "perilous policy."[47]

For the next two weeks, Lenin's spleen was vented on Kamenev and Zinoviev, as well as on the Provisional Government. At the enlarged Central Committee meeting of October 29, the policy advocated by Kamenev and Zinoviev was debated, along with that of Lenin, and the latter won approval (by a vote of nineteen to two, with four abstentions) in the form in which it had been adopted at the October 23 meeting. Kamenev resigned his membership in the Central Committee on the grounds that Lenin's position was "leading the Party and the proletariat to defeat." Together with Zinoviev, Kamenev published a declaration in the October 31 issue of the non-Party newspaper *Novaya zhizn'* stating that it was necessary to speak out against any attempt to seize power and characterizing it as a "desperate step." On the previous day, Lenin had denounced them—but not by name—as "two sad pessimists . . . spineless people" and their arguments as "philistine."

Upon learning of the publication of this declaration, Lenin wrote a letter "to the Party" in which he branded Kamenev and Zinoviev as "strikebreakers" and accused them of aiding the bourgeoisie in a manner "a thousand times meaner and a *million times more harmful* than were all the writings of Plekhanov in the non-Party press in 1906-07, which the Party so sharply condemned."[48] In this letter, intended only for Party members, Lenin told Kamenev and Zinoviev to found their own party.* Lenin's contention was that the Central Committee had decided upon an armed uprising and had been considering it since September. If Kamenev and Zinoviev had wished to speak out against this policy, he argued, they should have done so before the decision was made; once the matter was decided, any criticism was the equivalent of strikebreaking and "betrayal to the capitalists," since the die had been cast. They had sinned in that they had appealed to the rank-and-file Party membership

---

* These denunciations were not publicly disclosed until they were printed in *Pravda* on November 4, 1927, when Stalin was preparing to expel Kamenev, Zinoviev, and Trotsky from the Party.

over the heads of the central leadership. (However, it should be recalled that the decision in favor of an armed uprising had not been approved by a Party congress.) Lenin demanded that both Kamenev and Zinoviev be expelled from the Party.*

At its November 2 meeting, the Central Committee accepted Kamenev's resignation and obliged him and Zinoviev to make no statements against its decisions. On the same day, a Military Revolutionary Committee was organized in the Bolshevik-dominated Petrograd Soviet under the chairmanship of Trotsky, the President of that body. An attempt by the Provisional Government to close two Bolshevik newspapers on November 6 proved to be short-lived when the Party summoned forces of the Military Revolutionary Committee to stand guard at the printing plants. Lenin had set November 7 as the day for the seizure of power. The following day would have been too late, since Lenin, for tactical reasons, wanted the coup to coincide with the Second All-Russian Congress of Soviets scheduled to meet that same day. It was his strategy to seize the seat of the Provisional Government, the Winter Palace, along with other public buildings, in order to present the Congress of Soviets with a *fait accompli* before it could be organized as an effective force in the revolutionary situation.

The actual seizure of the Winter Palace by Lenin's paramilitary forces, accomplished at night, turned out to be surprisingly easy: the Palace was defended only by military cadets (Yunkers) and by members of a women's detachment. Kerensky had fled in the direction of the military front to organize support for the Provisional Government and had left his ministers to face arrest by the Red Guard. Late on the night of November 7, after the Bolsheviks had seized many public buildings, the Second All-Russian Congress of Soviets convened.[49] The Bolsheviks, in alliance with the Left Socialist Revolutionaries, claimed a majority. This led to a walkout of the other Socialist Revolutionaries and the Mensheviks, who formed the anti-Bolshevik

---

* Lenin employed his usual double standard and denied them the right to do what he himself had done when he suffered defeat at the Menshevik-dominated Fourth Congress and then proceeded to challenge the newly elected Central Committee.

Committee for Salvation with other groups. The next day, Lenin appeared at the Congress of Soviets and refused to consent to the formation of an all-Socialist coalition government, holding out, instead, for an exclusively Bolshevik Cabinet to be called the Council of People's Commissars.

Lenin headed the new government, which the fellow-traveling Left Socialist Revolutionaries did not enter. His one-time arch-enemy, the former pro-Menshevik Trotsky, held the foreign affairs portfolio. A new Central Executive Committee was announced with a Bolshevik majority, and the Congress of Soviets was adjourned in the early hours of the morning of November 9. Thus, the slogan "All power to the Soviets" was rendered meaningless and was, in fact, replaced by that of "All power to the Central Committee."

The Bolsheviks had obtained power by the will of their leader and through the impotence of the Provisional Government. Their opponents had too often mistaken their own words for action and had underestimated the effectiveness of Bolshevik demagogy. Florid oratory by Kerensky could no longer save the Provisional Government, as it had on previous occasions. A protracted civil war had begun, but Lenin's party was to demonstrate that a divided and exhausted majority is no match for a militant, ruthless, and well-organized minority.

CHAPTER V

LENINISM IN PRACTICE

The task of honest leaders of the people is inhumanly difficult. It is impossible to be a leader without being a tyrant to some degree or other. In all probability, more people were killed under Lenin than in Thomas Münzer's time. However, the resistance to the revolution headed by Lenin was organized in a broader and more powerful manner. It should also be borne in mind that with the development of "civilization," the value of human life manifestly declines.
—Maxim Gorky, V. I. Lenin (1931).

The more outstanding a man is, the more *dangerous* he is and the less deserving he is of "forgiveness," the French say. Only one who *belongs* to the inner circle can become a traitor.
—Lenin, in a letter to the Central Committee (November 1, 1917).

Socialism is, first of all, accounting. Socialism is not created by ukase from above. The state bureaucratic automatism is alien to its spirit; living, creative socialism is created by the popular masses themselves.
—Lenin, in the Central Executive Committee (November 17, 1917).

After thirty years of agitation and conspiratorial activity, almost half of which were spent abroad, Lenin was to have a little more than four years in which to impose his theories and schemes upon Russia before being felled, in May, 1922, by the first of three strokes. Ironically, he who was destined to rule Russia was, on occasion, aware of the limits to his knowledge of his native land. Once, on Capri, he had expressed these misgivings to Gorky: "I know Russia so little. Simbirsk, Kazan, Petersburg, exile, and—that is about all."[1] However, this lack of basic familiarity with the object of his experiment did not prevent Lenin from proceeding boldly on the basis of a general plan of action which had taken shape during his exile and life underground.

The purported goals of Bolshevism were most fully expressed in Lenin's *State and Revolution,* written in August and September of 1917, and in his lengthy article "Will the Bolsheviks Retain State Power?" published in October, 1917. In the earlier work, Lenin quoted Marx and Engels profusely on the class basis of the state and on the state as an instrument of oppression and exploitation. He took up Engels' phrase "the withering away of the state" (following the violent seizure of power by the Communists and the destruction of the bourgeois state apparatus). He quoted Engels' assertion that the "free and equal association of the producers will put the whole state machine where it will then belong: in the museum of antiquities, side by side with the spinning wheel and the bronze ax."[2] By attacking Kautsky, the Mensheviks, the Socialist Revolutionaries, the Provisional Government, the anarchists, and others, Lenin gave his *State and Revolution* the character of a polemic, as well as that of an exegetical work based upon Marx and Engels.

Lenin took recourse to one of his favorite topics, the Paris Commune, to illustrate what the proletariat would use in place of the destroyed bourgeois state machinery.[3] Praising the Commune's practice of paying public officials the wages of workingmen and subjecting them to recall, Lenin denounced Marxists for having forgotten this basic tenet. He declared sarcastically: "It is 'proper' to keep silent about it as if it were a piece of old-fashioned 'naïveté,' just as the Christians, after Christianity had attained the position of a state religion, 'forgot' the 'naïvetés' of primitive Christianity with its democratic-revolutionary spirit."[4] Lenin, forever the self-styled guardian of ideological orthodoxy, invoked a curious kind of reasoning to explain the withering away of the state. Once the modern counterpart of the Commune comes into its own, "the organ of suppression is now the majority of the population, and not a minority, as was always the case under slavery, serfdom, and wage labor. And, once the majority of the people *itself* suppresses its oppressors, a 'special force' for suppression is *no longer necessary.* In this sense, the state *begins to wither away*."[5] This formulation found further expression in the following statement in *State and Revolution*:

> To destroy officialdom immediately, everywhere, completely—this cannot be thought of. This is a utopia. But to *break up* at once the old bureaucratic machine and to start immediately the construction of a new one which will enable us gradually to reduce all officialdom to naught [*sic*]—this is *no* utopia, it is the experience of the Commune, it is the direct and urgent task of the revolutionary proletariat.[6]

The great miracle of creating a society without a conventional bureaucracy was to be wrought "under the leadership of the armed proletariat." In practice, this meant the Party.

Lenin's gross oversimplification of the problem of bureaucracy prior to the seizure of power is particularly well illustrated in his article "Will the Bolsheviks Retain State Power?" In it, he claimed that the problem could be reduced to the matter of "general state *accounting* of production and distribution of goods." He indicated, however, that the persons performing these accounting functions would be transformed into civil servants "by one decree" in the same way that "the watchdogs of capitalism, such as Briand and other bourgeois Ministers, transform striking railwaymen into employees."[7] Lenin wrote of "drawing the workers, the poor people, into the everyday work of managing the state." As an illustration of this principle in operation, he selected the example of the "wealthy" family being dispossessed of three of its five rooms and its unemployed members being compelled by the "detachment of workers' militia" to accept employment as keepers of accounts. When Lenin wrote of a "state apparatus of about ten if not twenty million,"[8] composed of "class-conscious workers" who would be part-time civil servants, he demonstrated the limited nature of his comprehension of the complexity of an industrialized, let alone socialist, society.

In analyzing Lenin's character, however, one should not let his strong utopianism obscure his shrewdness and considerable practical knowledge. Indeed, his success as a politician depended to a large extent upon his recognition of the need to break with the past and upon his suasive talents in promising fulfillment of a dream. Thus, Lenin combined fanaticism with pragmatism, persistence with flexibility. While he was a dedicated man who had forsaken a promising legal career for professional revolutionary activity, he was by no means a political ascetic.[9] Indeed, he was not averse to such pleasures as tramping in the woods with Krupskaya and, on occasion, going to concerts and to the theater. Yet, Lenin was notorious for his inability to relax for long—a condition which obviously stemmed from the fear of escaping from his inner compulsiveness. This fundamental aspect of his character emerges clearly in Gorky's oft-quoted account of Lenin's reaction to hearing Beethoven's *Appassionata* sonata performed at a private concert by Issay Dobroven, former chief conductor of the Imperial Opera. According to Gorky, Lenin first commented upon the incredible beauty of this work and upon the fact that it was wrought by man. Then, quickly changing his mood, he noted that he could not listen to music frequently because it "gets on one's nerves [and] makes one want to speak sweet nonsense and pat on the head people who, living in a filthy hell, can create such beauty." Applying this to politics, he added: "Today, it is impossible to pat anyone on the head—they will bite off your hand, and it is necessary to beat people on the head, beat them pitilessly, although our ideal is opposed to all coercion . . ."[10]

The incongruity of beating people over the head for the purpose of creating a paradise on earth—in the form of a future stateless and classless society in which houses were to be let without payment of rent—did not blind Lenin to the need for more immediate practical decisions. One of the most important of these was the decision to embark upon peace negotiations with the Central Powers—a step which was to provoke sharp disagreements within the Party. At the same time (on March 14 and 15, 1918), Lenin could tell Colonel Raymond Robins, the American Red Cross representative, that Soviet Russia would accept military aid from the United States if the peace treaty were not ratified by the Congress of Soviets. When it became necessary to organize resistance to the German war effort and to combat internal opposition to the Communist regime, Lenin did not hesitate to accept the military advice of Czarist army officers and to appoint one of their number, General Sergei Sergeyevich Kamenev, as supreme commander of all Soviet armed forces in July, 1919. Later, he was willing to offer concessions to foreign capitalists, although these agreements were of a highly conditional nature.[11] In this as in other matters, however, Lenin drew a line beyond which expedience was not to be allowed to encroach upon doctrine.

One of these "lines of no more concessions" brought a crisis within the Party ten days after the seizure of power, when five members of the Central Committee, together with their followers, resigned their Committee memberships on November 17, 1917. The five were: Kamenev, Zinoviev, Rykov, V. P. Nogin, and V. P. Milyutin. Three of them also withdrew from the Council of People's Commissars; Milyutin gave up the Commissariat of Agriculture, Nogin resigned as Commissar of Trade and Industry, and Rykov, who ultimately succeeded Lenin as Chairman of the Council of People's Commissars, gave up the Internal Affairs Commissariat. The issue that precipitated the withdrawals was the question of whether or not Lenin's government should be broadened to include all other socialist parties. The impetus for this demand came from the Left Socialist Revolutionaries, who were fellow-travelers of the Bolsheviks, and from the Executive Committee of the All-Russian Union of Railroad Workers and Employees (VIKZHEL). Negotiations between the Bolshevik Central Committee and VIKZHEL began after November 9, when the latter body, a key organization because of its influence over railroad workers, adopted a resolution regarding the necessity of broadening the government. Lenin's Central Committee appointed Kamenev and Sokol'nikov to negotiate with VIKZHEL. During this period, Lenin did not have complete control over the railroad workers, and when it became impossible to take over VIKZHEL, the Bolsheviks established a new organization, VIKZHEDOR.*

---

* The importance of this move lay in the key role of rail transportation in Russia and in the fact that railroad workers had to be subordinated to the Party if it was to govern the country.

During the negotiations of November 12-13, the Mensheviks and Socialist Revolutionaries demanded that Lenin and Trotsky be excluded from the new government and that it be headed by a Socialist Revolutionary such as Victor Chernov or Nikolai Dmitrievich Avksentiev. The Bolshevik delegation neither accepted nor rejected this proposition, but its position was the subject of discussion at the November 14 meeting of the Central Committee. The Committee was divided. Lenin's majority, which included Sokol'nikov, demanded that negotiations be continued only on some other basis. The minority, which apparently had as little confidence in the Party as Kamenev and Zinoviev had in Lenin's leadership on the eve of the seizure of power, insisted upon the need to include other parties in the government. The Central Committee resolution of November 14 denounced the notion of "petty trading for the incorporation into the soviets of organizations of the nonsoviet type." It rejected the idea of any concessions to the "ultimatums and threats of the minority" and contended that the Central Committee had not excluded anyone from the short-lived Second Congress of Soviets but was ready to share power. Denying the assertion that the Bolshevik government was "against a coalition with the peasants," the resolution declared that its agrarian law had been copied from the Socialist Revolutionaries.[12]

The Left Socialist Revolutionaries in the Central Executive Committee of the Congress of Soviets responded to this resolution with a declaration warning that the country was being pushed toward further civil conflict. At this same session of the Central Executive Committee, Zinoviev declared that the Bolshevik faction had not discussed the Central Committee's resolution; he and Kamenev introduced a series of amendments designed to please VIKZHEL and the other parties. Since the Bolshevik faction had voted against the Central Committee's resolution concerning the composition of the government, Zinoviev and Kamenev obviously were violating Party discipline. On November 16, the majority in the Bolshevik Central Committee presented the dissenters with an ultimatum demanding that they submit to Party discipline.[13] The members of the minority responded with their declaration of November 17, in which they resigned from the Central Committee and advanced the slogan "Long live the government of Soviet parties!" This declaration—published in *Izvestia* on November 18 and signed by Kamenev, Rykov, Milyutin, Zinoviev, and Nogin—contained the following statement: "We withdraw from the Central Committee in the moment of victory, in the moment of the prevalence of our party. We withdraw because we cannot calmly look on as the policy of the leading group in the Central Committee leads to the loss by the workers' party of the fruits of this victory, to the destruction of the proletariat."[14]

These were brave words, but the men who appended their names to them were no match for Lenin in a contest of wills. A second ultimatum of the Central Committee—drafted on November 18 or 19 and addressed to Kamenev, Zinoviev, D. B. Ryazanov (Gol'dendakh), and Yu. Larin—demanded that they either promise in writing to submit to the decisions of the Central Committee or "remove themselves from all public Party activity and abandon all responsible posts in the labor movement henceforward until [the convocation of] a Party congress."[15] An announcement drafted by Lenin and addressed to the Party membership was published in *Pravda* on November 20. It asserted that the Second Congress of Soviets had given the Bolsheviks a majority and that only a Bolshevik government could be a truly Soviet government. According to Lenin, only "enemies of the people" would dispute this.[16] He branded the members of the Central Committee minority "deserters" and reminded the Party that two of them, Kamenev and Zinoviev, had been "deserters and strikebreakers" in opposing the Bolshevik uprising.[17] This accusation had the desired effect. Zinoviev published a declaration in the November 21 issue of *Pravda* in which he announced his return to the Central Committee and called upon all members to submit to Party discipline. The other dissidents soon returned to the fold. Nevertheless, the issue of broadening the government was only the first of a series of incidents in which Lenin's leadership and policies were challenged within the inner ruling circle of the Party.

The next issue to threaten Party unity was the question of whether or not to conclude a peace treaty with the Central Powers. Lenin had removed General Nikolai Nikolaevich

Dukhonin from the supreme command on November 22, 1917, when the latter expressed reluctance to obey a directive ordering him to start peace talks with the Germans but not to conclude an armistice.* The appointment of an ensign, Nikolai Vasil'evich Krylenko, to the supreme command served as a sign of Bolshevik egalitarianism. A truce, to be effective for a period of ten days, was signed as early as December 5. The resumption of peace talks at Brest-Litovsk on December 13 led to the signing, two days later, of an armistice which was to be effective until January 14, 1918. During the January negotiations, the Central Powers demanded that Russia cede Poland, Belorussia, Lithuania, and most of Latvia; that Russian armies be completely demobilized; and that Russia make payments for the maintenance of Russian prisoners of war in Germany. Lenin was prepared to accept the most severe conditions, since his principal purpose was to neutralize the German threat to the Soviet regime's very existence—a threat which would become quite real in the event of continued Russian prosecution of the war. In a series of twenty-one theses, prepared on January 20, 1918, Lenin made it clear that he advocated peace at any price, on the assumption that a revolution in Germany would not occur soon enough to be of help to his regime if it were to pursue a policy of revolutionary war.†

---

* General Dukhonin met his death at the hands of Bolshevik sailors on December 3, 1917.

† Lenin's position at this time contrasts with an earlier statement made in a letter written to the Central Committee on September 26-27, 1917, when he was also advocating a separate peace with the Central Powers: "Only our Party, having at last won a victory in an uprising, can save Petrograd [from falling to the Germans], for if our offer of peace is rejected, and we obtain not even a truce, then *we* shall become 'defensists,' then we shall place ourselves *at the head of the war parties*, we shall be the most *'warring'* party, and we shall carry on a war in a truly revolutionary manner. We shall take away from the capitalists all the bread and all the boots. We shall leave them crusts. We shall dress them in bast shoes. We shall send all the bread and all the footwear to the front. And we shall save Petrograd. The resources, both material and spiritual, of a truly revolutionary war are still immense in Russia; there are ninety-nine chances in a hundred that the Germans will at last grant us a truce. And to secure a truce at present means to conquer the *whole world*."—Lenin, *Sochineniya* (2d ed.), XXI, 197 f.

The opposition to Lenin's views found expression in resolutions adopted by the Moscow and Petrograd Party organizations. Trotsky, who had been negotiating with the Germans at Brest-Litovsk, advocated a policy of neither fighting nor negotiating a peace treaty on the assumption that the armies of the Central Powers would not resume their advance into Russia. A meeting of sixty-three leading Party workers, held in Petrograd on January 21, 1918, expressed support for a revolutionary war by an absolute majority of thirty-two votes; Lenin's theses obtained only fifteen votes, and Trotsky's "no peace—no war" policy won sixteen votes.[18] However, at a meeting of the Central Committee held on January 24, Trotsky's position was adopted by a vote of nine to seven. At this meeting, Lenin dismissed Trotsky's proposal as an "international political demonstration"—implying that it was quite worthless as a practicable policy. He put the matter quite frankly when he declared that "we are making a turn to the right, which leads through a very filthy cattle barn, but we must do this."[19] He predicted correctly that a new German advance would inevitably impose peace—and on much harsher terms. The issue was not resolved by the end of January when the Third All-Russian Congress of Soviets adjourned after adopting an ambiguous resolution empowering the government to sign a peace treaty and, at the same time, approving Trotsky's policy of procrastination.

The bankruptcy of this policy became evident when the Central Powers signed a peace treaty with the Ukrainian People's Republic (the Central Rada) on February 9, 1918. This treaty gave the anti-Bolshevik Ukrainian government diplomatic recognition by the Central Powers and presaged the entry of German troops into Ukraine. It meant that Bolshevik armed units then invading Ukrainian territory would clash with the troops of the Central Powers. On February 10, Trotsky, Yoffe, the historian Pokrovsky, and the other members of the Bolshevik delegation at Brest-Litovsk announced to the Central Powers that Russia regarded the state of war as having been terminated and was fully demobilizing its side of the military front. The Bolshevik delegation then walked out, and one week later, on February 18, the Germans resumed their eastward advance. The

Central Committee was ready to accept the January terms of
the Central Powers on February 18. German forces seized most
of Belorussia and moved into Estonia. On February 24, the
Germans took Pskov, and on the following day marched into
Tallinn. By March 2, Narva fell. Capitalizing upon the impotence of their adversary, the Germans now insisted on new
conditions, including Bolshevik evacuation of the Baltic territories and recognition of the anti-Communist Ukrainian and
Finnish governments. An appeal adopted by the Council of
People's Commissars on February 21 and published the following day under the slogan "The socialist fatherland is in danger"
went unheeded.

The issue of a peace treaty was the subject of discussion at
Central Committee meetings on February 23 and 24. Lenin
argued that there was no alternative but to accept the German
conditions, since Russia no longer had an army and refusal to
sign would mean destruction of the Soviet regime. At the February 23 meeting, Lenin's position in favor of an immediate peace
received seven votes; four members opposed it, and four others
abstained. Lenin's partial victory prompted four of the Oppositionists within the Central Committee to resign their Party
and governmental posts, while reserving for themselves complete
freedom to agitate both within and without the Party. The
Oppositionists were: Bukharin, G. I. Lomov, A. S. Bubnov, and
Moisei Solomonovich Uritsky. Trotsky, who had abstained from
voting, spoke of resigning from the Commissariat of Foreign
Affairs. Lenin treated the Oppositionists with unusual moderation. When Stalin asked whether resignation of position did not
also imply resignation from the Party, Lenin answered in the
negative. He also disagreed with Stalin when the latter stated:
"It is not necessary to sign [a treaty], but peace negotiations can
begin."[20] Lenin's success in persuading a plurality to go along
with his demand that they sign a peace treaty should be attributed not only to his moderation in dealing with the Oppositionists,
but also to his threat to resign from the Central Committee and
the government if the purely verbal policy of the "revolutionary
phrase" were not abandoned.

Lenin followed up his victory in the Central Committee with

a clear-cut victory in the Central Executive Committee (of Soviets), which—by a vote of 116 to 85, with 26 abstentions—decided at 4:30 A.M. on February 24 to accept the German conditions. A meeting of the Central Committee held on the same day determined the composition of the Soviet peace delegation, but the Left Communists were in no mood to abandon the fight against the peace treaty. The Moscow Province (*oblast'*) Bureau of the Party quickly adopted a resolution expressing lack of confidence in the Central Committee—to which Lenin responded with an article entitled "Strange and Monstrous." The Petrograd City and Province Party committees, also a center of the prowar faction of Left Communists, began to publish a factional daily newspaper on March 5 under the title *Kommunist*. The first issue included articles signed by Karl Radek, Nikolai Bukharin, and Mikhail Pokrovsky. Other prominent Leftists included Inessa Armand, Alexandra Kollontai, A. S. Bubnov, Stanislav Kosior, Valerian Kuibyshev, D. B. Ryazanov, N. Osinsky (Valerian Valerianovich Obolensky), T. V. Sapronov, Eugene Preobrazhensky, G. Myasnikov, Georgii Pyatakov, M. S. Uritsky, Emilian Yaroslavsky, and Ivan Ivanovich Skvortsov-Stepanov.

The bitterness and extent of the opposition to Lenin led to a full-dress debate at the Party's Seventh Congress. This was a small and hastily convened gathering which met between March 6 and 8, 1918, and had only forty-six voting delegates—although the Party at that time claimed a membership of at least 270,000. Lenin spoke in defense of the conclusion of the March 3 peace treaty with the Central Powers, while Bukharin presented a co-report on behalf of the opposition urging a revolutionary war as the only correct policy. The Oppositionists even published their theses against a peace treaty on March 8. Lenin minced no words in criticizing his opponents for their arrogance in asserting that Germany's "inability" to advance made a treaty unnecessary; he blamed them for the fact that Soviet Russia now had to accept harsher terms than the Germans had offered in January. Lenin did not minimize the onerous nature of the treaty, but likened it to the treaty signed by the Germans at Tilsit in 1807. At that time, Lenin argued, Napoleon imposed harsh terms upon the Germans and even compelled them to provide troops for his further conquests; yet, Tilsit was the prelude to the liberation of the Germans from Napoleon's yoke.

Lenin explained to the Congress his philosophy of peace, noting that "peace is the means of accumulating strength" and that "history tells us that peace is a breathing space [*peredyshka*] for war, [and that] war is a means of obtaining at least a slightly better or worse peace."[21] His principal argument was that "everything will come in its time" and that it was necessary now to trade space for time by physically retreating. Any attempt to continue the current war would mean succumbing to the "provocation of the Russian bourgeoisie," which desired prolongation of the conflict as a sure means of bringing about the overthrow of the Bolshevik· regime. When Bukharin likened the Party to the Ukrainian nationalist leader Simon Petliura* and charged that the Party's policy was leading to the betrayal of Ukraine (by recognizing its independence at Brest-Litovsk), Lenin declared that it was "not worth talking about such obvious nonsense."[22] Trotsky's accusation that the Party had betrayed Finland was denounced by Lenin as "puerile talk."[23] The accusation of "infantilism" and "puerility" (*rebyachestvo*) was to become fairly common with Lenin in denouncing those who disagreed with him. He was to employ it in the title of an article published in *Pravda* in May, 1918, and directed against Bukharin and the "Left Communists." In 1920, he underlined his monopoly on adulthood and maturity when he entitled his criticism of tactically inflexible European Communists *"Left-Wing" Communism: An Infantile Disorder.*

However, he did not restrict himself to name-calling in dealing with the Oppositionists. It was at this time that he introduced the technique of compromising his opposition by having some of their number elected to the Central Committee. Thus, the Seventh Congress elected to the Central Committee such Left Communists as Bukharin, who was a full member, and M. S. Uritsky and G. I. Lomov, who were candidate-members. In this

---

* As the leader of the anti-Communist Ukrainian forces, Petliura was accused by Communists of having "betrayed" Ukraine because he did not wish to have his people ruled by Russians.

way, the Oppositionists had some of the ground cut from under them and were compromised by Lenin, who placed them in the position (as Central Committee members) of having to bear responsibility for a peace policy which they had opposed.[24] The Seventh Congress adopted a resolution favoring peace on the conditions offered by the Central Powers by a vote of twenty-eight to nine, with one abstention. The Oppositionists countered by refusing to take their places in the Central Committee, although when the formal cessation of hostilities with Germany demonstrated the validity of Lenin's policy in favoring a peace treaty, the Oppositionist movement quickly lost its strength.

At the same time that the breach among the Bolsheviks was being healed, the "coalition" between the Bolsheviks and the Left Socialist Revolutionaries broke up over the issue of the peace treaty. The Left Socialist Revolutionaries had cast their lot with the Bolsheviks when they refused to walk out of the Second Congress of Soviets along with the other SR's and the Mensheviks. This Socialist Revolutionary splinter movement had partially emerged in mid-June, 1917, when it expressed opposition to the bourgeois nature of the Provisional Government and to its foreign policy. The leaders of the fellow-traveling group included Boris D. Kamkov (Katz), Mark Natanson, and Maria Spiridonova. (Spiridonova had achieved notoriety as early as January, 1906, when, at the age of twenty, she assassinated General Luzhenovsky, a district police commandant in the Tambov province who had been unusually cruel in punishing rebellious peasants.) Spiridonova was not among the three Left Socialist Revolutionaries who accepted portfolios in the Bolshevik-controlled government on December 23, 1917. The three non-Bolshevik commissars were: Isaak Zakharovich Steinberg[25] (or Isaac Nachman), an attorney who held the justice portfolio; Prosh P. Proshyan, an Armenian who had served a six-year sentence at forced labor and was now Commissar of Posts and Telegraphs; and A. L. Kolegaev, Commissar of Agriculture, who was to break with the Left SR's in November, 1918, and become a Bolshevik.

The withdrawal of the Left Socialist Revolutionaries from Lenin's government was brought about not by the dissolution of the Constituent Assembly on January 18, 1918, but by the decision to sign a peace treaty with the Central Powers. Indeed, the Left Socialist Revolutionaries shared responsibility with the Bolsheviks for the dissolution of the Constituent Assembly following its single session on January 18. This was true not only because they continued to participate in the Bolshevik government after the dissolution, but also because their secession from the main body of Socialist Revolutionaries provided Lenin with a very convenient rationalization: while admitting that the Socialist Revolutionaries had the "largest following among the people and particularly among the peasantry," he could qualify his statement by saying that this was the case only from May to October, 1917. The unfortunate split in the ranks of the Socialist Revolutionaries, which assumed a permanent character *after* the elections to the Constituent Assembly, made it possible for Lenin to declare that the composition of the Assembly did not correspond to the "will of the electors in their mass."[26]

The Bolshevik logic regarding the Constituent Assembly's dissolution was based on Lenin's assertion that "the Soviets are above all Parliaments, above all Constituent Assemblies."[27] Dismissing the "formal juridical" point of view, Lenin resorted to the Scriptural injunction (Mark, 2:27) that "the sabbath was made for man, and not man for the sabbath."[28] The Left Socialist Revolutionaries had gone along with the Bolsheviks in spite of the fact that the latter had stolen their agrarian program. They desired a coalition of all Socialist parties, but entered the Bolshevik government knowing of Lenin's animosity toward the Socialist Revolutionaries and the Mensheviks. The Left Socialist Revolutionaries naïvely believed that the Bolsheviks would discredit themselves and that the Socialist Revolutionaries, with the words "love, brotherhood, trust" inscribed on their banner, would emerge triumphant. Possessed with a self-endowed moral superiority, the Left Socialist Revolutionaries had neither political acumen nor a systematic program nor a theory of political action.

The climax of the short-lived honeymoon between the Left Socialist Revolutionaries and the Bolsheviks came with the convocation of the Third Congress of Soviets during the latter part of January, 1918. However, the misalliance was terminated when the Left Socialist Revolutionaries withdrew from the government on March 15, 1918, after the ratification of the Brest-Litovsk Treaty by the Fourth Congress of Soviets (which also approved the transfer of the capital from Petrograd to Moscow).

By June 24, the Left Socialist Revolutionary Central Committee decided to put an end to Lenin's "breathing space" (the peace treaty) by employing terrorism. Reverting to the tactics of their predecessors, the People's Will movement of the 1880's, two Left Socialist Revolutionaries assassinated the German Ambassador, Count Wilhelm von Mirbach, on July 6, 1918.* This was followed, on July 30, by the assassination of Field Marshal Hermann von Eichhorn, commander of German occupation forces in Ukraine. The murder of Mirbach so upset the Bolsheviks that Lenin, Trotsky, and Commissar of Foreign Affairs Georgii Vasil'evich Chicherin went in person to the German Embassy to offer condolences.

In the Fifth Congress of Soviets, which was meeting at the time, the Left Socialist Revolutionaries were in a minority of less than 40 per cent. This fact, together with the assassination of Mirbach, gave Lenin an opportunity to suppress that strange band of fellow travelers which had left his "coalition" and was now openly rebelling against Bolshevik rule. Ironically, the Left Socialist Revolutionaries had turned against them the very police organ, the Vecheka or All-Russian Extraordinary Commission (also known as the Cheka), in which they had participated during the preceding winter.† This body had been established on December 20, 1917, and on February 22, 1918, it empowered local soviets to "arrest and shoot immediately" all members of "counterrevolutionary organizations"—a fact which makes it

---

* The documents of the German Foreign Ministry reveal that in the spring of 1918 the German Ambassador in Moscow, Count Mirbach, was spending money to keep the Bolsheviks in power, since it was not in Berlin's interest to have a prowar regime governing Russia. *See* Zeman, *op. cit.,* pp. 124–125, 128, 130, and 133.

† Regarding the participation of the Left Socialist Revolutionaries in Cheka activities, *see* I. N. Steinberg, *In the Workshop of the Revolution* (New York: Rinehart & Company, 1953), pp. 68 ff. *See also* Simon Wolin and Robert M. Slusser (eds.), *The Soviet Secret Police* (New York: Frederick A. Praeger, 1957), p. 33, n. 8.

clear that Lenin was prepared to use terror long before the Socialist Revolutionaries decided to employ it in an effort to disrupt the peace treaty with the Central Powers. The Cheka cracked down on the Left Socialist Revolutionaries, arresting all their delegates to the Fifth Congress of Soviets, as well as their Central Committee.

The head of the Cheka was then Dzierzynski. This secular ascetic, the son of a small Polish landowner, had joined the Social Democratic movement in Poland and Lithuania in 1893 and had become a member of the Russian Central Committee at the Stockholm Congress in 1906. It was not by coincidence that Lenin selected Dzierzynski as head of the Cheka; this Bolshevik grand inquisitor was given the post not only because of his ruthlessness, but also because he had been in jail or sentenced to hard labor during most of the period between 1905 and 1917 and was thus removed from the conflict which characterized Party life at that time. He and Lenin got along well because they had had little opportunity to clash. The Left Socialist Revolutionary and Commissar of Justice in Lenin's first government, I. Z. Steinberg, later reported that Dzierzynski had declared: "We don't want justice, we want to settle accounts."[29] In an interview during the summer of 1918, Dzierzynski asserted that the Cheka was not a court; he likened it to the Red Army in the civil war, since it "cannot reckon with whether or not it will inflict injury upon private individuals, but must concern itself with only one thing—the victory of the Revolution over the bourgeoisie . . . even if in so doing its sword accidentally falls on the heads of the innocent."[30]

The determination with which Dzierzynski suppressed the Left Socialist Revolutionaries brought attempts at revenge—the most notable of which was an attempt on Lenin's life on August 30, 1918. His would-be assassin, the Left Socialist Revolutionary Fanny (Dora) Kaplan, wounded him in the throat and lung as he was leaving the former Mikhelson factory in Moscow after having delivered a speech there. This was not the first attempt on Lenin's life; an earlier effort to assassinate him in February as he was riding in an automobile in Petrograd only wounded the Swiss socialist Fritz Platten. On June 20, the

Petrograd Commissar for Press, Propaganda, and Agitation, V. Volodarsky, was assassinated by a Socialist Revolutionary.* On the same day that Lenin was wounded, a student's bullet killed M. S. Uritsky, Chairman of the Petrograd Cheka and a former Menshevik and Trotskyite who had opposed the Brest-Litovsk Peace Treaty.

Ironically, only minutes before being wounded by Fanny Kaplan, Lenin had closed his speech with these words: "With us, there is only one way: victory or death!"[31] The assassination attempt of August 30 stiffened Lenin's determination to deal ruthlessly with those who stood in his way. He declared to Gorky: "Who is not with us is against us."[32] When Gorky spoke of the "cruelty of the revolutionary tactic and way of life," Lenin turned on him and declared: "But excuse me, we are not fools. We know: that which we want can be accomplished by no one but us. Could you possibly assume that if I were convinced of the opposite, I would be sitting here?"[33]

The hardening of Lenin's attitude was reflected in his diatribe entitled *The Proletarian Revolution and the Renegade Kautsky*. This work, written during October and November of 1918, was a rejoinder to Kautsky's *The Dictatorship of the Proletariat*, which was published in Vienna. Appalled by Bolshevik methods, Kautsky accused Lenin of violating democracy—a term which, as defined by Kautsky, meant that *all* citizens should be equal. Lenin countered by declaring that "exploited" and "exploiter"

---

* Volodarsky (born Moisei Markovich Goldstein in 1891) joined the ranks of the Bolsheviks after a brief membership in the Jewish Bund and in the Ukrainian Social Democratic *Spilka*. He had migrated to the United States in 1913 and, after working as a cutter in a Philadelphia clothing factory, participated in the publication of the radical Russian-language newspaper *Novyi mir* in New York City along with Bukharin, Trotsky, and Grigorii Isaakovich Chudnovsky. Volodarsky's brief but colorful revolutionary career reached its climax following his return to Russia in May, 1917. His colleague Chudnovsky met death at the hands of an army unit of the anti-Communist Ukrainian People's Republic in March, 1918, as he led a Bolshevik armed band bent upon imposing its rule over the Ukrainian peasantry. Ironically, all four publishers of *Novyi mir* were to meet violent deaths, although Bukharin and Trotsky were to wait more than two decades for their reward.

could not be equal on the grounds that the proletariat, as the majority, need not respect minority rights. Kautsky was particularly disturbed by Lenin's dispersal of the Constituent Assembly; Lenin, for his part, accused Kautsky of betraying Marxism and of being guided by the principle "Let justice be done, though the world perish" (*Fiat justitia, pereat mundus*). Against the popularly elected Constituent Assembly, Lenin counterposed the indirectly elected All-Russian Congress of Soviets—as though the latter could be more democratic.

With the usual Leninist venom, Kautsky was branded a "lackey of the bourgeoisie" and was accused of "swindling" and of "resinging Menshevik melodies." Lenin charged Kautsky with having forgotten that "*every* state is a machine for the suppression of one class by another." He was particularly annoyed by Kautsky's refusal to accept the Bolshevik definition of the dictatorship of the proletariat as a state form for the suppression of the bourgeoisie. According to Lenin, suppression was necessary because the bourgeoisie would offer "furious resistance." It is significant that Lenin rejected Kautsky's argument that Marx, in 1872, had admitted the possibility of a peaceful transition to socialism in England and America. This, said Lenin, was the "argument of a sophist—that is, to put it more simply, [the argument] of a swindler who cheats with the aid of quotations and references."[34]

Lenin's hatred of European socialists like Kautsky and his desire to spread Communism to Central Europe and beyond were factors which led to the founding of the Third International at its First Congress held in Moscow in March, 1919. It was quickly followed by the Eighth Congress of the All-Russian Communist Party (of Bolsheviks). (The Social Democratic label had been abandoned a year earlier.) Lenin opened the Eighth Party Congress on March 18 with his report of the Central Committee; already, at this Congress, there was "tumultuous, prolonged applause" and shouts of "Long live Comrade Lenin!" The establishment of the Comintern set the theme for the Congress and prompted Lenin to refer to the Russian Revolution as "the dress rehearsal or one of the rehearsals for the world proletarian revolution."[35] One of the principal achievements of the Eighth

Congress was the adoption of a new Party program which began
with extensive quotations concerning capitalism taken from the
1903 program. To these statements was added a résumé of
Lenin's doctrine of imperialism as an explanation of the phenomenon of war. Great hopes were held out in this program,
which remained on the Party's books long after Stalin's death.
It promised to liberate women "from the material burdens of
obsolete domestic housekeeping by replacing it with communal
houses, common dining rooms, central laundries, nurseries, and
the like."[36] The enthusiasm carried over into education, which
was to be free and compulsory for both sexes up to the age of
seventeen; the Party program promised to "supply all students
with food, clothing, footwear, and educational equipment at
state expense."[37]

In the economic sphere, the trade unions were promised that
"in their hands [would be] concentrated, in fact, the entire
administration of the whole national economy . . ." In agriculture, the 1919 Party program recognized that the "small peasant
holding will continue to exist for a long time" and recommended
various measures designed to increase productivity. At the same
time, it called for a decisive struggle against the kulaks (wealthy
peasants), as well as for an effort to entice the middle peasant
into "the work of socialist construction." In the field of finance,
the program recognized that "the destruction of money is impossible so long as Communist production and distribution of
goods is not fully organized." By equating money with the bourgeoisie and exaggerating the importance of nationalization of
the banks, the program promised "institution of a series of
measures broadening the area of money-less accounting and preparing for the abolition of money: compulsory depositing of
money in the public bank, the introduction of budget books,
the replacement of money by checks, short-term tickets granting
the right to obtain products, and the like."[38]

The 1919 program also promised much for living conditions
—such as, to "strive for the improvement of the housing conditions of the toiling masses," to liquidate congestion and unsanitary
conditions, to destroy worthless living quarters, to remodel old
dwellings, and to construct new ones. A maximum six-hour day
with no decrease in wages was promised in 1919 on the condition

of a general rise in labor productivity; workers would also be obligated to devote two additional hours, without compensation, to vocational and technical training and to the military art.

However, military affairs were not to be left to amateurs, and the Party program made it clear that the Red Army would avail itself of the services of the officer corps of the Czarist army. It was at the Party's Eighth Congress that the Military Opposition manifested itself. This rather sizable group had its beginnings in the Left Communism of the spring of 1918. Its members were disturbed by the abandonment of the voluntary principle and by the introduction of compulsory military service following the Seventh Party Congress. The appointment of Ioakim Ioakimovich Vatsetis, a former colonel in the Czarist army, as commander-in-chief on July 8, 1918, displeased these Bolsheviks —despite the fact that Vatsetis had played an important role in suppressing the Left Socialist Revolutionaries.

Many members of the Military Opposition were opposed to the establishment of a standing army and favored, instead, the organization of a people's militia. Lenin, Trotsky, and Stalin were in agreement on the need for a regular army if the civil war was to be won. Lenin warned that "the ruling class will never surrender its power to the oppressed class." In a frank statement of the Bolshevik position, he told the Eighth Congress:

> We have always said: "there are wars and wars." We condemned the imperialist war, but we did not reject *war in general* . . . We live not only in a state but in a *system of states,* and the existence of the Soviet Republic side by side with imperialist states for a protracted period of time is unthinkable. In the end, one or the other will be victorious. Until that end is at hand, a series of most frightful clashes between the Soviet Republic and the bourgeois states is inevitable.[39]

In this situation, Lenin argued, it was necessary to utilize every bit of military knowledge and experience bequeathed to the Soviet regime by the bourgeoisie. He accused the members of the Military Opposition of "pouring water on the mill of the Socialist Revolutionaries and Mensheviks" and appealed for "iron discipline" and respect for military leaders.

Ironically, the Military Opposition based its views on earlier statements made by Lenin regarding the need to replace the standing army with a people's militia. In an article published in the St. Petersburg Bolshevik newspaper, *Novaya zhizn'*, on November 16 (29), 1905, Lenin had declared:

> The experience of Western Europe has demonstrated the completely reactionary nature of the standing army. Military science has proved the complete feasibility of a people's militia which can rise to the military tasks of defensive as well as offensive warfare. Let the hypocritical or sentimental bourgeoisie dream of disarmament. So long as there are the oppressed and the exploiters in the world, we must strive not for disarmament but for universal popular armament.[40]

In the third of his five *Letters from Afar,* written on March 11 (24), 1917, Lenin described the people's militia as being composed of "all adult citizens of *both* sexes . . . [and] uniting in itself the functions of a popular army with the functions of the police with the functions of the principal and fundamental organ of state order and public administration."[41]

The members of the Military Opposition thus made the mistake of taking Lenin literally. This group—which included Yaroslavsky, G. Safarov, V. Smirnov, and Filipp Isaevich Goloshchekin—was defeated at the Eighth Congress, although it mustered support among many of the rank-and-file delegates. The Congress rejected the idea of an army based exclusively on partisan detachments on the grounds that this would be analogous to an attempt to return from large-scale industry to handicraft production. The abandonment of the practice of electing army officers was justified on the grounds that it was not needed in a "workers' and peasants' Red Army." The Eighth Congress, in addition to recognizing the need to employ former Czarist army officers who were willing to go along with the Soviet regime, decided that "kulak and parasitic elements" should be placed in special labor battalions.* Communists were to be systematically distributed throughout all military units and were to support the work of the political commissars who were defined

---

* Thus, the practice of employing forced labor, one of the principal characteristics of Stalinism, had its origin in Leninism.

as "the bearers of the spirit of our Party, its discipline, its firmness and courage in the struggle for the realization of the stated goal."[42]

The Eighth Congress made a fundamental decision in approving the formal establishment of a Politburo to be composed of five of the nineteen members of the Central Committee. The new Politburo consisted of Lenin, Stalin, Trotsky, Kamenev, and Bukharin. An Organizational Bureau (Orgburo), also composed of five members, was established; each of its members—Krestinsky, Stalin, Serebryakov, Alexander G. Beloborodov, and Stasova —was to be responsible for one aspect of the Central Committee's organizational work. The Orgburo was to make decisions regarding all organizational matters, and these were to be carried out by the Secretariat. Provision was also made for a responsible secretary, who was to be assisted by five technical secretaries. The first incumbent as responsible secretary was Nikolai Nikolaevich Krestinsky, an attorney who had been elected to the Central Committee *in absentia* at the Sixth Congress. The Eighth Congress resolution explicitly stated that the Politburo, the Orgburo, and the Secretariat were directly responsible to the Central Committee and were to report to it every two weeks at its regular plenary sessions. The Politburo was to make policy decisions in "urgent" matters, and the other fourteen members of the Central Committee were to have the right to participate in any Politburo meeting with a "consultative vote"—that is, with the right to speak but not to vote.

It is significant that the Party Statutes adopted at the Eighth Party Conference—which met early in December, 1919—did not contain the detailed provisions of the Eighth Congress' resolution concerning the responsibility of the Politburo, Orgburo, and Secretariat to make biweekly reports to the Central Committee. Nor did the Statutes contain the provision granting Central Committee members the right to attend Politburo meetings. Thus, the observation made at the Eighth Congress by Osinsky—who was later to play a prominent role in the Democratic Centralist Opposition—proved to be true almost as soon as it was spoken. Osinsky expressed the view that the fourteen Central Committee members who were not in the Politburo would be relegated to the status of secondary members. In this way, Lenin had laid the foundation for Stalin's subsequent circumvention of the Central Committee by means of the Politburo.

To Leninism must also be attributed the centralism which made Stalinism possible. The civil war served to justify the imposition of the "strictest centralism and the most severe discipline" upon the Party; the Central Committee was given complete control over the appointment of Party workers to specific assignments and was empowered to transfer them from one field of activity to another. The Eighth Congress recognized that Ukraine, Latvia, Lithuania, and Belorussia were separate Soviet republics. However, the resolution on the organizational question declared that this separate status was confined to the question of the form of state and had no bearing whatsoever upon Party organization, since there could be no thought of a federation of separate Communist Parties. Instead, the Eighth Congress called for a "single centralized Communist Party with a single Central Committee" and announced that "all decisions of the All-Russian Communist Party and its leading bodies are unconditionally compulsory for all parts of the Party, irrespective of their national composition." In order to remove any possible doubt, the resolution declared that the "Central Committees of the Ukrainian, Latvian, [and] Lithuanian Communists enjoy the rights of province [*oblast'*] committees of the Party and are completely subordinate to the Central Committee of the All-Russian Communist Party."[43]

This resolution of the Eighth Congress revealed the hollowness of Lenin's claim that Russian Communism recognized the "complete equality of nations" as provided for in the 1919 Party program. Yet this cruel hoax had to be perpetuated if Russian Communism was to extend its victories. It is for this reason that Lenin opposed Bukharin's proposal that the Party program contain a provision advocating the "self-determination of the toiling classes of all nationalities." Bukharin advocated this formulation in place of the slogan of national self-determination, which implied equality of treatment for all members of a nation irrespective of their social class. Instead, Lenin insisted that the Party pay lip service to national self-determination since it would facilitate the "self-determination of toilers." Lenin argued that this was the only way, since individual nations were at different stages of historical development and failure to recognize this would simply antagonize many non-Russians—especially the Finns.[44]

This kind of tactical distinction employed by Lenin in dealing with the nationality problem had a counterpart in the resolution concerning relations between the Party and the soviets (or organs of government). It was declared to be incorrect to "confuse the functions of the Party collectives with the functions of the state organs." The Party was to guide the activities of the soviets, but was not to replace them. At the same time, the Eighth Congress declared that "all Party members, irrespective of the important government posts which they may hold, are unconditionally under the control of the Party."[45] Ever fearful that the Party membership might become corrupted and be penetrated by the enemy, the Eighth Congress authorized the first large-scale purge. This involved reregistration of the entire membership—a task which was not completed until the end of September, 1919. During this period, the admission of new members was temporarily suspended, and Communists who wished to retain their membership had to surrender their Party cards and submit recommendations from two members of at least six months' standing who were known to the local Party committee as dependable persons.

The purge of 1919 resulted in the expulsion of approximately half the Party membership, which numbered more than 250,000 at the time of the Eighth Congress. However, this tremendous decline in membership was offset by a series of intensified recruitment drives conducted in various regions and known as the "Party week." As a result, more than 200,000 members were admitted. It is particularly significant that this occurred at a time when the Soviet regime was under heavy attack; General Anton Ivanovich Denikin's forces had advanced to Orel on the road to Moscow, and General Nikolai Nikolaevich Yudenich was menacing Petrograd. While fighting for its life in 1919, the Party permitted its ranks to swell—as it was to do a little more than two decades later when faced with the Nazi onslaught. The influx of 200,000 new members brought the total membership of the Party to the record figure of 350,000 at the end of 1919.

A membership rise of such proportions necessitated a tightening of the Party organization. It was with this purpose that the Eighth Party Conference, meeting in Moscow on December 2-4, 1919, with forty-five voting delegates, adopted new Party Statutes. The highly detailed 1919 Statutes, containing sixty-six paragraphs, replaced the very brief Statutes of fourteen paragraphs adopted by the Sixth Congress in August, 1917. A probationary period of candidacy was introduced for the purpose of verifying the personal qualities of the candidate and enabling him to become acquainted with the Party's program and tactics; workers and peasants were given a candidacy of two months, while all others had to wait six months. Recommendations by two members of at least six months' standing were also required. A graduated and progressive scale of dues was provided for in place of the 1917 requirement of at least 1 per cent of the member's income in addition to a 50-kopeck initiation fee. The 1919 Statutes raised the initiation fee to 5 rubles and created four categories of dues, ranging from 0.5 per cent to 3 per cent of the member's monthly income.

In spelling out the "democratic centralism" principle in greater detail, the 1919 Statutes provided for a reduction in the autonomy of local Party organizations. While the 1917 Statutes had provided for the unconditional right of every Party organization to publish political literature in its own name, the 1919 Statutes granted each the right to establish its own press, but only with the approval of the corresponding higher Party body. For the first time, the size of the Central Committee was fixed at nineteen members and twelve candidates. The tightening grip of the Central Committee on the lower Party committees was reflected in the provisions for at least two plenary sessions each month and for the establishment of the Politburo, Orgburo, and Secretariat. A new provision declared that the "Central Committee directs the work of the central Soviet [governmental] and social organizations through the Party factions" present within them.[46] Special sections within the Central Committee apparatus were provided for nationality affairs, for work among women and the youth, and for other kinds of activities.

The first mention was made in the Statutes of the Party "cell"—the primary grouping, which was to be composed of at least three Party members and was given the task of conveying Party "slogans and decisions" to the masses, recruiting new members, and supporting the local Party committee in its organizational and agitational work. Provision was also made for Party factions within "all non-Party congresses, conferences, institutions, and organizations" having at least three Party members; factions were given the task of enhancing the Party's influence in every sense and bringing all such bodies under Party control. The disciplinary requirements for membership were also tightened: "The strictest Party discipline is the first obligation of every member of the Party and of all Party organizations. Decisions of the Party centers must be fulfilled speedily and accurately."[47] Specific penalties were set forth for violations of decisions of higher Party organizations "and other offenses recognized as criminal by public opinion in the Party."[48] In the case of deviant lower Party organizations, the penalties ranged from censure to dissolution and "reregistration" (purging) of the membership; in the case of errant individual members, the penalties included censure within the Party or in public, suspension from Party and government posts, and expulsion from the Party with or without notification of the judicial authorities.

The existence of such disciplinary provisions in the Statutes did not prevent a controversy from manifesting itself at the Ninth Party Congress, which met from March 29 to April 5, 1920, and had 554 voting delegates representing almost 612,000 members. The source of the controversy and of the anti-Leninist opposition was the question of what role the trade unions were to play in the organization of the economy. The policies of "War Communism"—which involved conscription of manpower, total nationalization of industry and trade, rationing, and the requisitioning of agricultural products—had brought the economy to a standstill. The Communists in the Russian trade unions were disturbed by the willingness of the Congress to abandon the principle of collegiality in favor of a single responsible official (*yedinolichie*) in industrial management. The crux of the issue was whether or not the trade unions were to be independent of the Party's Central Committee. Krestinsky, the Central Committee secretary, put the matter bluntly when he declared that it was a question of whether the Central Committee apparatus or the Communist faction in the All-Russian Central Council of Trade Unions would control the disposition of personnel in the trade-union movement.

The Ninth Congress also approved the mobilization of civilian labor, which Trotsky advocated in accordance with his use of "labor armies"—instituted with his diversion of troops to the performance of economically useful labor when they were not needed on the civil-war fronts. One of the most outspoken advocates of discipline, Trotsky argued that the state had a right to conscript all labor, since its supposed aim—production for society—was pure. In addition to expressing the Bolshevik belief that the end justifies the means, Trotsky believed that compulsion was necessary: "As a general rule, man endeavors to avoid labor. It can be said that man is a rather lazy animal."[49] He contended that central economic planning could not tolerate the old "vagabond Russia" (*brodyachaya Rus'*), since the "laboring mass" would have to be "swiftly transferred, assigned, and dispatched in exactly the same way as soldiers."[50]

When Osinsky, of the Democratic Centralist Opposition, protested that he did not want workers in Russia to be attached to factories as they were in imperialist England during World War I, it was Bukharin who came to Trotsky's defense by glibly declaring that "militarization [of labor] is nothing more than the self-organization of the working class . . ."[51] Bukharin accused the trade-union group of wanting to replace the Council of People's Commissars with the trade unions. When A. G. Shlyapnikov, who was to become the leader of the Workers' Opposition, advanced the proposition that political authority belonged to the soviets and economic authority to the trade unions, while the Party was to exercise general leadership, Bukharin took issue on the grounds that "it is impossible to set off politics against economics." Bukharin employed the analogy of a machine in which the Party, although numerically the smallest element but still the vanguard, would represent the principal wheel: "If the cogs are properly set between the Party and the Soviet regime, between the Soviet regime and the trade unions, between the trade unions and the broad non-Party mass, the wheel of this machine—our Party—puts into movement the enormous machine, the broad group of the working class, and extends its influence to the broad strata of the peasantry."[52]

The ultimate consequence of the primacy of the Party found expression at the Ninth Congress in some of the charges voiced by the members of the Democratic Centralist Opposition. The Oppositionists were particularly concerned with rather arbitrary transfers of some of their number and charged that an exile system had been established for dealing with all who disagreed with Lenin. Lazar M. Kaganovich—soon to be placed in charge of the Bolshevik invasion of Turkestan—defended all transfers of personnel on the grounds that comrades remained too long in one spot and established a "pleasant company" (a clique based on the Soviet sin of "familyness" and mutual accommodation and protection), the existence of which was usually a certainty if things were too quiet. Lutovinov noted that the "Central Committee and the Orgburo in particular have been transformed from the highest leading organ into an executive organ for the most trifling and insignificant affairs—as, for example, the appointment of a superintendent for some institution, of the chief of a supply section, and the like—and on these has been spent nine-tenths of the time."[53]

V. N. Maximovsky, of the Democratic Centralist Opposition, declared: "It is said that the head of the fish begins to smell first. The Party from the top is beginning to yield to the influence of this bureaucratic centralism."[54] Timothy V. Sapronov made a similar charge regarding the growth of bureaucracy in the government as well as in the Party and referred caustically to the "dictatorship of Party officialdom."[55] Sapronov, who was later a member of the Soviet delegation to the Genoa Conference, went so far as to accuse Lenin of being an "ignoramus" (*nevezhda*) because he had allegedly supported the principles of collegiality and democratic centralism at the Eighth Congress, only to accuse their advocates at the Ninth Congress of being "ignoramuses." After charging Lenin with having introduced "vertical centralism," Sapronov asked him: "Do you think that the whole salvation of the Revolution lies in mechanical obedience?"[56]

Lenin answered Sapronov and the other Oppositionists with the assertion that the time for theorizing had passed and that it was now necessary to "manifest business ability and practicality." Democratic centralism was defined by Lenin in the following terms: "Representatives from localities gather and elect a responsible organ which must then govern."[57] In discussing the actual operation of the recently created Politburo and Orgburo, Lenin explained that they functioned without difficulty, since the secretary was a member of both bodies. More meaningful was his explanation that the function of the Orgburo was "the allocation of Party forces," while the Politburo was to concern itself with political questions. However, he added that "this division is to a certain extent artificial, [and] . . . it is impossible to carry out any policy without its being expressed in appointments and transfers [of personnel]."[58] Thus, every organizational question had political significance, and Lenin stated that any member of the Central Committee could insist that an organizational question be treated as a political question. In this way, the primacy of the Politburo was recognized, but the Ninth Congress debate over personnel transfers left no doubt as to the importance of the Party Secretariat.

The rigidity of the emerging central Party organization contrasted somewhat with the tactical flexibility which Lenin urged upon the Communists of Western Europe in his pamphlet *"Left-Wing" Communism: An Infantile Disorder*, written in April, 1920. The work carried an ironic dedication to David Lloyd-George for an address he had delivered to the Liberal MP's on March 18, 1920, on the need to unite with the Conservatives in order to prevent a Labour Party victory; Lenin referred to the speech as "almost Marxist and, in any case, extraordinarily useful for the Communists and Bolsheviks of the entire world." One purpose of the pamphlet was to persuade West European

Communists of the need to participate in "bourgeois parliaments" and to utilize even the most "reactionary" of trade unions for the purpose of furthering the victory of Communism. After emphasizing the "long, stubborn, desperate war . . . to the death" against the bourgeoisie and the need for "unconditional centralization and the most severe discipline," Lenin recounted the history of Bolshevism and its "fight against opportunism." He recalled the exclusion of the Left Bolsheviks from the Party for their refusal to participate in the Duma, as well as the "leftism" of Bukharin and Radek when they opposed the compromise Brest-Litovsk Treaty with the Central Powers. For Lenin, compromises were dictated by the circumstances—as when he referred to Brest-Litovsk as "our compromise with the bandits of German imperialism"—and were to be of a temporary nature.[59]

However, every compromise was not in itself desirable, and Lenin warned of the need to distinguish between the kinds of compromises which are permissible and those which are not. What Lenin was objecting to was the view of the "Left Communists" that all compromises should be rejected in principle; it was this blanket rejection of temporary compromises and the insistence upon tactical inflexibility that Lenin branded as "infantilism." He regarded the doctrinairism of the left as being younger and "a thousand times less dangerous and less significant than the error of right doctrinairism (that is, social chauvinism and Kautskyism)."[60] Yet, this did not mean that the "disease of Left Communism" need not be healed "with maximum energy," for its potential danger was great indeed. The principal significance of *"Left-Wing"* Communism lay in Lenin's insistence upon the doctrine of the multiplicity of means as being essential to the seizure of power:

> Everyone will agree that an army which does not train itself to wield all arms—all the means and methods of warfare that the enemy possesses or may possess—behaves in an unwise or even a criminal manner. But this applies to politics even more than it does to war. In politics, it is even less possible to foresee which methods of warfare will be

applicable and useful under certain future conditions. Unless
we master all means of warfare, we may suffer grave and
even decisive defeat . . .[61]

It is no coincidence that Lenin's advice to West European Communists on the need to participate in parliamentary elections
was published in the same year that the Soviet rulers invaded
Poland and also convoked the Second Congress of the Communist International.

As was to be expected, Lenin spoke to the Comintern Congress on parliamentarism, and the gathering condemned left
doctrinairism. Lenin also quoted John Maynard Keynes's *Economic Consequences of the Peace* with great relish and announced
that Soviet Russia had emerged the victor because there was
not a "shadow of unity" among her capitalist antagonists. The
lesson was not lost on Lenin, and he insisted that individual
Communist parties holding membership in the Comintern be
denied the right to decide questions of significance independent
of the Comintern; this, Lenin argued, had been the great weakness of the Second International, and he did not wish to repeat
it. At the very time that the Second Comintern Congress was
meeting between July 19 and August 6, 1920, Lenin was preparing for the invasion of Poland while advising Communists
to participate in bourgeois parliamentary elections. The Poles
had entered into an alliance with the anti-Communist government of the Ukrainian People's Republic, headed by Simon
Petliura, and had driven the Bolshevik forces out of Kiev on
May 6. However, by June 11, Lenin's forces had recaptured
the Ukrainian capital, and the end of July saw the establishment
of a Temporary Revolutionary Committee for Poland in the
Soviet camp—an abortive provisional government consisting of
Dzierzynski, Julian Marchlewski, and Felix Kon. On August 2,
a separate Galician Revolutionary Committee was established
under the direction of the Ukrainian Communist Volodymyr
Zatons'ky. However, the "miracle of the Vistula" in mid-August
of 1920 turned back the Bolshevik tide and saved Warsaw. The
Poles resumed the offensive and obtained very favorable terms
from Lenin, with the frontier delineated in the Treaty of Riga.

The Soviet defeat in Poland, bitter as it was, came at a time when the Workers' Opposition was gathering new strength for an all-out struggle with Lenin at the Tenth Party Congress. The Oppositionists demonstrated great enthusiasm and good organization at the Moscow Province Party Conference which met during the fourth week of November, 1920. On that occasion, Lenin rebuked the Oppositionists, gently confining himself to a warning concerning the danger of "opposition for the sake of opposition." Instead, he placed great emphasis on economic development and advanced his glib formula: "Communism is Soviet rule plus electrification of the entire country, because without electrification it is impossible to develop industry."[62] He predicted that electrification would require ten years at the very least, but the growth of the Opposition presented him with a more immediate task. The Moscow Province Conference ended in a serious split which could be resolved only at the approaching Tenth Party Congress.

The period immediately preceding the Tenth Congress had witnessed the appearance of numerous theses on the role of the trade unions. Lenin admitted at the Congress that he had not been able to read all the numerous platforms. When the Congress convened, three principal platforms emerged: that of Trotsky and Bukharin, which viewed the unions as state organs interested primarily in raising labor productivity; that of the Workers' Opposition, which took literally the provision in Point Five of the economic phase of the 1919 Party Program promising the trade unions control over the entire national economy; and that of Lenin and nine other members of the Central Committee. Although Trotsky and Lenin were in agreement on the need to combat the Workers' Opposition, Lenin's resolution paid lip service to the important role of the trade unions, but limited their function to the study of more efficient methods of production and the maintenance of labor discipline.

The Tenth Congress, which met between March 8 and 16, 1921, marked a new high for the Party, with 990 delegates representing 732,521 members. It also reflected the profound schism which had been developing in the Party since the Eighth Congress. In the report of the Central Committee, Lenin expressed pleasure over the fact that foreign troops had been expelled from the territory of the Russian Soviet Republic. He also indicated pride in the activities of the Comintern and in the attention which the twenty-one conditions for admission to it were receiving in Western Europe.* However, the principal burden of Lenin's report was that the Party had permitted itself the "luxury of discussions and controversies" and that this had worked great harm, since the Party's enemies had interpreted such discussion as a controversy, equating controversy with dissension and dissension with weakness. Lenin branded the Workers' Opposition as a "petty-bourgeois anarchist element" and warned of "what it means to weaken the Soviet apparatus when there are 2 million Russian *émigrés* abroad . . . [who] are now holding meetings in Berlin, Paris, London, and all capitals except ours."[63]

Probably the most telling document released by the Oppositionists was the pamphlet entitled *The Workers' Opposition*, written by the fiery Alexandra Kollontai, a former Menshevik and a latecomer to the ranks of the Opposition. Lenin was particularly incensed by this work, since it denied the dogma that his Party really represented the workers. Madame Kollontai contended that it was no coincidence that the Workers' Opposition did not contain any leaders of the Party: it was truly a movement of the workers, of the Party masses. When the Party leadership branded the Opposition as "syndicalism," Kollontai asked: "Who is right—the leaders or the working masses endowed with the healthy class instinct?"[64] The Opposition opposed Lenin's policy of utilizing the bourgeois specialists in

* Every Communist Party had to accept the twenty-one conditions before being granted admission to the Third International or Comintern. The conditions required every member party to: combat reformism and pacifism; obtain control of trade unions; subvert the armed forces of non-Communist states by agitation and propaganda; obtain the support of the peasantry and oppressed nationalities and colonial peoples; maintain an illegal Party organization in all countries in which the Party enjoyed legal status; compel Party members who were elected to parliamentary bodies to obey all directives of the Party's Central Committee; support all Soviet republics; purge the Party's membership periodically; recognize the principle of democratic centralism; and accept decisions of all Comintern congresses as binding. These conditions were laid down by the Second Congress of the Comintern, meeting in Moscow in August, 1920.

the economy, since it held that the workers could actually
manage industrial enterprises. Madame Kollontai branded the
old specialists as "servants of capital," incapable of serving a
new master. She was also disturbed by the growth of bureaucracy
and regarded the Party's rejection of collective management in
favor of one-man management as being contrary to the dictatorship of the proletariat. Instead, she insisted upon the establishment of "workers' democracy" by means of the expulsion of
"all nonproletarian elements" from the Party. She also voiced
the demand of the Workers' Opposition that all "nonworking
elements" be removed from administrative positions in the Party
and from all Party committees. The practice of making appointments in the Party—a characteristic of bureaucracy—was to be
replaced by the elective principle, along with "strict account-
ability before the rank and file."

Lenin employed several different tactics in dealing with the
Workers' Opposition. For the most part, he was harsh—as when
he accused the Oppositionists of engaging in "purest demagogy"
and asked them what concrete suggestions they could make to
reduce the bureaucracy rather than merely denouncing it. He
sardonically asked Shlyapnikov and Madame Kollontai why they
had not taught the Party how to combat bureaucracy when they
held Cabinet posts. At the same time, he employed moderation
of sorts when he stated that it was necessary to "sift out the
healthy from the unhealthy in the Workers' Opposition" and
admitted that the movement was "permeating the broad
masses."[65] But Lenin also scolded the Oppositionists when he
declared: "Enough, it is impossible to play with the Party in
this way." While admitting that the Party was "ill," he contended that Oppositionism was now inappropriate: "We have
spent enough time in discussion, and I must say that it is now
much better to 'discuss with rifles' than with theses put forth
by the opposition. There is no need for an opposition now, comrades, it is not the time!"[66]

The Tenth Congress was no time for an opposition to be tolerated. The Kronstadt Revolt of sailors and workers—in what
had been a Bolshevik stronghold in 1917—broke out while the
Congress was in session. As many as 140 delegates had to leave

the Congress and take up arms against the rebels. At the Congress, Madame Kollontai accused Lenin of having "evaded the question of Kronstadt," thus implying that the Workers' Opposition had behind it a groundswell of popular opinion which Lenin was presumably ignoring. However, in fairness to Lenin, it should be said that he was aware of the prevailing mood; it was precisely this recognition which induced him to launch the New Economic Policy at the Tenth Congress. The Kronstadt Revolt was a symptom of widespread dissatisfaction, based as it was on demands for free elections to the soviets, abolition of the Communist Party's monopoly of power by means of a political amnesty, and a restoration of the "anarchists and left socialist parties."[67] Lenin was quick to brand the Kronstadt Revolt as the work of "White generals" as well as of the Socialist Revolutionaries—despite the fact that the rebels did not voice the SR demand for the Constituent Assembly. On the surface, Lenin argued, it appeared that the rebels wanted a Soviet regime "with minor changes," while in reality they were being used by the Whites. Lenin put the matter bluntly in a statement published on March 26, 1921: "Believe me, only two governments are possible in Russia: the Czarist or the Soviet."[68] In true Communist fashion, Lenin posed absolute alternatives.

If opposition to the regime from outside the Communist Party had to be eliminated, it was no less necessary to root it out from within the Party. Shlyapnikov attempted to explain to Lenin what had happened to the Party:

> We must state that in spite of the existence of unity in form, there is not in the Party an organizational tie between the members of the Party and its leading organs. I am able to say this not only on my personal experience, but on the basis of the state of affairs in the locales, and every one of us knows very well about this. Vladimir Ilyich, we do not have in our Party that former fusion [*spaika*] which we had in the past, in no less difficult moments in the life of our Party in the prerevolutionary period. ... It is this, Comrade Lenin, which gave birth to what you here call the Workers' Opposition![69]

Lenin was not one to be moved by Shlyapnikov's claim that the Party had been swamped by alien elements. Nor was deference to this argument necessary, since Lenin had the votes with which to defeat the Workers' Opposition. Shlyapnikov could only warn Lenin: "Do not go too far in the struggle against us. It may be that you will crush and break us here, but from this you can only lose."[70] In the end, Madame Kollontai contented herself with a laconic rejoinder to Lenin's attack upon her pamphlet: "Jupiter, thou art angry—which means thou art wrong."[71]

Lenin's annoyance with the Workers' Opposition did not prevent him from moving against it with apparent circumspection. Although attacking the Opposition vigorously, he took the seemingly conciliatory step of including in the membership of the new Central Committee two Workers' Oppositionists, Shlyapnikov and I. Kutuzov, as full members—as well as one candidate-member. Lenin also chose among the new candidate-members Osinsky, a representative of the unorganized Democratic Centralist Opposition (which did not present a separate platform to the Tenth Congress). It was only on March 16, after the new Central Committee had been elected, that Lenin introduced two of the briefest and most significant resolutions in the Party's entire history. Many of the delegates were not present on that momentous last day of the Tenth Congress; final preparations were already being made for the storming of rebellious Kronstadt on Kotlin Island—an operation in which the troops, under the command of the future Marshal Mikhail N. Tukhachevsky, had to be driven onto the ice at gunpoint. The two resolutions directed against the Workers' Opposition were particularly harsh in view of the fact that its members were not a disciplined group but were merely attempting to achieve their aims within the Party, without questioning the Party's right to play the leading role.

One of the resolutions, entitled "Concerning the Syndicalist and Anarchist Deviation in Our Party," condemned the views of the Workers' Opposition as "not only theoretically false, but in practice [they] serve as an expression of petty-bourgeois and anarchist wavering, in practice [they] weaken the tested guiding line of the Communist Party and, in fact, aid the class enemies of the proletarian revolution."[72] The enforcement of this condemnation was spelled out in a momentous resolution "Concerning the Unity of the Party," which directed the Central

Committee to "carry out the complete destruction of all factionalism." Violations of Party discipline and the rebirth of factionalism were to be punished by expulsion from the Party. Nor were members of the Central Committee exempted from this provision, which was made public by Stalin only in January, 1924, at the Thirteenth Party Conference. They could be demoted to the status of candidacy or even expelled from the Party by a two-thirds vote of the Central Committee and of the Central Control Commission meeting jointly.[73]

Thus, the Tenth Congress established a formal procedure for combatting factionalism which Lenin's successor was soon to employ against his rivals. In practice, this was to mean that whoever was in a position to pack the Central Committee could dispose of any minority within that body and within the Party at his pleasure. The fundamental premise of a democratic society —enabling any minority to continue to state its case in an attempt to win a majority—was denied to the Party membership by Lenin and his followers in 1921. Three years earlier, the democratic principle of majority rule had been denied to Russia by the same men at the time of the dissolution of the Constituent Assembly. Those who at that time had participated in depriving others of their rights were now branded as deviationists and consigned to an inferior, onus-bearing status. The stage was now set for far more ambitious and frightening future hunts for new heretics against Marxist-Leninist orthodoxy.

CHAPTER VI

STALIN'S RISE TO POWER

Before us is the entire world of the bourgeoisie, which is only seeking a form by which to strangle us. Our Mensheviks and SR's are nothing more than the agents of this bourgeoisie.

—Lenin, March 27, 1922.

But there are things about which it is impermissible to joke; there are such things as the unity of the Party.

—Lenin, March 28, 1922.

Yes, comrades, I am a blunt and rude person; that is true, I do not deny it. [*Laughter.*]

—Stalin, December 23, 1925.

The road to despotism in its twentieth-century variant known as Stalinism cannot be understood apart from the development and strengthening of the Party's administrative apparatus, which began in 1921. The Tenth Congress, held in the same year, had elected as Responsible Secretary Vyacheslav M. Molotov (Skryabin), who had served as secretary to the editorial board of *Pravda* prior to World War I. Molotov, Yaroslavsky, and Mikhailov replaced three followers of Trotsky who had been elected to the Secretariat in 1920: Nikolai Krestinsky, Eugene Preobrazhensky, and Leonid Serebryakov. These three were not only ousted from the Secretariat at the Tenth Congress, but they were not even re-elected to the Central Committee or to the Orgburo. This is not to say that they had been gentle with the Workers' Opposition, since they had developed the system of personnel transfers to a high degree. However, they were not sufficiently tough to suit Lenin; nor were they reliable, in view of their loyalty to Trotsky. Krestinsky was sent to Germany as Soviet envoy in October, 1921; Serebryakov was transferred to work in the field of transportation; and Preobrazhensky returned to editorial work on *Pravda* and prepared to become the principal theoretician of Trotskyism.

Prior to assuming the Secretaryship, Molotov had carried out a number of assignments in the name of the Party's central organization. In 1919, he had been sent to Nizhni Novgorod to serve as chairman of the province executive committee; following his appointment as secretary of the Party province committee in the Donets Basin, he became secretary of the Central Committee of the Communist Party of Ukraine in 1920. Although Molotov had the backing of Lenin in 1921, he was already committed to Stalin, whose unique status as a member of both the Politburo and the Orgburo gave him a growing voice in Secretariat affairs. The decline of the Central Committee, brought about by the growth of the Party's administrative apparatus, was reflected in two decisions taken by the Tenth Congress. One of these reduced the frequency of Central Committee plenary sessions from two per month (as provided for in the December, 1919, Statutes) to one every two months; the other resolution provided that five of the twenty-five Central Committee members be engaged exclusively in inspecting the province Party committees.[1]

The trend toward a Party bureaucracy operated by experts was to some extent related to the New Economic Policy (NEP) adopted at the Tenth Congress. This was evident at the Eleventh Congress, which met from March 27 to April 2, 1922, and was the last such meeting to be attended by Lenin. He had been failing physically during much of the preceding year; on August 9, 1921, he had written to Gorky, complaining: "I have become so fatigued that I cannot do anything."[2] In December, he had taken a leave in the village of Gorki near Moscow and was able to attend the Eleventh Congress; the first paralysis (which affected his right side as well as his speech) did not occur until May 26, 1922. Despite a rapidly developing sclerotic condition, Lenin was able to deliver a spirited defense of his New Economic Policy.

The NEP, which lasted from 1921 to 1928, was made necessary by the utter failure of the economic policies of the period of

"Militant Communism" ("War Communism") which preceded it. The civil war period, during which most of the Czarist territorial patrimony was recovered, was characterized by an inflation which caused money transactions to be replaced by barter. By 1920, industrial production declined to less than one-sixth of the 1913 level, and foreign trade came to a complete halt. The lack of manufactured goods and the worthlessness of the ruble provided no incentive for the peasantry to grow crops. The situation had also been aggravated by the Communist attempt to introduce the class war into the countryside in 1918 by creating the Committees of Poor Peasants (*kombedy*), designed to pit the poorer peasantry against the so-called "middle" and "wealthy" peasants. The Committees of Poor Peasants were used to aid the Communist requisitioning squads by putting the finger on peasants who had concealed grain and produce and were thus part of the "village bourgeoisie." The food requisitioning was designed to feed the industrial workers in the cities, the populations of which were experiencing grave difficulties. The peasantry, resisting Communist rule, refused to grow crops, hid part of the harvest, and killed and consumed much of the livestock. These conditions led to the terrible famine of 1921-22.

The sole solution was to grant certain concessions which would restore a measure of public confidence, provide economic incentives, and create political stability. The introduction of a fixed tax in kind on agricultural products, in place of the hated requisitioning, enabled the regime to placate the peasantry, which could now hire labor and lease land but could not sell the latter. In retail trade and light industry, a new but heavily taxed class of small businessmen and entrepreneurs (Nepmen) arose. However, the overwhelming bulk of industry remained in the hands of the Soviet state, as well as all banking, transport, and foreign trade.

This new course, which permitted a bare minimum of small-scale capitalism, was also said by Lenin to require Communists to "learn to trade" and to acquire business acumen. This was the period of the Genoa Conference—the first such international meeting attended by Soviet delegates, who, according to Lenin, came "not as Communists, but as tradesmen [*kuptsy*]."[3] Trade

with the outside world and the attempt to create a bond between
the peasant economy and the future socialism by means of a
limited free market were avowedly aimed at using capitalism
in the interests of Communism. Lenin put it this way: "We will
be able to rule the economy when and if the Communists are
able to build this economy with the hands of others and will
themselves learn from this bourgeoisie and direct it along the
lines which they will."[4] However, this would require the development of a professional Soviet commercial class. It was probably
inevitable that the spirit of the times should cause the criterion
of professionalization to be applied not only to the economy but
to the Party itself. This was of particular importance in view of
the fact that the Party, in adopting the NEP, had granted some
substantial, though temporary, concessions.

Speaking at the Eleventh Congress on March 27, 1922, Lenin
characterized this period as a "retreat," and he issued the following warning:

> . . . To retreat following a victorious grand offensive
> is very difficult; here there are absolutely different relation-
> ships; there [in advancing], even if discipline is not main-
> tained, all are pushing ahead and flying forward; here [in
> retreating], discipline must be more planned and is a hun-
> dred times more necessary, because when an entire army
> retreats . . . it does not see where to halt but sees only
> retreat—here, it is sometimes sufficient for a few panicky
> voices to cause all to flee. Here, the danger is tremendous.
> When such a retreat occurs with an actual army, machine
> guns are set up and then, when a proper retreat becomes
> disorderly, the command is given: "Fire!" And correctly so.[5]

At this time, Lenin also declared that it was necessary to end
the retreat and regroup the Party's forces. Too much freedom
could be a dangerous thing. If the peasant was permitted to
trade freely what he produced above the tax in kind, it did not
follow from this that free trade unions were to be allowed or that
the Party would "permit trade in political literature which is
Menshevik and SR and which is maintained with money of the
capitalists of the entire world."[6]

Although the NEP appeared to be a period of relaxation,

Lenin regarded it as fraught with danger for two principal reasons: the Party could lose its vigor, and it could make too many concessions. Therefore, an even tighter discipline would have to be maintained, and violations—though they might be prompted by the best of intentions—would have to be punished "severely, cruelly, [and] mercilessly." To this end, the Eleventh Congress renewed the condemnation of the Workers' Opposition pronounced at the Tenth Congress. The Opposition had refused to dissolve and had taken its case to the Comintern at that body's Third Congress in June, 1921, when Madame Kollontai delivered the protest aimed at Lenin's policies. In February, 1922— on the eve of the Eleventh Party Congress—the Workers' Opposition had appealed to the Executive Committee of the Comintern in the hope of obtaining its support against the Central Committee. This was the so-called "Declaration of the Twenty-Two," whose signers included Shlyapnikov, S. P. Medvedev, Kuznetsov, and Madame Kollontai. Their complaint was that the Party had ceased being a workers' party, had admitted the bourgeoisie to its ranks, was lacking in democracy, and was dominating the trade unions; the Oppositionists also charged that the Central Committee had been infiltrating their ranks with spies. Since the Comintern did Lenin's bidding, it rejected the appeal of the twenty-two.

The experience with the Workers' Opposition between the Tenth and the Eleventh Congresses dictated a strengthening of the Central Control Commission, the Party body charged with enforcing discipline, and its local counterparts. These local commissions were established in September, 1920, under the secretaryship of Krestinsky, who did not have much taste for this kind of activity. The chairmanship of the Central Control Commission was soon assumed by Aaron Alexandrovich Sol'ts, an old Marxist who came from a merchant's family and later ascended to the Soviet Supreme Court. Most of the members of the Workers' Opposition, who had been so voluble at the Tenth Congress, were not elected as delegates to the Eleventh Congress. The Samara province Party organization, a stronghold of the Opposition, was purged and the entire committee replaced; its secretary, Yu. K. Milonov, had warned in vain at the Tenth

Congress that the upper layer of the Party was "hardening" and being transformed into a caste.

The fact that fewer such outbursts marked the Eleventh Congress did not mean that the work of the control commissions had been completed. Shlyapnikov was present to express shock over Lenin's machine-gun metaphor and to gloat over Lenin's failure to oust him from Party membership (the motion had received three votes less than the necessary two-thirds majority at a joint session of the Central Committee and the Central Control Commission held on August 9, 1921). Now, the Eleventh Congress refused to support the expulsion of Shlyapnikov, Medvedev, and Madame Kollontai; and a proposal to abolish all local control commissions was defeated by 223 votes to 89. Yet, the drive against Oppositionists was to continue, and the Eleventh Congress empowered each control commission to establish a "small investigatory apparatus of tested comrades who know the Party."[7] In addition, some of the control commission members were to be freed from all other activities; in the case of the Central Control Commission, the full-time contingent was to consist of three of the five members and two candidates.

A full-scale purge of the Party during the latter half of 1921 resulted in the expulsion of nearly 170,000 members, approximately one-fourth of the entire membership. In an article published on September 21, 1921, Lenin wrote of the purge in glowing terms and of the need to "cleanse the Party of swindlers, of persons who have become bureaucrats, of the dishonest, of unsteady Communists, and of Mensheviks who have recolored their 'facade' but have inwardly remained Mensheviks."[8] So profound was the distrust and antipathy toward the former brethren, the Mensheviks, that Lenin announced that approximately 99 per cent of their number admitted to the Party after 1918 would have to be expelled and that each Menshevik remaining in the Bolshevik Party would have to be checked three or four times.

It was in this period of purges and tightening Party discipline that Stalin was elected General Secretary by the Central Committee on April 3, 1922. That this was done with the apparently unqualified approval of Lenin is evident from the latter's statement to the Eleventh Congress on March 28, 1922. On that occasion, Lenin rose to Stalin's defense when Preobrazhensky asked how Stalin could simultaneously head two people's commissariats, be a member of the Politburo and the Orgburo, and participate in the work of approximately ten Central Committee commissions. The reference here was to Stalin's positions as head of the Commissariat of Workers' and Peasants' Inspectorate (*Rabkrin*) and as Commissar for Nationalities. He held the latter post from November, 1917, until early in 1923, when it was abolished after the establishment of the U.S.S.R. *Rabkrin* was Stalin's bailiwick from March, 1919, to May, 1922. It was there that he acquired much of his authority and set about extending the tentacles of his control over the various branches of the state apparatus, under the guise of administrative efficiency.

While it is true that Lenin had expressed some criticism of Stalin's direction of *Rabkrin* in a statement on September 27, 1921 (first published in 1929), at the Eleventh Congress (six months later) he was defending the head of *Rabkrin* as a "person with authority." He declared that Stalin was the sole person capable of dealing with the nationality problem in practice and was an official "to whom any national representative could go and relate in detail the problem at hand."[9] Lenin stated flatly that Preobrazhensky could not find a man more qualified than Stalin for the nationalities' post. This support enabled Stalin to be elected General Secretary in place of his own man, Molotov. The new Central Committee which elected Stalin included such of his followers as Voroshilov, Kalinin, Yaroslavsky, Rudzutak, Ordzhonikidze, as well as Molotov; Stalinist candidate-members included Anastas Ivanovich Mikoyan, Kirov, Manuilsky, and Badaev.

The presence of a substantial number of Stalin's followers in the Central Committee was not the only sign of his growing influence. These same followers were being appointed to key positions in the Party apparatus. Molotov remained in the Secretariat as Stalin's principal deputy, along with Valerian Kuibyshev, who was later to become Chairman of the Central Control Commission as well as head of *Rabkrin*. Lazar Kaganovich was placed in charge of the Organization and Instruction Department of the Central Committee apparatus, which was charged with sending directives and supervisory agents to local Party bodies. The regional bureaus also were important instruments of control, and here again Stalinists were in evidence. Mikoyan headed the North Caucasus Bureau, Jan Rudzutak was in charge of the Central Asian Bureau, and Stanislav Kosior directed the Siberian Bureau. Sergei Kirov was sent to Azerbaidzhan to serve as secretary of the Central Committee of the local Communist Party. The number of Stalin's appointees was legion. It was thanks to this following that Stalin ultimately laid claim to Party leadership.

Stalin's position was immensely enhanced less than two months after he had assumed the General Secretaryship when Lenin suffered his first stroke on May 26, 1922. The human dynamo, who had set for himself the modest goal of overturning the entire world, had at last burned out at the relatively early age of 52. This had come about despite Lenin's continuous preoccupation with physical health.[10] The paralyzed shell of a man was to linger for another twenty months before a merciful death finally claimed him. By the autumn of 1922, Lenin had rallied sufficiently from his first stroke to deliver short addresses before the Central Executive Committee in October and before the Moscow Soviet and the Fourth Congress of the Comintern in November (the latter one in German). He was also able to grant two rather extensive interviews to British correspondents. This brief period of recovery was cut short by a second stroke on December 16, 1922, which paralyzed his right arm and leg. It was at the time of this second stroke that Lenin's appraisal of Stalin changed drastically.

During the summer of 1922, Stalin had visited Lenin at the village of Gorki near Moscow and supposedly had himself photographed with the ailing leader—or else had a photomontage prepared. In an article published in *Pravda* on September 24, 1922, Stalin recounted two of his visits to Lenin and confidently observed that the "old fighter" would soon be returning to action.[11] The general tone of the brief article—brief, said Stalin, because of the insistence of the editors—hardly reflected the ambitions and inner thoughts of its author. However, appearances were deceiving and merely served to conceal tensions which had arisen within the Politburo between some of its members and the new General Secretary.

In the general disillusionment which Lenin experienced as he lay ill in 1922—a disillusionment stemming from the inevitable growth of the Soviet bureaucracy and the General Secretary's arbitrariness—the situation in Georgia was an important factor. The independent Georgian Republic, which was governed by the Mensheviks, was the last of the non-Russian territories of the former Russian Empire to come under Soviet rule. This was finally accomplished through an invasion of Georgia by the Red Army in February, 1921. Military action was preceded by Soviet-style diplomacy and subversion. In a treaty signed on May 7, 1920, Moscow granted recognition to the Menshevik government of independent Georgia and then sent Sergei Kirov as its envoy to Tbilisi for the purpose of reorganizing the Georgian Communists and employing diplomatic protests in a war of nerves directed against the Georgian government. A secret provision in the treaty obligated the Georgian government to amnesty the Bolsheviks whom it had arrested; upon being released, these Bolsheviks immediately made plans for a Communist take-over in Georgia.

Moscow's policy toward Georgia was the handiwork of Stalin and his henchman on the spot, Serge Ordzhonikidze, a former pupil of Lenin's in the Longjumeau Party School near Paris and the secretary of the Transcaucasian Territorial Committee of the Party in 1921. It appears that this pair presented Lenin with something of a *fait accompli* at the time of the armed invasion of Georgia. Lenin, of course, was in favor of Communist rule in Georgia, but apparently he was willing to wait a bit longer than Stalin and Ordzhonikidze were. However, once the invasion proved to be successful and the Menshevik government had to abandon the country to the invader, Lenin accepted the situation but counseled Ordzhonikidze to pursue a policy of moderation in dealing with the numerous Mensheviks in Georgia. He advised concessions to the Georgian intelligentsia and to small tradesmen, and he actually suggested a bloc with some of the Mensheviks.

Lenin particularly warned against having Georgia, Armenia, and Azerbaidzhan copy the Russian model to the letter, and he was anxious for the states of the Caucasus to enter into commercial relations with Western Europe and America.[12]

Most of Lenin's advice was disregarded by Stalin and Ordzhonikidze; a fierce resistance developed in Georgia to the tactics which they employed in riding roughshod over local sensitivities. In October, 1922, the Central Committee of the Communist Party of Georgia resigned in a body as a protest. Lenin then decided that it would be necessary to launch a campaign against "Russian great power chauvinism." He appointed a special commission of three non-Russians—Dzierzynski, Vikentii Semenovich Mitskevich-Kapsukas, and D. Z. Manuilsky—to conduct an on-the-spot investigation in Georgia. When this commission of Russified non-Russians took a position in defense of Stalin and Ordzhonikidze and against the Georgian Communists led by Philip Makharadze, Lenin—though ill—was undeterred in his criticism of chauvinist actions. On December 30-31, 1922, he dictated a statement in which he bitterly attacked Stalin, Ordzhonikidze, and Dzierzynski; this statement was later carried out of the Soviet Union by Trotsky when he went into exile abroad. In this document, Lenin, conscious of the excesses committed by the Russians against the non-Russian nationalities, demanded that the non-Russian languages be used in public administration and that a lenient policy be adopted toward the understandable sensitivities of these peoples. He asked whether the Soviet administrative apparatus had not merely been "borrowed from Czarism and only thinly anointed with Soviet chrism."[13] Lenin also singled out for criticism Dzierzynski's "100 per cent Russian attitude" and noted that "assimilated non-Russians always overdo in the matter of 100 per cent Russian attitudes"—a criticism particularly applicable to the Georgian Stalin.

Five days earlier, on December 25, 1922, Lenin had dictated his Testament, in which he expressed some concern over the possibility of a split in the Party based upon personality conflicts. He correctly sensed that the relationship between Stalin and Trotsky constituted "a big half of the danger of that split," but incorrectly proposed that it could be avoided "by raising the number of members of the Central Committee to 50 or 100." Ironically, it was precisely the expansion of the Central Committee that both reflected and strengthened Stalin's bid for absolute power. However, Lenin was unable to designate a successor. His characterization of Stalin included the observation that the General Secretary "has concentrated enormous power in his hands; and I am not sure that he always knows how to use that power with sufficient caution." Lenin referred to Trotsky as "the most able man in the present Central Committee," but criticized "his too-far-reaching self-confidence and . . . disposition to be too much attracted by the purely administrative side of affairs." Kamenev and Zinoviev were not praised in the Testament, but Lenin instead made reference to the "October episode"—to their having opposed the seizure of power in 1917 —although he noted kindly that "it should no more be used against them personally than should the non-Bolshevism of Trotsky." Significantly, both Trotsky and Stalin were to violate this provision of the Testament at different times in their dealings with Kamenev and Zinoviev. The Testament described Bukharin as "not only the most valuable and most important theoretician of the Party, but he also may legitimately be considered the favorite of the whole Party; but his theoretical views can only with the greatest reserve be regarded as fully Marxist, for there is something scholastic in them (he never has studied, and I think never has fully understood dialectics)."[14]

By both praising and damning various candidates to succeed him, Lenin did not come to grips with the crucial problem of succession. Several days prior to the dictating of the Testament—on December 22, 1922—Stalin had employed "vile invectives and threats" in a quarrel with Lenin's wife. The following day, Krupskaya wrote to Kamenev asking him and Zinoviev to "protect me from rude interference with my private life . . ."[15] Obviously, the cause of tension was the Georgian affair and Lenin's determination to do something about it. Krupskaya had written a letter to Stalin in words dictated by Lenin, and it was this missive which precipitated the outburst of rudeness from Stalin. Particularly revealing as to the circumstances of the quarrel is the following sentence in Krupskaya's letter: "What one can and what one cannot discuss with Ilyich [Lenin]—I know better than any doctor, because I know what makes him nervous and what does not; in any case, I know better than Stalin." Soon after this manifestation of Stalin's rudeness—on January 4, 1923—Lenin dictated the famous Postscript to his Testament:

> Stalin is too rude, and this fault, entirely supportable in relations among us Communists, becomes insupportable in the office of General Secretary. Therefore, I propose to the comrades to find a way to remove Stalin from that position and appoint to it another man who in all respects differs from Stalin in one superiority—namely, that he be more tolerant, more loyal, more polite, and more considerate to comrades, less capricious, etc. This circumstance may seem an insignificant trifle, but I think that from the point of view of preventing a split and from the point of view of the relation between Stalin and Trotsky which I discussed above, it is not a trifle, or it is such a trifle as may acquire decisive importance.[16]

Despite the importance of the matter—or, more correctly, because of it—neither Lenin's Testament nor the crucial Postscript was discussed in the Central Committee until sixteen months later—in May, 1924, following Lenin's death.

The break between Lenin and Stalin was to become complete when Lenin sent him a letter on March 5, 1923, demanding that "you weigh carefully whether you are agreeable to retracting your words and apologizing or whether you prefer the severance of relations between us."[17] Stalin's problem was largely solved four days later when Lenin suffered his third and most serious stroke, which paralyzed the entire right side of his body and greatly impaired his speech. It was a disillusioned Lenin who succumbed to this stroke, and the source of his dismay lay in his having finally concluded that the Soviet state apparatus, after five years of operation, had acquired many of the less desirable characteristics of the bureaucracy of Imperial Russia. In his last article, entitled "Better Less, But Better" and published in the March 4, 1923, issue of *Pravda,* Lenin placed the blame squarely on Stalin's *Rabkrin* and declared that no Soviet institution enjoyed less confidence or was more poorly organized.[18] Although the article did not mention Stalin by name, it was obviously directed against him.

However, the fact that Stalin was not explicitly denounced by Lenin, except in the Postscript to the highly secret Testament, enabled him to retain the strongest position enjoyed by any of Lenin's lieutenants. One other factor helped him: the fear among the lieutenants that Trotsky was the most ambitious and most dangerous contender for Lenin's mantle. This distrust of Trotsky made it possible for Stalin to form a triumvirate with Kamenev and Zinoviev. This proved to be an unbeatable—if temporary—combination, for it effectively isolated Trotsky during 1923 and provided Stalin with a protective cover against the charges raised by the dying Lenin.

The initial success of the triumvirate lay in the influence of its members. Stalin controlled the Secretariat of the Central Committee. Zinoviev headed the Petrograd (soon to be renamed Leningrad) Party organization and was Chairman of the Executive Committee of the Comintern. Kamenev headed the Moscow Soviet. All three were members of the Politburo, Zinoviev having temporarily replaced Bukharin in that body in 1921, following the Tenth Congress. Of the three, Zinoviev had the longest tenure as a Central Committee member, dating from 1907, while Stalin became a member in 1912, and Kamenev in April, 1917. Trotsky, who had been considered a Menshevik until 1917, when he finally returned to the Bolshevik fold, remained in the Politburo and also headed the Commissariat of War. Although the real rivals were Stalin and Trotsky, much of the antagonism at this time was between Zinoviev and Trotsky. In the latter part of 1920, it was Zinoviev who led the criticism against Trotsky because of the latter's arbitrariness and approval of compulsion in dealing with labor. However, the conflict between Trotsky and the triumvirs did not yet come out into the open at the Twelfth Congress of the Party, which met between April 17 and 25, 1923.

Lenin had attended every Party congress except the first in 1898 and the sixth in 1917. Now, as he lay paralyzed and awaiting death, it became necessary to select one of the members

of the Politburo to present to the Congress the report of the
Central Committee. Trotsky, already suspected of Bonapartist
tendencies, demurred when Stalin suggested that he speak for
the Central Committee. Stalin declined to deliver the report
since he had to present the organizational report in his capacity
as General Secretary. In the end, the rather hazardous honor
fell to Zinoviev. It soon became clear that the Twelfth Congress
was in Stalin's hands. On the very first day, he succeeded in
deflecting Lenin's criticism of his operation of *Rabkrin* by placing
the blame on shortcomings in personnel. He then used this as a
reason for obtaining from the Congress greater powers for
the Secretariat's Evaluation and Assignment Department
(*Uchraspred*), which maintained personnel dossiers and effected
transfers. Prior to this, *Uchraspred* had confined itself to the
personnel of the province and district Party committees; now
it would extend to the various sectors of the economy its evaluation system of "studying each worker bone by bone."[19] In this
way, Stalin succeeded in turning the situation to his own advantage by enhancing his control over not only the Party apparatus
but the civil service and the economy as well.*

Stalin went to great pains to create the impression of agreement with and loyalty to Lenin. Noting that many of the delegates were quoting extensively from Lenin's writings, Stalin
modestly stated that he "would not want to quote my teacher,
Comrade Lenin, since he is not here and I fear that I may cite
him incorrectly and inappropriately."[20] He then proceeded to
quote two lines from Lenin, in accordance with the practice—

---

* It was at this time, just prior to the Twelfth Congress, that the
regime's police began to be turned against the Party membership with
the arrest of the Tatar Communist Mirza Sultan-Galiev. Originally an
official in Stalin's Commissariat of Nationalities Affairs, Sultan-Galiev had
great hopes that Pan-Islamic anticolonialism and Tatar nationalism could
be reconciled with Soviet Russian rule. However, by 1922, he had become
disillusioned with the NEP and the Russian dominance of the Communist
Party. Stalin ordered his arrest, following police interception of his mail,
on the grounds that he had been in contact with anti-Soviet Turkic elements (including Zeki Validov-Togan and the insurgent Turkestanian
Basmachis). Sultan-Galiev's case was taken up at a special conference
called by Stalin in June, 1923, and he was released after a "confession"
of guilt. In November, 1929, he was rearrested and then disappeared.

to which he was to adhere throughout his career—of justifying his opinions and policies with quotations from Lenin. Stalin also tried to mute rumors of a split within the Central Committee by declaring that no split existed, although he added that the possibility of a split could not be excluded.

In order to make certain that he would come out on top in the event of a split within the Party's inner ruling circle, Stalin succeeded in having the Twelfth Congress increase the size of the Central Committee from twenty-seven to forty members. Candidate-members promoted to full membership included Kirov, Komarov, Manuilsky, and Mikoyan; among the new members were Lashevich, Karl Radek (Sobelsohn), Uglanov, Kharitonov, and Tsyurupa. The ranks of the candidate-members included such Stalinists as Kaganovich, S. V. Kosior, Orakhelashvili, and Skrypnyk. Stalin justified the broadening of the Central Committee on the grounds that the "nucleus of ten to fifteen persons" which provided leadership in the twenty-seven–member Central Committee would "have every chance of becoming ossified and of being cut off from the masses" unless it were surrounded by the "new generation of future leaders." He also argued that the nucleus within the Central Committee was "becoming old, is in need of replacement"—although, ironically, he was a member of that nucleus. He alluded to Lenin's illness and noted that the "other members of the basic nucleus of the Central Commitee have become rather worn out."[21] Stalin also spoke of the need to bring "independent" people into the Central Committee—people "free from personal influence, free from those habits and traditions of struggle within the Central Committee which have developed and which sometimes create alarm within the Central Committee."[22]

It was impossible to challenge these arguments. Who could question the desirability of introducing new blood into the Central Committee? On the surface it was a laudable measure, although Stalin would now, in fact, be able to reward his faithful followers by placing them in the enlarged Central Committee. Another measure in kind which Stalin succeeded in getting the Twelfth Congress to adopt concerned the establishment, within the Central Committee apparatus, of a school for training be-

tween 200 and 300 secretaries of Party district committees.
These trainees would then go to the country as additional emis-
saries of the Party's General Secretary to supplement those who
were already doing Stalin's bidding at the province committee
level. Still another measure which strengthened Stalin's hand
was the decision of the Twelfth Congress to increase the size of
the Central Control Commission from seven to fifty members.
This enabled Stalin to reward more of his followers with new
positions and to enhance the powers of the body designed to
"enforce the Party line in all respects." The Central Control
Commission was to meet every other month just before the
plenary session of the Central Committee, and its members and
candidate-members were to have a consultative vote at the all-
Russian Party conferences.* Thus, Stalin's authority to deal with
Oppositionists was substantially enlarged.

The fact that Stalin commanded a majority in the Twelfth
Congress made it impossible for Trotsky to fulfill Lenin's request
that he undertake the defense of the Georgian Communists
whom Stalin had treated harshly when they expressed opposition
to the establishment of a Transcaucasian Soviet Federation. Lenin
had originally hoped that the matter could be resolved satisfactorily within the Central Committee and had written a strictly
confidential letter to Trotsky on March 5, 1923, requesting him
to lead the opposition to Stalin.[23] The difficulty lay in the fact
that Trotsky, confronted by the triumvirate within the inner
ruling circle, had been rather effectively isolated. Nor did Trotsky
have Lenin's unqualified blessings for what would certainly
become a showdown involving much more than the Georgian
affair and Stalin's treatment of the Georgian Communists who
disagreed with him. Lenin's secret Testament certainly did not
extend to Trotsky the kind of confidence and plenipotentiary
powers which he would have needed in a final battle with Stalin.

In the end, Trotsky chose not to fight. The only Politburo
member to speak in defense of the non-Russian nationalities

* The conferences of the Party were conclaves which met during the
periods between Party Congresses. The last conference, the Eighteenth,
met in February, 1941. The October, 1952, Party Statutes, which replaced
those of March, 1939, contained no provision regarding the conferences.

was Bukharin. Together with Rakovsky, he proposed that the Congress eliminate from its resolution any reference to the danger of local (non-Russian) nationalism as opposed to the much more dangerous "Russian great power chauvinism." In this debate, Stalin employed a tactic which was never to fail him throughout the long struggle against his rivals—that of referring to differences of opinion which had formerly existed between Lenin and Stalin's opponents. He noted that Bukharin had "sinned against the nationalities for years, rejecting the right to self-determination," and that it was now appropriate for him to be repenting, although, according to Stalin, he had gone from one extreme to the other.[24] Within a matter of months, this same tactic was to be utilized by Stalin against Trotsky, who had had numerous disagreements with Lenin in the period prior to 1917. And it was to be invoked later against Stalin's fellow triumvirs, Kamenev and Zinoviev.

It became clear at the Twelfth Congress that Stalin was the leading figure in the triumvirate, and Zinoviev began to consider means by which the powers of the General Secretary could be circumscribed. With this in mind, Zinoviev organized the famous cave meeting in the Caucasian watering place of Kislovodsk in September, 1923. The participants were Zinoviev, Bukharin, M. M. Lashevich, Grigorii E. Yevdokimov, and Voroshilov. At this meeting, Zinoviev and Bukharin considered two possibilities: one was to limit the Secretariat to the performance of technical functions and to deprive it of control over appointments; the other was to "politicize" the Secretariat by introducing two additional Politburo members into its ranks for the purpose of limiting Stalin's influence. They considered adding Trotsky to the Secretariat, with the third member to be either Kamenev, Zinoviev, or Bukharin. The proposal was sent to Stalin via Ordzhonikidze, and Zinoviev received in response a telegram from Stalin written "in a coarse but friendly tone."

Stalin indicated that he would come to the Caucasus and discuss the matter. In the end, it was agreed not to touch the Secretariat itself, but to add three Politburo members to the Orgburo: Trotsky, Bukharin, and Zinoviev. However, this was a hollow measure because the three new members were either unable or unwilling to attend Orgburo meetings. Stalin's proposal gave the appearance of a willingness to compromise; by this time, however, the Secretariat had actually supplanted the Orgburo, and it is doubtful whether attendance at Orgburo meetings would have enabled the new members to have any knowledge of or control over the day-to-day business of the Secretariat in the vital matter of appointments and directives. The Kislovodsk cave meeting did not become public knowledge until December, 1925, at the Fourteenth Party Congress, when Voroshilov revealed that it had occurred, admitted that he had been present, and declared that "only harm, only confusion could come from such a combination." Zinoviev was then compelled to explain the purpose of the meeting and to justify his conduct.

The differences between Zinoviev and Stalin in the autumn of 1923 were temporarily muted by more immediate problems: notably, the discontent among factory workers over wage levels which led to the outbreak of a number of strikes. Even more important was a growing dissatisfaction among certain Party members over the fact that the Party had acquired a tremendous bureaucratic apparatus which the rank and file could not control. There was also some dissatisfaction with the NEP and with the rise of a new entrepreneurial class, which some of the less flexible Party members regarded as a betrayal of the Party's purpose. Others were disturbed over the growing disparity between the lower agricultural prices and the much higher prices of industrial goods (known as the "scissors" crisis—the term being derived from a graphic representation of the two price curves). These various tendencies coalesced in the "For Democratism" group, which demanded the right to form groupings within the Party in order to facilitate meaningful debate of the issues confronting it. In October, 1923, the Oppositionists issued an appeal—the so-called "Declaration of the Forty-Six"—which criticized economic conditions and described the regime within the Party as "utterly intolerable," declaring that the Party had been replaced by a political machine.[25] Among the signers were Pyatakov, Preobrazhensky, Serebryakov, Sapronov, Osinsky, Jacob Naumovich Drobnis, Mikhail Abramovich Rafail, Arkadii Osipovich Alsky, and V. M. Smirnov. Although Trotsky did not sign the declaration, it was clear to all that these were primarily his followers, and it was suspected that he was directing them from behind the scenes. Once again, Kamenev and Zinoviev failed to understand where the real danger lay; once again, they sided with Stalin, their future destroyer.

Although condemning the "Declaration of the Forty-Six," the Central Committee agreed to permit a free discussion within the Party. Trotsky finally made a public pronouncement on December 8, 1923—in the form of a letter to all Moscow borough Party organizations—in which he outlined his "New Course." This letter was designed to explain the vote he had cast in favor of the Central Committee resolution of December 5 condemning bureaucracy in the Party. Adopted unanimously, the resolution had been meant to smooth over the serious disagreements which had developed within the Party. Trotsky's letter of December 8 was an attempt to rally the youth of the Party against the "old guard" in the name of "democracy" and in opposition to bureaucracy and terrorism in the Party. At last, the conflict between Trotsky and Stalin was brought out into the open and the lines drawn. Zinoviev demanded that Trotsky be expelled from the Party, but the calculating Stalin restrained him. Trotsky and his followers would be dealt with at the All-Russian Party Conference which was to meet on January 16-18, 1924, with 128 voting delegates—a conclave packed by the Party machine which Trotsky had now denounced in public.

Stalin's address to the January, 1924, Party Conference was built around the definition of six alleged errors which were committed by Trotsky and which "led to the aggravation of the inner Party struggle." Trotsky's first error was his article of December 8, 1923, which Stalin described as a "new platform opposed to the unanimously adopted resolution of the Central Committee." Stalin accused Trotsky of "going over the head of the Central Committee" and of violating Party discipline.[26] The second error was that Trotsky had "conducted himself equivocally, bluntly ignoring the will of the Party, which wished to know his true position, and diplomatically evading the question . . ." Stalin asked whether Trotsky was for the Central Committee or for the Opposition. He noted that much was said of Trotsky's illness, yet Trotsky had managed to write three articles and publish a pamphlet when all that was required from him was two lines indicating whether he was for or against the Opposition. The third error was that Trotsky had "placed the Party apparatus in opposition to the Party" with the slogan of a struggle against the *apparatchiki* (Party bureaucrats). Stalin declared flatly that "Bolshevism cannot accept the opposition of the Party to the Party apparatus" and that the Party was "unthinkable without the apparatus."

The fourth of the six errors committed by Trotsky consisted in his allegedly having placed the Party youth in opposition to the cadres on the grounds that the latter were in danger of degenerating. Stalin noted that it was amusing "how one of the members of the Central Committee [Trotsky], who only yesterday was fighting against the Bolsheviks hand in hand with the opportunists and Mensheviks, how he now . . . attempts, if only in a conjectural form, to affirm that the cadres of our Party, having been born, matured, and strengthened in the struggle against Menshevism and opportunism . . . find themselves facing degeneration." As Trotsky's fifth error, Stalin cited his plea that the youth of the Party, the students, be regarded as an "infallible barometer" since they had reacted so sharply against bureaucracy in the Party. Stalin, aware that much of Trotsky's support rested among the students of Moscow, suggested that if this were the case, then the doors of the Party should be thrown wide open to the student youth. He accused Trotsky of having taken the formula of the proletarian Party and turned it upside down. Leaning upon Leninism, Stalin referred to the controversy over Party membership at the Second Congress, when Lenin had refused to throw open the door to "nonproletarian elements." Stalin then charged that Trotsky wished to "break with the organizational line of Bolshevism."

Trotsky's sixth and last error, according to Stalin, was his desire to permit "freedom of groupings." Trotsky distinguished between factions and groupings and approved of the ban on the former, while believing that the latter should be permitted. Stalin argued that there was only an external difference between a grouping and a faction, and that Trotsky wished to "legalize factions and, first of all, the faction of Trotsky." He branded Trotsky's assertion that groupings arose because of the bureaucratic regime in the Central Committee as an "un-Marxist approach," since groupings could be attributed to the existence in the country of various economic forms ranging from the "embryonic forms of socialism to the Middle Ages." Stalin also ascribed groupings to the existence of NEP "capitalism" in Soviet Russia and to the tripartite composition of the Party (workers, peasants, and intelligentsia). He implied that Trotsky's position carried with it the destruction of the Party. He noted sarcastically that it was "somewhat amusing" to hear speeches on democracy from Trotsky—that same Trotsky who at the Tenth Congress had wanted to "shake up the trade unions from above" and who now wanted to "shake up the Leninist cadres in the Party." Stalin also noted that, among the Oppositionists, Preobrazhensky had opposed Lenin on the issue of the Treaty of Brest-Litovsk in 1918 and in the trade union discussion, and that Sapronov had called Lenin an "ignoramus."

It was on this occasion that Stalin read to the Oppositionists the secret Point Seven of the Tenth Congress resolution "Concerning the Unity of the Party," which provided for expulsion in the event of a violation of Party discipline. Although critical of the program of Trotsky's Opposition, the resolution referred to it only in quotation marks as if to question its role as a *bona fide* opposition. The resolution also included a passage which emphasized the value of the recent Party-wide discussion, in spite of the "petty-bourgeois deviation" of the Opposition. At the same time, it included an affirmation that "Party unity is assured to a greater extent than ever before," coupling this with a threat to "destroy politically anyone who makes an attempt on the unity of the Party ranks."[27]

Following this serious defeat, Trotsky, who had been running a fever, set off for the Caucasus to recuperate. On January 21, 1924, Lenin died, and the cult of Leninism was born. The bizarre spectacle of an embalmed corpse on permanent display in a mausoleum was soon to give this Communist cult a spurious religious character. Trotsky had no role in the genesis of the cult, although his role as the "devil's advocate" helped its founding.

Trotsky had been informed of Lenin's death as his train stopped in Tbilisi; he later charged that Stalin deliberately misinformed him as to the day of the funeral in order to prevent him from being present. Trotsky proceeded to Sukhum for his rest cure on the advice of the Politburo. Lenin's funeral took place on January 27. On the preceding evening, a singular event had taken place at the memorial session of the Second U.S.S.R. Congress of Soviets: Stalin, astutely grasping the significance of the moment and speaking on behalf of the Party, took a sixfold oath couched in quasi-ecclesiastical language. He swore to: "hold high and preserve in purity the great title of member of the Party . . . guard the unity of our Party like the apple of our eye . . . guard and strengthen the dictatorship of the proletariat . . . strengthen with all our might the union of workers and peasants . . . strengthen and broaden the union of republics . . . [and] keep faith with the principles of the Communist International."[28] In each instance, the vow was prefaced by this phrase: "In leaving us, Comrade Lenin ordained us to . . ." Comrade Lenin, in fact, had left in writing a very different kind of last testament—one aimed directly at the General Secretary who was now assuming the role of Lenin's most faithful pupil.

Stalin was spared the embarrassment of having the Testament published when the Central Committee—meeting in May, 1924, prior to the Thirteenth Congress—decided that the document would not be read to the Congress, but would instead be divulged and appropriately explained only to certain delegates. Ironically, it was Zinoviev who saved Stalin by making the motion that the Testament not be published. Meanwhile, Stalin had strengthened his claim to be *the* true disciple of Lenin. Prior to the Thirteenth Congress, he published his *Foundations of Leninism,* originally prepared as lectures for delivery at Sverdlov University. In an exercise akin to theological exegesis, Stalin employed a catechistical style in which he presented dogmatic answers to his own loaded questions. After defining Leninism as "Marxism of the epoch of imperialism and proletarian revolution," Stalin surveyed its historical roots, method and theory, the dictatorship of the proletariat, the peasant question, the nationality problem, and strategy and tactics. In discussing the so-called "proletarian revolution," he attacked Trotsky's idea of the permanent revolution by contending that Lenin had criticized its adherents for underestimating the role of the peasantry. For this reason, according to Stalin, Lenin regarded the "permanentists" as semi-Mensheviks, since the Mensheviks had also rejected the role of the peasantry.[29] However, Stalin did not on this occasion attack Trotsky by name.

The discussion of the Party in Stalin's *Foundations of Leninism* placed great emphasis upon its organizational aspect, defining it as a "single *system* of these organizations, their formal unification in a single whole, with the subordination of the minority to the majority, with practical decisions obligatory for all members of the Party."[30] In emphasizing the Party as a "unity of will" incompatible with the existence of factions, Stalin had only to cite Lenin's admonition that "whoever weakens, if only in the slightest, the iron discipline of the Party of the proletariat (particularly in the period of its dictatorship) in fact aids the bourgeoisie against the proletariat."[31] This was intended as a warning for those Trotskyite Oppositionists who were to attend the Thirteenth Congress.

It is significant that Stalin dedicated to the "Leninist levy" this, his first effort to systematize and rigidify Lenin's doctrines. This levy resulted in the admission of approximately 250,000 new members to the Party, bringing it to a new high of 440,365 members and 361,439 candidates in 1925. The decision to open the ranks, particularly to workers, was taken at a plenary session of the Central Committee at the end of January, 1924. The Leninist levy was really anti-Leninist in that it broadened the Party membership, whereas Lenin had consistently warned against an excessively large Party. Stalin repeated this warning in an address delivered on June 17, 1924, when he criticized those who wished to increase the membership to 1 or 2 million. At that time, he expressed concern that the Party would not be able to "digest" what it had seized. According to Stalin, 60 per cent of the membership was "politically illiterate" prior to the Leninist levy, and this element had increased to 80 per cent following the levy. Nevertheless, Stalin hailed this influx of members as proof of the Party's "democratic" character.[32] Its

real purpose was to make more human material available to the
Secretariat and, at the same time, to swamp the Oppositionists
led by the reluctant Trotsky.

When the Thirteenth Congress met on May 23-31, 1924,
the Opposition found itself in an even weaker position than it
had been at the January Conference. Trotsky was not even a voting delegate. The triumvirate of Stalin, Zinoviev, and Kamenev
remained united, and Zinoviev demanded that Trotsky recant
his errors. Stalin took the position that Trotsky needed only to
submit to Party discipline without any recantation. When Trotsky
finally decided to address the Congress, he made a conciliatory
statement to the effect that the Party was always right. Stalin,
who was far less critical of Trotsky at this time than Zinoviev
was, gave the impression of good sense and moderation when he
declared that the "Party is not seldom wrong" (*Partiya neredko
oshibaetsya*) and that "Ilyich [Lenin] instructed us to teach the
Party correct leadership on the basis of its own errors."[33] At
the same time, he was unmistakably harsh toward the Opposition in general, threatening it with purging on the grounds that
this was the only means of strengthening the Party. He noted
that "it is no accident" that the Mensheviks and SR's were
sympathizing with the Opposition. Yet, Stalin gave the appearance of being conciliatory toward the Oppositionists when he
declared that their "petty-bourgeois deviation" could be cor-
rected if they did not insist upon clinging to their errors.

Stalin was in a position to make good his threat. He had
succeeded in having the Central Committee increased from forty
to fifty-three members and from seventeen to thirty-four candidate-members. Among the newly promoted members were Lazar
Kaganovich and Stanislav Kosior, two of Stalin's most faithful
lieutenants. More important than the increase in size was the
fact that Stalin would be able to reduce the influence of the
other members of the Politburo—whether temporarily allied
with him or not—by claiming that the Central Committee was
the more significant body. At the Thirteenth Congress, he
announced: the "center of gravity has shifted from the Politburo and the Orgburo to the plenum [plenary session of the
Central Committee]."[34] Stalin noted that between 100 and 120

persons were attending these plenary sessions, which were being
held jointly with the members of the Central Control Commission. In this way, the other members of the Politburo were
gradually reduced to impotence, while Stalin claimed that his
packing of the Central Committee was proof of Party democracy
and declared: "Before our very eyes, there are new people growing and flourishing, tomorrow's leaders of the working class—
in this lies the inestimable importance of our broadened plenary
sessions."[35]

If the Oppositionists and the other members of the Politburo
needed an additional indication of where Stalin was taking the
Party, they could find it in the resolution of the Thirteenth Congress trebling the membership of the Central Control Commission from 50 to 150. Not only were numerous new positions
open to Stalin's followers by way of patronage, but the instrument for "cleansing" the Party was now strengthened immeasurably. The Congress stipulated that seventy of these members
were to be freed from all other duties and to be assigned for
"permanent work" in the Commission and in the Workers' and
Peasants' Inspectorate; fifty members were to be workmen who
would remain at the workbench following their election; and
thirty members were to remain in the principal regional centers
to work with local organs of state and Party control.[36]

Faced with such measures and with the continued—though
declining—unity of the triumvirate, Trotsky was to experience
still another defeat at the Fifth Congress of the Comintern in
June and July of 1924. This was only natural since Zinoviev
was its head and the Communist Party of the Soviet Union
controlled the organization's purse strings. Following this last
defeat, Trotsky set about to publish some of his writings dealing
with the 1917 seizure of power; to these he added a lengthy introduction, *Lessons of October*. The central theme of the
work was that the revolutionary situation is a fleeting phenomenon which must be seized upon and utilized at the proper
moment. In his introduction, Trotsky was critical of Comintern
failures during 1923 in Germany and in Bulgaria. However, the
significance of this work lay in the fact that Trotsky, in discussing the events of 1917, placed great emphasis upon Kamenev's

and Zinoviev's disagreement with Lenin on the advisability of seizing power in November (October by the Julian calendar).

The resurrection by Trotsky of the old "strikebreaker" charges which Lenin had leveled against Kamenev and Zinoviev aroused them to greater fury. Only Stalin benefited from the acrimonious exchange between them and Trotsky. The General Secretary could sit back and observe the scene with satisfaction, while his opponents discredited each other. Now Kamenev and Zinoviev became even more dependent upon Stalin since they required his support, although Lenin's widow also came to their defense. Stalin obliged them with a temporary clean bill of health, but he did this in his own best interest, his immediate task being to discredit Trotsky totally. On November 26, 1924, *Pravda* published the text of an address which Stalin had delivered a week earlier under the title "Trotskyism or Leninism?" Stalin was not entirely an innocent bystander, since Trotsky, without mentioning him by name, had alluded to the disagreements between Lenin and the editors of *Pravda* (then published under Stalin's direction) prior to Lenin's return to Russia in 1917. Stalin claimed that the disagreements of 1917 were not important and accused Trotsky of "rejoicing at the misfortunes of others" and of claiming incorrectly that the Bolsheviks were almost two parties in 1917.

More important, as far as Stalin was concerned, were the differences which plagued the Party in 1924. The "legends" which he accused Trotsky of circulating had as their alleged purpose the "substitution of Trotskyism for Leninism."[37] Stalin defined Trotskyism in terms of three criteria: the theory of permanent revolution; lack of faith in "Bolshevik partyness, in its monolithic nature, in its enmity toward opportunistic elements"; and lack of confidence in the leaders of Bolshevism and an attempt to discredit and "uncrown" them. Stalin quoted from an anti-Leninist letter which Trotsky had written to Chkheidze in April, 1913, in which he had declared that Leninism was "built on lies and falsifications" (because Lenin had just expropriated the title of Trotsky's Vienna newspaper, *Pravda*). Trotsky's August Bloc of 1912 was recalled by Stalin, along with Lenin's condemnation of it as Liquidationist. The theory of permanent revolution was denounced as ignoring the poor peasantry of Russia and as being designed to deprive the Russian proletariat of "its ally." Now it was Stalin's turn to read Trotsky one "lesson of October" which the latter had ignored: namely, that collaboration between Trotsky and the Bolsheviks was possible only if he abandoned his "old baggage" and subscribed to Leninism.[38] The only difficulty was that Leninism had now become a monopoly of the Party's General Secretary.

Trotsky's *Lessons of October* not only revealed his vulnerability but also made it possible for Stalin, with the support of Kamenev and Zinoviev, to have him removed from his post as Commissar of War (Chairman of the Military Council) in January, 1925. With Trotsky substantially weakened, Stalin now embarked upon a course which won him the support of three other members of the Politburo—Bukharin, Rykov, and Tomsky. The April, 1925, Party Conference made an effort to appeal to the "middle peasants"* by easing their tax burden and removing certain restrictions on the hiring of agricultural labor and on the accumulation of capital. Stalin justified these measures on the grounds that socialism could not be established in Russia without peasant support. Bukharin, the leading advocate of this policy, argued that the peasantry should be permitted to prosper so that it could pay for the industrialization of the country and provide food for the new cities. While Stalin appeared to be in substantial agreement with Bukharin, he did have some reservations regarding the danger of the development of a rural bourgeoisie. Kamenev and Zinoviev opposed the decisions of the Conference, and within six months the break between them and Stalin was to become irreparable.

Zinoviev was so incensed by the new rightist peasant orientation that he likened Bukharin to the Czarist minister Peter A. Stolypin, who had attempted to create a numerous and prosperous landowning peasantry as a social basis underlying a limited Russian autocracy.[39] The debate over what was alleged to be a "pro-kulak" policy came into the open at the Fourteenth Congress, which met on December 18-31, 1925, resulting in the

---

* A "middle peasant" was defined as one who neither hired laborers nor hired himself out.

emergence of a new quadrumvirate in which Stalin was far stronger vis-à-vis Bukharin, Rykov, and Tomsky than he had been in the now-dissolved triumvirate. Stalin had attempted to prevent a full airing of the controversies which plagued the Central Committee; he proposed an agreement with the Opposition on December 15 under which members of the Politburo would not speak against each other at the Congress, certain issues would not be discussed, and Zinoviev's Leningrad Party organization would receive a position in the Secretariat.[40] However, Zinoviev would not be bought off; aided by Lenin's widow and by Kamenev and Finance Commissar Sokol'nikov, he insisted upon a debate of all outstanding issues confronting the Party.

The report of the Central Committee, delivered to the Fourteenth Congress by Stalin, did not indicate that he was seeking a quarrel, although he obviously was prepared for one. Stalin donned the robes of a theoretician when he devoted a substantial part of his address to the international situation and expounded five categories of "contradictions." It was on this occasion that Stalin advanced the notion of "peaceful coexistence," which he viewed as a temporary condition resulting from a "partial or temporary stabilization of capitalism." While admitting that there was an ebb in the revolutionary tide in Western Europe, he insisted that the stabilization of capitalism had developed from a "rotten" basis. At a time when Stalin was presumably rejecting the notion of permanent revolution, his report had much to say on the existence of "two camps" (the non-Soviet camp headed by the United States and Great Britain) and on the "capitalistic encirclement." According to Stalin, the Dawes Plan was "pregnant" with a new European war.[41]

Stalin flattered his audience and the country by arguing that peaceful coexistence had been made necessary by the fact that the establishment of the U.S.S.R. had deprived capitalism of one-sixth of the earth's land surface. Europe, said Stalin, required peace in order to obtain access to Russian markets and raw materials. Although no detailed plan was announced, it was made clear that the Soviet Union would become economically self-sufficient and acquire its own industry. At the same time, Stalin defended the policy adopted in April, 1925, of encourag-

ing the middle peasantry on the grounds that this group constituted a majority, and he declared that attempts to circulate
statistics to the contrary were "worse than counterrevolution."[42]

This defense of the Party's policy toward the peasantry was
appropriately accompanied by quotations from Lenin. Indeed,
the heated debate centered on the question of who was the
better Leninist. Kamenev and Zinoviev launched an all-out attack
against Stalin and Bukharin. This brought into the open the
entire story of the September, 1923, Kislovodsk cave meeting
which had been directed against Stalin's control over the Secretariat. Kamenev created an uproar when he denounced the
emergence of a leader (*vozhd'*) and questioned Stalin's qualifications and worthiness. The General Secretary's followers immediately staged a noisy demonstration on his behalf. The die was
now cast. Earlier, Krupskaya had attempted to conciliate the
minority and Stalin's majority by noting pointedly that the
majority may not always be right: "In the history of our Party,
there were congresses in which the majority was wrong."[43] She
cited as an example the Stockholm Congress of 1906, when the
Mensheviks had been in a majority. Kalinin made the following
retort: "The idea that the truth remains the truth is admissible
in a philosophical club, but in the Party the decisions of the
Congress are obligatory also upon those who doubt the correctness of the decision."[44]

Stalin contented himself with pointing out an alleged error
in Krupskaya's assertion that the NEP was "in substance, capitalism." This, said Stalin, was "regular nonsense"—although,
on this occasion, he did beg Krupskaya's pardon before uttering
the statement.[45] He justified the extension of the NEP on the
grounds that Lenin had initiated the policy and had known full
well what dangers it contained. He referred to the Oppositionists
derisively as "cave people" (recalling the Kislovodsk cave meeting organized by Zinoviev). He accused Kamenev of approaching the question of aid to the peasantry as a "liberal" and not
as a Marxist, and charged him with engaging in "slander against
the Party" when he contended that it was pursuing a pro-kulak
policy. Stalin accused Zinoviev of having deviated in underestimating the middle peasantry and denounced him as a vacil-

lator. This denunciation was prompted by the fact that Zinoviev had recently paid lip service to the policy of an alliance with the middle peasant, but Stalin cast doubt on the firmness of his profession. Nor did he hesitate to remind the Congress of the "errors of certain comrades" (meaning Kamenev and Zinoviev) who had violated decisions of the Central Committee and who were hardly worthy of criticizing Bukharin's far less important error of telling the peasants to "enrich yourselves"—a formulation which Stalin himself never approved, although he was now in alliance with Bukharin.

Stalin's success was due largely to his effective mask of moderation. Thus Trotsky, who remained aloof from the Kamenev-Zinoviev opposition at the Fourteenth Congress, was not the subject of any of Stalin's attacks. Stalin revealed how Kamenev and Zinoviev had wanted to oust Trotsky from the Politburo and the Party and how this had been prevented, although Trotsky was removed from the post of Commissar of War. He then went on to explain, more prophetically than he realized, that "we did not agree with Zinoviev and Kamenev because we knew that a policy of head chopping is fraught with great dangers for the Party, that the method of head chopping, the method of bloodletting—and they were demanding blood—is dangerous, is contagious: today they cut off one, tomorrow another, the day after tomorrow a third—what will be left of the Party?"[46] Thus spoke the General Secretary who was to become the greatest of all head choppers. Yet, he was able to mislead and deceive his new allies of the Right, to flatter them into thinking that they were indispensable to him, and to pose as the advocate of a "collective leadership" reposing in the Central Committee. At the same time, he declared to Kamenev and Zinoviev that "the Party desires unity"—with them if they so wished, or without them if that was their choice.

This made it clear that Stalin would define the conditions under which Kamenev and Zinoviev, the leaders of the so-called "New Opposition," would remain within the Party's leadership— or even within the Party itself. There was also the mute testimony furnished by the enlargement of the Central Committee from fifty-three to sixty-three full members and from thirty-four to forty-three candidate-members. The Central Control Commission was increased from 150 to 163 members. Zinoviev remained in the Politburo, as did Trotsky—although obviously on sufferance—while Kamenev was demoted to candidate's rank for having attacked Stalin at the Fourteenth Congress. Sokol'nikov was dropped from the ranks of the Politburo candidates. Voroshilov, Molotov, and Kalinin became full members of the Politburo as a reward for having spearheaded the attack on Kamenev and Zinoviev; in this way, the full membership of the Politburo was increased to nine. Stalin and his three new cohorts could, with the aid of the Right (Bukharin, Rykov, and Tomsky), outvote Zinoviev and Trotsky. Significantly, the five candidate-members included—in addition to the demoted Kamenev—the Stalinists Rudzutak, Dzierzynski, and Petrovsky.

Stalin's victory at the Fourteenth Congress was followed by the publication early in 1926 of his *Problems of Leninism*—an attack on Kamenev and Zinoviev that was dedicated to the Leningrad Party organization, from which the latter was being removed as a leader. Trotsky was not criticized in this work, since he had been relatively quiet during 1925 and had even accommodated Stalin by falsely denying the existence of Lenin's Testament in September of that year, following its publication in Max Eastman's book, *Since Lenin Died*. During this period, Trotsky had immersed himself in administrative matters pertaining to industry and electrification, just as Malenkov was to do exactly thirty years later when deprived of the Premiership by Khrushchev. It was only in the spring of 1926, following the April plenary session of the Central Committee, that Trotsky, Kamenev, and Zinoviev decided to join forces against Stalin. By this decision, Trotsky only compromised himself further since he was now allying himself with two men who had been his worst detractors, and Stalin needed only to quote what they had said about each other in the preceding five years in order to make them appear ridiculous. Under this "unprincipled deal" and "mutual 'amnesty' at the expense of the Party"—as Stalin characterized it—Kamenev and Zinoviev adopted Trotsky's economic program, and he, in turn, forgave them their sins for which he had denounced them in *Lessons of October*.

As in the past, Stalin now employed organizational measures against the Oppositionist bloc. In February, 1926, Zinoviev was replaced as Leningrad province committee secretary by Sergei Kirov, and the entire local leadership was also replaced. In April, Yevdokimov—the one Zinovievite to be included in the Secretariat after the Fourteenth Congress, as a concession to the Leningrad Opposition—was transferred "at his own request" and replaced by the Stalinist Nikolai Shvernik. In July, 1926, at a plenary session of the Central Committee, even greater changes occurred when Lashevich, a follower of Zinoviev, was removed from his post as deputy to Voroshilov in the War Commissariat on the grounds that he had tried to organize support for the Oppositionist bloc within the army. Zinoviev was expelled from the Politburo at the same time for using the Comintern Executive Committee against Stalin; he was replaced in the Politburo by Rudzutak. The July, 1926, Central Committee plenary session also increased the number of Politburo candidate-members from five to eight, adding Ordzhonikidze, Andrei Andreyevich Andreyev, Kirov, Mikoyan, and Kaganovich to the three incumbents (N. A. Uglanov, Petrovsky, and Kamenev).

The application of organizational pressure prompted the Oppositionist bloc to sue for peace. On October 16, 1926, its members announced their willingness to submit to Party discipline (although with some mental reservations) in the interests of preventing a complete break. Stalin, instead of convening the annual Party congress late in 1926, decided to call a conference which met from October 26 to November 3 and was attended by only 194 voting delegates and more than three times as many nonvoting delegates. The Oppositionists had capitulated in order to gain some time, but Stalin was in no mood to show them any mercy.

He heaped scorn and ridicule upon their heads and branded them the "Social Democratic deviation." He announced that the two groups of Trotskyites and Zinovievites had strength so long as they fought each other, but once they entered into a bloc they "castrated themselves."[47] He cruelly quoted Lenin on Trotsky, Trotsky on Lenin, Trotsky on Kamenev and Zinoviev,

and Zinoviev and Kamenev on Trotsky.* The charge of "Social
Democratic deviation" was based on the contention that the
Oppositionists were denying the socialist character of the Russian Revolution in questioning the possibility of building "socialism in one country." As proof that Lenin believed this possible,
Stalin cited his teacher's statements at the beginning of the NEP
which indicated that he regarded that policy as a step toward
the establishment of socialism in Russia. He had also found an
appropriate quotation in Lenin's 1915 article "Concerning the
Slogan of a United States of Europe." Stalin was particularly
severe with Karl Radek, well known for his rather heavy humor,
who had asked—in something more than jest—whether the
theory of socialism in one country, if valid, might not permit
the establishment of socialism "in one county" or "in a single
street."[48]

Stalin countered by demanding less chatter and more construction. He insisted that the Oppositionists capitulate unconditionally and told them to listen as he read them eight demands
concerning what the Party would not tolerate. In concluding, he
again turned on Zinoviev, recalling that he had once boasted
of his ability to put his ear to the ground and hear the footsteps
of history; Stalin said that this might be true, although Zinoviev
seemed unable to hear certain "details"—such as that the Party
had "long ago turned its back on the Opposition."[49] Stalin
offered his opponents the following advice: "Honorable Oppositionists, have your ears treated." Ridicule alone was not enough,
and Zinoviev was shortly compelled to resign the Chairmanship
of the Comintern. A joint plenary session of the Central Committee and Central Control Commission, meeting on October 23,
1926, had removed Trotsky from full membership and Kamenev
from candidacy in the Politburo. In Trotsky's place, the Stalinist

---

* Later—in the January 21, 1932, issue of *Pravda*—Stalin published an
article said to have been written by Lenin early in 1911 in which Trotsky
is referred to contemptuously as "Iudushka" (Little Judas). The sobriquet
was apparently taken from the novel of Mikhail E. Saltykov-Shchedrin,
The Golovlev Family, in which the character Porfiry Golovlev bears this
nickname because of his unmitigated hypocrisy. (*See* Lenin, *Sochineniya*
[4th ed.], XVII, 25. This article is not to be found in the three earlier
editions of Lenin's works.)

Valerian Kuibyshev was elected; he had served his master well as Chairman of the Central Control Commission and had expressed his adulation for him at the Fourteenth Congress when he declared that only Stalin was capable of leading the Party "from victory to victory." Another Stalinist, Stanislav Kosior, replaced Kamenev in the Politburo. Ordzhonikidze left the Politburo to serve Stalin as Chairman of the Central Control Commission, and his seat was taken by Vlas Chubar'.

The final defeat of the Oppositionist bloc came during 1927, when Zinoviev and Trotsky decided to attribute the Soviet failure in China to Stalin's policies, thus attempting to discredit him. The violent break between the Kuomintang, led by Chiang Kai-shek, and the Chinese Communists was regarded by the Oppositionists as proof of the incorrectness of Stalin's advice to the Communists to enter the Kuomintang as individuals. For his part, Stalin merely cited Lenin's position that temporary alliances between Communists and the so-called "nationalist bourgeoisie" of colonial and semicolonial countries were permissible. Yet, in spite of the fact that Stalin had miscalculated in China by assuming that Chiang Kai-shek would serve as a willing tool of the Communists in 1927, the Oppositionists were unable to unseat him with their demand that soviets be established in China.* In large part, their failure was due to Stalin's control of all media of information (except word of mouth) and to his firm entrenchment.

The last desperate step of the Oppositionists was taken in the autumn of 1927 when they resorted to secret meetings in homes and to several large public meetings in order to take their case "to the workers." The public meetings were, almost without exception, broken up by hecklers and strong-arm men in the service of the Party machine. Stalin had given Zinoviev and Trotsky what was to be his final ultimatum on the occasion of the joint plenary session of the Central Committee and Central Control Commission early in August, 1927. On that occa-

---

* Neither Stalin nor Trotsky had any firsthand knowledge of China. They viewed it in terms of Russian developments—Stalin seeing China as possessing "feudal vestiges" and a mercantile class, while Trotsky emphasized the rise of capitalism and the growth of a Chinese proletariat.

sion, he demanded "peace and not a temporary truce" which
would only sharpen the struggle in the future.

The deterioration of Trotsky's and Zinoviev's positions in
1927 can be understood only in terms of the war scare and
the false threat of foreign intervention which they helped nourish and which Stalin cynically employed to create a controlled
panic for the purpose of provoking the Opposition. Trotsky had
unwisely exposed himself in a letter which he wrote to Ordzhonikidze, Chairman of the Central Control Commission, on July 11,
1927. In this letter, he expounded his disastrous Clemenceau
thesis: in the event of war, he argued, the Oppositionists would
conduct themselves as Georges Clemenceau did in 1917, when
the Germans were only 80 kilometers from Paris and he attacked
the French Government for its failure to prosecute the war,
assumed the Premiership himself, and led the country to victory.
Trotsky argued that it was not "defeatism" to insist that the
"political line of the ignorant and unscrupulous cribbers must
be swept out like rubbish—namely, in the interests of the victory
of the workers' state."[50] In response, Stalin referred to Trotsky
as "this operatic Clemenceau" and pointed out that the "rubbish" to which he had referred was the "majority of the Party,
the majority of the Central Committee, the majority of the
Government." Although Stalin minimized the weight of the
Opposition—"this little group in which the leaders outnumber
the army"—he still hinted at treason and insisted upon its total
capitulation, declaring that anyone who really believed in the
"unconditional defense of our country" would not have written
as Trotsky had.

The conditional capitulation—announced on August 8, 1927
—merely served as a prelude to the final unequal round in this
protracted and verbose struggle. The illegal meetings and the
use of a clandestine printing shop, which constituted the last
effort of the Opposition, led to the expulsion of Zinoviev and
Trotsky from the Central Committee on October 23, 1927. All
that remained for the Oppositionists was to "go to the streets"
on the occasion of the tenth anniversary of the seizure of power,
on November 7, 1927. When this was attempted in Moscow,
the Trotskyite demonstrators had their placards (denouncing the

bureaucracy, the kulaks, and the NEP) torn to pieces by the
Central Committee's representatives. Trotsky's automobile was
shot at, and one of its windows was shattered. This demonstration was the last straw as far as Stalin was concerned. On
November 12, Trotsky and Zinoviev were expelled from the
Party. On November 16, Adolf Yoffe, one of Trotsky's closest
associates, committed suicide.

All that remained was to convene the Fifteenth Congress
during the first half of December, 1927. On that occasion, 898
voting delegates and 771 nonvoting delegates assembled to vilify
the doomed Oppositionists. The Congress voted to exclude from
the Party seventy-five members of the Trotskyite Opposition and
twenty-three followers of Sapronov. The expelled Trotskyites
included Kamenev, Lashevich, Pyatakov, Radek, Rakovsky,
Rafail, Safarov, and Smilga. This was the exclusive victory of
the apparatus which had been created by Stalin as his own
instrument in the intra-Party struggle. It had at last equated
itself with the Party; it had become the Party. Whoever challenged the supremacy of the machine hereafter would be branded
an "oppositionist" or "factionist" and would have invoked against
him Lenin's portentous Tenth Congress resolution "Concerning
the Unity of the Party," with its provision for expulsion. Stalin
had only to quote to the Fifteenth Congress Lenin's previous
injunction: "We need no opposition now . . . we have had
enough opposition, it is now time to put the lid on opposition."[51]
It was now only a question of the kind of "lid" which would be
fashioned by the General Secretary and his cohorts.

CHAPTER VII

STALINISM

We are not liberals. For us, the interests of the Party are above formal democratism.

> —Stalin, at the Fourteenth Party Congress
> (December 23, 1925).

But what is democracy in the Party? Democracy for whom? If by democracy is meant freedom for a pair or two of intellectuals who are separated from the revolution to chatter without end, have their press organ, etc., then we do not need such "democracy" because it is democracy for an insignificant minority breaking the will of the vast majority.

> —Stalin, at the Fifteenth Party Congress
> (December 3, 1927).

A revolution is undoubtedly the most authoritarian thing there is, an act whereby one part of the population imposes its will upon the other part by means of *rifles, bayonets, and cannons—all very authoritarian means*; and the victorious party must perforce *maintain its rule by means of the terror* which its arms inspire in the reactionaries.

> —Lenin, quoting Engels on the Paris Commune, in "The Proletarian Revolution and the Renegade Kautsky" (1918).

The policies and practices which comprised the reign of Stalin and bear his name constitute a phenomenon which was, in part, singularly consistent and yet contradictory. Stalinism created in the Soviet Union a heavy industry—at a cost which sane men would regard as prohibitive—but denied to the bulk of the population the fruits of this herculean effort in terms of consumer goods and made the queue for food purchases a national institution. Stalinism almost brought Soviet Russia to defeat in 1941-42, but by 1945 it had surpassed even the dreams of the Czars in achieving for the country a status and power position of the first rank in the international arena. While based initially upon a borrowing of technical knowledge from the West and the hiring of foreign technical and scientific personnel, Stalinism also led to the lowering of the iron curtain in the post–World War II period in an effort to isolate its subjects from the influences of the outside world. Stalinism was to proclaim the liquidation of "exploiting" classes in the Soviet Union by fiat in 1936, but it created instead a society possessing numerous strata and marked income differentials. It launched vicious campaigns against religious beliefs and practices in the late 1920's and the 1930's—only to arrive at a *modus vivendi* with the Russian Orthodox Church in September, 1943, while continuing to advocate atheism. Stalinism claimed to represent the "international proletariat" at the same time that it based itself on a revival of Russian chauvinism and cruelly punished any genuine defense of the national identity of its non-Russian subject peoples. It permitted and even encouraged Russian nationalism, while condemning that of the non-Russians as "bourgeois nationalism."

Despite these and many other contradictions and zigzags in Stalinism, certain of its salient characteristics do permit a definition of the phenomenon. Stalinism meant, above all else, the victory of the organization man—of the Party apparatus.[1] Stalinism spawned a titanic bureaucracy of state and Party, together with a vast hierarchy in which no one could be certain of his position from one hour to the next. It led to the creation of a police state without parallel and to the cultivation of paranoia on a mass scale—ultimately reaching the depths of depravity in the nightmarish Yezhovshchina (named after Nikolai Yezhov, the head of the NKVD) in 1937-38. Stalinism presented the spectacle of a cult, calling itself the "workers' party" and engaging in the adulation of a living mortal on a scale which rivaled that of the Pharaohs and the Roman emperors. The personal dictatorship and the cult of the despot which issued from the so-called "dictatorship of the proletariat" ended with the *vozhd'* living in fearful isolation in the Kremlin, not deigning to have a look at the country or to familiarize himself with objective conditions, but still retaining a sufficiently tight control over his army of subordinates.

The origins of this system were outlined in the preceding chapter. Intellectually, Stalin's opponents were his superiors, although in due time he was able to give the appearance of being a theoretician. Stalin's real forte lay in his ability to manipulate men—including his rivals—and to harness the ambitions of his own subordinates. He proved himself to be a master of intrigue, dividing and misleading both his opponents and his allies. Adept at dissimulation, he was also aided by his rivals' errors. From the beginning, Zinoviev and Kamenev had miscalculated in thinking that Trotsky was more dangerous than Stalin. When they allied themselves with Trotsky in 1926, it was far too late, and Stalin already enjoyed the support of the Right wing in the Politburo—with which he could quickly dispense once he had removed Trotsky from the scene by exile and compelled Kamenev and Zinoviev to recant their heresy as a condition for their readmission to the Party. Stalin was also aided by Trotsky's temperament and by the strange ailment, with its inexplicable high temperature, that afflicted Trotsky during much of the struggle for power.

In addition to the more important question of who was to dominate the Party, the Stalin-Trotsky controversy centered on the issue of how socialism could be established in the Soviet Union. Trotsky, in advocating his old doctrine of permanent revolution, insisted that Soviet socialism could be wrought only through further revolutionary activity and the establishment of Soviet-type regimes in Western Europe. Seeking some kind of substantial weapon to use against Trotsky, Stalin gradually drifted to the extreme of the opposite position and ended by asserting that it was possible to build "socialism in one country." However, in April, 1924, Stalin had declared flatly in his *Foundations of Leninism* (at the end of Part Three) that the "final victory of socialism" could not be achieved in one country, but would require the "victory of the revolution in at least several countries." By December 17, 1924, Stalin had modified his position to indicate that socialism could be achieved in one country, although he did add a few face-saving qualifications. The formula "socialism in one country" was first adopted at the Fourteenth Party Conference in April, 1925, in a resolution dealing with the Comintern and the international situation.[2] In advocating "socialism in one country" without committing himself as to the tempo with which it was to be established or the cost involved, Stalin nevertheless was adopting a position which appeared to be far more realistic than that of Trotsky at a time when the revolutionary tide in Europe was ebbing and capitalism apparently was becoming stabilized.

Stalin's doctrine was also somewhat flattering to the Russian ego: it stressed self-reliance and the Russian ability to "go it alone" without waiting for the more advanced and more numerous industrial labor forces of Western Europe to place themselves completely at the disposal of the Russian pundits of Marxism-Leninism. Conversely, Trotsky's position implied that the Russians could not "go it alone" and that the Russian Revolution would stagnate if it did not burst from its confines and sweep all of Europe. The failure of Communism in the Europe of the mid-1920's made Trotsky's position less tenable. Yet, in spite of the fierceness of the Stalin-Trotsky controversy, there was more to unite these two men from a doctrinal point of view than to divide them. Stalin never rejected Trotsky's thesis regarding the need for a Communist world victory. Both continued to believe in the permanence of world revolution—indeed, their disagreement was over tactics and methods and not over ultimate goals.

Stalin made this clear in his address to the Fifteenth Party Conference on November 1, 1926. In discussing the possibility of constructing socialism in the Soviet Union, Stalin asked rhetorically whether it could be regarded as the "complete and final victory." He answered firmly in the negative and then proceeded to raise the specter of a foreign intervention aimed at restoring the old order. Stalin warned:

> We do not live on an island. We live in a capitalistic encirclement. This circumstance—that we are building socialism and in this way are revolutionizing the workers of the capitalistic countries—cannot but elicit hatred and enmity from the entire capitalist world. To think that the capitalist

world can view with equanimity our successes on the economic front, successes revolutionizing the working class of the entire world, means to succumb to an illusion. Consequently, so long as we remain in the capitalistic encirclement, so long as the proletariat has not won at least in a series of countries, we cannot consider our victory as final . . . For this reason, in order to win definitely, it is necessary that we strive for the replacement of the present capitalistic encirclement by the socialist encirclement, that we strive for the victory of the proletariat in at least a few more countries . . . That is why we view the victory of socialism in our country not as an end in itself, not as something self-sufficient, but as an aid, as a means, as a path to the victory of the proletarian revolution in other countries.[3]

Proceeding from this assumption, Stalin argued persuasively that Trotsky's denial of the possibility of building "socialism in one country" actually constituted a retreat from Communist world revolution. Thus, Stalin insisted that Trotsky's doctrine of permanent revolution was "objectively" a betrayal of what it professed to stand for.

This kind of dialectical legerdemain, by which Trotsky's permanent proletarian revolution became a permanent reaction, could be accomplished only through the very substantial enlargement of the Party membership which was to become one of the principal characteristics of Stalinism. Yet, the great sin—if we are to believe what Lenin said at the Second Congress in 1903—was to broaden the membership of the Party excessively and to open its doors to "nonproletarian elements." In the end, this is precisely what occurred under Stalin, the self-styled "Lenin of today." Beginning with the Leninist levy, Stalin admitted to membership tens of thousands of ordinary workingmen; but the industrialization of the country and the increased demand for managerial personnel soon removed many of these new members from the proletarian ranks. However, the appeal exercised in its time by Stalin's "proletarianizing" of the Party and by his demi-myth of maintaining "ties with the masses" should not be underestimated.

Stalin's departure from the Leninist norm of a numerically

rather small party should be viewed only in terms of the total balance between what Stalinism inherited from Leninism and what it contributed by way of innovation. In the period of "de-Stalinization" following Stalin's death—as among ex-Stalinists and Trotskyites in an earlier day—it was fashionable to stress the alleged distinctions between Leninism and Stalinism. These differences included the "cult of the person" as practiced in honor of Stalin—something which the more modest Lenin would undoubtedly have found to be repulsive. The cult had its beginning in 1925, when Tsaritsyn was renamed Stalingrad; on the other hand, Petrograd had not been renamed in honor of Lenin until after the latter's death. Lenin had little more than contempt for Russia's past. Stalin, in the end, glorified this past, made a hero out of Ivan the Terrible, and buttressed his regime with the psychological props of Russian chauvinism. Another distinction lay in Stalin's eagerness to shed blood within the Party in the 1930's, contrasted with Lenin's reluctance to do so except in a case such as that of the police spy Roman Malinovsky.[4] Lenin appeared to believe in annual Party congresses and, for the most part, welcomed and enjoyed a lively debate, although democratic centralism, that ingenious device for muting discordant views, was his work. Stalin consistently violated the statutory provisions regarding the frequency of Party congresses: he permitted more than thirteen years to elapse between the Eighteenth and Nineteenth Congresses.

These differences, significant though they may be, are eclipsed by the Leninist heritage to Stalinism. Stalin obtained from Lenin the centralist, antifactional conception of the Party, as well as the Tenth Congress resolution on Party unity, with its provision for expulsion. Stalin inherited from Lenin the principle of periodic purges of the Party membership, and it was Lenin who established the Central Control Commission which proved so useful to Stalin. The practice of enlarging the Central Committee, which Stalin employed for his own personal advantage, had actually been initiated by Lenin, under whom the membership increased from fifteen members and eight candidates in 1918 to twenty-seven members and nineteen candidates in 1922. Stalin's frequent use of the practice of co-optation of members to the

Central Committee in place of election by the Party Congress was based upon solid precedent: Lenin had Stalin co-opted to the Central Committee in 1912. Both men employed the threat to resign—Lenin in 1918, and Stalin in 1924 and 1932.

Both Lenin and Stalin invoked the argument of capitalistic encirclement and the bogey of a restoration of the White Guards in order to throttle their critics within the Party. Both men were outspoken, bitter, and heartless in polemics, headstrong and self-righteous. Both believed in the ultimate victory of Communism on a world-wide scale, and in the use of strategic retreat and maneuver in order to attain this goal. Lenin's obsession with political orthodoxy and doctrinal loyalty made it easy for Stalin to carry the process to its logical outcome: the shedding of blood within the Party. Lenin had never hesitated about shedding the blood of the "class enemy"; he had believed also that enemies would attempt to infiltrate the Party's ranks. Once it was conceded that the class enemy or "inimical elements" (in other words, anyone who questioned the general line of the Party as set down by the Secretariat) had penetrated the Party's membership, it was relatively easy for Stalin to pose as the righteous executioner. Thus, Lenin provided the basic assumptions which— applied by Stalin and developed to their logical conclusion— culminated in the great purges.

Indeed, purges became the panoply of Stalinism. Originally satisfied with expelling oppositionists and sending some of their number into exile following the Fifteenth Congress in December, 1927, Stalin was ultimately to demand the blood of everyone who had ever had a sustained disagreement with him. The number of "dissidents" grew as Stalin changed his position with amazing rapidity. His victory at the Fifteenth Congress was aided by, although not dependent upon, his alliance with the Right, led by Bukharin, Rykov (Lenin's successor as Premier), and Tomsky, the trade union chief. The "super-industrialists" of the Trotskyite-Zinovievite Oppositionist bloc, whose spokesman was Preobrazhensky, were expelled from the Party.[5] The Right thought that it had now obtained from Stalin a clear commitment to pursue a slow policy of industrialization, to be financed through the increased agricultural output prompted by concessions to the peasantry. Thinking that they could take Stalin at his word, members of the Right blithely joined in the attack upon the Trotskyite-Zinovievite Left Opposition at the Fifteenth Congress.

The resolution on "socialist construction" adopted unanimously at the Fifteenth Congress was deliberately vague and said nothing about the degree and tempo of industrialization, the cost involved, or the source from which the revenue was to be derived. It merely empowered the Central Committee to prepare a draft of the First Five-Year Plan for submission to the next Congress of Soviets meeting in 1928. In agriculture, the Fifteenth Congress had condemned the Trotskyite-Zinovievite Opposition for its hostility toward the middle peasant and private agriculture; the resolution paid lip service to collectivization, to the establishment of state farms, and to the amalgamation of small, uneconomical holdings; but it did not provide for the all-out war against the kulak and the middle peasant which Stalin was to initiate shortly.

The first three months of 1928 passed rather quietly in the Party. The beginning of the break between Stalin and the right came following the joint plenary session of the Central Committee and Central Control Commission which was held on April 6-11, 1928. This meeting was concerned primarily with agriculture and more specifically with the decline of grain deliveries to the state, which had resulted in a deficit of 130 million poods (2,340,000 short tons) by January, 1928. The Party admitted that the decline in grain deliveries could be attributed to the small amount of industrial goods available for sale to the peasants. Grain surpluses existed, but the peasant had little incentive to sell, since the price offered by the state was low, there was much distrust of the currency and state organs of credit, and the "goods famine" made it difficult to purchase anything with the proceeds from grain sales. The kulaks (or wealthier peasants) were accused of combining with the upper ranks of the middle peasants and with the Nepmen speculators in order to drive up the price of grain and break the Government's price policy by withholding grain from the state procurement agencies.

The Party interpreted this as a sign that capitalism had become too strong in the countryside and that a campaign would have to be launched against the kulak. However, Stalin made a false promise when he stated that "only enemies of the Soviet regime can think of the abolition of the NEP."[6] An ominous note crept in after the April, 1928, plenary session when Stalin complained of the overabundance of small peasant households (about 25 million), which he regarded as individually inadequate and primitive. He contended that fertilizer, farm machinery, and agronomy could be introduced only into large-scale agriculture. The solution proposed by Stalin was the establishment of huge collective and state farms, composed of the poor and middle peasantry, aimed against the successful larger-scale individual farmer or kulak.[7] In other words, collective farms were to be established, the kulak was to be combatted, but the NEP was to be miraculously retained at the same time.

Another ominous note which marred the first months of 1928 was the so-called "Shakhty trial," in which approximately fifty engineers in the Donets Basin, including three Germans, were arrested for allegedly having attempted to retard the country's economic development, especially its coal production. The sabotage, supposedly carried on for five years under the very eyes of the Soviet police and security organs, allegedly included the flooding of mines, the deliberate mining of veins poor in coal, and the destruction of machinery. This first of a lengthy series of show trials to which the country and the world were to be treated had as its purpose the perpetuation of a "state of siege" psychology and a preoccupation with enemies both internal and external—characteristics that were also inherited from Leninism. It was an obvious extension of Stalin's 1927 war scare which he had so effectively employed against the Trotskyite-Zinovievite Opposition. By attributing alleged sabotage to "international capital," Stalin was preparing the groundwork for the establishment of an imaginary linkage between the foreign enemies of the Soviet regime and past and future oppositionists.

Since 1925, Stalin had been talking like Bukharin and had defended the latter against attacks by the Trotskyite-Zinovievite Opposition. Bukharin's position, which stressed the financing of industrialization by providing an incentive for the peasantry to produce tremendous surpluses, was championed by Stalin until the Left Opposition had been disposed of. If Stalin were to be believed, the principal errors of the Left Opposition lay in its refusal to support the alliance between the industrial workers and the poor and middle peasantry and in its insistence that the NEP be terminated. The break between Stalin and the Right, which began in 1928 and deepened in 1929, did not arise over any disagreement concerning the desirability of collectivized, large-scale agriculture or over the policy of favoring the kulak (although Bukharin was soon accused of being too conciliatory toward the kulak). Everyone agreed that large-scale agriculture and state ownership were preferable to small holdings, but disagreement was to arise over questions of timing and tempo.

Stalin had accused the Left Opposition of desiring too rapid an industrialization; the Rights were to be accused of wanting industry to be developed at too slow a pace. It was not before mid-October of 1928 that Stalin publicly indicated the danger of a Right opposition. Prior to this, as at the July Central Committee plenary session, Stalin spoke out of both sides of his mouth. He advocated a campaign against the kulak, but denied that the Party intended to intensify the class struggle in the villages, since that would lead to civil war, which the Party wished to avoid.[8] At the same time that he argued in this manner on behalf of the advantages of collectivized agriculture, he criticized those who thought that the "individual peasant household had exhausted itself, that it was not worth supporting." "These people," said Stalin, "have nothing in common with the line of our Party."[9] Yet, on the same occasion he attacked those who thought that agriculture began and ended with the individual peasant holding.

This doubletalk quickly acquired meaning when the Central Committee decided in July to establish a number of new state grain farms which were to produce 100 million poods (1,800,000 short tons) of grain annually. Bukharin, thoroughly alarmed, promptly contacted Kamenev on July 11 and expressed his fear of Stalin as an "unprincipled intriguer" and a "Genghis Khan" interested only in enhancing his own power. On September 30,

1928, Bukharin published in *Pravda* a lengthy article, entitled "Notes of an Economist," in which he restated his position that industry could only develop commensurately with agriculture. According to Bukharin, both the grain shortage and the "goods famine" could be remedied if individual peasant holdings were permitted to flourish. He warned that industrialization must not be accomplished in such a way as to become parasitical and lead to the "debasement of agriculture."[10]

Yet, this was precisely the policy which Stalin was adopting as he advocated the simultaneous revolution in industry as well as in agriculture: industrialization was to be accomplished at the expense of the peasantry. In an unusually frank statement, made on July 9, 1928, Stalin declared that the peasantry was paying "not only the usual taxes, direct and indirect, but it is *overpaying*, in the first place, on the relatively high prices for industrial goods, and is being more or less *underpaid* on the low prices of agricultural products." He conceded that this "additional tax on the peasantry" was "something in the nature of a 'tribute,' something like a supertax which we are compelled to levy temporarily [*sic*] in order to maintain and develop further the present tempo of development . . . and to abolish entirely this supertax, these 'scissors' between the city and the village."[11] Thus, Stalin held out the hope that the peasants' position would be alleviated, while the policy toward which he was actually moving was designed to make the peasants pay even more: they were compelled to enter collective farms in order to finance his program of industrialization, which would surpass by far the "superindustrialization" advocated by the ousted Trotskyite-Zinovievite Oppositionists.

The leadership of the Moscow Party organization became a stronghold of the Right in opposition to Stalin's economic policies. Proceeding cautiously at first against his enemies, Stalin invited himself to address the joint plenary session of the Moscow Party Committee and Control Commission on October 19, 1928. He noted that there was a "danger of a Right, openly opportunist deviation in the Party" and attributed it to an "underestimation of the strength of our enemies, the strength of capitalism."[12] Stalin attempted to persuade his audience that

there was actually a possibility of a "capitalist restoration" in
Soviet Russia—more than a decade after the Communists had
seized power. The danger, according to the General Secretary,
lay in the continued existence of "small-scale production." With
typical oversimplification, Stalin declared that the Right was
moving in the direction of Social Democracy and away from
the "revolutionary line of Marxism." Thus, he now accused the
Right of precisely the same sin which he had attributed to Trotsky
and Zinoviev at the Fifteenth Party Conference on November 1,
1926—i.e., having advocated "permanent revolution" and
questioned the possibility of "constructing socialism in one country."[13] The Right and the Left were branded with the same label.

At this point, Stalin did not name the deviationists; in fact,
he criticized those who, he claimed, had urged him to do so.
This was as calculated a stratagem as was his statement to the
Moscow Party Committee meeting that there was no deviation
of the Right or the Left in the Politburo. In this way, Stalin
wished to give the country the impression that there was unanimous support in the Politburo for the policies which he was
advocating. *Pravda* published the text of this address on October
23, 1928, but it could not dispel what Stalin had referred to as
the "gossip" regarding a split within the Politburo.

He again denied the rumors of a Politburo split at the Central Committee plenary session on November 19, but attacked
the Right and particularly the Commissar of Finance, Moses
Frumkin, whom he accused of being niggardly in the matter of
the budget appropriation for capital outlays in industry. Frumkin
allegedly wished to grant no more than 650 million rubles, while
the Supreme Council for the National Economy had requested
825 million; in the end, the Central Committee decided upon
800 million rubles. According to Stalin, Frumkin's offense was
not his niggardliness, since that was to be expected of a Commissar of Finance, but rather his opposition to the tempo of
industrial development demanded by the General Secretary.
While insisting that the Right constituted the "principal danger"
to the Party, Stalin did not attack Bukharin at this time. Instead,
he ostensibly attempted to persuade the Right to acquiesce in his
plans by not terming its members a "faction" and by expressing

doubt that they would go so far. Stalin again feigned moderation by restraining those who supposedly wished to remove the Oppositionists from their Party posts. Stalin declared that the Right could be dealt with by means of a "developing ideological struggle," although he coupled this with a threat to employ organizational measures (removal from posts) if the Right violated Party decisions.[14]

Anyone who disagreed with Stalin was charged with favoring the growth of "capitalism in the villages" or the laissez-faire policy of the French liberals. By equating the Right with the Left and labeling each as "petty bourgeois" in origin, Stalin could deny that his own position was that of a centrist. In this way, Stalin meant to demonstrate that his position was the only true Leftist one representing the "Leninist line." In a sense, this was very true because his policy of rapid industrialization was stolen from Trotsky. It was in November, 1928, that Stalin insisted upon the maintenance of a rapid tempo of development in industry as well as in agriculture when he denied that the "tension of the plans" could be dispensed with. He alluded to "sober and even-tempered people in the Politburo and in the Council of People's Commissars" in order to imply that the forced tempo was feasible. The rapid tempo was justified on the grounds that the Soviet regime had inherited a "frightfully backward" technology in Russia. It was on this occasion that Stalin advanced the theme that the Soviet Union should "overtake and surpass" the capitalist countries in technology and economic achievement.

Such a program was found to attract a great many supporters within the Party in spite of the sacrifices which it entailed —and especially since the sacrifices would be borne primarily by the non-Party masses. Industrialization was financed by means of confiscations, hidden taxes on an unprecedented scale, uninterrupted inflation, compulsory state loans, the lowest of wages, and the rationing of food. The "goods famine" worsened in spite of all promises to the contrary. Imports of machinery were paid for with wheat exports—which, in the conditions of the early 1930's, meant dumping on the international market. Foreign exchange was also obtained through the *Torgsin* stores, in which purchases of scarce commodities could be paid for only in foreign currencies or in precious stones and metals, since these shops established by the Soviet regime would not honor the regime's debased currency. Thus, Stalin launched at a fantastic rate a program of capital accumulation based upon expropriations, artificially induced famine, forced savings, and deprivations in consumption; in this way, he made himself the greatest of all capitalists.

The helplessness of the Right when confronted with this program was even greater than that of the Trotskyites and Zinovievites in 1926 and 1927. By aiding Stalin in his campaign against the Left, the Right had unwittingly dug its own grave. From the outset, the Right had lacked the necessary numerical strength to become a true opposition. The Fifteenth Congress in December, 1927, had increased Stalin's Central Committee from sixty-three to seventy-one members and from forty-three to fifty candidate-members, while the Central Control Commission membership was increased from 163 to 195. Only three of the nine full members of the Politburo belonged to the Right. Stalin's majority was assured when he quickly succeeded in swinging the slightly wavering Kalinin and Voroshilov behind him. He was able to crush the Right within a few months—in contrast to the period of more than three years it had taken him to dispose of the Left.

The Right had compromised itself when it supported the resolution on economic development adopted at the November, 1928, Central Committee plenary session. Stalin obtained its support by including in the resolution a section, which he had no intention of honoring, providing for the development of the individual households of poor and middle peasants and for an increased supply of consumer goods as a means of stimulating agricultural production.[15] The Right, and Rykov in particular, thought that it had won a concession from Stalin, but events were soon to demonstrate again the General Secretary's ability first to deceive and then to oust his opponents.

In February, 1929, Stalin openly attacked Bukharin in the Politburo, accusing him and Sokol'nikov of having engaged in factional "behind-the-scenes negotiations" with Kamenev in order to "organize a bloc of the Bukharinites with the Trotskyites against the Party and its Central Committee."[16] Stalin noted pointedly that "Lenin was a thousand times right when he wrote to Shlyapnikov as early as 1916 that Bukharin 'is devilishly unstable in politics.' "[17] Stalin criticized Bukharin for having wanted to resign the editorship of *Pravda* and his leadership of the Comintern. Tomsky had wanted to resign from his trade union post, but by this time Rykov had retracted his resignation of the Chairmanship of the U.S.S.R. Council of Commissars. Earlier, at the end of November, 1928, Stalin had used the organizational weapon against the Right in the Moscow Party Committee when he obtained the removal of two of its leaders, Uglanov and Kotov. Like Bukharin, Uglanov was a veteran of the fight against Trotsky.

The first direct attack on Bukharin was made by Stalin on April 22, 1929, in a lengthy address delivered before the Central Committee and the Central Control Commission meeting jointly on the eve of the Sixteenth Party Conference. This was one day prior to Bukharin's removal from the chairmanship of the Comintern Executive Committee (announced in July). Stalin began by expressing contempt for the "complaints and wails" which arose as the result of this falling out among Old Bolsheviks. He warned that "ours is not a family circle, not an association of personal friends, but a political party of the working class," and he declared that the "interests of personal friendship cannot be placed above the interests of the cause."[18] Indeed, Stalin gave a new definition of "Old Bolshevik" when he asserted: "If an Old Bolshevik has turned from the path of revolution, has let himself go, and has become tarnished politically, though he may be a hundred years old, he does not have the right to call himself an Old Bolshevik, he does not have the right to demand of the Party respect for his person."[19]

Following this scathing introduction, Stalin proceeded to discuss all the alleged errors of Bukharin, whose group he accused of "living in the past" and of being characterized by "blindness, perplexity, [and] panic in the face of difficulties."[20] The July 11, 1928, meeting of Bukharin, Sokol'nikov, and Kamenev was recalled, and Stalin asked whether there was one

Party line or two. Bukharin was accused of having failed to comprehend the nature of the class struggle, of having preached the peaceful transformation of the "capitalism" of the kulak into socialism. This represented a deliberate distortion of what Bukharin had written.* Stalin then denounced Bukharin for having confused the greater resistance offered by the capitalist elements with an increase in their relative weight. Intensified resistance on the part of the kulak, Stalin argued, meant not that he was becoming stronger, but the opposite. Stalin also accused Bukharin of seeing only the middle peasant in the countryside and of being blind to the existence of the poor peasants and the kulaks; Trotsky's alleged crime was that he had failed to see the middle peasant and saw only the kulak and the poor peasant. Thus, only the General Secretary, in his own biased judgment, had correct and peripheral vision in the countryside.

Other errors heaped upon Bukharin's head included his alleged failure to perceive the dual nature of the NEP and to comprehend the limits to the "freedom" which it permitted. Stalin was particularly incensed by the use which the Right had made against him of his frank statement of July 9, 1928, regarding the imposition upon the peasants of "something in the nature of a 'tribute.' " The Right had asserted that Stalin's policy of overtaxing the countryside was "military-feudal exploitation of the peasantry." Stalin, in response, had succeeded in discovering one instance in which Lenin had employed the word "tribute," and this was quoted when Bukharin insisted that it was an "unfortunate word."[21] Resorting inevitably to the *ad hominem* argument, Stalin quoted from Lenin's Testament the passage in which Lenin recognized Bukharin's abilities but doubted the completely Marxist nature of his theorizing as well as his understanding of dialectics.[22] Earlier disagreements between

---

* Actually, Bukharin advocated increased pressure and the imposition of higher taxes upon the kulak, but he opposed the establishment of compulsory collective farms, hoping that they would be joined on a voluntary basis. In this, he differed from Stalin, who believed in collectivization by use of bayonets. Bukharin also advocated higher agricultural prices, lower prices on industrial commodities, and the extension of credits to farm cooperatives.

Bukharin and Lenin were resurrected, including the former's opposition to the Brest-Litovsk Treaty of March, 1918.

When Bukharin attempted to argue that his group was no opposition, Stalin insisted that it was and declared that it had "betrayed" the "working class" and the "revolution" in refusing to combat itself.[23] Again simulating moderation, Stalin said that he did not agree with "certain comrades" who were demanding the immediate exclusion of Bukharin and Tomsky from the Politburo. This sanction would be imposed, Stalin warned, "in the event of the slightest attempt at noncompliance with decisions of the Central Committee."[24] The threat was fulfilled in Bukharin's case on November 17, 1929, when he was removed from the Politburo by the plenary session of Stalin's Central Committee, while Rykov and Tomsky were given a temporary reprieve. Tomsky had lost his trade union post in June, 1929, and was to be expelled from the Politburo in July, 1930. The April, 1929, Party Conference had approved the First Five-Year Plan, and by the end of the year Stalin openly called for the "liquidation of the kulaks as a class" in condemnation of what he had termed the "bourgeois-liberal policy" of Rykov and Bukharin, who had opposed the application of "extraordinary measures" against the kulak.

Why had the Right Opposition been crushed so quickly, especially after its victory at the Eighth Trade Union Conference in December, 1928, when Kaganovich had failed to engineer the ouster of Tomsky? In large part, it was the victory of Stalin the practitioner and organization man over Bukharin the theorist. The Right was doomed from the beginning because it could not organize to present its program as an alternative to that of Stalin and the Central Committee apparatus. Its failure was caused by the ban on all blocs and factions—a ban which its members had once favored, but which now prevented the Right from presenting its case to the rank and file and to the public at large without violating Party discipline. Stalin's control of the Party press and his power to assign new deputies to Bukharin, Rykov, and Tomsky in order to keep himself thoroughly informed on their activities also contributed to the weakness of the Right. In addition, the Rightist leadership was found wanting in unity; the benign Rykov, though disturbed by Stalin's growing power, wished to avoid a break and hesitated to go all the way with Bukharin and Tomsky. The secondary Rightist leaders also proved to be undependable; Uglanov, Kotov, and others recanted and broke with Bukharin at the time of his expulsion from the Politburo. Thus, the Right was routed in 1929 even before it could form a genuine faction.

On the occasion of the twelfth anniversary of the Bolshevik seizure of power, Stalin was to characterize 1929 as the "year of the great turning point"—the year in which the "retreat" of the NEP had been halted and reversed in accordance with the Bolshevik principle that every retreat is merely a preparation for a further advance. The year was a turning point in many respects. In February, Trotsky was forcibly deported to Turkey after having spent a year in exile in Alma-Ata. The year also witnessed the recantation of such Trotskyites as Preobrazhensky, Serebryakov, Smilga, Drobnis, and Beloborodov, who asked for readmission to the Party in view of the fact that Stalin had adopted their program of rapid industrialization and collectivization. Others, like Christian Rakovsky, were treated harshly for their unwillingness to repent quickly. Stalin demanded greater "criticism and self-criticism" from the Party. This was a phrase which he had begun to employ in 1924. When it became a Party principle, it was to be applied to everyone except Stalin himself. The year 1929 closed very appropriately with the celebration of Stalin's fiftieth birthday, on December 21, in a plethora of panegyrics. Stalin responded with this declaration: "I am prepared in the future as well to give to the cause of the working class, to the cause of the proletarian revolution and world Communism all of my strength, all of my abilities, and, in case of need, all of my blood, drop by drop."[25] There was soon to be much generosity with blood, but it was to be the blood of others and not that of the General Secretary.

Stalin was now supreme, a law unto himself. He had arrived at this position by employing against his opponents and rivals within the Party some of the same methods which they had earlier employed against countless numbers of persons outside the Party. Now in a position to impose his (really the Trotskyite) policies on the country, he ordered the use of force and deportations as the means for collectivizing agriculture. These excesses were cleverly attributed by Stalin to his subordinates in the Party ranks by means of the "Giddiness from Success" article, published in the March 2, 1930, issue of *Pravda,* which heralded a retreat on the collectivization front. More than 60 per cent of the collectivized peasants left the farms after the publication of this article, but usually without the tools and livestock which they had contributed when compelled to join. However, the relief provided by Stalin's "retreat" was only temporary. The campaign was soon resumed, with the term "kulak" given a broad definition meaning anyone who expressed doubt regarding the value of collectivized agriculture. By the end of 1932, the majority of peasant households (60 per cent) were collectivized. In an environment dominated by force and reduced incentives, it was natural that grain production in 1932 declined to approximately 70 per cent of the 1913 level. Any humane government would have imported grain or at least sharply reduced the vast grain exports with which the Soviet regime was financing the importation of machinery from the West. Stalin not only did not adopt either course but, when foreign relief agencies offered to help the starving, denied that a famine existed.

The winter of 1932-33 brought to the Soviet Union, but particularly to the Ukrainian Soviet Republic, a famine unique in historical annals—one in which the peasantry starved while the limited food supply was expropriated by the regime for rationing in the cities. The dispossessed peasantry came to the cities to beg for food and to die. As the number of the famine's victims climbed into the millions, the regime censored all references to this man-made tragedy in the dispatches of foreign correspondents stationed in Moscow. Travel to the Ukrainian Soviet Republic was forbidden. In order to take people's minds, if not their stomachs, off the famine, the regime concocted the Metropolitan-Vickers trial in April, 1933, in an attempt to blame British "sabotage" activities for certain failures in Soviet industry.

Earlier, in December, 1930, the arrest of eight technical

specialists headed by Professor Leonid Konstantinovich Ramzin had precipitated the resignation of Rykov from the Chairmanship of the Council of Commissars and his replacement by Molotov. Rykov was also expelled from the Politburo. Ramzin's so-called "Industrial Party" was accused of engaging in sabotage, and its members were also linked with the moderate approach to industrialization advocated by the Right. At the Sixteenth Party Congress, in June, 1930, the members of the Right had had to confess their sins in humility before an unfriendly audience composed of delegates selected by Stalin's *apparat*. Stalin ridiculed them for mistaking a "cockroach" for a "thousand furious beasts"—that is, for having overestimated the obstacles in the way of the new program and for allegedly having predicted the collapse of the Soviet regime as a result of Stalin's policies.[26]

The Sixteenth Congress, held two and one-half years after the Fifteenth, did not witness any debate or clash of opinions or programs. Stalin, now a theoretician and a specialist on "contradictions," held forth on the international issues of the day as he saw them. He spoke of the end of the "stabilization of capitalism" and depicted the world as being on the threshold of Communism, when it was, in fact, much closer to the threshold of fascism. The League of Nations was denounced by Stalin as "rotten," although within four years the Soviet Union was to join it. France was declared to be the "most aggressive and militaristic country in the world," but within four years Moscow was to seek alliance with it. Stalin also restated the Soviet claim to Bessarabia, along with a denunciation of the diplomacy and "provocational acts and adventurist attacks" of the Western powers. Bukharin's thesis, which allegedly held that capitalism could peacefully grow into socialism, was again denounced by Stalin, who declared that "development has moved and will continue to move according to Lenin's formula—'who [will defeat and destroy] whom.' "[27]

Although the Right was defeated, new enemies had to be sought and the compulsive drive of Stalinism sustained. The modest goal of "overtaking and surpassing" the world of capitalism required the adoption of the slogan "Technics decide everything." At the Fifteenth Congress in 1927, Stalin had falsely boasted that the Soviet Union had the "most large-scale and concentrated of all existing industries in the world."[28] Yet, three years later, in the famous address to industrial officials delivered on February 4, 1931, Stalin was to declare that "we are fifty to a hundred years behind the leading countries." In demanding "genuine Bolshevik tempos" of industrial development and the liquidation of Russian backwardness, Stalin offered the following justification: "You are mighty—it means you are right; consequently everyone must take heed of you."[29]

Stalin was to restate this theme at the Seventeenth Party Congress on January 26, 1934; in discussing foreign policy, he observed that "in our time the weak are not reckoned with—only the strong are reckoned with." It was on this occasion that he publicly opened the door to an agreement with Nazi Germany. After stating that Moscow was "not elated" over the establishment of the fascist regime in Germany, Stalin hastily added: "But the question here is not one of fascism, if only, for example, because fascism in Italy did not prevent the U.S.S.R. from establishing the best relations with that country."[30] He declared that the world should not be "thrust into the chasm of a new war" for the sake of the preservation of the Versailles Treaty.

As an "authority" on conditions in the "capitalist world," of which he knew nothing, Stalin interpreted the rise of Nazism in Germany as an indication of the "weakness of the bourgeoisie . . . [since it] is no longer strong enough to rule by the old methods of parliamentarianism and bourgeois democracy, in view of which it is compelled in internal politics to resort to terroristic methods of rule."[31] This statement revealed far more about Stalinism than it did about Germany, since Stalin had now placed the Party on the threshold of a reign of terror. The Party had condoned the use of terror against the "class enemies" —against the peasantry, the clergy, and the intelligentsia. Now, in a kind of ironic retribution, the Party was to become the victim of its own instrument.

Although the Left and Right Oppositions had been defeated and the Seventeenth Congress had given Stalin an ovation and hailed him as a "genius," he still groped about for new enemies— as if to demonstrate that their destruction was his staff of life.

While admitting to the Congress that "there is no one left to be beaten," Stalin warned that the remnants of the ideology of the Party's enemies, of the "opportunists of all hues," remained "in the heads of individual members of the Party, who often make themselves known."[32] He singled out the "national deviationists" in the non-Russian republics, referring to the "falling into sin of Skrypnyk," the Ukrainian Communist Commissar of Education who had committed suicide in July, 1933, in protest against Stalin's policies which had brought on the famine and had led to the arrest of much of the Ukrainian intelligentsia on the charge of "bourgeois nationalism." The Seventeenth Congress witnessed the turning point in Stalin's nationality policy. Prior to 1934, he had condemned Russian great-power chauvinism as the principal danger; now local non-Russian national deviations were condemned as equally dangerous. This marked the beginning of Stalin's orientation toward Russian nationalism. Stalin's tone was ominous as he spoke of "enemies both internal and external" and denounced those in the Party who thought that the classless society could be attained by means of a "spontaneous process" instead of through an intensified class struggle.

It was at the Seventeenth Congress in January, 1934, that Stalin stressed the importance of the "selection of people and the verification of fulfillment" in organizational work.[33] His preoccupation with the shifting of personnel and the replacement of the Party membership through the purge—key elements in Stalinism—found expression in his address of May 4, 1935, delivered to Red Army Academy graduates. On that occasion, he announced that the earlier slogan, "Technics decide everything," was to be replaced by a new one, "Cadres decide everything." By this, Stalin meant that the possession of technical skills was not enough in itself and that in order to utilize technology fully, more attention would have to be paid to the recruitment of proper personnel—an essential element in totalitarianism. Stalin couched his argument in terms of a cynical plea that people, workers, and cadres be valued. Illustrating his point with an anecdote supposedly based upon an experience during his period of Siberian exile, Stalin recounted how some of the inhabitants of the area had expressed greater concern for the care given a mare than for the fate of a drowned man. When he reproached them for their callous attitude, they were said to have justified it on the grounds that it was far easier to produce people than it was to produce a mare.[34] Unfortunately, nothing actually remained of this solicitude for human life which Stalin professed to have felt as an exiled revolutionary.

While paying lip service to the values that should be placed on human life, Stalin had launched in 1935 what was to become a wave of mass arrests and executions, accompanied by the incongruous slogan "Life has become better, life has become happier." This horrendous blood bath was precipitated by the still not fully explained assassination of Sergei Kirov on December 1, 1934. Kirov had served as secretary of the Leningrad province Party organization since 1926, when he replaced Zinoviev in that post and purged the organization of the latter's followers. Stalin had made him a full member of the Politburo in 1930, and he had also become a member of the Secretariat in 1934 following the Seventeenth Congress. Kirov's assassin, Leonid Nikolayev, had been arrested for suspicious conduct and released only a month and a half before he obtained entry to his victim's office in the Smolny in Leningrad—this, it must be remembered, in a country where security precautions were most elaborate and arrested persons were not readily released. One of the important police officials involved in the case was killed in a mysterious automobile "accident" on the day following Kirov's assassination. Stalin journeyed to Leningrad and conducted a personal interrogation of Nikolayev, who was then shot, along with a number of alleged accomplices, without the benefit of a public trial.[35] It is possible that Nikolayev was motivated by the desire for vengeance, as a result of attentions which Kirov had allegedly paid his wife. This explanation may be valid, although it does not eliminate the interest which Stalin may have had in Kirov's demise. Nor does it contradict the remarkable facts of Nikolayev's earlier release and the light sentences given the responsible Leningrad NKVD officials following the assassination (although the latter were shot in 1937, presumably in order to prevent them from revealing their roles in this event). Whether or not the assassination was motivated by Stalin's fear of a somewhat popular rival, it provided the pretext for the arrest of thousands of "Kirov's assassins" in cities all over the country. A chain reaction was set off, and the terror did not come to a halt until four years later. Fear, hatred, suspicion, denunciation, and perversity fed the human holocaust; the purge consumed Party members and officials, as well as non-Party people. In 1956, Khrushchev was to confirm the execution by Stalin, mostly in 1937 and 1938, of 98 of the 139 members and candidate-members of the Central Committee elected at the Seventeenth Congress (ironically called the "Congress of Victors").

The most spectacular parts of the purges of the thirties were the three show trials of Old Bolsheviks and certain other obscure defendants. The first of these, the trial of the sixteen who allegedly comprised the "Trotskyite-Zinovievite Terrorist Center," took place in August, 1936. The defendants—who included Kamenev, Zinoviev, G. E. Yevdokimov, S. V. Mrachkovsky, and I. N. Smirnov—were accused of having assassinated Kirov and of having planned other terrorist acts, although the Kirov assassination had originally been attributed to "White Guards."* Kamenev and Zinoviev had actually been tried on this charge in January, 1935, and had received prison sentences. However, since there is no legal right protecting persons against double jeopardy in the Soviet Union, they were taken from prison and were brought to trial again on the same charges. The death penalty was imposed upon all sixteen defendants. In 1935, Zinoviev had admitted to Stalin a partial responsibility for Kirov's assassination on the grounds that the earlier opposition of Zinoviev and his followers had placed the assassin Nikolayev and his "accomplices" on the road to crime. In thus attempting to come to terms with Stalin, Zinoviev had merely forged a weapon

---

* Two groups of alleged "White Guard terrorists" were arrested and tried in Leningrad (thirty-nine persons) and in Moscow (thirty-three persons), according to the December 6, 1934, issue of *Pravda*. In Kiev, twenty-eight Ukrainians (including the prominent writers Kost' Burevii, Oleksa Vlyz'ko, Hryhorii Kosynka, and Dmytro Fal'kivs'kyi) were shot to death following a trial of thirty-seven persons held on December 13–15, 1934.

for his own destruction—just as he had done in 1928 and in 1933, when he recanted.

The second show trial was that of the seventeen alleged members of the so-called "Anti-Soviet Trotskyite Center" in January, 1937. These included Karl Radek, L. P. Serebryakov, Sokol'nikov, Jacob N. Drobnis, and a number of technical specialists. The defendants were accused of engaging in espionage, "wrecking," the planning of terrorist acts, and of having established a "parallel center" which had collaborated with the defendants in the first trial. Twelve of the accused were executed, and four of them, including Radek and Sokol'nikov, were sentenced to long prison terms. This second trial—which was public, as the first one had been—was followed in June, 1937, by the secret trial and execution of Marshal Tukhachevsky, the Red Army's Chief of Staff, and seven other generals. The Assistant Commissar of War, Jan Borisovich Gamarnik, is said to have committed suicide. Marshals Vasilii Konstantinovich Blucher and Alexander Ilyich Yegorov, who had signed Tukhachevsky's death warrant, were soon purged also. Significantly, none of the arrested generals was given a public trial or apparently prepared for the orgy of self-vilification which had been inflicted upon the purged politicians.

The third and least successful show trial, that of the "Bloc of Rights and Trotskyites," was held in March, 1938. The twenty-one defendants included Bukharin, Rykov, Krestinsky, Grigorii Fedorovich Grin'ko, Rakovsky, two Uzbek Communists (Akmal Ikramov and Faizula Khodzhayev), and three physicians. Also among them was Genrikh G. Yagoda, a bookkeeper who had joined the Party in 1907, became a member of the presidium of the *Cheka* in 1920, and succeeded Vyacheslav Rudol'fovich Menzhinsky in 1934 as head of the OGPU-NKVD. Tomsky was not among the defendants, having committed suicide on August 23, 1936. They were accused of engaging in espionage, wrecking, and terrorist activities, and of wanting to dismember the Soviet Union and restore capitalism. Eighteen of the defendants were sentenced to death; the other three, among them Rakovsky, received prison sentences.

The three show trials were accompanied by organized "hate sessions"—mass meetings which demanded that no mercy be given the doomed defendants. The former Menshevik Andrei Vyshinsky served as state prosecutor in all three trials and enhanced his career at the expense of the defendants' blood. The rules of evidence were nonexistent, and hearsay and utterly false testimony were admitted into the record.[36] The trials were not public in the full sense of the word, since certain sessions were held *in camera*. The prosecution did not have to prove guilt, since it operated under the principle that the accused is assumed to be guilty until he proves his innocence.

Yet, the defendants did not protest their innocence. The only exception was Krestinsky, the former Soviet envoy to Berlin, who retracted in open court the confession that he had given his interrogators in the chambers of the NKVD. However, on the following day, Krestinsky quickly retracted his retraction and his initial plea of "not guilty." Certain defendants employed various other means, some of them rather subtle, to make denials and cast doubt on the authenticity of their own testimony.[37] There were such techniques as being too cooperative with Vyshinsky in the examination by the prosecution, being exceedingly vague regarding vital details, and agreeing to obviously false statements. There was also the question asked by Yevdokimov: "Who will believe a single word of ours?" On occasion, Bukharin rather effectively parried Vyshinsky's questions. However, the defendants admitted, for the most part, to having engaged in espionage for years on behalf of Britain, France, Germany, and Japan; to having planned and committed terrorist acts in certain instances, to having attempted to wreck the nation's economy and military capabilities; and to having wanted to restore capitalism, dismember the Soviet Union, and cede territory to Germany and Japan. Yagoda and the physician L. G. Levin claimed that they had taken part in the medical murder of Maxim Gorky, Gorky's son, and Valerian Kuibyshev, and in the attempted murder of Yezhov, Yagoda's successor.

The fantastic nature of the testimony and the "evidence" in the three trials would have made the entire matter ridiculous were it not for the lives involved—however despicable and unworthy some of the defendants may have been. Ironically, every one of the prominent defendants had cast his lot with Stalin at one time or another—now to be rewarded by death or imprisonment. The basically cooperative attitude of the defendants in the three trials obviously cannot be attributed to any single cause. All of the accused were in the custody of the NKVD for lengthy periods, during which they were appropriately conditioned for the roles assigned to them. This was accomplished by means of protracted and systematic interrogation, leading to mental and physical exhaustion, and may have been facilitated by "negotiations" of sorts carried on between the defendants and the arrangers of the show trials. It is possible that promises as well as threats played some role in the preliminary arrangements, since some of the accused were undoubtedly concerned over the fate of members of their families and may have cooperated in the hope of sparing them. Some of the obscure defendants, who were not even known to the prominent accused persons, were undoubtedly *agents provocateurs* planted by the NKVD. While the NKVD was known to employ torture, there is no direct evidence to indicate that it was used in these three cases, although the possibility cannot be ruled out. It should also be borne in mind that the defendants had been subjected to Party discipline for many years and had adhered to it far more often than they had violated it. By 1936, it was clear to everyone that Stalin was the Party, and this fact must certainly have been brought home to the helpless defendants as they were confronted by their interrogators and had impressed upon them the need to cooperate with the prosecution. The accused were caught in a horrible trap of their own making, and they knew it. Since the breaking point of men varies, it is also not surprising that some of the defendants were implicated by others who succumbed to "persuasion" more quickly. It is also possible that most of the defendants were prepared to concede that they would have committed the alleged crimes had they been in a position to do so. They were induced to perform one last service for the Party— to confess and die a "useful" death.

Whether the crude details of the three show trials were concocted by Stalin or by the police themselves, it is clear that the sentences were reviewed and approved by Stalin before being imposed upon the defendants. The harsh sentences may possibly indicate in embryonic form the dementia which characterized the last years of Stalin's rule. There was cruel irony here in the fact that Radek and Bukharin, defendants in the second and third trials respectively, had helped to write the new Stalin Constitution in 1936, the "democratic" provisions of which now failed to save them. Yet, there was a rationale behind the General Secretary's sadism: he undoubtedly believed it necessary to destroy these former opponents who might pose an alternative to his system of rule. It was not enough that they be compelled to grovel in the dirt and admit heinous crimes and thoughts; it was necessary that they be physically destroyed as traitors and spies. The trials were also useful in that they linked the internal enemy with the external foes of the Stalinist regime, the foreign powers referred to in the testimony. On a more personal level, Stalin disliked such men as Bukharin, Rakovsky, Kamenev, and Krestinsky for their knowledge of foreign languages and their worldly sophistication, which the misanthropic dictator did not possess—although he far surpassed them in cunning. But personal animosity, which might partially explain Stalin's desire to exterminate many of the Old Bolsheviks, does not explain the great purges of his lieutenants and of the rank and file in the thirties.

The total Party membership, including the candidates, passed the 1-million mark in 1926 and rose steadily until it reached 3,555,338 in 1933. A decline then set in, and by 1937 and 1938 the total membership had fallen to slightly below the 2-million mark (1,920,002 members and candidates in 1938). Admission to the Party was suspended from December, 1932, to November, 1936, as the result of a Central Committee decision.[38] A general verification of all Party documents was decided upon by the Central Committee on May 13, 1935, and between February 1 and May 1 of the following year new membership cards were issued. It was charged that carelessness had characterized admission to the Party and that "enemies" and "foreign spies" had penetrated its ranks. The search for "adventurists, crooks, double-dealers, and other counterrevolutionary elements" who had obtained Party membership cards was intensified.[39]

In the midst of these mass expulsions, a plenary session of the Central Committee, meeting in February and March, 1937, adopted a resolution which called for the restoration of intra-Party "democracy," election of Party committee members, and abandonment of the practice of co-optation.[40] A report by Andrei A. Zhdanov, who was rapidly emerging as Stalin's favorite lieutenant at that time, cited many instances of co-optation, but did not explain why it was being employed so frequently. Part of the answer lay in the fact that the Party was being decimated and the simplest procedure was to co-opt new committee members in place of those who had been arrested. Similarly, co-optation rather than election was made necessary by the frequent arrival of new Party officials assuming secretaryships in the local organizations on orders from Moscow. An ominous note crept into the plea for the restoration of democratic centralism when Zhdanov warned that the enemies of the Soviet regime were renewing their activities as a result of the "freedom" granted under the new Stalin Constitution.[41]

This theme was further developed by Stalin in his speech of March 5, 1937. Here the *vozhd'*, who had just expelled Bukharin and Rykov from the Party, dwelt on enemies, encirclement, double-dealing, the presence of Trotskyites in the Party, and the need for greater vigilance. The purge ground on through 1937, taking its inevitable toll. However, by January, 1938, the Central Committee had adopted a resolution criticizing the "errors" of local Party organizations in expelling members and "formal bureaucratic attitudes" in handling appeals for reinstatement. As in the "Giddiness from Success" article, Stalin was blaming subordinates for errors resulting from policies for which he himself was responsible.

At the Eighteenth Party Congress, on March 10, 1939, Stalin was to admit that "serious errors" had occurred in far greater numbers than had been supposed. While reporting that there were 270,000 fewer members in 1939 than there had been at the time of the previous Congress in 1934, Stalin rationalized the decline (which, in fact, was far greater) on the usual grounds that quality had been gained at the expense of quantity.[42] Growth of the total Party membership was to continue under Stalin—

in spite of the institutionalized purging—until its ranks swelled
to 3,965,530 members and 1,794,839 candidate-members at the
close of World War II. At the time of Stalin's death, the membership numbered more than 6 million, and there were 868,886
candidates.

This wholesale "cleansing" of the Party served to enhance
Stalin's position. Thousands upon thousands of vacancies and
new positions were created as the result of the purges and the
Party's unprecedented growth in membership.[43] The new incumbents were bound to the General Secretary since he had
made them what they were and he could just as easily break
them. Indeed, the manipulation of subordinates throughout the
Party echelons constituted one of the principal characteristics of
Stalinism. As the show trials demonstrated only too vividly,
Stalin had absolutely no respect for a person's past achievements
and contributions to the Party—an attitude which had been
expressed by him as early as the Seventeenth Congress in January, 1934. On that occasion, Stalin denounced the "conceited
magnates [who] think they are irreplaceable and that they can
with impunity violate the decisions of the leading [Party]
bodies."[44] Thus, no one was to be irreplaceable except Stalin
himself.

For the prominent Old Bolsheviks who had been expelled
and executed, Stalin substituted a whole retinue of lieutenants
who had joined the Party no later than 1907. He rewarded some
of them with positions in the Politburo, but they did not fare
too well. There was, for example, Jan Rudzutak, who had served
in the Politburo from 1926 to 1931 and from 1934 to 1936, and
had headed the Central Control (Purging) Commission in 1933
—only to disappear in 1938. Stanislav Kosior, who became a
candidate-member of the Politburo in 1927 and a full member
in 1930, disappeared in 1938—the reward for his services to
Stalin in imposing collectivization upon Ukrainian agriculture.
Vlas Chubar', who became a member of the Politburo in 1935
(the only Ukrainian to attain full membership under Stalin),
also disappeared in 1938. Valerian Kuibyshev, who had succeeded Stalin as the chief of *Rabkrin* in 1923 and had become
a member of the Politburo in 1927, died in 1935 at the age of

forty-seven, ostensibly of heart disease. Gregory (Sergo) Ordzhonikidze, an old acquaintance of Stalin's who had become a
Politburo candidate-member in 1926 and had served as a full
member from 1930 to 1937, died under mysterious circumstances
in 1937—either murdered or driven to suicide.* Robert I. Eikhe,
a candidate-member of the Politburo, was arrested in April, 1938,
and executed on February 4, 1940. Paul P. Postyshev, a candidate-member of the Politburo and Nikita Khrushchev's predecessor as Stalin's satrap in the Ukrainian Communist Party (though
he served only as Second Secretary), was quietly removed from
his Kiev post in March, 1937, and consigned to oblivion.
Gregory Petrovsky, the grand old man among the Ukrainian
Communists and a candidate-member of the CPSU Politburo,
disappeared in 1938, only to reappear miraculously in 1953.
Several of these men probably met their fate for having bravely
expressed their opinion—at the February-March, 1937, plenary
session of the CPSU Central Committee—that the purge had
gone too far.

This opinion was not shared by their jailer, Nikolai I.
Yezhov, who had served Stalin in a number of different capac-
ities: in 1929-30, he was Deputy Commissar for Agriculture, and
from 1930 to 1934 he was in charge of the Cadres Department
in the Central Committee apparatus; in 1935, Yezhov became
one of the secretaries of the Central Committee, as well as the
Chairman of the Commission on Party Control. Succeeding
Yagoda as the head of the NKVD in September, 1936, he
supervised the intensified purges and liquidations of 1937 and
1938. It was during his tenure that the second and third show
trials were prepared and an important self-incriminatory role
was appropriately assigned to Yagoda. Although Yezhov became
a candidate-member of the Politburo in October, 1937, his
removal "at his own request" from the post of head of the
NKVD was announced on December 8, 1938, after he had
performed the gruesome task assigned to him by Stalin. He was

---

* Abel Yenukidze, another fellow Georgian, was removed from the
Central Committee and from the Secretaryship of the Central Executive
Committee (of the Congress of Soviets), was expelled from the Party in
June, 1935, and was executed.

appointed People's Commissar of Water Transport in March, 1938, but was quickly consigned to oblivion—in all probability, executed—since he knew far too much and was expendable.

In addition to the purging of even the highest of the lieutenants—to say nothing of the expendable rank and file of the Party—Stalin employed the very effective practice of encouraging rivalries among his subordinates. In this way, he preserved for himself the role of arbiter. Thus, he permitted—and probably encouraged—the seesawing conflict between Malenkov and Zhdanov in the 1940's. Zhdanov moved to the forefront of Stalin's retinue in 1946 with a campaign for ideological purity and obtained the temporary removal of Malenkov from the Secretariat.* After Zhdanov's death on August 31, 1948, following the excommunication of Tito from the Cominform, Malenkov made a comeback to the extent of being selected by Stalin to present the report of the Central Committee to the Nineteenth Congress in October, 1952, under the watchful and suspicious eyes of his aged mentor. Zhdanov's demise was followed in early 1949 by that of the economist Nikolai Voznesensky, the chief of the State Planning Commission (*Gosplan*) and the youngest Politburo member, having entered that body as a candidate-member in 1941. Other Zhdanovites who were removed from high positions included: Colonel-General I. V. Shikin, chief of the Main Political Administration of the Army since July, 1946; A. A. Kuznetsov, a member of the Secretariat in Zhdanov's time; Mikhail I. Rodionov, Chairman of the R.S.F.S.R. Council of Ministers; and P. S. Popkov, Secretary of the Leningrad Party organization.[45] All except Shikin were executed.

---

* The campaign for ideological vigilance included attacks upon the lyric poetess Anna Akhmatova and the well-known humorist Mikhail Zoshchenko. The latter was singled out by Zhdanov in September, 1946, for his story "Adventures of a Monkey," written in 1945. This harmless tale takes place in 1941, at the outbreak of the war with Germany. A monkey escapes from a small zoo and goes to the town of Borisov, where it encounters such unpleasant features of Soviet life as the queue, ration cards, the bathhouse, and the weakness for alcohol. While being pursued, the monkey expresses a preference for life in the zoo. Zhdanov took Zoshchenko to task for allegedly having permitted the monkey to pass judgment on Soviet social conditions and to insult the Soviet people.

It is not impossible that Voznesensky's demise bore some relationship to a disagreement over economic policy, particularly in view of his assertions (in his book, *The Economy of the U.S.S.R. During World War II*) that the state economic plan "possesses the force of a law of economic development"—a view later criticized by Stalin. Yet, it is clear that Voznesensky's promotion to full membership in the Politburo occurred at a time (in 1947) when Zhdanov was enjoying a marked advantage over Stalin's other lieutenants and led the drive for ideological conformity and the establishment of the Cominform. Voznesensky's mysterious removal from the Politburo was followed by a Central Committee decree attacking his book.

This was not the only change in the Politburo following World War II. The Soviet titular executive, Supreme Soviet Presidium Chairman Mikhail Kalinin, died in 1946. During the same year, Georgii Malenkov and Lavrentii Beria became full members. Beria had been a candidate-member since 1939, following his appointment as NKVD chief; prior to that, he had been a Party chief in the Caucasus. Malenkov had risen in the ranks of the Central Committee apparatus, where he had been employed since 1925. Nikolai Bulganin—a political Army Marshal, former economic administrator, Mayor of Moscow, and head of the State Bank—became a candidate-member of the Politburo in 1946 and was advanced to full membership in 1948. Alexei Kosygin, an economic administrator, became a Politburo candidate-member in 1946 and was promoted to full membership in 1949.

These were the men added to the Politburo which had emerged from the Yezhov purges and had survived World War II. In addition to Stalin, Voroshilov and Molotov, this body included Lazar M. Kaganovich (added in 1930), A. A. Andreyev (added in 1932), and Nikita S. Khrushchev (who gained membership along with Zhdanov in 1939, following his appointment as Ukrainian Party chief). Andreyev, a veteran Party secretary, was removed from the Politburo in 1952 after having been made a scapegoat for failures in agriculture. In March, 1951, Khrushchev was rebuked for his advocacy of agro-cities (which would have peasants living in apartment houses), but was not removed from the Politburo. The earlier removal of Zhdanov and Voznesensky probably benefited Beria and Malenkov to some degree.

This behind-the-scenes warfare among Stalin's lieutenants took place in the absence of any Party congress. The practice of co-optation persisted in spite of promises to abolish it—such as the one made by Zhdanov before the Central Committee in February, 1937. Indeed, the Central Committee fell into a state of desuetude during the last decade of Stalin's reign. It was replaced by the Politburo, and during the war an even smaller body, the State Defense Committee, suited Stalin's purposes. This group originally consisted of Stalin, Molotov, Malenkov, Beria, and Voroshilov; Mikoyan, Voznesensky, Kaganovich, and Bulganin were later added to it. Khrushchev's report to the Twentieth Congress in 1956 indicated that Stalin ruled without the Politburo most of the time, but occasionally employed subcommittees for certain categories of problems, and these groups actually replaced the parent body which had itself superseded the Central Committee.

The decline of the Party's responsible central bodies had occurred as a consequence of the destruction of the cadres of the old Leninist Party and their replacement by a new elite of Party bureaucrats and economic managers subject to Stalin's discipline. The old Party, like the Comintern, died during the Yezhovshchina, and what survived it was a far cry from what Lenin had predicted in his *State and Revolution* in 1917. As Stalin's personal Secretariat came to rely more and more upon the secret police, any distinction between the Party and an arbitrary police apparatus of mammoth proportions became blurred.

Stalin's Party became even more compromised when it allied itself with Hitler's Nazi regime in August, 1939, and precipitated World War II by agreeing to partition Poland. The pledge of "neutrality" given to Hitler enabled the Nazi regime to direct all its energies against the Western democracies, but it also was to Stalin's advantage since his "land of socialism" was in no condition to face a war, having been bled white during the purges. Stalin refused to believe that Hitler would attack and took no military measures to forestall the Nazi onslaught, but merely awaited it in the hope that it would not confront the Soviet regime with a supreme test. When the blow came on June 22, 1941, it was to lead to mass defections and incredible defeats as the Wehrmacht reached the gates of Moscow by October, besieged Leningrad, and drove into the easternmost reaches of the Ukrainian Republic.

Since the Nazis did not provide any genuine alternative to Stalin's regime and pursued cruel occupation policies, it is not surprising that the Party was able to increase its membership by 640,238 during the second half of 1942, as the battle of Stalingrad began to take shape. It is reported that during the war years the number of admissions to Party candidacy was two and one-half times that in the corresponding prewar period (i.e., after the Yezhovshchina).[46] It is known that the Party doubled in size between the Yezhovshchina and the Eighteenth Party Conference in February, 1941 (from 1.9 to 3.8 million), and it appears that the war years witnessed the admission of some 4.7 million new members. By the end of the war, the Party had a total membership of approximately 5.8 million.

The tremendous influx of new members required intensified indoctrination and careful screening during the immediate postwar period. It also placed the officer corps of the Soviet Army directly under Party discipline, since 86 per cent of the officers had been enrolled in the Party. Though the tyrant and his lieutenants were aging, the Party rank and file had become youthful, thanks to the purges and the war: in 1946, 63.6 per cent of the membership was under thirty-five years of age.

The wartime changes in the Party's membership were accompanied by the acquisition of a new Soviet colonial empire in Eastern Europe which brought Communism as far as the Elbe River. It was as though Stalin's prediction of a "Soviet Germany, Poland, Hungary, and Finland" (made in a letter to Lenin on June 12, 1920)[47] was being fulfilled. The new Communist regimes, established wherever Soviet bayonets were present, were formed by Communist *émigrés* who had been returned to the countries of their birth in 1945 in the baggage trains and airplanes of the Soviet Army.

This extension of Soviet influence beyond the frontiers of the so-called "land of socialism" occurred in spite of (or more likely, because of) the nominal dissolution of the Comintern in the spring of 1943, as Stalin began to assume the temporary pose of an old-fashioned Russian nationalist. Yet, such an empire inevitably created problems, despite the common world outlook and training in operational tactics shared by Communists. Coordination was effected by the Soviet ambassadors accredited to the countries of Eastern Europe, by special representatives of the Soviet Party apparatus, and by the presence of the Russian military. Soviet colonialism was most blatant in the appointment of Soviet Marshal Constantine Rokossovsky as Polish Minister of Defense.

The Cominform, or so-called "Communist Information Bureau," founded in Poland in September, 1947, was designed to maintain Soviet influence over the new satrapies, although it also had a foreign-policy function in combatting the Marshall Plan of American economic aid to Europe which had been announced in June of that year. The Cominform was an extension of Zhdanov's Soviet domestic campaign for ideological purity and anti-Westernism in the name of a refurbished and more bellicose Marxism-Leninism-Stalinism. Significantly, the North Korean, Mongolian, East German, and Albanian Communist Parties were not included in this new organization, which embraced all the other East European regimes and the Communist Parties of France and Italy. The inclusion of the latter parties was understandable in view of the anti–Marshall Plan strikes and unrest which occurred in Western Europe following the formation of the Cominform. The establishment of Cominform headquarters in Belgrade was regarded as appropriate, since Tito's Yugoslav Communists were probably the most anti-American and pro-Soviet in their foreign policy. The Communist seizure of power in Czechoslovakia in February, 1948, less than five months after the founding meeting, also gave notice of the Cominform's militancy and destroyed the last remnants of the illusion that Communists could be trusted in a coalition government.

However, the Cominform soon lost much of its apparent

"anti-imperialist" purpose and became an instrument of the anti-Tito campaign following Yugoslavia's expulsion from that body in June, 1948. The headquarters was removed to Bucharest, and Tito was reluctantly placed on his own road to socialism. The Kremlin's excommunication of Tito and his followers stemmed from a miscalculation by Stalin, who assumed that it would prompt the "healthy forces" among the Yugoslav Communists to take control. This did not happen, for Tito had built up his party apparatus during the war and had received very little aid from the Russians (and much from the British and Americans). Yet, he did owe his start to Stalin, who had purged Tito's predecessor, Gorkic, and whose Comintern in 1937 had designated Tito as caretaker-secretary of the Yugoslav Communist Party, then on the verge of dissolution.

The tensions which characterized Soviet-Yugoslav relations in 1948 prior to the excommunication included the following issues: the efforts of the Soviet Ambassador in Belgrade to engage in espionage at the expense of Tito's Party; Tito's ambitious plans for a Southeast European Federation, which was to include Rumania (and ultimately Hungary and a Communist Greece) and had the support of Georgii Dimitrov, the Bulgarian Communist and Comintern leader; Tito's plans for a rapid industrialization of Yugoslavia and his unwillingness to serve as a mere source of raw materials for the Soviet Union; Tito's reluctance to accept Moscow's terms for the establishment of Soviet-Yugoslav joint-stock companies; the higher salaries which had to be paid to Soviet military and economic advisers stationed in Yugoslavia; and Tito's practice of keeping Soviet personnel in Yugoslavia under the surveillance of his secret police.

All these issues were indicative of Tito's desire to be master in his own country, although he and his cohorts professed loyalty to Moscow after their excommunication. While Tito did not defect, he would not recant unconditionally. However, Stalin would not negotiate and demanded total submission—which undoubtedly would have involved Tito's being replaced by a more "reliable" and more subservient satrap. This did not prevent Tito from launching a collectivization campaign in 1949 in an effort to demonstrate his orthodoxy (he had been accused of pursuing a pro-kulak policy). This measure nearly wrecked the Yugoslav economy, which was saved only by American agricultural exports. Tito also aligned himself with the Soviet bloc against Britain, France, and the United States at the Danube River Conference held in Belgrade during August, 1948.

Yet, none of these measures would placate Stalin in his dealings with his pocket-size Yugoslav counterpart, who now had to make his own way. Tito soon declared himself to be a better Leninist than Stalin. The Kremlin now tightened its grip upon the states remaining in the Cominform and also extended its control over Albania, which had previously been a Yugoslav satellite. There followed during 1949 a witches' sabbath in which alleged "Titoists" and "national deviationists" were purged and executed. These included Koçi Xoxe in Albania, Laszlo Rajk in Hungary, and Traicho Kostov in Bulgaria. Wladyslaw Gomulka, the First Secretary of the Polish Communists, alone escaped with his life. The Communist Party of Czechoslovakia was shaken by the liquidation in 1952 of Party Secretary Rudolf Slansky and his followers and of the Slovak Communist Vladimir Clementis.

The Soviet Communist Party was not immune from the terror, fear, and suspicion which it had exported to Eastern Europe in the name of Communism. As the year 1952 wore on, an atmosphere of tension was to grip Stalin's Party in what were to be the last months of his eventful and bloody reign.

Thus, it came as somewhat of a surprise when Stalin convened the Nineteenth Party Congress in October, 1952—after a lapse of thirteen and one-half years since the preceding Congress. Yet, there was a sinister purpose in this action. Evidence which has come to light since Stalin's death indicates that Stalin, with the apparent aid of Malenkov, was preparing to rid himself of most of the Politburo members whom he had promoted during the thirties. The first step toward this goal was the replacement of the Politburo by the much larger Presidium of the Central Committee, provided for by the Nineteenth Congress. Whereas the Politburo had had nine members and two candidate-members, the new Presidium was composed of twenty-five members and eleven candidate-members. The Orgburo was abolished, since its functions had long ago been taken over by the Secretariat. The

Party also changed its name from All-Union Communist Party (of Bolsheviks) to Communist Party of the Soviet Union. In this way, "Bolshevism" was declared to be extinct as an official term.

Stalin left no last testament: his few words to the Nineteenth Congress were directed primarily to foreign Communist parties. His last published work, *Economic Problems of Socialism in the U.S.S.R.*, which appeared on the eve of the Nineteenth Congress, was a disjointed document covering many different questions inadequately. Yet, it contained a warning which might be considered testamentary. The warning was expressed in connection with Stalin's reaffirmation of the Marxist "law of value" as still being operative under Soviet socialism, although for Marxists this "law" was, strictly speaking, applicable only to the precapitalist and capitalist economies, since it was related to trade, to commodity exchange, and to cost-price relationships. What Stalin was referring to was the fact that remnants of a private market and a system of purchasing and selling persisted in the Soviet Union—especially in agriculture, where the peasant could still trade the surplus from his small private plot.

It was in the course of insisting that the "laws of political economy under socialism are objective laws . . . and operate independently of our will" that Stalin offered his warning:

> The fact is that we, the leading core, are joined every year by thousands of new and young cadres who are ardently desirous of assisting us and . . . proving their worth, but who do not possess an adequate Marxist education, are unfamiliar with many truths that are well known to us, and are therefore compelled to grope in the darkness. They are staggered by the colossal achievements of the Soviet regime, they are made dizzy by the extraordinary successes of the Soviet system, and they begin to imagine that the Soviet regime can "do anything," that "nothing is beyond it," that it can abolish scientific laws and form new ones. What are we to do with these comrades? How are we to educate them in the spirit of Marxism-Leninism?[48]

Stalin's sole suggestion—and a not very impressive one—was that the "so-called 'generally known' truths" be reiterated sys-

tematically. Yet, what is significant here is that this was possibly
a slightly wiser Stalin than the one who had brashly told the
Moscow Party organization on April 13, 1928, that "there is no
fortress in the world which . . . the Bolsheviks cannot take."[49]
The Stalin of 1952 was an old ruler who, though psychopathic
in certain respects, undoubtedly understood some of the limits
of Soviet power, although he had acquired this insight at a rather
great cost which was borne by his subjects. Within five months,
the "man of steel" was to go the way of all flesh, but what
would matter was whether or not his lieutenants also compre-
hended the limits of the vast power which they would inherit—
a power over which they would quickly begin to struggle
for control.

CHAPTER VIII

STALIN'S HEIRS

Accomplished leaders do not fall from the skies. They are raised up only in the course of struggle.

—Stalin, in a speech to the Polish Commission of the Comintern (July 3, 1924).

If we look at the history of our Party, it will become clear that always at certain serious turns in our Party a certain part of the old leaders fell off the Bolshevik Party truck, making room for new people. A turn is a serious matter, comrades. A turn is dangerous for those who do not sit firmly in the Party truck. During a turn, not everyone can maintain his equilibrium. Having made a turn with the truck, you look— and several have fallen off. [*Applause.*]

—Stalin, at the Fifteenth Party Congress (December 7, 1927).

It is, of course, a bad thing that Stalin launched into deviations and mistakes which harmed our cause. But even when he committed mistakes and allowed the law to be broken, he did that with the full conviction that he was defending the gains of the Revolution, the cause of socialism. That was Stalin's tragedy. But in the fundamental, in the main thing—and for Marxist-Leninists the fundamental and main thing is the defense of . . . the cause of socialism and the struggle against the enemies of Marxism-Leninism— in this fundamental and main thing, I . . . would to goodness every Communist could fight as Stalin fought. The enemies of Communism have deliberately invented the word "Stalinist" and are trying to make it sound abusive. For all of us, Marxist-Leninists . . . Stalin's name is inseparable from Marxism-Leninism. Therefore, each one of us, members of the Communist Party of the Soviet Union, strives to be as faithful to the cause of Marxism-Leninism . . . as Stalin was faithful to this cause.

—Khrushchev, in a speech at the Chinese Communist Embassy in Moscow (January 17, 1957).

Stalin's timely death—said to have occurred at 9:50 P.M. on March 5, 1953, after an illness of four days caused by a massive brain hemorrhage—abruptly brought to an end a period of mounting internal tension which had pushed the country to the brink of a blood bath. The tension had begun soon after the conclusion of the Nineteenth Party Congress in the autumn of 1952, when several economic administrators were executed in Kiev for allegedly having participated in various forms of graft. This was a rather harsh penalty to be imposed for this type of offense; also significant is the fact that the sentence was passed by the Kiev military tribunal. The Communist Party organization of the Ukrainian Republic, headed by Nikita S. Khrushchev until the end of 1949, came under attack for having permitted the alleged crimes to be committed. It is also possible that this campaign was aimed at Anastas I. Mikoyan, chief Soviet trader, who was responsible for the country's commercial apparatus. However, the fact that the executed defendants were Jewish was to take on added significance in January, 1953.

It became clear that a witches' sabbath was in the making when Tass, the official Soviet news agency, announced on January 13, 1953, that nine professors of medicine and practicing physicians had "confessed" to having committed "medical murder" in the deaths of former Politburo member Andrei Zhdanov and Colonel-General Alexander S. Shcherbakov, former chief of the Main Political Administration of the Soviet Army. Six of the nine physicians were Jewish, and it was alleged that they were "connected with the international Jewish bourgeois-nationalist organization 'Joint,' established by American intelligence . . ." This was a reference to the American Joint Distribution Committee, a Jewish charitable organization. Others of the physicians were said to have been "old agents of British intelligence."[1] It was also charged that the physicians had plans to eliminate Marshals Alexander M. Vasilevsky, Leonid A. Govorov, and Ivan S. Konev, as well as General of the Army Sergei M. Shtemenko and Admiral G. I. Levchenko.

The charges appeared to herald a new mass purge—one with a definite anti-Jewish, although ostensibly anti-Zionist, bent. Seasoned observers recalled the role which "medical murder" had played in the third show trial of March, 1938, in which three physicians were among those accused of having murdered Gorky and Kuibyshev and of having attempted to poison Yezhov. But the 1953 purge extended far beyond the medical profession. Economists had to recant the praises they had heaped upon purged Politburo member Nikolai Voznesensky's book on the Soviet wartime economy—a book in which serious "errors" were discovered.[2] The campaign against espionage, embezzlement, sabotage, and ideological heresy was couched in terms of the need to combat "carelessness" and "gullibility." Stalin's assertion at the February-March, 1937, Central Committee meeting was quoted to the effect that the "class struggle" does not die down with the so-called "elimination" of the "exploiting classes," since the "class enemy" supposedly becomes more dangerous as he grows weaker.

Apprehension, uncertainty, and fear gripped the population and the Party leadership, as well as the rank-and-file membership, in the last months of Stalin's reign. Stalin, a "good" atheist, never had given much thought to his own death and had apparently considered longevity as simply another "scientific" problem. Thus, it is not surprising that he failed to designate a successor at the time of the Nineteenth Congress. Yet, it would appear that Malenkov enjoyed as much of a blessing as Stalin was willing to dispense to any of his lieutenants: he had, after all, been chosen to deliver the report of the Central Committee to the Congress. At the same time, there can be little doubt that Stalin wanted to make the position of his lieutenants appear as unstable as it undoubtedly was. This he accomplished by the abolition of the old Politburo and the establishment of the new Presidium of the Central Committee, with twenty-five members and eleven candidate-members. The new members of this enlarged body included Semion D. Ignatiev, Minister of State Security (MGB), whose organization concocted the January, 1953, "doctors' plot"; Dem'yan S. Korotchenko, of the Ukrainian Party organization; Vasilii M. Andrianov, secretary of the Leningrad Province Party Committee and protégé of Malenkov; Leonid G. Mel'nikov, Khrushchev's successor as First Secretary of the Communist Party of Ukraine; Panteleimon K. Ponomarenko, Nikolai A.

Mikhailov, Averkii B. Aristov, and Mikhail Suslov—all members of the Secretariat; Vasilii V. Kuznetsov, trade union official and diplomat; Otto V. Kuusinen, Russified Finnish Communist and an old Comintern hand; and Matvei F. Shkiryatov, Chairman of the Party Control Committee.

The old Politburo members—Khrushchev, Beria, Bulganin, Molotov, Voroshilov, Malenkov, Kaganovich, and Mikoyan—were obviously being swamped by Stalin's introduction of new blood into what was supposed to be the Party's ruling body. In addition, the Secretariat was enlarged from five to ten members; the newcomers were A. B. Aristov, N. A. Mikhailov, P. K. Ponomarenko, and the new Presidium candidate-members Leonid I. Brezhnev and Nikolai G. Ignatov. Possibly, Malenkov would have been the only one to gain from this great personnel shuffle—if there had been time for it to be fully consummated. The "doctors' plot" was a weapon to be employed against Beria, since it supposedly pointed to impermissible laxity in the security organs. Molotov had been relieved of his post as Foreign Minister in March, 1949, and replaced by Andrei Vyshinsky, although he continued to hold a Deputy Premiership. Mikoyan was replaced by Mikhail A. Menshikov as Minister of Foreign Trade at the same time, but remained a Deputy Premier. In fact, Khrushchev recalled later (in February, 1956) that Stalin had informed the Central Committee at its first meeting following the Nineteenth Congress in 1952 that Molotov and Mikoyan had been guilty of certain wrongdoings. Khrushchev suggested that had Stalin "remained at the helm for another several months, Comrades Molotov and Mikoyan would probably have not delivered any speeches at this [Twentieth] Congress." To this he added: "Stalin evidently had plans to finish off the old members of the Political Bureau."[3] It was revealed also that Stalin, in the last years of his life, suspected Voroshilov of being an "English agent," often forbade him to attend Politburo meetings, and showed his annoyance with Voroshilov whenever the Marshal was allowed to attend.

Thus, it is clear that Stalin died not a moment too soon as far as the old Politburo members (his senior lieutenants) were concerned. Approximately six hours passed between the actual

announcement of Stalin's death and the time he was said to
have expired. These must have been busy hours for the dead
dictator's uneasy heirs. Alexander N. Poskrebyshev, Stalin's
personal secretary, had to be disposed of by the new rulers, and
the Kremlin garrison had to be dealt with. But the transcending
task was to agree upon some sharing of the inheritance, however
temporary. Malenkov assumed the Premiership, which Stalin
had held since 1941, and also retained his post in the Secretariat.
Vyshinsky, the Soviet representative at the United Nations in
New York City, was summarily informed that he had been
demoted to the post of Deputy Foreign Minister. Molotov at
long last had his sweet revenge and again assumed the position
of Foreign Minister, as well as that of First Deputy Premier along
with Beria, Bulganin, and Kaganovich. The MGB (Ministry of
State Security) was merged with the MVD and given to Beria.
Mikoyan headed a unified ministry dealing with both internal
and external trade. Nikolai Shvernik was rather unceremoniously
replaced by Voroshilov in the post of President of the Presidium
of the Supreme Soviet, and was himself placed in charge of the
trade unions. Bulganin, a political marshal, became Minister of
Defense, but the Army received recognition with the appointment
of Marshals Georgii K. Zhukov and Alexander M. Vasilevsky
as First Deputy Ministers.

More important, Stalin's enlarged Presidium of the Central
Committee was declared dead. A smaller Presidium, composed
of ten members and four candidate-members, was established
in its place. The new body included all the old Politburo members except Andrei A. Andreyev, who had been ousted from the
Politburo by Stalin for having espoused the numerically smaller
work group (the *zveno* or link) in the collective farms, and
Alexei M. Kosygin, who had been demoted to candidate's rank
in the 1952 Presidium and was now dropped. The two 1952
Presidium members who were retained in the new post-Stalin
Presidium were Maxim Z. Saburov, former *Gosplan* chairman
and now Minister of Machine Building, and Mikhail G. Pervukhin, Minister of Electric Power Stations and Electrical Industry. The four candidate-members were Shvernik, Ponomarenko,
Mel'nikov, and Mir-Dzhafar Bagirov, the First Secretary of the

Azerbaidzhanian Republic Communist Party. The ten-member
Secretariat was reduced in size with the removal of Ponomar-
enko, N. G. Ignatov, Leonid Brezhnev, and others. Khrushchev
was replaced by Nikolai Mikhailov as First Secretary of the
Moscow Party organization so that he could concentrate exclu-
sively on Central Committee matters. He was joined in the
Secretariat by the former head of the MGB, Semion D. Ignatiev;
Peter Pospelov, Director of the Marx-Engels-Lenin Institute; and
Nikolai N. Shatalin, a former official in the Cadres Department
of the Central Committee apparatus.

With these basic, if temporary, steps in the distribution of
power taken, plans for Stalin's funeral could now be made by
a commission headed by Nikita Khrushchev. Stalin's name was
carved on Lenin's mausoleum in large letters below that of Lenin
in preparation for the interment. The strange funeral took place
in Red Square on Monday, March 9, 1953, following the pro-
cession from the Hall of Columns on Hunters' Row in which
fourteen marshals of the Soviet Union carried Stalin's medals
and decorations on cushions. Funeral addresses were delivered
by Malenkov, Beria, and Molotov—each of whom expressed
grief and loyalty to Lenin's and Stalin's teachings and heaped
praise upon their late mentor. Malenkov promised "peace" and
a "happy life" and declared that "we have everything needed
for the construction of a complete Communist society."[4] Beria
spoke of the need to "unceasingly intensify and sharpen the
vigilance of the Party and of the people against the intrigues
and machinations of the enemies of the Soviet state."[5] He also
spoke of Malenkov as the "talented disciple of Lenin and the
faithful companion in arms of Stalin." Significantly, Molotov
made no such bows to Malenkov.

The mentor's embalmed corpse having been placed alongside what is said to be the corpse of Lenin, the heirs could now
turn to the more pressing problems of fully determining the
succession. There is little doubt that Malenkov made an effort
of sorts to don Stalin's mantle. Significantly, Malenkov did not
mention the Central Committee even once in his oration at
Stalin's funeral, while Beria and Molotov both spoke of the need
to "rally around the Central Committee." Beria referred to the

Central Committee no fewer than five times in his brief address. More evidence that Malenkov wished to be regarded as Stalin's successor is the famous photomontage published in *Pravda* on March 10, 1953, the day following Stalin's funeral. This shows Stalin, Mao Tse-tung, and Malenkov—the latter with his right hand resting upon his ample paunch. The photomontage was made from a large group photograph taken on February 14, 1950, on the occasion of the signing of the Sino-Soviet treaty of alliance and mutual assistance. Malenkov had eliminated from the picture all of his fellow Politburo members who had also been present at the signing of the treaty. This highhanded act undoubtedly did not sit very well with the other members of the new "collective leadership." A plenary session of the Central Committee held on March 14, 1953, decided to "grant the request" of Malenkov that he be relieved of his duties as a secretary of the Central Committee.

A new five-man Secretariat was also decided upon at that time. On March 21, *Pravda* published the list of its members in the following (nonalphabetical) order: N. S. Khrushchev, M. A. Suslov, P. N. Pospelov, N. N. Shatalin, and S. D. Ignatiev. Shatalin was also promoted from candidacy to full membership in the Central Committee, although he was to be eased out of the Secretariat in late 1954 or early 1955. Ignatiev was soon to be exiled from Moscow and given the post of First Secretary of the Party organization in the Bashkir A.S.S.R. The published list of Secretariat members made it clear that Khrushchev was its ranking member. At the March 15, 1953, session of the Supreme Soviet, it was Khrushchev who nominated Voroshilov for the post of President of the Presidium of the Supreme Soviet. Malenkov was approved as Premier after being nominated by Beria.

However, Beria's position as head of the unified Interior Ministry and as master of the huge internal army and the security organs cast a growing shadow over the other members of the collective leadership. The initial strength of Beria's position was demonstrated sharply during the period of more than three full days between the time of Stalin's death and the end of the funeral. From March 6 to March 9, Beria was for all practical

purposes in control of Moscow: his MVD troops had entered
the city by the thousands and had been deployed with tanks
and trucks along the concentric boulevards surrounding the inner
city, as well as along the avenues and streets connecting the
boulevards. The grip which he temporarily had on the city must
have given some pause to his colleagues as well as to the Army.
Yet, Beria did not seize power when he had an apparent opportunity to do so; possibly, his hand was stayed by his own
unwillingness to risk civil war at the time of Stalin's funeral.
However, this apparent moderation could hardly, in itself, be
reassuring to his colleagues.[6]

Beria remained a threat that had to be liquidated. He had
taken measures obviously designed to enhance his rather low
popularity in the country. He announced on April 4, 1953, that
his Interior Ministry had, after a "thorough verification," found
all the members of the January "doctors' plot" to be innocent.
Fifteen physicians were exonerated—curiously enough, six more
than had originally been accused of "medical murder." Dr. Lydia
Timashuk, who had revealed the alleged "crimes" of the physicians, was deprived of the Order of Lenin which she had been
awarded ten weeks earlier. The leaders of the former MGB
were accused of having separated themselves from the people
and the Party. The former Minister of State Security, Semion D.
Ignatiev, was charged with having "displayed political blindness"
and having permitted himself to be misled by his deputy, M. D.
Ryumin. Ignatiev escaped with a demotion from the Secretariat,
while Ryumin was ultimately executed. Ryumin's execution was
not announced until July 23, 1954; the protracted delay may
have been due to efforts to determine who else, in addition to
Stalin, in the inner ruling circle of the Party was behind the
"doctors' plot." In the end, Ryumin had to be executed because
he undoubtedly knew too much.

Beria quickly grasped the opportunity which the exposé of
the "doctors' plot" offered him and appointed some of his lieutenants as Ministers of Internal Affairs in the non-Russian
republics. Thus, Paul Ya. Meshik became MVD chief in the
Ukrainian Republic, and V. G. Dekanozov, the former Soviet
Ambassador to Nazi Germany, was appointed head of the MVD

in the Georgian Republic. In April, Beria restored his previously ousted Georgian friends, but they were to remain in office only a few months. More important is the fact that Beria apparently attempted to pose as a defender of the national rights of the non-Russian peoples. In May, 1953, Gregory Petrovsky, the former nominal head of the Ukrainian Soviet Government who had disappeared during the Yezhovshchina, was brought out of obscurity and decorated. In June, the First Secretary of the Communist Party of Ukraine, Leonid G. Mel'nikov, was removed from his post for having attempted to Russify institutions of higher learning in the western regions of the Ukrainian Republic. He was replaced by Alexei I. Kirichenko, secretary of the Odessa Province Party Committee and one of Khrushchev's close lieutenants.

The indictment against Beria included the charge that he had attempted to create hostility among the various nationalities of the Soviet Union; he was also accused of having attempted to sabotage Soviet agriculture—which, translated into non-Communist language, may mean that he advocated some concessions to the peasantry. There was also the ludicrous charge that Beria had been a British agent since 1919. The tactics of Stalin's successors in dealing with Beria were worthy of the late master himself. Though he was arrested during the latter part of June— probably on June 26—this fact was not announced until July 10. Beria is said to have been executed in December, 1953, along with six of his lieutenants: Meshik, Dekanozov, B. Z. Kobulov, S. A. Goglidze, L. E. Vlodzimirsky, and Vsevolod N. Merkulov.*

The demise of Beria did not augur well for the future of the collective leadership. However, "collegiality" continued to be the watchword during the remainder of 1953 and throughout 1954. It was necessitated by the fact that Stalin had not publicly designated a successor prior to his death. In addition, none of the lieutenants had sufficient power to proclaim himself to be Stalin's successor. Collective leadership was also an old and respectable line; Stalin himself had adumbrated the concept when he told the German writer Emil Ludwig, in referring to

---

* Merkulov had served as Minister of State Control in the post-Stalin Cabinet organized in March.

the Central Committee, that "in this areopagus is concentrated the wisdom of our Party."[7] Stalin made this statement on December 13, 1931, at a time when he had already established his personal dictatorship. Thus, it was almost a foregone conclusion that one of the members of the collective leadership would dispose of his colleagues and wrest supremacy for himself in the name of "collective leadership"—as Khrushchev actually did in June, 1957, when he employed the Central Committee against the Presidium.

It is doubtful whether there can be genuine collective leadership under Communism. Collegial authority in decision-making assumes collegial responsibility for failure. Yet, the Party, if it is to divest itself (as it must) of blame for failures, must perforce find convenient scapegoats. Individuals can serve as scapegoats, while the Party itself cannot. Collective leadership in the post-Stalin era, therefore, merely testified to the weakness and uncertainty of Stalin's heirs—to the absence of an arbiter in the ruling circle in 1953, and to a common fear of Beria. The outward signs of congeniality—for example, Malenkov, Khrushchev, Molotov, and Mikoyan vacationing together in August, 1954, at Sochi on the Black Sea—only obscured a new and ruthless struggle for power.

Only six months after this vacation—in February, 1955—Malenkov was compelled to resign the Premiership. Certain events which had occurred in December, 1954, throw some light on Malenkov's ouster. On December 24, the Soviet press announced the execution of Victor S. Abakumov, one of Beria's lieutenants and Ignatiev's predecessor as chief of the MGB. Executed along with Abakumov were three of his associates: A. G. Leonov, the former head of the MGB investigation unit for cases of special importance, and two of his deputies, V. I. Komarov and M. T. Likhachev. Abakumov and his aides were accused of having fabricated the so-called "Leningrad case"—the liquidation in 1949 of former associates of the late Andrei Zhdanov. Their unsaintly victims had included, among others, Nikolai Voznesensky, A. A. Kuznetsov, Mikhail I. Rodionov, and Peter S. Popkov.[8] Abakumov allegedly had acted on orders from Beria, who, it was now charged, had persuaded Stalin that the alleged culprits should be shown no mercy. What is of importance here is the timing of the announcement—one year after Beria's execution and six weeks prior to Malenkov's resignation from the Premiership. The question of Malenkov's complicity in the "Leningrad case" naturally arises. The activities of Abakumov occurred in 1949, at a time when Malenkov's position was immeasurably strengthened following his return to the Secretariat after Zhdanov's death. By May Day of 1949, Malenkov was Stalin's right-hand man—and not merely because he stood at Stalin's right as they viewed the passing parade from the convenient vantage point of the reviewing stand on Lenin's mausoleum. Malenkov and Beria shared a common interest in dealing harshly with Voznesensky and other followers of Zhdanov, and they did this with Stalin's blessings. The removal of Abakumov as MGB chief in late 1951 or early 1952 merely points to the fact that Beria was already at that time beginning to experience the decline which resulted in the "doctors' plot" aimed at him.

Malenkov had been so close to Stalin in 1949 that he could hardly avoid implication in the "Leningrad case." Khrushchev, on the other hand, had still been serving as First Secretary of the Communist Party of Ukraine at that time, and had not come to Moscow to assume the duties of secretary of the province Party committee until the end of 1949. His hands, therefore, were relatively clean. The revelation in the 1954 version of the "Leningrad case," as extracted from Abakumov and others, must certainly have weakened Malenkov's hand and helped to bring about his resignation. Another, and possibly more important, cause of Malenkov's resignation of the Premiership was the debate which developed in December, 1954, over the issue of whether or not continued primacy should be given to the development of heavy industry at the expense of light industry and consumers' goods.

On December 21, 1954—the occasion of the seventy-fifth anniversary of Stalin's birth—a rather unusual conflict in editorial policy manifested itself between *Pravda*, the Party organ edited by Dmitrii Shepilov, and *Izvestia*, the Government newspaper. *Pravda*, speaking for Khrushchev's Secretariat, came out

strongly in favor of continuing the Stalinist policy of giving
preference to the development of heavy industry, which was
termed the "very foundation of a socialist economy and a firm
basis for the further development of the national economy."
Izvestia, representing Malenkov's position, declared that the
"principal task . . . is the maximum satisfaction of the constantly increasing material and cultural needs of all members of
society." Malenkov's policy of increased production of consumers'
goods, first announced in August, 1953, and supported at that
time by Khrushchev, was now under heavy attack.

The issue was decided at the January 25, 1955, plenary session of the Central Committee in favor of Khrushchev's Leninist-
Stalinist line. Khrushchev even went so far as to liken the
light-industry policy to that of the Bukharin-Rykov deviation,
denouncing it as "slandering of the Party."[9] On February 8, a
clerk read Malenkov's brief letter of resignation to the Supreme
Soviet in Malenkov's presence. In this curious and obviously
artificial document, Malenkov pleaded guilty to many sins and
recognized the correctness of the heavy-industry line. He spoke
of the "need to have in the post of the Chairman of the Council
of Ministers another comrade with greater experience in state
work." Although Malenkov had been responsible for increasing
Soviet aircraft production during World War II, he now referred
to his "insufficient experience in local work and the fact that
I did not have occasion, in a ministry or some economic organ,
to effect direct guidance of individual branches of the national
economy." As if these falsehoods were not enough, Malenkov
had to admit "guilt and responsibility for the unsatisfactory state
of affairs which has arisen in agriculture." This was sheer nonsense. Khrushchev himself had for several years been playing a
far more important role in agriculture than Malenkov. In a final
gesture of contrition, Malenkov declared that "in the new sphere
entrusted to me, I will, under the guidance of the Central Committee . . . perform in the most conscientious manner my duty
and those functions which will be entrusted to me."[10]

The resignation was accepted, and Khrushchev nominated
Bulganin for the Premiership. Yet, Khrushchev was soon to adopt
as his own Malenkov's program of making additional consumers'

goods available to the goods-starved population. Malenkov had to be content with the Ministry of Electric Power Stations, which he was to hold until June, 1957. Thus fell the man who more than any other had dealt with cadres and personnel matters in Stalin's name. Malenkov's access to the dossiers of Party members and his influence over personnel appointments began in 1934. His was a career made exclusively in the Party apparatus— one which began when he joined the Central Committee apparatus in 1925, following the completion of his higher education. Significantly, Malenkov's decline apparently began when he assumed the Premiership and permitted himself to be ousted from the Secretariat.

Yet, the policy of granting limited concessions while maintaining the dictatorship of the Party—a policy initiated during Malenkov's Premiership—continued during Bulganin's tenure. Coming on the heels of an extremely harsh and repressive regime, this policy involved substantial gains for the post-Stalin regime at an almost negligible cost. An amnesty in March, 1953, led to the release of various categories of criminals, but did not apply to any political prisoners. Parts of the Kremlin were opened to the public. A large department store (GUM)—which was to serve as a national show place, since there was no comparable store in any other Soviet city—was reopened in the old commercial buildings on Red Square opposite the Kremlin. A large store specializing in children's toys was constructed on Dzierzynski Square across the way from the grim Lubyanka Prison and MVD headquarters. Certain cities were opened to foreign tourists, and a more liberal tourist visa policy was adopted. The collective leadership made an elaborate show of rubbing elbows with the populace. Tuition was abolished for qualified students in institutions of higher learning.

In foreign policy, the collective leadership initiated a series of bold and calculated moves which also brought substantial gains at little cost. The long-awaited Austrian State Treaty, providing for the withdrawal of Soviet troops from Austria, was concluded in May, 1955. This was quickly followed in June by Khrushchev's and Bulganin's visit to Belgrade to "apologize" for Tito's excommunication from the Cominform in 1948 and to effect a "reconciliation" (which soon encountered difficulties). In September, 1955, Moscow established diplomatic relations with the Federal Republic of Germany as a result of negotiations conducted by Khrushchev, Bulganin, and Molotov. The Soviet military base at Porkkala in Finland was evacuated and returned to the Finns—an obvious move to make Soviet demands for the return of the United States overseas base system more "legitimate." October, 1956, saw the resumption of diplomatic relations with Japan and the conclusion of a "Declaration of Peace" in lieu of a peace treaty, permitting postponement of any settlement regarding the territorial issues outstanding between the Soviet Union and Japan. In July, 1955, came the Geneva "summit meeting" with Eisenhower, Sir Anthony Eden, and Edgar Faure— attended by both Khrushchev and Bulganin. The Soviet Union undertook the sale of arms and military jet aircraft to Egypt, Syria, and Yemen, in spite of its oft-proclaimed professions of peace. An imaginative program was begun in which long-term loans were made at low interest rates to a number of under-developed countries, and technicians were sent abroad in substantial numbers. But the bloody suppression of the Hungarian popular rebellion in November, 1956, revealed another and apparently more permanent side of Soviet policy.

The change in the Soviet regime's appearance—if not in its substance—can be attributed in large part to the forceful and wily nature of the Party's First Secretary, Nikita Sergeyevich Khrushchev. Unlike Molotov and Malenkov, Khrushchev did not come from a middle-class family. Born in 1894, the son of a coal miner in the Kursk province, Khrushchev received little formal education. He worked first as a herdsman and then as a coal miner. Joining the Party in 1918, he participated in the civil war on the southern front as a "political worker" and then went to work in the coal mines of the Donets Basin. It was only by attending a *rabfak* (adult workers' school) that he completed his elementary and secondary education in 1925. He quickly became a district (*raion*) Party committee secretary and then carried out various Party assignments in Stalino and Kiev.

Khrushchev's great opportunity came in 1929 with his assignment as a student in the Stalin Industrial Academy in Moscow, where he became secretary of the Party committee and acquired some prominence as a Stalinist in combatting the Right Opposition. His reward came late in 1931, when he was appointed a borough (*raion*) Party committee secretary in Moscow. In 1932, he became Second Secretary of the Moscow City Party Committee (Kaganovich was First Secretary), and in 1934 he assumed the First Secretaryship in the city Party organization and the Second Secretaryship in the Moscow province Party organization; by 1935, he was First Secretary of both the city and province Party committees. It was during this period that he became associated with Bulganin, then the Chairman of the Moscow City Soviet. The Seventeenth Congress in January, 1934, brought Khrushchev a seat in the Central Committee, and four years later he was fortunate enough to be among the 30 per cent of its membership which survived the great purge. But he did more than merely survive: he advanced over the corpses of his comrade Party members. In January, 1938, Khrushchev became a candidate-member of the Politburo, replacing Paul P. Postyshev not only in that post but as Stalin's principal satrap in the Party organization in the Ukrainian Republic. In 1939, he became a full member of the Politburo.

Khrushchev was sent to Kiev to preside over the last stages of the purge and to teach the Ukrainians the Russian language. Thus, he informed the Fourteenth Congress of the Communist Party of Ukraine in June, 1938:

> Comrades, now all peoples will learn the Russian language because the Russian workers—and first of all, the workers of Peter [Petrograd] and the workers of Moscow—raised the banner of revolt in October, 1917. [*Prolonged applause.*] The Russian workers set an example to the workers and peasants of the whole world, showing them how it is necessary to struggle, how it is necessary to deal with your enemies . . .[11]

Khrushchev declared that all peoples would learn Russian "in order to master better the teachings of Lenin and Stalin, to learn how to vanquish their enemies." He remained at the head of the Party in Ukraine for the better part of a decade—except for the wartime period and the short time from March to December, 1947, when Kaganovich held the First Secretaryship in Ukraine and Khrushchev headed the Kiev government. This decade undoubtedly provided Khrushchev with invaluable experience, since it enabled him to exercise control over a functioning Party organization, maintain some ties with the "grass roots," and acquire henchmen whom he could reward for services rendered him.

His appointment in December, 1949, as First Secretary of the Moscow Party organization and as a member of the Secretariat gave Khrushchev a new advantage. It brought him to the very center of Party life, and with Malenkov's removal from the Secretariat in 1953, he gained control of that vital body. As First Secretary, a title he assumed in September, 1953, he was in a position to place his own men in control of regional and local Party organizations. This was to give him control of the Party Congress and enable him to pack the Central Committee. As early as July, 1955, following Malenkov's loss of the Premiership, Khrushchev was able to advance his lieutenant, Alexei I. Kirichenko, to full membership in the Presidium. Kirichenko, in his capacity as First Secretary of the Ukrainian Party organization, placed behind Khrushchev the entire Party apparatus of the Ukrainian Republic. In addition, Khrushchev had at his disposal the apparatus of the Russian Republic Bureau of the Central Committee, established by the Twentieth Congress in February, 1956, and placed under his Chairmanship.

Yet, it would be erroneous to assume that Khrushchev's primacy was based exclusively upon manipulation of personnel, even though this tipped the scales in his favor. As First Secretary, he controlled the entire Party press, and he was also able to win over many of Malenkov's followers. His success must also be attributed in part to a strong political instinct, a capacity for developing new programs, and a certain measure of daring. He enhanced his prestige as a result of journeys made with Bulganin to Communist China, India, Burma, Afghanistan, and England—as well as to the countries of Eastern Europe. He made a real effort to solve the Soviet Union's agricultural problems by reducing somewhat the burdens of the peasantry and by intro-

ducing the cultivation of corn (maize) in order to increase livestock production. He undertook a great gamble in bringing the
so-called "virgin and fallow lands" of Siberia and Kazakhstan
under cultivation in spite of unfavorable soil conditions and
limited rainfall. In 1957, he boldly abolished more than 100
economic ministries in Moscow and in the union republics and
established in their place 105 regional economic councils—a
move which increased somewhat the decision-making authority
of local industrial managers, but still left them subject to the
discipline imposed by the highly centralized Party apparatus.
While he did not appreciably reduce the overloaded bureaucracy
in Moscow, he did manage to shift many economic administrators to the provinces. However, Khrushchev's most effective
and most dangerous gambit was the so-called "de-Stalinization"
campaign.

What began with veiled critical references to the "cult of
personality" in July, 1953, developed into the lengthy "secret"
address which Khrushchev delivered before 1,436 delegates to
the Twentieth Congress on the night of February 24-25, 1956.
This remarkable document—remarkable for its half-truths and
falsehoods, as well as for some of its revelations—was procured
through a Communist source and made public by the United
States Department of State on June 4, 1956. Moscow verified
the authenticity of this text by using it as a basis for a discussion
carried on between various foreign Communist Parties and the
Communist Party of the Soviet Union.[12] Additional confirmation
was provided by a Central Committee resolution of June 30,
1956, entitled "On Overcoming the Cult of Personality and Its
Consequences."[13] This resolution paraphrased certain passages
from Khrushchev's speech and attempted to answer foreign
critics who argued that the Stalinist cult was a natural outgrowth
of the Soviet system and of Leninist norms of Party life. Foreign
Communists had also contended that Stalin's henchmen who
were now denouncing him posthumously were also guilty and
should share responsibility for his crimes, as well as sharing the
credit for his successes.

The June 30 resolution attempted to justify—although not
very convincingly—the fact that Stalin's heirs had acquired bold-

ness only after Stalin's death. Calling themselves the "Leninist core of the Central Committee," these heirs explained that since the "successes of socialist construction" were attributed to Stalin, "it is clear that anyone who spoke out against Stalin in this situation would not have received the support of the people."[14] This damning admission merely serves to confirm the ceaseless effort of the lavishly financed Party propaganda apparatus of the Central Committee to persuade its listeners that black is white, that night is day, that the dictatorship of a single party is democratic, and that Stalin was in his time the "Lenin of today," though he established a cult and committed untold crimes.

The Central Committee resolution protested that the failure of Stalin's heirs to de-Stalinize while Stalin was living "is not at all a matter of a lack of individual courage." It pretended that "many of the facts and incorrect actions of Stalin, particularly in the area of violations of socialist legality, became known only recently, only after the death of Stalin, principally in connection with the unmasking of the Beria gang and the establishment of Party control over the organs of state security."[15] This could be credible only if it were assumed that Khrushchev and his lieutenants, as well as the persons whom he ousted from the Central Committee, had been asleep for the two decades preceding 1953. The hypocrisy of this stage of the de-Stalinization process was evident in Khrushchev's warning to his select audience at the close of his address:

> We cannot let this matter get out of the Party, especially not to the press. It is for this reason that we are considering it here at a closed Congress session. We should know the limits; we should not give ammunition to the enemy; we should not wash our dirty linen before their eyes.[16]

If the Party were really divesting itself of the Stalinist heritage, Khrushchev's address would not have been delivered and disseminated in such a manner. However, the truth is that the de-Stalinization campaign could not be conducted in any other way, since the heirs were themselves thoroughly compromised. Each of them owed his position to Stalin, and Khrushchev was alive in 1956 and denouncing Stalin only because Stalin had spared him.

Khrushchev had survived because he had served Stalin faithfully and had sung his praises as a practitioner of the personality cult. With Stalin dead, Khrushchev could safely denounce him.[17] Yet, the crimes of Stalin, as far as Khrushchev was concerned, were those committed against members of the Party. Khrushchev was not concerned with the victims of Stalinism who were not Party members. The excesses of the collectivization campaign in the countryside were quite proper from Khrushchev's point of view. Nor was he concerned with the Trotskyites, Zinovievites, Right Oppositionists, and non-Russian "bourgeois nationalists." Khrushchev regarded Stalin's campaigns against these groups as "indispensable." But the Party members who had not been deviationists from Stalinism and still had perished were generously offered "posthumous rehabilitation" by Khrushchev in 1956. These included Postyshev, Chubar', Kosior, Rudzutak, and Voznesensky. The victims of the 1936-38 Moscow show trials were not granted this dubious honor.

Although Khrushchev's denunciation of certain of Stalin's excesses stands as probably the most damning indictment of Communism to come from the lips of a Communist ruler, we should not be blinded to the calculated nature of this official posthumous denigration of Stalin. Here was a deliberate attempt to attribute a portion (but not all) of the excesses and bloodshed of two decades to the character of one man—all this in order to remove responsibility for these crimes from the Party itself. One must ask whether the absolute power wielded by Stalin could have been acquired so easily without the Leninist organizational principles of the Communist Party of the Soviet Union and its lack of respect for minority views within its membership and for majority opinion outside it. Thus, Khrushchev attacked the Stalinist personality cult, but not the power cult of the Communist Party itself.

There was another purpose in delivering this secret speech, and that was to detract from Malenkov, Molotov, and Kaganovich in order to make it appear that they shared greater responsibility for Stalin's crimes and had been closer to the despot then Khrushchev. This was done obliquely. Thus, Kaganovich, Molotov, "and other members of the Politburo" were said to have received a telegram from Stalin dated September 25, 1936, which ordered them to remove Yagoda from the post of chief of the Commissariat of Internal Affairs and to appoint Yezhov in his stead. Khrushchev also indicated that in 1942, when he had attempted in vain to persuade Stalin to abandon an impossible plan to encircle Kharkov, he was unable even to speak to the dictator, but had to converse with Malenkov over the phone; though Stalin was present, he would not speak directly with Khrushchev, but only through Malenkov. The recounting of this episode was designed to imply that no one was closer to Stalin than Malenkov.[18] According to Khrushchev, only Bulganin, Mikoyan, and himself had been aware of Stalin's crimes and errors. Khrushchev even asked his listeners to believe that he had contradicted Stalin to his face by defending Marshal Zhukov's reputation when the dictator made certain disparaging remarks about the Army commander.[19]

If Khrushchev's attack upon Stalin was useful in the struggle for power within the Soviet Party, it proved to be much less so to those Communist rulers in Eastern Europe who were endeavoring to pursue a policy of firmness in dealing with their restless subjects. It is not coincidental that the ferment which caused Russian control to be challenged in Hungary and Poland during the autumn of 1956 came on the heels of the de-Stalinization campaign. This unrest in Eastern Europe also stemmed from Khrushchev's assertion at the Twentieth Congress that there were various "roads to socialism"—a statement which the Poles and Hungarians took quite literally. Khrushchev also contributed to the Soviet Party's difficulties when he endeavored to effect a reconciliation with Tito's Yugoslavia. The Khrushchev-Bulganin visit to Belgrade in May and June of 1955, the legitimacy conferred on Tito in Khrushchev's report at the Twentieth Congress, the dissolution of the Cominform in April, 1956, at Tito's request, and Tito's visit to Moscow in July, 1956—preceded by Molotov's removal from the Foreign Ministry—all served to give the impression that heresy and self-respect could be made to pay dividends.

However, the other states of Eastern Europe would not be permitted to adopt Yugoslavia's course, since Tito would not give his blessings to the Warsaw Pact of May, 1955, but continued to condemn all blocs—whether Soviet or Western—and to seek a reduction of Soviet influence in Eastern Europe. Thus, when Imre Nagy, under the pressure of public opinion, endeavored to take Hungary out of the Warsaw Pact in November, 1956, and give the country a neutral status under United Nations protection, he was overthrown by Soviet bayonets and tanks. Having attempted to pursue a separate Hungarian "road to socialism," Nagy paid with his life in 1958.

After the suppression of the Hungarian revolt, Moscow could well appreciate the blessing which the Chinese Communist Party in Peking bestowed upon this sanguinary operation. But Tito's condemnation of the October 24 Soviet intervention in Hungary and the fact that he granted temporary refuge to Nagy and his followers were not appreciated by either Moscow or Peking—though Tito did later voice approval of the November 4 Soviet intervention in Hungary. Indeed, Moscow's reliance upon Peking for support in the Hungarian affair (Khrushchev repaid it by approving Mao's bloody suppression of the Tibetan revolt in 1959) indicated a somewhat changed role for what had been the sole fountainhead of all Communist wisdom and authority.

The Communist Party of China represents a rather unique phenomenon, for it governs a country whose population is between two and three times as great as that ruled by the Soviet Party. The Chinese Party is also the world's largest Communist Party, with a membership half again as large as that of the Soviet Party (18 million as against 10 million members, respectively, in 1963). Mao Tse-tung, like Tito, seized power without much direct Soviet aid and built an apparatus of his own. While these characteristics did not reduce China's economic dependence upon the Soviet Union for machine tools, atomic weapons, technical personnel, and credits, they did serve to indicate that Moscow's primacy in the Communist bloc could be challenged ultimately or at least diminished. The efforts of the Chinese to impose a "higher" form of Communist social organization in the autumn of 1958 in the form of barracks-type communes indicated a desire on the part of Peking to be more orthodox than Moscow and to move closer to defining the meaning and form of an advanced Communist society. This was in contrast to the Soviet attitude toward the problem—at least insofar as it found expression in a programmatic document.

At the Twentieth Congress, Khrushchev promised a new Party program, to be ready by the time of the Twenty-First Congress, in place of the obsolete 1919 program drafted by Lenin. However, programs were of less immediate importance in 1956 than the question of who would control the Central Committee and its Presidium. At the Twentieth Congress, the size of the Central Committee was increased from 125 to 133 members, and from 110 to 122 candidate-members. Khrushchev's tenure as First Secretary had led to the removal of at least thirty-seven members and forty-nine candidate-members from the Central Committee elected at the Nineteenth Congress in 1952. Because of these and other vacancies, Khrushchev was able to add to the Central Committee no fewer than forty-one new full members and to promote no fewer than twelve from the ranks of the candidate-members. The turnover among the candidate-members was even greater, 71 of the total of 122 being new to the Central Committee.[20]

The Presidium elected by this new Central Committee in 1956 had eleven members and six candidate-members. The former included the surviving old Politburo members, plus Pervukhin and Saburov, and the two additions of July, 1955, Alexei I. Kirichenko and Mikhail A. Suslov. For a brief period, Khrushchev and Suslov were the only Secretariat members who were also members of the Presidium, although Khrushchev soon took measures to increase the number after the Twentieth Congress. The candidate-members of the Presidium were: Marshal Georgii K. Zhukov; Leonid I. Brezhnev, a former Dniepropetrovsk province committee secretary in the Ukrainian Party organization, as well as a former First Secretary in Moldavia and Kazakhstan; Nuritdin A. Mukhitdinov, First Secretary of the Party in Uzbekistan; Dmitrii T. Shepilov, Editor-in-Chief of *Pravda*; Ekaterina A. Furtseva, former secretary of the Moscow City Party Committee; and the veteran second-stringer,

Nikolai M. Shvernik. It was after the Twentieth Congress that Khrushchev brought Furtseva and Brezhnev into the Secretariat. Shepilov remained in the Secretariat until June 2, 1956, when he briefly assumed the post of Foreign Minister. He had been made a Secretariat member in July, 1955, along with Averkii B. Aristov, former First Secretary of the Khabarovsk Territory Party Committee, and Nikolai I. Belyaev, former First Secretary of the Altai Territory Party Committee.

Khrushchev's control of the Secretariat and his success in packing the Central Committee in 1956 paid off in June, 1957, when he was confronted with opposition to his policies in the Presidium. Some reports at the time indicated that he was even outvoted in the Presidium, and the number of subsequent ousters has tended to confirm this contention. He dealt with the matter by convening a plenary session of the Central Committee which, unsurprisingly, gave him its support. This enabled him to oust the key oppositionists—Molotov, Kaganovich, Malenkov, and Shepilov—not only from the Presidium, but from the Central Committee as well. Lenin's Tenth Congress resolution on Party unity was conveniently cited as justification. Pervukhin was demoted to the status of a candidate-member of the Presidium and sent off to East Berlin in February, 1958, as Ambassador to the Communist regime. Maxim Z. Saburov was dropped from the Presidium; earlier, in December, 1956, he had been forced to assume the blame for faulty estimates underlying the Sixth Five-Year Plan. The Central Committee, meeting from June 22 to 29, 1957, issued an indictment of this so-called "anti-Party group" which indicated that its members (and others) had opposed certain of Khrushchev's foreign and domestic policies, including the decision to cultivate the "virgin lands," the decision to establish the 105 regional economic councils, and the decision to abolish the tax on the individual peasant plot. Molotov was accused of "narrow-mindedness" in foreign policy and of having opposed the conclusion of the Austrian State Treaty, the "normalization" of relations with Yugoslavia, and the establishment of diplomatic relations with Japan.[21] Kaganovich and Malenkov were accused of having supported Molotov on certain foreign policy issues. Undoubtedly, these opponents of Khrushchev's policies had blamed him for the Hungarian revolt and for the rise of Gomulka in Poland, since his secret attack upon Stalin had been followed by unrest in the Soviet empire. However, the ousted oppositionists apparently acted out of weakness rather than strength. All of them, with the exception of Molotov (who abstained), voted for their own expulsion from the Central Committee.

Seizing upon this opportunity, Khrushchev consolidated his control by enlarging the Presidium to fifteen members and nine candidate-members. Of the eleven members in the Presidium following the Twentieth Congress, only six remained: Khrushchev, Bulganin, Voroshilov, Mikoyan, Suslov, and Kirichenko. Four of the nine new full members were promoted from the ranks of the candidates: L. I. Brezhnev, Marshal Zhukov, Madame Furtseva, and Shvernik. The other five new full members were taken either from the Central Committee or from the Secretariat: A. B. Aristov, N. I. Belyaev, Nikolai G. Ignatov, Frol R. Kozlov, and Otto V. Kuusinen—the last-named appointed to the Secretariat.[22] Thus, Khrushchev created a new Presidium for himself almost overnight, rewarded faithful followers, and was prepared to deal with anyone who dared to challenge him. When Marshal Georgii Zhukov expressed concern over political controls imposed upon the armed forces, Khrushchev sent him to Yugoslavia and Albania on a three-week state visit in October, 1957. Upon his return to Moscow, Zhukov discovered that he had been removed from his post as Minister of Defense and ousted from the Presidium of the Central Committee; he was also subjected to abusive personal attack and called a "would-be Bonaparte."[23]

The significance of Khrushchev's victory of June, 1957, lay in the fact that it brought into the fourteen-member Presidium a total of ten Secretariat members—nine as full members, and one (Peter N. Pospelov) as a candidate-member. It also signified the elimination of all of Stalin's heirs and pallbearers except Khrushchev and the pliable Armenian, Mikoyan. It only remained for Khrushchev to permit himself what had been forbidden to Malenkov: simultaneous tenure of the First Secretaryship of the Party and the Premiership. This Khrushchev accomplished on March 27, 1958, when he eliminated Bulganin and had

his name placed in sole nomination for the Premiership by
Voroshilov.

Thus, Khrushchev assumed the Premiership after only five
years as head of the Secretariat; Stalin, it may be recalled, had
been content to wait nineteen years as General Secretary before
becoming the head of the Government in 1941. Of course, there
are significant differences between the two men. Stalin was only
forty-two years old when he became General Secretary, while
Khrushchev was fifty-nine. Stalin did not introduce a woman
into the Politburo, as Khrushchev did. Nor did Stalin place so
many non-Russians—including an Uzbek—in the Party's ruling
body, as Khrushchev did after June, 1957. Khrushchev sold
agricultural machinery to the collective farms—something which
Stalin expressly forbade in his last published work in 1952. Stalin
dissolved the Society of Old Bolsheviks, whereas Khrushchev
released from jails and brought out of obscurity the few surviving Old Bolsheviks and rehabilitated some of the many who
had been purged. Khrushchev also packed the Presidium with
Secretariat members in 1957 to an extent never practiced by
Stalin. Nor was Stalin ever received in the White House in
Washington by the U.S. President, as Khrushchev was in September, 1959.

However, these differences between Stalin and Khrushchev
should not be permitted to obscure certain very basic similarities.
Both men claimed to be Leninist—although Khrushchev utilized
stratagems like de-Stalinization which seem to contradict a Leninist policy. Both men rose to power exclusively within the Party
apparatus and achieved supremacy because of their control of
the Secretariat. Both men initially simulated willingness to share
power, only to dispose of their colleagues in the end. Stalin rid
himself of his fellow triumvirs, Kamenev and Zinoviev; Khrushchev did the same with Malenkov and Beria. Both Stalin and
Khrushchev resorted to bloodshed, and Khrushchev employed
it even earlier in his Secretarial career—against Beria, Ryumin,
Abakumov, and many others. Both men owed their power to
a mentor: Stalin was Lenin's protégé, and Khrushchev was
Stalin's. There is a difference, however, in that Khrushchev
denounced and defamed the man who had given him his career,

while Stalin did not. Both Khrushchev and Stalin appropriated their opponents' programs: Khrushchev adopted Malenkov's promise of more consumers' goods and the view (expressed in March, 1954) that nuclear deterrence made a world war less likely; Stalin appropriated Trotsky's policy of rapid industrialization, subordination of the trade unions to the state, and the export of Communism abroad.

Both Khrushchev and Stalin effected great changes in personnel and in the membership of the Central Committee. Both rose to power by employing the Central Committee against the smaller Politburo (Presidium) and then packing the latter body with their own men. Both men introduced great changes and launched grandiose projects, while preserving the internal content and hard core of Bolshevik doctrine. Both men insisted upon giving a priority to the development of heavy industry at the expense of the population, depriving the people of inexpensive consumers' goods. And both men insisted upon maintaining sustained tempos under the compulsive psychology of overtaking and surpassing the non-Communist world.

CHAPTER IX

THE KHRUSHCHEV ERA

From history we have not a few examples when one or another political leader at a certain stage in his life did well and began to play an important role but then, as it were, cooled and even began gradually to fade. Such phenomena occur for various reasons: in one case the man may run out of strength; in another he may divorce himself from life, become conceited and not work; another may turn out to be unprincipled, a spineless time-server, a waverer in the struggle for the Party's cause. Meanwhile in the course of struggle there emerge new political leaders who oppose everything that impedes the development of the new, overcoming the resistance of the old. There occurs something comparable to what in astronomy is termed the light of extinguished stars. At a great distance certain stars appear to be shining, as it were, although in reality they have long since become extinguished. The difficulty with some people who have become stars on the public horizon is that they believe themselves to be radiating light when they have long since become smoldering embers.

—Khrushchev, discussing the "anti-Party group" at the Twenty-second Congress (October 17, 1961).

An important task of the [Party and state] control organs consists of halting window-dressing, false imputations, localism, squandering and stealing of state-owned material wealth and the like. . . . This disease [bribery] has permeated certain central departments and institutions, has infected certain leading workers with Party cards in their pockets. . . . In return for bribes state funds are squandered, orders for apartments are issued illegally, plots of land are allocated, pensions are granted, students are admitted to institutions of higher education and even diplomas are awarded.

—Khrushchev, at a Central Committee plenary session (November 19, 1962).

The Party solemnly proclaims: the present generation of Soviet people shall live in Communism.

—The 1961 Program of the CPSU.

The era associated with the name of First Secretary and Premier Nikita Khrushchev began as an antidote to the alleged policies of the "anti-Party group of Malenkov, Kaganovich, Molotov, and Shepilov who joined them"—as they were initially identified in the official formula. Subsequently, in addressing the Twenty-second Party Congress on October 17, 1961, Khrushchev confirmed that the group had actually consisted of eight members and included Premier Bulganin, Marshal Voroshilov, and First Deputy Premiers Pervukhin and Saburov.[1] Under the circumstances, it had been impossible in 1957 for Khrushchev to oust the entire group of his opponents from the Presidium of the Central Committee; it would have been embarrassing to admit at that time that the First Secretary had only been able to enlist the support of First Deputy Premier Mikoyan and Central Committee secretaries Suslov and Kirichenko.

Although Khrushchev's victory in the momentous Central Committee plenary session of June 22-29, 1957, enabled him to press the campaign against the "remnants of the cult of personality" and to pursue new policies, it was still necessary to discredit the members of the "anti-Party group" and to remove their followers from responsible positions and from the Moscow scene. Thus some of Malenkov's associates in the Soviet governmental apparatus were being removed even prior to the Central Committee session, as a result of the economic reorganization that abolished a number of ministries and transferred many ministers and officials from Moscow to the provinces to staff the new regional economic councils. Malenkov, who had been Premier only thirty months earlier, was exiled to Eastern Kazakhstan and appointed director of the Ust'-Kamenogorsk Hydroelectric Station. Molotov was removed from the post of Minister of State Control and appointed Ambassador to the Mongolian People's Republic, where he was kept under surveillance. Kaganovich and Shepilov were also relegated to humble posts in remote areas. Pervukhin was sent to East Berlin as Ambassador to the Communist East German regime. Several of Malenkov's followers, including P. K. Ponomarenko, were also sent abroad as ambassadors.

Bulganin's turn to be implicated publicly in the "anti-Party group" came in the December, 1958, Central Committee plenary session, at which he was required to confess his guilt and to denounce the others. The former Premier had been dropped from the Presidium of the Central Committee in September, 1958, and sent to head the Stavropol Regional Economic Council after a brief period—from April to August—as chairman of the State Bank (a post which, ironically, he had held in the late 1930's prior to his rise in the hierarchy).

The campaign of vilification and the self-abasement were to persist at the extraordinary Twenty-first Party Congress, which met between January 27 and February 5, 1959. This Congress had only one item on the agenda: to approve, but not debate, the "control figures" for Khrushchev's Seven-Year Plan (1959-65), which replaced the Sixth Five-Year Plan adopted at the Twentieth Congress in 1956. Khrushchev, in his report on the "control figures," boldly predicted that the Soviet Union would lead the world both in over-all industrial output and in per capita production by 1970—if not earlier. At the same time, Khrushchev conceded that in 1958 labor productivity in United States industry was more than double that of the Soviet Union and in agriculture it was three times as great; he thus made his sweeping forecast conditional upon a sharp rise in Soviet labor productivity.[2]

Khrushchev and other spokesmen assured the Congress that there were "at present no persons confined in prisons for political reasons."[3] This, however, begged the question as to how "political crimes" were being defined. Speaker after speaker at the Twenty-first Congress denounced the "anti-Party group of Malenkov, Kaganovich, Molotov, Bulganin, and Shepilov," although there were differences in the degree and nature of the denunciations.[4] Party secretary O. V. Kuusinen attacked Molotov as a "pseudo-theoretician" and condemned the "fruitless dogmatism" and "inside-out revisionism" of Khrushchev's opponents.[5] Alexei I. Kirichenko—who was to be removed unceremoniously from his Central Committee secretaryship the following year—denounced the oppositionists as "political intriguers and double-dealers" who were "sitting up to their ears in the mud of conservatism." In the course of the castigation he revealed June

18, 1957, as the date of the action against Khrushchev's "Lenin-ist general line for the creative application of Marxism-Leninism in the practice of Communist construction."[6]

Not one word was uttered in defense of the "anti-Party group." Pervukhin and Saburov were called upon to recant their "errors," although neither was a delegate to the Congress. Pervukhin, still officially a candidate-member of the Presidium, claimed, in partial extenuation, that he had helped unmask the "splitters and factionalists" at the June, 1957, Central Commit-tee plenary session, and thanked the Central Committee and its Presidium for enabling him to demonstrate at an important post the ability to "atone for my guilt before the Party." However, he was subsequently attacked at the Congress for having opposed, together with Molotov and Shepilov, the 1957 economic reor-ganization; he was also accused of lying when he claimed to have aided the Central Committee in June, 1957.[7]

In a brief statement that was not greeted by any applause, Saburov also confessed his "error" and claimed that he had been permitted to retain his seat in the Central Committee—though ousted from the Presidium—because he had deserted the "anti-Party group" during the plenary session. He expressed approval of the decision by which he was demoted to the post of factory director in the city of Syzran'.

In the final denunciation of the "group" at the Twenty-first Congress, the Soviet academician-propagandist Mark B. Mitin uttered a highly revealing Soviet-style epitaph: "The shameful bankruptcy of the anti-Party group of splitters and factionalists . . . and the complete victory of the Leninist line of the Central Committee have conclusively confirmed the remarkable state-ment of Lenin that life is the best teacher, that life always tells who is right."[8] Yet the highest representatives of the "Leninist line" were to have their ranks depleted and replaced within the next three years, despite the appearance of unity and stability.

The new lieutenants whom Khrushchev had brought into the Secretariat and Presidium following the June, 1957, crisis remained in office after the Twenty-first Congress. Since the extraordinary congress was not a regular meeting, it did not elect a new Central Committee. The first change occurred in January, 1960, with the demotion of N. I. Belyaev from the post of First Secretary of the Communist Party of Kazakhstan to the position of secretary of the Stavropol Party organization. At the same time, A. I. Kirichenko was removed from his post in the Central Committee Secretariat and demoted to secretary of the Rostov-on-the-Don Party committee. In May, 1960, Belyaev and Kirichenko were ousted from the Presidium. To replace them, Khrushchev promoted from candidate to full membership in the Presidium N. V. Podgorny, the Ukrainian Party First Secretary, D. S. Polyansky, Premier of the Russian Republic, and A. N. Kosygin, Deputy Premier of the U.S.S.R. No reason was given for the ouster of Kirichenko, who in 1958-59 was very close to Khrushchev and was even regarded as a likely successor to the First Secretary. His removal was preceded by criticisms of Party cadres in the non-Russian republics—for which the Ukrainian Kirichenko was apparently responsible. Kirichenko's career provided a graphic example of how rapidly a Party official can rise and fall.

The enlarged ten-member Secretariat that had come into being in July, 1957, was halved by Khrushchev in May, 1960, with the removal of A. B. Aristov, N. G. Ignatov, P. N. Pospelov, and Mme. Furtseva. Leonid Brezhnev temporarily left the Secretariat and the Presidium in July, 1960, after becoming Chairman of the Presidium of the Supreme Soviet (chief of state) in May, replacing the aged and compromised Voroshilov. Voroshilov was also removed from the Presidium; the other four remained in the Presidium for the time being. The five-man Secretariat that remained consisted of Khrushchev, M. A. Suslov, F. R. Kozlov, O. V. Kuusinen, and N. A. Mukhitdinov. In 1960, only Khrushchev and Suslov remained from the Secretariat installed after the Twentieth Congress in 1956. Only Khrushchev, Mikoyan, and Suslov remained of the eleven-member Presidium elected by the Central Committee in 1956.

First Secretary Khrushchev's success in retaining his Party post as well as the Premiership was based on his ability to control the territorial (union republic, *oblast'*, and *krai*) Party organizations. This enabled him to control the election of delegates to the Party Congress and, in turn, to control the election of the Central Committee. As Chairman of the Central Committee's Bureau for the Russian SFSR, established in February, 1956, to serve as an organizational bureau for the largest republic, Khrushchev reinforced his control of that vital sector of the Party apparatus.

If there were any doubts regarding the effectiveness of Khrushchev's control of the Party leadership after May, 1960, they were laid to rest by the Twenty-second Congress, which met October 17-31, 1961. This lengthy Congress was unusual in a number of ways. It adopted a new Party program and new Statutes; it reflected fissures in the structure of international Communism; it approved the removal of Stalin's embalmed body from the Lenin-Stalin Mausoleum in Red Square. The Congress heaped more abuse upon the defeated "anti-Party group." It was preceded and accompanied by the launching of Soviet multistage rockets fired into the Central Pacific target area, a distance of 8,000 miles from the launching site. A series of nuclear-weapons tests was conducted during the Congress, and Khrushchev announced the detonation of a 50-megaton hydrogen bomb.[9]

The Twenty-second Congress was also distinctive because it was held in the Kremlin's newly completed "Palace of Congresses," a modern structure of marble pylons and glass, which seats 6,000 persons. An auditorium of this size was required because the Twenty-second Congress was of unprecedented size, with 4,408 voting delegates (of whom 4,394 were in attendance) and 405 nonvoting delegates (possessing the so-called consultative vote). This was more than three and a half times the size of any of the three previous congresses, the last of which, the Twenty-first, had 1,269 voting and 106 nonvoting delegates. The increase in size was due to the change in the ratio of delegates to Party members; at the Nineteenth and Twentieth Congresses, the ratio was 1 to 5,000; at the Twenty-first Congress, it was 1 to 6,000. For the Twenty-second Congress, the ratio was set by the Central Committee at 1 to 2,000. The change in the norm of representation was justified as promoting the "development of intra-Party democracy."[10] It also represented an effort to replenish and revive the Party's forces, just as the prolongation of the anti-Stalin campaign indicated an attempt to refurbish the Party's image and the new program an endeavor to restock its ideological arsenal.

Khrushchev's lengthy Report of the Central Committee and his address on the new Party program required the better part of two whole days. Although the Report dealt with international issues and Soviet economic development in generally boastful tones, it admitted that the Party had experienced a fateful struggle between the remnants of the Stalinist "cult of personality" and the true "Leninist course" advocated by Khrushchev. The proponents of the "cult of personality" were said to have threatened "severance of the Party from the masses, from the people, serious violations of soviet democracy and revolutionary legality, delaying the economic development of the country, reducing tempos of Communist construction and consequently a worsening of the welfare of the toilers."[11] Despite—or because of—this crisis, Party membership was reported to have increased by a third between 1956 and 1961 with the admission of 2.5 million new members. The total membership of 9,716,005 consisted of 8,872,516 full members and 843,489 probationary candidate-members.[12] Khrushchev reported that during the preceding six years "more than 200,000 persons" had been expelled from the Party "for various reasons."[13]

The perpetuation of the anti-Stalin campaign and the renewed attacks upon the "anti-Party group" were made in a number of partial revelations by a select group of speakers. The new formula for identifying the "anti-Party group" involved a rearrangement and expansion of the list of offenders, which now read as follows: "Molotov, Kaganovich, Malenkov, Voroshilov, Bulganin, Pervukhin, Saburov, and Shepilov who joined them."[14] It was conceded that the group had an "arithmetical majority" in the Presidium in June, 1957. The replacement of Malenkov by Molotov as the group's leader was probably due to the fact that the latter had addressed a statement to the Party in defense of his own position. Molotov was alleged to have prepared a factional platform in which Khrushchev's new Party program was branded as "pacifist and revisionist" and "antirevolutionary," ignoring the inevitability of serious political conflicts with the "imperialist countries." The former Soviet Foreign Minister and Premier was accused of rejecting the policy of "peaceful coexistence" and of advocating adventurism and war.[15] However, Molotov's "platform" (or letter) was not published, and he was not permitted to address the Twenty-second Congress. Indeed, a number of speakers (of whom the most prominent were N. M. Shvernik, O. V. Kuusinen, B. N. Ponomarev, and P. A. Satyukov) proposed that the leaders of the "anti-Party group" (Molotov, Kaganovich, and Malenkov) be expelled from the Party because of their complicity in Stalin's crimes.[16]

Molotov was accused of having permitted "violations of socialist legality" during his tenure as Chairman of the Council of Commissars in the 1930's and of having approved Stalin's March, 1937, contention that the "diversionists and wreckers" were feigning loyalty to the Soviet regime. He was held responsible for the arrest and execution of an old Bolshevik and member of the first Soviet Government, G. I. Lomov. Molotov was also singled out for attack because of his stubborn refusal to admit the "incorrectness" of his views and the harmfulness of the "anti-Party group." Khrushchev claimed that his opponents had wanted to place Molotov in the leadership in 1957.[17] Although it was conceded that Molotov had "worked under Lenin," his reputation as a theoretician and as a Leninist was challenged on the grounds that Lenin had never spoken of Molotov's "theoretical merits" and had not referred to him in his 1922 Testament.[18]

Malenkov was accused of having conspired with Yezhov to liquidate the leading cadres of the Communist Party of Belorussia in 1937. He was also charged with responsibility for the 1949 "Leningrad case," for the deaths of Central Committee secretary A. A. Kuznetsov and Politburo member N. A. Voznesensky, and for a purge of the Party apparatus in Armenia.[19]

Kaganovich was accused of having been "supervigilant," even prior to the assassination of Kirov in 1934, and of having used "blackmail and provocation." He was held responsible for the execution of numerous railroad officials whom he had allegedly accused of "Trotskyite-Japanese wrecking" activities. Khrushchev's Ukrainian lieutenant, N. V. Podgorny, branded Kaganovich a "genuine sadist" and accused him of having advocated a campaign against Ukrainian nationalism in 1947 when he temporarily replaced Khrushchev as the First Secretary of the Ukrainian Communist Party. Podgorny denied that there was any need for such a campaign because Khrushchev had supposedly been training Ukrainians "in the spirit of internationalism" since 1938.[20]

It would be naïve to believe that only the leaders of the "anti-Party group" were implicated in Stalin's crimes, as is suggested by the manipulation of selected archival data at the Congress and the convenient omission of other data. Indeed, the release of biased and fragmentary data at the Twenty-second Congress by Khrushchev and his lieutenants makes it impossible to reconstruct the events of June, 1957, with any real degree of accuracy. However, several accusations made at the Congress place the "Leninist collective leadership" of 1953-57 in a new perspective. Thus Bulganin was accused by Shelepin, then head of the secret police (Committee for State Security, or KGB), of having, as Premier, used his bodyguard to prevent the entry of Central Committee members (Khrushchev's supporters in Moscow) into the Kremlin building in which the Presidium was meeting with Khrushchev in the minority.[21] *Pravda* editor Satyukov accused his predecessor D. T. Shepilov of keeping a book in which he "entered various pieces of gossip concerning leading [Party] workers" and then allegedly using such information in an attempt to cause Presidium members to quarrel among themselves.[22]

Marshal Voroshilov was the sole member of the "'anti-Party group" to attend the Twenty-second Congress as a delegate; he was even included in the Presidium of the Congress, an honorary body. He was criticized especially for having condoned the execution in 1937 of Soviet military leaders.[23] However, it was noted that he had "recognized his errors in time." Voroshilov was quoted as stating that he had been "confused by the devil"[24] and was described by Khrushchev as "walking about the Congress like a beaten man." The First Secretary recalled: "But you should have seen him at the time when the anti-Party group raised its hand against the Party. Then Voroshilov was a man of action [who] came forth, so to speak, in full regalia and armor, almost as though on a charger."[25] D. S. Polyansky quoted Voroshilov as telling the Central Committee in June, 1957: "You are young yet, and we will set your brains right" (*my vam mozgi vpravim*).[26]

Khrushchev asserted that the opposition had sought to utilize Voroshilov's not inconsiderable authority before the Central Committee and that he had joined the opposition (despite his dislike of Molotov, Kaganovich, and Malenkov) allegedly to prevent the "exposure of [his and] their illegal acts in the period of the cult of personality." Voroshilov submitted a statement, read to the Congress on October 26, 1961, in which he admitted that he had supported certain spokesmen of the group "in the beginning," but that he fully understood the seriousness of his "errors."[27] Khrushchev suggested that Voroshilov be treated differently from the "other active members of the anti-Party group," ostensibly because he had "to a certain extent aided the Central Committee" in the confrontation at the plenary session. The First Secretary recommended that Voroshilov, although properly criticized, be treated with "magnanimity."[28] It was obviously to Khrushchev's advantage to split his opponents, to obtain the support of the oldest among them (who had joined the Party in 1903), and to demonstrate a degree of forbearance after publicly humiliating Voroshilov.

Denied the right to state their case before a Party congress or even to publish a single newspaper article in their own behalf, the other members of the so-called "anti-Party group" could only suffer in silence. According to Shelepin, its members were "political corpses who . . . do not represent even a shadow of danger" to the Party.[29] Yet apparently there were compelling reasons why Khrushchev's opponents should have been given so much attention—in terms somewhat reminiscent of Stalinism—four years after they had been so thoroughly defeated. The new campaign contained few revelations and cannot be said to have been conducted in the interests of historical objectivity. The charge that the opponents were motivated by the desire to conceal their own culpability in Stalin's crimes ignores the very real reasons for their dissatisfaction with Khrushchev's leadership. Indeed, what is revealing is that the oppositionists put aside their various disagreements in 1957 in order to unite in an effort to oust Khrushchev; apparently they distrusted him more than they disagreed among themselves.

Yet even in defeat, the "anti-Party group" was useful to the First Secretary as a post-Stalin counterpart of previous deviationist or factional movements within the Party. By continuing to denounce the "cult of personality" and to blame past shortcomings on Stalin and the "conservatives"—rather than on the Communist Party or the Soviet system—Khrushchev was endeavoring to make his own regime appear better by contrast. The campaign was also resumed with the intention of discrediting and compromising the "anti-Party group" once and for all by unalterably associating its leaders with Stalin's crimes. It served to deprive any potential rival of the possibility of employing the Stalinist variety of orthodoxy as a weapon with which to oust the First Secretary. It served as a reminder of the fate which awaits "factionalists" who challenge the Party apparatus. Finally, the campaign reinforced the impression of a break with the fairly recent past: It was related to the issuance of the new Party program, the developing Sino-Soviet controversy, and the need for the Soviet Union to acquire a new image.

The effort to obliterate nearly two decades of Stalinist excesses and injustice assumed a symbolic form in the decision by the Twenty-second Congress to remove Stalin's body from the mausoleum in Red Square and inter it in an ordinary grave near the Kremlin wall. The action, taken on October 30, 1961, was supposedly prompted by popular demand, as expressed by Leningrad Party secretary I. V. Spiridonov, Moscow city Party secretary P. N. Demichev, and Ukrainian Party secretary N. V. Podgorny. Nor was Stalin's native Georgian Republic omitted from this unique ritual; G. D. Dzhavakhishvili, Chairman of the Georgian Council of Ministers, was called upon to assert that the Communist Party of Georgia "fully approves and supports" the transfer of Stalin's remains. Podgorny, who declared that the proposal had the support of "all Communists of Ukraine and of the entire Ukrainian people," submitted the resolution, which was adopted unanimously (and to the accompaniment of "stormy, prolonged applause") in accordance with prevailing Soviet practice.

One other delegate was selected to speak in support of the resolution. She was Dora Lazurkina, a Party member since 1902, who was arrested in 1937 and spent nearly two decades in prison, concentration camp, and exile. Lazurkina claimed that she had defended Stalin during all that time, attributing her own misfortune and that of others to "wreckers," and that it was only as a result of the Twentieth Congress that she "first learned the grievous truth about Stalin." Her moment of triumphant justice came when she told the Twenty-second Congress: "I always carry Ilyich [Lenin] in my heart and always survived, comrades, in the most trying minutes only because I had Ilyich in my heart and took counsel with him, so to speak. [*Applause.*] Yesterday I consulted with Ilyich as though he stood before me alive and [he] said: it is unpleasant for me to be beside Stalin who brought so much misfortune to the Party. [*Stormy, prolonged applause.*]"[30]

Another aspect of the effort to overcome the past was the adoption of new Party Statutes by the Twenty-second Congress. Although the new Statutes did not differ markedly from those adopted in 1952, there were several significant changes. The Party was now described in the Preamble as the "tested vanguard of the Soviet people"—in accordance with the abandonment of the "dictatorship of the proletariat" formula as inappropriate for a regime that is said to be moving from socialism into Communism. The Preamble also included an explicit provision condemning factionalism and groupings, and defining "ideal and organizational unity" as the "inviolable law of life of the CPSU." A new duty of Party members was that of "struggling for the creation of the material-technical basis of Communism" and raising labor productivity, mastering technique, and improving their own qualifications.

A new provision (Article 25) required the "systematic renewal" of the membership of Party committees. This provision stipulated that the members of the Central Committee and its Presidium be elected "as a rule to not more than three consecutive terms," and that one-fourth of the members be replaced at each Party congress. However, this was qualified by the following special provision: "Some Party workers by virtue of their recognized authority, high political, organizational, and other qualities may be elected successively to the leading organs for a longer period of time." In such instances a three-quarters vote is required. In the case of subordinate Party committees the rate of "systematic renewal" was fixed at one third for union republic central committees, territorial Party committees (*kraikoms*), and provincial Party committees (*obkoms*); for city Party committees (*gorkoms*) and district or borough Party committees (*raikoms*) it was fixed at one half. In actual practice, the 1961 provision for renewing committee membership was not an innovation, since it had been applied generously in the past—in the absence of a provision in the Party Statutes—as a result of the policy of systematic purging.

The Central Committee elected at the Twenty-second Congress contained 175 full members and 155 candidate-members, compared with the 133 members and 122 candidate-members elected at the Twentieth Congress in 1956. A high rate of turnover was evident in the fact that only 66 of the 133 full members elected in 1956 were re-elected in 1961. Of the 109 full members who were newly elected in 1961, only 27 were promoted from the ranks of the candidate-members. The other 82 new full members who had not been promoted from among the candidate-members included such figures as Alexei Adzhubei (Khrushchev's son-in-law and editor of *Izvestia*), Yuri Andropov (Central Committee department head), Leonid Ilichev (Central Committee secretary), and the writer Mikhail Sholokhov.

The Presidium elected by the Central Committee after the Twenty-second Congress consisted of eleven members and five candidate-members. Four of the fourteen full members of the preceding Presidium were not re-elected in 1961: A. B. Aristov, N. G. Ignatov, N. A. Mukhitdinov, and E. A. Furtseva. The survivors—in addition to Khrushchev and Secretariat members F. R. Kozlov, M. A. Suslov, and O. V. Kuusinen—included L. I. Brezhnev, A. N. Kosygin, Mikoyan, N. V. Podgorny, D. S. Polyansky, and N. M. Shvernik. Five of the nine Presidium candidate-members were not re-elected in 1961: Jan E. Kalnberzins, A. P. Kirilenko (dropped temporarily), D. S. Korotchenko, M. G. Pervukhin, and Peter N. Pospelov.* One candidate-member, Gennadi I. Voronov (secretary of the Orenburg *oblast'* committee of the Party prior to 1960, and subsequently First Deputy chairman of the RSFSR Bureau of the Central Committee and Premier of the RSFSR), was promoted to full membership in the Presidium. Voronov's rise was rapid; he had been made a Presidium candidate-member only in January of 1961. Thus the tradition of a substantial rate of turnover was maintained by Khrushchev as a means of rewarding younger and possibly more loyal followers and demonstrating the expendability of second- and third-rank members of the inner leadership.

However, the "permanent renewal of cadres"—to use Khrushchev's phrase—does not necessarily provide a guarantee against the "abuse of authority" and the possibility of a revival of the "cult of personality" which, understandably, were matters of concern at the Twenty-second Congress. Khrushchev reassured the delegates: "In the draft program and Statutes—these principal Party documents—are formulated theses, which must create guarantees against relapses of the cult of personality, which must raise in its path a reliable barrier (*shlagbaum*)."[31] The First Sec-

---

* The candidate-members newly elected by the Central Committee after the Twenty-second Congress were Sharaf Rashidov (Uzbek Party First Secretary, replacing the ousted Mukhitdinov) and V. V. Shcherbitsky, Ukrainian Premier and a former Ukrainian Party secretary. However, Shcherbitsky was removed in December, 1963, and was succeeded as candidate-member by Peter E. Shelest, Ukrainian Party First Secretary. Candidate-members re-elected in 1961 were Soviet trade union chief Victor Grishin, Georgian Party First Secretary V. P. Mzhavanadze, and Belorussian Party First Secretary Kiril T. Mazurov.

retary insisted that the "systematic renewal of elected organs must henceforth become the inviolable norm of Party life, the norm of state and public life."[32] In his concluding remarks to the Congress Khrushchev declared:

> It is necessary that in the Party there always be a situation in which any leader would be accountable to the Party, to its organs, so that the Party could replace any leader when it deems this necessary. . . . We Communists value highly and support the authority of correct and mature leadership. We must protect the authority of leaders (who are) acknowledged by the Party and the people. But every leader must understand the other side of this matter never to swagger [*kichit'sya*] as a result of his position, to remember that in holding one or another post, this person is only fulfilling the will of the Party. . . . Of course, by force of many reasons much authority is concentrated in the hands of one person holding this or another leading post. A leader raised up [*vydvinutyi*] by the Party and the people must not abuse authority. . . . But there is one matter that cannot be stipulated in any statutory paragraphs—the collective of leaders must understand well that it is impossible to permit a situation in which any authority, even the most estimable, can cease to reckon with the opinion of those who promoted him.[33]

Although the First Secretary was unwittingly ironic—in view of the treatment meted out to some of his erstwhile colleagues in the *kollektiv*—his concern for a crucial problem was laudable. However, the 1961 Statutes, although recognizing the "principle of collective leadership" (in the Preamble), did not once mention the post of First Secretary, let alone define and circumscribe the powers of the office. Nor were fixed and limited terms of office really stipulated for high Party officials. The Preamble also contained a warning that "any manifestation of factionalism and group activity is incompatible with Marxist-Leninist Party principles and Party membership."[34] The inclusion of an injunction against "revisionism and dogmatism" provided a means of disgracing or even punishing those who might in the future chal-

lenge the correctness and the orthodoxy of the Party's current
general line.

As if to purge the specter of the so-called "cult of personality," the Twenty-second Congress adopted the long-awaited and
much-heralded 1961 Party program, which replaced Lenin's
archaic 1919 program. Such a document had been promised by
Stalin at the Eighteenth Congress in March, 1939, and at the
Nineteenth in October, 1952, but in each case the special commission that was established brought forth nothing. At the Twentieth Congress, Khrushchev had promised a new program for the
Twenty-first Congress, but was unable to produce it in 1959.

The 1961 program, an excessively verbose document when
compared with the brief programs of 1903 and 1919, provided
no real enlightenment regarding the details of daily living in a
truly Communist society. Half the new program was devoted to
international relations as viewed from Moscow. In the remaining
half an effort was made to create the impression that Communism is humanistic and concerned exclusively with the welfare
of mankind. The establishment of the "material-technical basis"
for Communism in the Soviet Union was promised by 1980, with
full Communism to follow in the indefinite future. Steel production of 250,000,000 tons annually by 1980 was predicted in the
program—but no mention was made of the possible impact of
future technological changes upon living patterns and consumer
needs.

Various amenities were promised by 1980 at public expense.
These included free education, free medical service and drugs,
free municipal public transportation, a rent-free apartment for
each family and for newlyweds, "gradual introduction" of free
mid-day meals at schools and enterprises. Public catering was
seen as taking precedence over home cooking by 1970-75. The
program did not promise abolition of the indirect taxes needed
to finance these benefits. Nor did it promise the abolition of
money (as Lenin's 1919 program had), but rather the "strengthening of the monetary and credit system." Enterprises are to be
operated profitably. Yet the promised benefits are conditional,
the program warned, upon the absence of "complications in the
international situation and the resultant necessity of increasing

defense expenditures." Thus there was included a ready-made explanation for any possible failure to fulfill the program's promises.

Lest the old Leninist notion of the "withering away" of the state be misunderstood, the 1961 program declared that the state "as an organization of the entire people will survive until the complete victory of Communism." One of its purposes is to "exercise control over the measure of work and the measure of consumption" and to "instill in the people conscious discipline and a Communist attitude to labor." Khrushchev had told the Twenty-first Congress that the Communist society would be "planned" and "highly organized." In addition to repeating the hackneyed formula that a Communist society is one in which each person is rewarded "according to his needs," Khrushchev embellished upon the new program in his own inimitable way:

> You know of the great industry of the bees: every bee brings its drop of nectar to the hive. Figuratively speaking, Soviet society represents, as it were, a great Communist hive. In our society each person must, by his labor, increase the public wealth. . . . But as among bees there are drones whom the bees and the beekeeper seek to drive out, so in our Soviet collective there are people who, while not giving anything to society, wish to live at its expense. There are still people among us who are inclined to regard Communism as a society of idleness and inactivity. Unfortunately, in oral and in printed propaganda the society of the future is frequently portrayed in a one-sided and simplified manner as though no one will either sow or reap under Communism but only eat pies. [*Animation*.] Such a conception of Communism is peculiar to people who are poor in spirit, Philistines and parasites.
>
> Communism and labor are inseparable. The great principle "He who does not work does not eat" will be in operation under Communism and in fact will become a sacred principle for all. . . . In labor are revealed people's abilities and talents, man's genius. In labor lies mankind's immortality. [*Applause*.][35]

As if in accordance with the beekeeper analogy, the program provided for the enhancement of the Party's role and not for its "withering away" during the period of "full-scale Communist construction." Defining the Party, in Lenin's words, as "the brain, the honor, and the conscience of our epoch," the program paraphrased key provisions from the 1961 Statutes. It also denounced the "cult of personality and the violations of collectivism in leadership," without explaining their causes, and modestly asserted that "the achievement of Communism in the U.S.S.R. will be the greatest victory mankind has ever won throughout its long history."

According to the program, this victory is to entail the "complete unity" of the nations of the U.S.S.R. and, ultimately, the creation of a "single world-wide culture of Communist society." In the section on nationality policy, a dialectical treatment was much in evidence. Thus the union republics were promised an extension of their rights, while the boundaries between them were said to be "increasingly losing their former significance." Nations were said to "flourish" under socialism, but all manifestations of nationalism, "parochialism," "national egoism," and "idealization of the past" were to be eliminated. The Party pledged itself to "promote the free development of the languages of the peoples of the U.S.S.R." and to prevent all "privileges, restrictions or compulsions in the use of this or that language." Yet, the program described the Russian language as "the common medium of intercourse and cooperation between all the peoples of the U.S.S.R.," and Khrushchev, in presenting the program, referred to Russian as the "second native language" of the non-Russian peoples of the Soviet Union and the means of their obtaining access to "world culture."[36] While conceding that "even after Communism has been built in the main, it would be premature to declare the fusion of nations," Khrushchev made it clear that Communism "will not conserve and perpetuate national differences" and will "root out even the slightest manifestations of nationalistic survivals."[37] As if to presage the disagreement which would mar the proceedings at the Twenty-second Congress, Khrushchev, in discussing the international "socialist commonwealth," declared: "Nationalism, irrespective of the covering in which it might appear, constitutes the most dangerous political and ideological weapon used by international reaction against the unity of the socialist countries."[38]

An attempt to symbolize the unity of the socialist camp was the belated dedication of a monument to Karl Marx in Moscow's Sverdlov Square on October 30, 1961. The erection of countless statues of Lenin and Stalin in the Soviet Union had for decades prevented the erection of a statue of Marx. Ironically, the dedication followed Chinese Premier Chou En-lai's expression of disagreement with Khrushchev's policy toward Albania. Khrushchev had openly denounced the Albanian Communist regime of Enver Hoxha for having opposed the campaign against the "cult of personality" and for ruling Albania by Stalinist methods and even allegedly seeking to restore the "cult" in the CPSU. After expressing concern for the "fate of the heroic Albanian people," Khrushchev insisted that Albania "must abandon its erroneous views and return . . . to the path of unity with the entire international Communist movement."[39]

This treatment of Hoxha—which was comparable to Stalin's treatment of Tito—prompted Chou En-lai to criticize "public one-sided censure of any fraternal party," and to insist that disputes between Communist parties be settled "on the basis of mutual respect for independence and equality." Chou declared that the exposure "before the face of the enemy" of disputes between two fraternal parties "cannot be viewed as a serious Marxist-Leninist approach."[40] The Chinese not only refused to censure the Albanians, but obviously abetted them in their defiance of Khrushchev. Other Soviet speakers repeated and enlarged upon Khrushchev's condemnation of the Albanian leadership, and Chou left the Congress early (on October 23) and returned to Peking after first laying a wreath on Stalin's tomb. Khrushchev responded by further denouncing Albania for its failure to publish in full the new CPSU Program (allegedly done to create a "distorted impression" of it), for its "anti-Soviet calumny," and for "pouring filth over our Party." He accused Hoxha of employing repressive measures against those Albanian Communists who advocated "Soviet-Albanian friendship" (and who, by implication, wanted to oust Hoxha). Khrushchev pointedly told the remaining members of the Chinese delegation: "If the Chinese comrades wish to apply their efforts to normalizing the Albanian Workers' Party's relations with the fraternal parties it is doubtful that anyone can better aid in the resolution of this task than the Communist Party of China."[41]

The deterioration of Soviet-Albanian relations had its origin in the Soviet decision to seek a *rapprochement* with Tito's Yugoslavia in 1955. Since Albania would probably have been absorbed by Yugoslavia had Tito not been excommunicated by Stalin in 1948, the Albanians could not view with favor the Soviet flirtation with Yugoslav "revisionism" following the May, 1955, visit of Khrushchev and Bulganin to Belgrade. In the spring of 1956, the Soviet Union had also sought, but in vain, the posthumous rehabilitation of Koçi Xoxe, the Albanian Minister of the Interior, whom Hoxha had executed in 1949 as a Titoist.[42] The Hungarian rebellion of 1956, for which the Albanians held Tito largely responsible, was viewed by Hoxha as proof of the incorrectness of Khrushchev's anti-Stalin campaign. The deterioration in relations could not be checked by Khrushchev's lengthy visit to Albania in late May and June, 1959. Khrushchev's apparent encouragement of pro-Soviet and anti-Hoxha elements in the Albanian Workers' (Communist) Party in April, 1956, and in 1960, resulted only in Hoxha's ruthless purging of his enemies. The intentional snubbing of Albanian Premier Mehmet Shehu by Khrushchev and other East European Communist leaders at the U.N. General Assembly in October, 1960, reflected the seriousness of the dispute. Soviet pressure on Albania (the denial of credits and the withdrawal of specialists) during 1960-61 resulted in Hoxha's seeking economic aid from Peking.*

Hoxha's defiance of Khrushchev was made possible by Al-

---

* In a broader context, the Soviet-Albanian dispute could also be attributed to the fact that the Albanian Communists had established their regime without Soviet aid (although with some Yugoslav direction and support). In their centuries-old dislike for and fear of their neighbors (Serbs, Macedonians, Greeks), the Albanians have cultivated nationalism and xenophobia, which have left their mark on the Communists. The Albanian political tradition has been characterized by violence and fierce recriminations. A small country with limited resources, Albania has depended on foreign subsidies and probably was not satisfied with the amount of economic aid received from the Soviet Union.

bania's geographic remoteness from the Soviet Union and the impossibility of a Soviet military intervention of the kind that occurred in Hungary in 1956. Nor could Hoxha have defied the Kremlin had he not enjoyed the support of Peking—an ally not too close to Albania geographically, but of sufficient stature to be reckoned with by Albania's enemies. Unimpressed by Khrushchev's fulminations at the Twenty-second Congress, Hoxha responded with a speech on November 7, 1961, in which he heaped scorn and ridicule upon "N. Khrushchev and his group," while at the same time professing belief in "Albanian-Soviet friendship."[43] Various accusations were leveled by Hoxha against Khrushchev: The Soviet leader had become fearful of "imperialism"; he was delaying the solution of the German question; he had fostered the "illusion" that Communists could come to power by obtaining a parliamentary majority; he had disrupted international Communist unity by publicly attacking Albania; he had not invited Albania to the Twenty-second Congress so as to prevent the refutation of his "baseless slanders and accusations"; he had denied the equality and independence of all Communist parties; he was discrediting the Soviet Union by his criticism of J. V. Stalin, by exaggerating Stalin's errors and neglecting his great merits; he had created a "cult" of his own personality; he had joined Albania's enemies as a result of his "anti-Marxist position" and had claimed that the "traitorous clique of the Yugoslav revisionists" was building socialism; he had "not refrained from any measures" in attempting to bring Albania to its knees.

Hoxha's attack on Khrushchev was followed on November 25, 1961, by the recall of the Soviet Ambassador in Tirana, Iosif V. Shikin. When the Albanians demanded a sizable reduction in the size of the Soviet diplomatic mission in Tirana, Moscow (on December 3, 1961) withdrew all of its diplomatic and commercial representatives from Albania and demanded the withdrawal of Albanian diplomatic personnel stationed in Moscow. However, tiny Albania's defiance of the Soviet colossus, although based on Albanian interests, was an integral part of the growing Sino-Soviet dispute.

The Sino-Soviet relationship had begun to deteriorate following the Twentieth Congress of the CPSU, despite the fact that Soviet economic aid to China had been increased. One source of friction was Khrushchev's arbitrariness in issuing important doctrinal pronouncements regarding the changing character of "imperialism," the possibility of preventing World War III, and the existence of "various roads to socialism"—including the possibility that a Communist regime might be established by free parliamentary elections rather than by civil war. Khrushchev undertook to make such theoretical revisions at the Twentieth Congress without consulting Mao Tse-tung (who regarded himself as a fully qualified theoretician) or leaders of other Communist parties. The anti-Stalin campaign and Khrushchev's desire to entice Yugoslavia back into the fold also were potential sources of friction, in view of Chinese unwillingness to regard decisions taken by one party—even the CPSU—as binding on all other Communist parties.

An uneasy compromise resulted from the November 14-16, 1957, Moscow meeting of twelve ruling Communist parties. The Communist leaders issued an imprecise and contradictory Declaration that condemned "dogmatism and sectarianism," but defined "revisionism or right opportunism" as the "principal danger." However, it was agreed that "each Communist party defines which danger is for it the principal danger at a given time." Yugoslav "revisionism" was condemned—a victory for the Chinese—and a "parliamentary" road to socialism was recognized, although a "nonpeaceful transition" was also regarded as a possibility, depending on "concrete historical conditions."[44]

The Chinese were willing to accept Soviet leadership of the Communist movement if they could exercise sufficient influence over CPSU policy. Khrushchev, after endeavoring to win over Tito's Yugoslavia, launched a campaign against Yugoslav "revisionism," in 1958, in which the Chinese, Bulgarians, and Albanians joined. Tito's refusal to join the Warsaw Pact, his demand for equality, and the issuance of a new Yugoslav Party program led to renewed Soviet economic pressure on Yugoslavia and to attacks by Khrushchev at the Twenty-first Congress in

January, 1959. In attacking Tito, Khrushchev denied that there were any disagreements with Peking, while conceding that China's "methods of building socialism are in many respects different from ours."[45]

The Sino-Soviet differences included the introduction of agricultural communes in China in 1958 and the "great leap" designed to lead to rapid industrialization. Thus there emerged the danger that China would claim to have achieved "Communism" before the Soviet Union. Khrushchev now declared that the transition from socialism to Communism would be gradual and not abrupt—even though involving intensive effort—and would require the achievement of economic abundance.[46] A series of events in 1959 further clouded Sino-Soviet relations: Khrushchev's official visit to the United States, the Soviet refusal to support China in its border dispute with India, and the cool reception Khrushchev received during his visit to Peking in early October, following his visit to the United States.

In 1960, the relationship reached a turning point. In April, Peking published an anthology, *Long Live Leninism,* in which it attacked Khrushchev's views on the danger of war and the possibility of a peaceful transition from capitalism to socialism. Khrushchev responded with a surprise attack on the Chinese position on war and peace in June, 1960, at the Third Congress of the Rumanian Workers' (Communist) Party in Bucharest.[47] Soviet technical personnel were withdrawn from China and Sino-Soviet trade declined sharply as Moscow endeavored to exercise economic pressure and impede Chinese industrial development. A month-long conference of eighty-one Communist parties, held in Moscow in November, 1960, resulted in a verbose Statement, an unsatisfactory compromise that meant various things to various Communists. Like the Declaration of 1957, the Statement condemned "dogmatism and sectarianism," as well as "revisionism, Right-wing opportunism," and specifically denounced the Yugoslavs. A significant passage, typical of the new compromise, was the following: "All the Marxist-Leninist parties are independent and have equal rights; they shape their policies according to the specific conditions in their respective countries and in keeping with Marxist-Leninist principles, and support each other."[48] The Moscow Conference revealed many disagreements between the new Sino-Albanian axis and Moscow. Peking refused to accept the CPSU Twentieth Congress as binding on other parties; it refused to regard peaceful coexistence as more than a tactical maneuver; it reserved for itself the right to propagate its viewpoint within the world Communist movement. Albania's Hoxha and Shehu walked out of the Conference after Hoxha denounced Khrushchev's policies.

The 1961 program of the CPSU ignored the Chinese contribution to the "building of Communism." But Khrushchev's denunciation of the Yugoslav "revisionist positions" at the Twenty-second Congress (despite a *rapprochement* in foreign policy between Belgrade and Moscow) did not prevent the Chinese from protesting his treatment of Albania. Yet 1962 witnessed an improvement in Soviet-Yugoslav relations, as well as a visit by Tito to Moscow in December, following a visit by Soviet chief of state Leonid Brezhnev to Belgrade in September and October—all to the accompaniment of shrill attacks by Peking and Tirana against "modern revisionists" (now including Khrushchev). Mutual recriminations were intensified during 1963 as a result of the June 14 letter of the Chinese Communist Party to the CPSU—which the Chinese began to distribute within the Soviet Union without official permission when Moscow refused to publish it. This document covered nearly the entire range of fundamental differences dividing the two parties. On July 14, 1963, *Pravda* belatedly published the Chinese letter and a lengthy "Open Letter" of the CPSU that attempted to refute the Chinese contentions. Bilateral Sino-Soviet talks held in Moscow during July ended in complete deadlock. The serious nature of the Sino-Soviet differences was fully evident in the February 14, 1964, report to the CPSU Central Committee delivered by M. A. Suslov, who denounced the "splitting activities" and the "anti-Leninist positions" of the Chinese and expounded on "the danger of a petty-bourgeois, nationalist, Trotskyite deviation."[49]

The issues dividing Peking and Moscow involved differences

of degree that tended at times to become differences in kind. One area of disagreement dealt with the relative strength and character of "imperialism" and the danger of war. Peking held that the Soviet Union had exaggerated the possibilities of avoiding war so long as "imperialism" exists and had allowed itself to be "blackmailed" by the "imperialist" nuclear powers. Moscow contended that war could be prevented and that war would harm rather than promote the Communist cause. Basic to the dispute was a disagreement over the significance of nuclear weapons and the degree of risk entailed in launching local "wars of liberation" that could escalate into global nuclear war. In Peking's view, the Soviet Union should assume greater risks in promoting the revolutionary struggle (the spread of Communism) in Asia, Africa, and Latin America, since global war was not likely to ensue from such undertakings. The Chinese advocacy of a more militant concept of coexistence was based on a rejection of the Soviet view of the possibility of a peaceful road to socialism; in Peking's view, civil wars and armed revolutionary struggle were viewed as the more likely course of development.

Nor did Peking approve of Soviet internal developments. It criticized the Twentieth Congress and the posthumous denigration of Stalin. It rejected Khrushchev's replacement of the "dictatorship of the proletariat" by a "state of the whole people" as being contrary to Marxism-Leninism. It also accused the Soviet Union of "great power chauvinism" in its treatment of Albania (the Soviet Union claimed that Peking was using Tirana as a "mouthpiece"). Peking refused to condone Moscow's efforts to bring the "Yugoslav revisionist clique" into the socialist commonwealth and condemned such efforts as violations of the November, 1957, Moscow Declaration and the December, 1960, Moscow Statement. The CPSU insisted that Yugoslavia was a socialist state despite "differences on a number of ideological questions."

At the bottom of this controversy—frequently conducted in semi-esoteric language and by proxy—has been the Chinese desire to obtain adoption of its line. To this end, the Chinese assumed the role of defender of the principle of the equality of parties in challenging Soviet hegemony—as Tito had challenged it earlier, but for different reasons. After all, Khrushchev had conceded at the Twenty-first Congress that "all Communist parties are independent and develop their policies proceeding from the concrete conditions of a given country."[50] The different positions of Moscow and Peking have reflected the age of the respective regimes and the fact that the Chinese leadership was closer to the revolutionary experience of seizing power. In all likelihood, Peking overestimated the political significance of the 1957 Soviet successes in rocketry, and readily assumed that Moscow could be persuaded to adopt a high-risk policy and press its supposed advantage in promoting the revolutionary struggle against the "imperialists." Thus there was disagreement over the tempo which the revolutionary struggle should assume and the role of violence in it. In the background there undoubtedly lurked Chinese resentment over dependence on the Soviet nuclear capability and the inadequacy of Soviet economic aid—while Moscow made large loans to various non-Communist regimes which, in Chinese eyes, were far less worthy of support than China.

The spectacle of the world's two largest Communist parties each claiming to be the true repository of ideological orthodoxy while censuring the other "fraternal" party indicated that the Communist world was plagued by serious contradictions. Although the Twenty-second Congress and the 1961 CPSU program devoted much attention to the "contradictions" which allegedly characterize relations between "capitalist" states, they offered no satisfactory analysis of the new Communist contradictions. Clearly, Khrushchev's efforts to develop "creative" theory, while simultaneously claiming to combat "dogmatism" and "revisionism" (as practiced by those who disagree with him), played no small role in the advent of this phenomenon.

At the Twentieth Congress, Khrushchev was said to have enriched theory and modified Leninist doctrine by declaring that a world war (fought with nuclear weapons) was "not fatalistically inevitable," because of the power of the "peace-loving socialist states." Stalin's concept of "peaceful coexistence" was redefined in terms of an economic race with "capitalism" and a more intensive ideological struggle with the old order; there was to be no coexistence of ideologies. Khrushchev also proclaimed the end of the "capitalistic encirclement" of the Soviet Union—a cardinal concept of Stalinism—because of the enhanced position of the Soviet Union as a great power and the emergence of a "world socialist system" and the "forces of peace."[51]

Recognizing the destructive nature of nuclear warfare, Khrushchev conceded that the costs of such a war for the Soviet Union would far outweigh the possible gains. In lieu of war as the gravedigger of "capitalism," he proposed a relentless economic competition in which the Soviet Union would outproduce its archantagonist and win followers throughout the world. The significance of this formulation lay in its definition of Communism primarily in terms of economic productivity and material abundance. The tendency to equate Communism with a form of state-controlled industrialization has, ironically, left Khrushchev open to the charge of "revisionism." It also has neglected the possibility that industrialization (with or without Communist rule), like any solution to mankind's situation, creates problems even as it solves them.

Perhaps in an attempt to divert men's minds from such thoughts, Khrushchev sought to provide a hazy glimpse, though not a blueprint, of the promised land of the 1961 Party program. Of more immediate consequence was his abandonment of the "dictatorship of the proletariat" formula in an effort to depict Communism as an all-embracing popular movement. Another of Stalin's formulations abandoned by Khrushchev was that the class struggle intensifies as the class enemy grows weaker (expounded in March, 1937). The campaign against the "cult of personality"—apart from its use as a weapon in the post-Stalin power struggle—was intended to prove that the Soviet dictator need not be adulated or deified and that Communism need not be based primarily on terror.

Because Khrushchev's contribution to Communist theory was not based on systematic works, but on speeches and policy statements, it understandably acquired a somewhat fragmentary character. As a policy-maker, Khrushchev did not hesitate to improvise and to adopt a pragmatic and flexible approach to many problems. Thus he undertook numerous official visits abroad and also sent Brezhnev, Mikoyan, Marshal Malinovsky, and his son-in-law, Adzhubei, on missions to foreign lands. These journeys were taken not only to engage the Soviet Union's enemies in disputation, but to attempt to win support wherever possible by promoting a new image of the Soviet regime and also to become better acquainted with the non-Communist world. As Adzhubei told the Twenty-second Congress, "self-isolation is easier, contacts are more difficult, but it is contacts that are necessary . . ."[52] Khrushchev personally received numerous foreign dignitaries, ambassadors, and correspondents. Soviet exports were increased greatly as a result of a substantial foreign-loan program extended to various neutralist states. Petroleum, armaments, machinery, technical expertise, and gold became important export items—the gold to balance trade deficits. A new Soviet merchant marine and large fishing fleets made their presence felt on the high seas. "Delegation diplomacy" and cultural exchanges were expanded in the pursuit of political ends.

Characterizing Soviet foreign policy as "active and flexible," Khrushchev seemed to be seeking a *détente* with the United States. This led to the conclusion of a partial, unenforced nuclear-test-ban treaty (signed in Moscow on August 5, 1963), which banned tests in the atmosphere, in outer space, and underwater, but permitted them underground. The treaty, which followed five years of frustrating negotiations over enforcement and test detection, was not signed by Peking or Paris. Earlier, Khrushchev had dusted off the Soviet Union's 1927 proposal for complete and rapid general disarmament (including the abolition of military academies and war ministries) and presented it to the U.N. General Assembly in September, 1959. The absence of effective controls made this proposal as meaningful as the Kellogg-Briand Peace Pact, which had attempted to outlaw war as an instrument of national policy. However, the Soviet Union and the United States did sign an agreement on June 20, 1963, providing for the establishment of direct telegraphic communication between the White House and the Kremlin.

In the cultural sphere, concessions were alternately granted and retracted as the desire for freedom among artists continued to challenge the canons of "socialist realism." Although a more tolerant attitude toward jazz and abstract art was evident at times, and although a school of younger critical poets made its appearance, the Party was ready at all times to censure deviant literature. Indicative of the harsh treatment was that accorded the poet and novelist Boris Pasternak. Pasternak, who was awarded the Nobel Prize in literature in October, 1958, first accepted the honor and then declined it after being told that he would be expected to remain abroad if he received the prize. The first Soviet writer to be awarded a Nobel Prize, Pasternak was expelled from the Union of Soviet Writers. Pasternak's difficulties resulted from the publication abroad of his novel, *Doctor Zhivago*, a work that raised many basic questions regarding the value of the Soviet revolution. A lesser-known literary figure, Yevgeny Yevtushenko, exemplified how a poet who espoused the ideas of truth and justice could be used by the regime. The publication of his poem "Stalin's Heirs" in the October 21, 1962, issue of *Pravda* was useful to Khrushchev in the campaign against his opponents. However, when Yevtushenko exceeded the limits of Party tolerance he was publicly reprimanded, in the spring of 1963.

The vagaries of literary controls had their economic counterparts in the administrative reorganizations of 1957 and 1962, in periodic personnel shake-ups, and in the extension of the death penalty in May, 1961, to so-called economic crimes such as theft, embezzlement, and the operation of clandestine private enterprises. Countless Central Committee plenary sessions devoted to agricultural production could not solve this chronic problem. Various proposals, such as the cultivation of corn, bringing more than 100 million acres of virgin lands under grain cultivation, increasing the number of state farms, expanding Party control over farming, and increasing chemical fertilizer production reflected the seemingly unending search for a solution. When Soviet grain production declined, in 1963, Khrushchev did not hesitate to expend gold and foreign exchange for large-scale purchases from Australia, Canada, and the United States.

Lest there be any ideological backsliding, a ponderous new textbook, *Foundations of Marxism-Leninism,* edited by O. V. Kuusinen, made its appearance in 1959. This volume replaced the chapter on dialectical and historical materialism in Stalin's *Short Course History.* Renewed attention to ideological indoctrination was also evident in the early 1960's, with the intensification of atheistic propaganda and attacks on the clergy reminiscent of the repressive measures employed by Stalin in the 1930's. The continuing effort to eradicate religious beliefs belied the apparent "liberalism" of the Khrushchev regime in other sectors of public life.

Yet Khrushchev's distinctive political style managed to convey the impression of a somewhat different regime. The First Secretary's practice of visiting every populated region of the Soviet Union, his innumerable interviews, broadcasts, and television appearances, his volubility at receptions, luncheons, and banquets, and his occasional studied clowning endowed his regime with a degree of novelty and a certain air of informality.[53] At the same time, much of the old political style remained, with its concern for the achievements of milkmaids and swineherds, its exhortations to increase production. Although always the center of attraction, Khrushchev consciously avoided the extreme forms of the "cult of personality." This did not prevent his receiving credit for Soviet satellite, rocketry, and manned-spaceflight successes, nor his being referred to as an "outstanding Marxist-Leninist." Khrushchev pontificated on countless subjects, including the Soviet pea, potato, and buckwheat crops, fertilizers, the social structure of "capitalist" states, nuclear weapons, and electrification of railroads. He did not hesitate to interrupt speakers with embarrassing questions at Party congresses.

Khrushchev's role was enhanced as a result of the publication in 1962 of a second edition of the official 1959 *History of the CPSU.* The new edition, reflecting the line taken at the Twenty-second Congress, systematically belittled and criticized Stalin's role in the Party and demeaned or ignored the lengthy services of Molotov and Kaganovich. However, the Party history, prepared on Khrushchev's orders and designed to demonstrate his loyalty to "Leninism," could hardly present a balanced appraisal of its principal sponsor; this would have required a treatment of various events and decisions which, in retrospect, may not redound to Khrushchev's credit. These include the 1956 rebellions in Hungary and Poland, the ineffective six-month Berlin ultimatum of November, 1958, the erection of the Berlin Wall in 1961, and the rash and unilateral decision to attempt to excommunicate defiant Albania from the socialist camp. The question of the ultimate profitability of the expensive and speculative virgin-lands program continued to lurk in the background. Whether or not the costly Soviet foreign-loan program would pay high dividends would also affect the ultimate verdict on Khrushchev's leadership. His reckless and clandestine attempt to emplace missiles and bombers armed with nuclear weapons in Cuba in 1962 resulted in a nuclear confrontation with the United States. This prompted Peking to condemn Khrushchev's "adventurism" and his "capitulationism"; indeed, Khrushchev has contributed significantly to the division of the world Communist camp that has characterized his era.

Yet the First Secretary's ability to survive his errors is a tribute to his amazing resilience and dexterity. His merits include cunning, an ability to improvise, a certain degree of frankness, a recognition of the need to abandon or modify tactics, and a basic soberness despite manifestations of bellicosity and tactlessness. Khrushchev's efforts to learn about the outside world have somewhat reduced the vast area of ignorance about the West that characterizes large segments of the Soviet political elite. If he shocked the diplomatic world at the U.N. General Assembly in October, 1960, by removing his shoe and pounding the desk with it in order to express his disapproval of a speaker, it simply reaffirmed—in a novel way—Soviet denial of freedom of speech.[54]

If Khrushchev effected a revolution in Soviet political style, he has also had a profound impact upon the Party. His preeminent position was reflected in his removing from the Secretariat the lieutenants whom he had installed in 1957, replacing them with a new group as a result of the gradual enlargement of the Secretariat after the Twenty-second Congress. The five-member Secretariat of 1960 was enlarged to nine in November, 1961, with the addition of four new positions. Five new members were added—one of whom replaced Mukhitdinov. The new secretaries were Leonid Ilichev, former editor-in-chief of *Pravda,* who served in the Foreign Ministry prior to 1958 and subsequently as head of the Propaganda and Agitation Department of Central Committee; Boris Ponomarev, editor of Khrushchev's *History of the CPSU* and a specialist on foreign Communist parties; Alexander N. Shelepin, former Komsomol First Secretary and head of the Soviet secret police from December, 1958, until November, 1961; Peter N. Demichev, former First Secretary of the Moscow Party Committee. Ivan Spiridonov, former Leningrad Party secretary, was also appointed in November, 1961, but was relieved of his post in April, 1962, to become Chairman of the Supreme Soviet's Council of the Union.

The Secretariat was increased to twelve members at the November, 1962, Central Committee plenary session. The newcomers were Yuri V. Andropov, specialist on East European Communist parties and Soviet Ambassador to Hungary, 1953-57; Vasilii I. Polyakov, agricultural specialist; Alexander P. Rudakov, heavy-industry expert; Vitalii N. Titov, Kharkov *oblast'* Party secretary from 1953 to 1961 and subsequently chief of the Central Committee's Department of Party Organs for Union Republics. The Secretariat was also reorganized, with the establishment of a number of commissions dealing with agriculture (with Polyakov as chairman), industry and construction (Rudakov), Party organizational problems (Titov), chemical and light industry (Demichev), and ideology (Ilichev). A new joint Party and governmental control body, the Committee of Party and State Control of the Central Committee and Council of Ministers, was headed by Shelepin, with Iosif V. Shikin as deputy chairman.

In November, 1962, the Central Committee approved a far-reaching reorganization of the Party's structure by extending the functional principle upward from the primary Party organizations. Prior to this the territorial principle had been the basis of the union republic, *krai, oblast', raion,* and city Party organizations while the primary Party organizations were found in various enterprises, ministries, universities, and the like. The reorganization, based on the "production principle," provided for the establishment of two parallel Party committees in nearly every *oblast'*—one for agriculture and the other for industry. *Oblasts* not having highly diversified economies continued to have a single Party committee (*obkom*). Each union republic Central Committee was to have two bureaus (one for agriculture and the other for industry or industry and construction). A similar division was effected in governmental organization at the *oblast'* and *krai* levels with the establishment of separate soviets for agriculture and industry.

The 1962 reorganization reflected Khrushchev's preoccupation with economic production and increased Party involvement in industry and agriculture. It also resulted in the consolidation of rural *raion* Party committees so that several rural *raions* now constituted a Production Administration with a parallel Party Committee and Bureau concerned largely with fulfilling agricultural production quotas. By creating two Party hierarchies, united at the union republic level, the authority of the central Party organization was enhanced since the organization at the provincial level was divided and its autonomy correspondingly reduced. Additional evidence of aggrandizement of the center at the expense of the locale was provided by the establishment of a Central Asian Bureau of the CPSU Central Committee; this intermediate body, located in Tashkent and headed by a Russian, Vladimir G. Lomonosov, rather than by a Turkic Communist, further reduced the autonomy of the Uzbek, Tadjik, Turkmen, and Kirghiz republic Party bodies. The promised "extension of the rights of the union republics" was not to be fulfilled in Party organization.

Khrushchev's impact on the Party transcended personal style and organizational changes. His effort to revitalize the Party made the Congress both a far larger and a more helpless body than it had been under Stalin, but it also increased mass participation—though of a passive nature. Party organizations were established on nearly every collective farm, and more workers and peasants were admitted to membership. The Party's unprecedented size was paralleled by the growth of the Central Committee's membership. Although Khrushchev restored the practice of holding regular Central Committee plenary sessions (at least two per year; in 1958, as many as six sessions were held), he also adopted the practice of frequently devoting these sessions to agricultural and industrial development. He not only enlarged the Central Committee membership, he swamped it by inviting to certain plenary sessions large numbers of specialists, Party apparatus officials and *oblast'* and city Party secretaries, ministers of union republics, planning officials, and newspaper and magazine editors. Thus Khrushchev enhanced as well as demeaned the status and role of the Central Committee.

Yet the Party's continued supremacy over such vital sectors as the military, economic management, and the secret police was demonstrated in various ways. The military were subjected to renewed Party discipline and indoctrination with the replacement in May, 1962, of Marshal Filipp I. Golikov by Alexei A. Yepishev as chief of the Defense Ministry's Main Political Administration; Golikov, a professional army officer, was replaced by a Party official who had served as Soviet Ambassador to Yugoslavia. The 1962 reorganization testified to the Party's ability to interfere in economic decision-making and management. The removal of General Ivan A. Serov, a professional security police officer, from the chairmanship of the Committee for State Security (KGB) in December, 1958, placed the secret police under the direction of Party officials. Serov's successor, A. N. Shelepin, remained as KGB chairman until November, 1961, when he joined the Secretariat and was replaced by V. E. Semichastny.

The renewal of leading cadres became the hallmark of the Khrushchev regime, which also endeavored to create the impression of championing and promoting younger cadres against old, "conservative" elements. However, responsible senior appointments in the Secretariat were given in June, 1963, to such tested Presidium members as L. I. Brezhnev and N. V. Podgorny.

Brezhnev's appointment was unusual in that he rejoined the Secretariat while retaining the chairmanship of the Presidium of the Supreme Soviet for another year. In July, 1964, he was succeeded in the latter post as chief of state by Anastas Mikoyan. Brezhnev's return to the Secretariat also followed the sudden withdrawal from public life of Frol Kozlov, who was said to be ill. The appointment of Podgorny brought to the Secretariat a specialist on agriculture and food processing who had headed the Ukrainian Communist Party as First Secretary since 1957 and had acquired much experience between 1953 and 1957 as second secretary under his unfortunate predecessor, Kirichenko. Those who were rising to still greater heights in the Soviet hierarchy could take cognizance of Suslov's February 14, 1964, address, in which the expulsion from the Party of Molotov, Malenkov, and Kaganovich was announced. It was as if to confirm an unwritten law of Soviet politics that while new men are advanced and acclaimed, their predecessors are demoted and disgraced, either quietly or in public.

The tortuous and yet obvious development of the Party recounted in the preceding pages should give pause to all who would view this phenomenon in the same light as a conventional political party. The record of the Party's dealings with its members and with many who have acted in its name and have dutifully attempted to do its bidding indicates that admission to its ranks has involved oppressive obligations, unexpected personal compromises, and untold risks. The Party has in many ways been a twentieth-century golden calf, although there is much in its past to suggest a Moloch. Whether the Party can divest itself of this dark heritage—a heritage that stems directly from its self-centered philosophy of history—remains one of the crucial questions of the century.

NOTES

CHAPTER I

From Marxism to Factionalism

1. The authoritative text of Nechaev's *Catechism of a Revolutionary* is contained in the Soviet historical journal *Bor'ba klassov*, No. 1–2 (1924), pp. 268–272. All excerpts from it presented here are translated from that text, which was decoded and was published with an explanation of the ingenious code which Czarist police officials were unable to decipher before finding the key in the notebook of a Nechaevite.

2. This statement is not invalidated by the fact that Stalin on one occasion—December 13, 1926, at a plenary session of the Executive Committee of the Comintern—employed the pejorative term *Nechaevshchina* in attacking Zinoviev for allegedly having equated the dictatorship of the proletariat with the dictatorship of the Party. This, claimed Stalin, would "tear the Party away from the masses, lead to bureaucratization of the Party to the highest point, transform the Party into an infallible force, implant in the party a Nechaev regime."—J. V. Stalin, *Sochineniya*, IX, 79. An explanatory note (p. 366) describes Nechaev as a terrorist "anarchist-Bakuninite"—although Bakunin wanted to have nothing to do with him—who advocated a "narrow conspiratorial organization, severed from the masses, in which the will and opinions of its members were absolutely crushed." Ironically, this definition of Nechaev's position is appropriately applicable to the Communist Party, which, in the name of so-called "democratic centralism" and "iron discipline," has treated its membership in precisely the manner described.

3. Nechaev, *Narodnaya rasprava*, No. 2 (1870), p. 9, as quoted in Alexander Gambarov, *V sporakh o Nechaeve; k voprosu ob istoricheskoi reabilitatsii Nechaeva* (Moscow: *Moskovskii rabochii*, 1926), p. 121. This latter, Soviet work, published in the very year when Stalin made his one derogatory reference to Nechaev, is a successful but unfashionable attempt to document Nechaev's role as a precursor of the CPSU.

4. Lenin told Maxim Gorky in 1918, following the attempt on his life by the Left Socialist Revolutionaries: "He who is not for us is against us. People independent of history—it is a fantasy. If it is acknowledged that at one time there were such people, there are none now and cannot be any. They are not needed by anyone."—Gorky, *V. I. Lenin* (Moscow-Leningrad: Gosizdat Khudozhlit, 1931), p. 31.

5. Tkachev, *Izbrannye sochineniya na sotsial'no-politicheskie temy* (Moscow: izdat. Vsesoiuz. o-va. politkat i ss-ros, 1933), III, 225. *See also*

Michael Karpovich, "A Forerunner of Lenin: P. N. Tkachev," *Review of Politics*, July, 1944, pp. 336–350.

6. Tkachev, *op. cit.*, III, 66.
7. V. I. Lenin, *Sochineniya* (2d ed.), XXI, 362 ff.
8. Tkachev, *op. cit.*, III, 223.
9. *Ibid.*, I, 51.
10. In referring to Tkachev, whom he regarded not altogether correctly as having been overly concerned with terror, Lenin said that a terrorist organization "would, in fact, divert our army from drawing closer to the crowd which unfortunately is still not ours, and which unfortunately still does not ask us or asks us very little concerning when and how to commence military activities."—Lenin, *op. cit.* (2d ed.), IV, 495.
11. *See* Oliver H. Radkey, *The Election to the Russian Constituent Assembly of 1917* (Cambridge, Mass.: Harvard University Press, 1950), p. 16.
12. Lenin was still attacking Mikhailovsky and other Populists in January, 1898, while in Siberian exile, in his article "Which Heritage Do We Renounce?"—Lenin, *op. cit.* (2d ed.), II, 321–330.
13. G. Zinoviev, *Istoriya Rossiiskoi Kommunisticheskoi partii (bol'shevikov), populyarnyi ocherk* (Moscow: Gosizdat, 1923), p. 33.
14. Vera Zasulich had originally acquired notoriety as a revolutionary when she shot and wounded F. F. Trepov, the principal municipal official in St. Petersburg, for having ordered the flogging of a political prisoner. Her acquittal by a jury in 1878 resulted in her flight to Switzerland; in 1879, she returned to Russia, where she joined the Black Repartition group. After resuming exile in Switzerland in January, 1880, she remained abroad until 1905. Her previous acquaintance with Nechaev (in 1868) had led to her arrest in 1869 after she permitted him to use her address in contacting his agents.

    Deutsch was arrested in Germany in 1884 while preparing a shipment of illicit literature to Russia. He received a sentence of thirteen years and four months at hard labor when the Germans extradited him to Russia.
15. Quoted in Lev Deich (Leo Deutsch) (ed.), *Gruppa 'Osvobozhdenie Truda'; iz arkhivov G. V. Plekhanova, V. I. Zasulich i L. G. Deicha, Sbornik No. 1* (Moscow: Gosizdat, 1923), p. 134.
16. Zinoviev, *op. cit.*, p. 34.
17. *See* V. Volosevich, *Samaya kratkaya istoriya VKP(b)* (5th ed.; Leningrad: "Priboi," 1928), p. 14.
18. *Programma Sotsial-demokraticheskoi gruppy 'Osvobozhdenie Truda'* (Geneva, 1884), pp. 8 ff.
19. Zinoviev, *op. cit.*, pp. 16–18.
20. Krupskaya noted that Lenin once told her of this period that he had engaged in agriculture at the insistence of his mother and that "my

relations with the *muzhiki* [peasants] became abnormal."—N. K. Krupskaya, *Vospominaniya* (Moscow: Gosizdat, 1926), p. 32.

21. Krupskaya, *op. cit.*, p. 16.
22. *See* Mikhail S. Balabanov, *Istoriya revolyutsionnogo dvizheniya v Rossii ot dekabristov k 1905 godu* (Kharkov: Gosizdat Ukrainy, 1925), p. 345.
23. Lenin, *op. cit.* (2d ed.), II, 179.
24. *See* Volosevich, *op. cit.*, p. 28.
25. Lenin, *op. cit.* (2d ed.), II, 186.
26. *Ibid.*, II, 477 ff. The "Credo" was printed together with Lenin's "Protest."
27. *Ibid.*, II, 491.
28. *Ibid.*, II, 492.
29. *Ibid.*
30. *See* Krupskaya, *op. cit.*, p. 46.
31. Martov, *Zapiski Sotsialdemokrata, Letopis' Revolyutsii*, No. 4 (Berlin: Z. J. Grschebin Verlag, 1922), I, 13. Martov spoke French as well as modern Greek during the years in Constantinople; his mother was Viennese and had not yet learned Russian. His grandfather founded the first Jewish newspapers in Russia, published in Russian, Hebrew, and Yiddish.
32. Lenin, *op. cit.* (2d ed.), IV, 19.
33. *Ibid.*, IV, 24.
34. *Ibid.*, IV, 25.
35. *Ibid.*, IV, 30.
36. *Ibid.*, IV, 109.
37. *Ibid.*, IV, 108.
38. *Ibid.*, IV, 456.
39. *Ibid.*, IV, 380.
40. *Ibid.*, IV, 423.
41. *Ibid.*, IV, 447.
42. *Ibid.*, IV, 501.
43. *Ibid.*, V, 18 and 35.
44. Krupskaya, *op. cit.*, p. 88.
45. *Ibid.*, p. 97.
46. *Ibid.*, p. 97.
47. Balabanov, *op. cit*, p. 440.
48. Lenin, *op. cit.* (2d ed.), VI, 32.
49. *Ibid.*, VI, 32 ff.
50. *V.K.P.(b) v rezolyutsiyakh i resheniyakh s'ezdov, konferentsii i plenumov Ts.K.* (5th ed.; Moscow: Partizdat, 1936), Part I, p. 26.
51. Balabanov, *op. cit.*, p. 440.
52. Lenin, *op. cit.* (2d ed.), VI, 411.
53. *Ibid.*, VI, 18.
54. *Ibid.*, VI, 34.

55. *Ibid.,* VI, 36.
56. *Ibid.,* VI, 41.
57. *Ibid.,* VI, 92.

CHAPTER II

The Widening Rift

1. Lenin, *op. cit.* (2d ed.), VI, 441, n. 113.
2. Lenin, *op. cit.* (4th ed.), VII, 145.
3. *Ibid.,* VII, 147.
4. *Iskra,* No. 57 (January 15, 1904), 10.
5. Lenin, *op. cit.* (2d ed.), VI, 272.
6. *Ibid.,* VI, 303.
7. *Ibid.,* VI, 310.
8. *Ibid.,* VI, 206.
9. *Ibid.,* VI, 205 f.
10. *Ibid.,* VI, 272.
11. *Ibid.,* VI, 292.
12. *Ibid.,* VI, 293.
13. *Ibid.,* VI, 328.
14. *Ibid.,* VI, 343.
15. M. Lyadov (Mandelstamm), a participant at this conference, noted in his memoirs that it was held "not in August, as is generally written, but in September; however, it was decided for conspiratorial purposes to call it the August Conference."—M. Lyadov, *Iz zhizni partii, nakanune i v gody pervŏi revolyutsii, vospominaniya* (Moscow: Un-tet imeni Sverdlova, 1926), p. 56.
16. *V.K.P.(b) v rezolyutsiyakh* . . . (5th ed.), Part I, p. 37.
17. *Ibid.,* Part I, p. 39.
18. Lenin, *op. cit.* (2d ed.), VI, 343.
19. Lenin, *op. cit.* (4th ed.), VII, 428 f.
20. *Ibid.,* VIII, 124.
21. Lenin, *op. cit.* (2d ed.), VII, 80.
22. *Ibid.,* VII, 84 f.
23. *Ibid.,* XXIX, 266.
24. J. V. Stalin, *Sochineniya,* I, 65, 70, 71, and 73.
25. Lenin, *op. cit.* (2d ed.), XXVIII, 452.
26. *V.K.P.(b) v rezolyutsiyakh* . . . (5th ed.), Part I, p. 46.
27. *Ibid.,* Part I, p. 47.
28. Lenin, *op. cit.* (2d ed.), V, 113 f. In the spring of 1903, Lenin published his pamphlet *To the Village Poor,* written in simple language as a propaganda instrument and prompted by the widespread peasant uprisings of the previous year. Lenin contended that the poor peasantry must in the long run ally itself with the urban factory workers.

While recognizing that the poor peasantry could temporarily unite with the wealthier peasants against the landowners in demanding return of the *otrezki*, he contended that this alliance would be valid only in the first phase. In the second phase, Lenin argued, their interests would cease to coincide, as nationalization of *all* land and creation of a socialist society would be involved. In this envisaged second stage, the wealthier and poorer peasants would part company; the former would ally with the landowners (presumably to defend the sanctity of private property), while the latter would supposedly have to fight the entire village bourgeoisie (logically as champions of socialist property, but probably as partisans of the acquisitive spirit). Lenin warned that "whoever confuses the first step [return of the *otrezki*] with the last step [nationalization] harms this struggle and unconsciously obstructs the vision of the village poor." (*Ibid.,* V, 307.) Thus, in the agrarian question as in all other issues, timing and thinking in terms of stages were to be of the utmost importance. The nearsighted might foolishly accept the short-range goal as the long-range goal and in this way contribute to the creation of conditions over which they would soon have no control.

29. *Ibid.,* VIII, 186.
30. *Ibid.,* VIII, 62.
31. V. Volosevich, *Samaya kratkaya istoriya VKP(b)* (Leningrad: "Priboi," 1928), p. 45. Cf. Lyadov, *op. cit.,* p. 125.
32. *50-letie Vladimira Ilyicha Ulyanova-Lenina, 1870—23 aprelya—1920* (Moscow: Gosizdat, 1920), p. 27.
33. Lenin, *op. cit.* (2d ed.), IX, 345–359.
34. Quoted in L. Martov, *Istoriya Rossiiskoi Sotsial-Demokratii* (Moscow-Petrograd: "Kniga," 1923), p. 163.
35. Lenin, *op. cit.* (4th ed.), XI, 14.
36. Martov, *op. cit.,* pp. 207 f. Cf. Lenin, *op. cit.* (4th ed.), XI, 144 and 206. The Menshevik Yu. Larin (Mikhail Alexandrovich Lurye), who was to join the Bolsheviks in July, 1917, after a career as a Liquidator, wrote in defense of this proposal a pamphlet entitled *A Broad Workers' Party and a Workers' Congress.* According to Lenin, Larin's proposal was for a workers' party embracing 900,000 of the 9 million members of the Russian proletariat. Regarding the workers' congress, Lenin said: "Certainly we will participate if there is one. We participated in the Zubatov and Gapon workers' movement for the purpose of struggling for social democracy." (Lenin, *op. cit.* [4th ed.], XII, 350 and 353.)
37. Martov, *op. cit.,* p. 183.
38. Lenin, *op. cit.* (4th ed.), X, 254. In a report on the Fourth Congress written in May, 1906, Lenin declared that "the *complete* victory of the bourgeois revolution in Russia will provoke almost inevitably (or, at the very least, in all likelihood) a series of such political shocks in

Europe which will be a powerful impetus to the socialist revolution."
(*Ibid.*, X, 305.)

39. *Ibid.*, X, 269 f.
40. *Protokoly ob"edinitel'nogo s"ezda RSDRP* (Moscow-Leningrad: Gosizdat, 1926), p. 247.
41. *Ibid.*
42. Lenin, *op. cit.* (4th ed.), X, 134.
43. *V.K.P.(b) v rezolyutsiyakh* ... (5th ed.), Part I, p. 80.
44. *Ibid.*, Part I, p. 69.
45. Lenin, *op. cit.* (4th ed.), X, 139.
46. *V.K.P.(b) v rezolyutsiyakh* ... (5th ed.), Part I, p. 84.
47. *Ibid.*, Part I, pp. 73–76. Cf. Lenin, *op. cit.* (4th ed.), X, 284–288.
48. Lenin, *op. cit.* (4th ed.), X, 341.
49. Lyadov, *op. cit.*, pp. 152 ff.
50. Quoted in Sh. M. Levin and I. L. Tatarov (eds.), *Istoriya RKP(b) v dokumentakh* (Leningrad: Gosizdat, 1926), I, 418 f.
51. *Ibid.*
52. Lenin, *op. cit.* (2d ed.), X, 19.
53. *Ibid.*, X, 29.
54. *V.K.P.(b) v rezolyutsiyakh* ... (5th ed.), Part I, p. 88.
55. *Ibid.*
56. *See* Lenin, *op. cit.* (2d ed.), X, 501 ff., n. 188.
57. Lenin, *op. cit.* (4th ed.), XI, 406.
58. *Ibid.*, XI, 408.
59. *Ibid.*, XI, 423 and 426.
60. *Ibid.*, XII, 20.
61. *Ibid.*, XII, 382.
62. *Ibid.*, XII, 389 and 407.
63. *Ibid.*, XII, 389.

CHAPTER III

From Faction to Party

1. K. D. Gandurin, *O Londonskom s"ezde RSDRP 1907 goda* (Moscow-Leningrad: Molodaya Gvardiya, 1931), p. 30.
2. *Ibid.*, pp. 33 f.
3. *Ibid.*, p. 39.
4. *See* Lenin, *op. cit.* (2d ed.), XI, 570. Cf. N. Semashko, *Pyatyi s"ezd* (5th ed.; Kharkov: "Proletarii," 1930), p. 4.
5. *See* Gandurin, *op. cit.*, pp. 6, 8, 47, 55.
6. Lenin, *op. cit.* (4th ed.), XII, 423; and *op. cit.* (2d ed.), XI, 575 f., n. 144. *See also Protokoly pyatogo s"ezda RSDRP* (Moscow: Partizdat, 1935), pp. 465 and 515.
7. *Supra*, pp. 70–72.

8. *V.K.P.(b) v rezolyutsiyakh* ... (5th ed.), Part I, p. 107.
9. *Ibid.*, Part I, p. 101.
10. *Ibid.*, Part I, p. 108.
11. *Ibid.*, Part I, p. 106.
12. *Ibid.*, Part I, p. 110.
13. Lenin, *op. cit.* (2d ed.), X, 471, n. 71 and 72. Lenin specifically justi-
    fied terrorist attacks and armed robbery on the Party's behalf—not
    only against the government, but also against private persons—in an
    article, "Partisan Warfare," which was published in the September
    30 (October 13), 1906, issue of *Proletarii*. However, he did insist that
    this type of activity was to be but one of many forms of struggle.—
    Ibid., X, 80–88. For an English translation of this little-known article,
    see *Orbis, A Quarterly Journal of World Affairs,* II, No. 2 (July,
    1958), 194–208.
14. For details of this raid, as well as data regarding the fabulous career
    and prison record of the ringleader (known as Kamo), *see* B.
    Bibineishvili, *Kamo* (Moscow: "Staryi bol'shevik," 1934); and S. F.
    Medvedeva Ter-Petrosyan, *Geroi revolyutsii (tovarishch Kamo)*
    (Moscow-Leningrad: Gosizdat, 1925). Kamo (whose real name was
    Semion Ter-Petrosyan) came from Gori, Stalin's birthplace, and had
    joined the Party in October, 1901. His group of raiders, disguised as
    soldiers, seized the funds with the aid of bombs as the money was
    being transferred from the post office to the state bank. The money
    from the Tbilisi raid went to Kuokkala in Finland (renamed Repino
    in 1948; now in the Leningrad *oblast'*), where Lenin and Bogdanov
    were staying at the time (*Kamo*, p. 129). In December, 1906, Kamo
    had attempted to smuggle arms into Russia from Rumania, but the
    ship proved to be unseaworthy, and 2,000 firearms as well as 650,000
    bullets—purchased with funds obtained in a 1905 raid—did not reach
    their destination. Following the Tbilisi raid of June 13, 1907, Kamo,
    who was a master at disguise, arrived in Berlin on a passport identi-
    fying him as a representative of an insurance concern. However, he
    was soon arrested by the German police, and explosives were dis-
    covered in his luggage. Kamo is said to have feigned insanity in order
    to deceive his captors, although his behavior leads one to doubt
    whether it was necessary to simulate such a mental condition. The
    Germans surrendered him to the Russians in October, 1909; he was
    later placed in a psychiatric hospital in Tbilisi, from which he escaped
    in August, 1911, after patiently sawing bars for three months. Kamo
    went to Lenin in Paris and then to the Balkans for a rest. He soon
    returned to Russia, but when an attempt at a new raid failed, he was
    arrested and received a sentence of twenty years at hard labor. The
    collapse of the Russian monarchy in March, 1917, led to his release.
    When the Bolsheviks seized power, Kamo was no longer in his ele-
    ment and actually became a nuisance since he could not very well

organize expropriatory raids against the Soviet regime. Death came to him in a rather inglorious manner in Tbilisi when an automobile struck him down on his bicycle late at night on July 14, 1922.

15. Semashko, *op. cit.*, p. 16; and Gandurin, *op. cit.*, p. 46. For a photographic reproduction of the promissory note, *see Protokoly pyatogo s"ezda RSDRP,* facing p. 696.
16. Lenin, *op. cit.* (4th ed.), XII, 398.
17. For a detailed account of the plot and the dissolution of the Second Duma, *see* Alfred Levin, *The Second Duma; A Study of the Social-Democratic Party and the Russian Constitutional Experiment* (New Haven, Conn.: Yale University Press, 1940), chap. 14.
18. Lenin, *op. cit.* (2d ed.), XII, 454, n. 19.
19. Krupskaya, *Vospominaniya o Lenine* (Moscow-Leningrad: Gosizdat, 1931), pp. 163 f.
20. Lenin, *op. cit.* (4th ed.), XIII, 411.
21. *Ibid.,* XIII, 412.
22. *Ibid.,* XIII, 416.
23. This interesting review is reproduced in an appendix in Lenin, *op. cit.* (2d ed.), XIII, 329–333.
24. *Ibid.,* XIII, 265 and 266.
25. *Ibid.,* XIII, 270.
26. *Bol'shevik,* No. 7 (April 1, 1937), pp. 7 f.
27. A. V. Shcheglov, *Bor'ba Lenina protiv Bogdanovskoi revizii marksizma* (Moscow: Sotsekgiz, 1937), p. 111.
28. Lenin, *op. cit.* (2d ed.), XIII, 100.
29. *Ibid.,* XIII, 117.
30. *Ibid.,* XIII, 111.
31. *Ibid.,* XIII, 280.
32. *Ibid.,* XIV, pp. 499 f., n. 30.
33. Martov, *Spasiteli ili uprazdniteli? Kto i kak razrushal RSDRP* (Paris: Sotsialdemokrat, 1911), p. 19.
34. Lenin, *op. cit.* (2d ed.), XIV, 483, n. 1.
35. *Ibid.,* XIV, 60.
36. *V.K.P.(b) v rezolyutsiyakh* . . . (5th ed.), Part I, p. 144.
37. *Ibid.,* Part I, p. 148.
38. Lenin, *op. cit.* (2d. ed.), XIII, 282.
39. A. Lunacharsky, "Ateizm," in *Ocherki po filosofii marksizma* (St. Petersburg, 1908), p. 159.
40. *Teatr; Kniga o novom teatre* (St. Petersburg, 1908), p. 27; quoted in I. K., "Bogostroitel'stvo M. Gor'kogo," *Moskovskii yezhenedel'nik,* September 6, 1908, p. 10.
41. *V.K.P.(b) v rezolyutsiyakh* . . . (5th ed.), Part I, p. 152.
42. Lenin, *op. cit.* (2d ed.), XIV, 120 f.
43. *Pis'ma V. I. Lenina A. M. Gor'komu, 1908–1913 gg.* (Leningrad: Gosizdat, 1924), p. 72.

44. *Ibid.*
45. *Ibid.*, p. 77.
46. Lenin, *op. cit.* (2d ed.), XIV, 389.
47. M. Lyadov, *Po povodu partiinogo krizisa, Chastnoe zayavlenie* (Paris: "Vperyod," 1911), p. 13.
48. *V.K.P.(b) v rezolyutsiyakh* . . . (6th ed.; Moscow: Partizdat, 1941), Part I, p. 179.
49. *Ibid.*, Part I, p. 184.
50. Lenin, *op. cit.* (2d ed.), XV, 533 ff.
51. *Ibid.*, VI, 84 f.
52. *Ibid.*, XVI, 617.
53. *Ibid.*, XVI, 553; XVII, 120 and 134.
54. *Ibid.*, XVI, 595 f.
55. *Ibid.*, XVI, 618.
56. *Ibid.*, XVI, 328.
57. Stalin, *op. cit.*, II, 303.
58. *Ibid.*, II, 330.
59. *Ibid.*, II, 301.
60. *Ibid.*, II, 313.
61. See *Padenie tsarskogo rezhima, stenograficheskie otchety doprosov i pokazanii, dannykh v 1917 g. v Chrezvychainoi Sledstvennoi Komissii Vremennogo Pravitel'stva* (Leningrad: Gosizdat, 1924–27), III 286 and 466. This stenographic report of the Investigatory Commission established by the Provisional Government provides much data on Malinovsky's activities.
62. Lenin, *op. cit.* (2d ed.), XVII, 497 ff.
63. *Pis'ma V. I. Lenina A. M. Gor'komu, 1908–1913 gg.* (Leningrad: Gosizdat, 1924), p. 58.
64. Lenin, *op. cit.* (2d ed.), XVIII, 55 f.
65. *Ibid.*, XVIII, 193 f.
66. *Ibid.*, XIX, 357.

CHAPTER IV

The Seizure of Power

1. Lenin, *Sochineniya 1917 goda* (Moscow: Partizdat, 1937), I, 56.
2. *Ibid.*, I, 3.
3. Lenin, *Sochineniya* (2d ed.), XII, 162.
4. *Ibid.*, XII, 163.
5. *Ibid.*, XV, 157 ff.
6. *Ibid.*, XII, 164.
7. *Ibid.*, XXII, 205.
8. *Ibid.*, XX, 74. *See also* Z. A. B. Zeman (ed.), *Germany and the*

Revolution in Russia, 1915–1918; Documents from the Archives of the German Foreign Ministry (London: Oxford University Press, 1958) pp. 38–40.

9. Lenin, *Sochineniya* (2d ed.), XX, 74.
10. *Ibid.* (4th ed.), XXIII, 287.
11. *Ibid.*, XXIII, 317.
12. A. Shlyapnikov, *Semnadtsatyi god* (Moscow-Petrograd: Gosizdat, 1923), Book I, pp. 212 f.
13. Lenin, *Sochineniya* (2d ed.), XX, 88.
14. *Ibid.*, XX, 132 f.
15. *Ibid.*, XX, 134.
16. *Ibid.*, XX, 239.
17. *Ibid.*, XX, 277.
18. Stalin, *op. cit.*, III, 57.
19. *See* Lenin, *Sochineniya* (2d ed.), XX, 534–535, 539 ff.
20. Sergei Petrovich Mel'gunov, *Zolotoi Nemetskii Klyuch Bol'shevikov* (Paris, 1940), pp. 104 ff. This is the most thorough and careful study of the tangled question of whether or not the Bolsheviks received German financial aid. Although not the final word, it examines all the evidence available at the time of writing. Cf. B. V. Nikitine, *The Fatal Years, Fresh Revelations on a Chapter of Underground History* (London: Hodge, 1938); the memoirs of an agent of the Provisional Government's hastily organized counterintelligence unit.
21. Lenin, *Sochineniya* (2d ed.), XXI, 549.
22. *Ibid.*, XXI, 563.
23. This significant document was published in the April, 1956, issue of *International Affairs* (p. 189), the journal of the Royal Institute of International Affairs. *See also* the explanatory article by George Katkov, "German Foreign Office Documents on Financial Support to the Bolsheviks in 1917," pp. 181–188, same issue, as well as the rejoinder by Kerensky, published in the October issue. The document may also be found in Zeman, *op. cit.*, pp. 94 f.
24. Lenin, *Sochineniya* (2d ed.), XXI, 32.
25. *Ibid.*, XXI, 33.
26. *Ibid.*, XXI, 38.
27. *Ibid.*, XXI, 35.
28. *Shestoi s"ezd Rossiiskoi Kommunisticheskoi Partii (bol'shevikov)* (2d ed.; Moscow: Gosizdat, 1927), p. 303.
29. *Ibid.*, p. 25.
30. *Ibid.*, pp. 62 ff.
31. Stalin, *op. cit.*, III, 168 f.
32. *Ibid.*, III, 179.
33. *Ibid.*, III, 177.
34. *Shestoi s"ezd . . .*, p. 35.
35. *Ibid.*, p. 300.

36. *V.K.P.(b) v rezolyutsiyakh* ... (6th ed.), Part I, p. 264.
37. Lenin, *Sochineniya* (2d ed.), XX, 68.
38. *Ibid.*, XXI, 42.
39. *Ibid.*, XXI, 116.
40. *Ibid.*, XXI, 193.
41. *Ibid.*, XXI, 194 and 196.
42. *Ibid.*, XXI, 229.
43. *Ibid.*, XXI, 241.
44. *Ibid.*, XXI, 294.
45. *Ibid.*, XXI, 319 f.
46. *Ibid.*, XXI, 329.
47. *Ibid.*, Vol. XXI, Documentary Appendix; for English translation, *see* Lenin, *Toward the Seizure of Power* (New York: International Publishers, 1932), Book II.
48. Lenin, *Sochineniya* (2d ed.), XXI, 350 f.
49. For a colorful eyewitness account of the events on the streets and in the Soviet in Petrograd, *see* John Reed, *Ten Days That Shook the World* (first published in 1919). Reed's book is, at best, the account of an observing and sympathetic journalist; but it does not deal with internal Party developments, and Reed did not have access to documents which were published later. Lenin wrote a brief introduction to the book. Banned by Stalin, this work has since been republished by Khrushchev.

   A more reliable eyewitness account is to be found in N. N. Sukhanov, *Zapiski o Revolyutsii* (7 vols.; Berlin: Z. I. Grzhebin, 1922-23). Much of this fascinating account has been translated into English by Joel Carmichael and published as *The Russian Revolution, 1917* (New York: Oxford University Press, 1955). Sukhanov was tried with other Mensheviks in 1931, was sentenced, and then disappeared. Ironically, the October 23, 1917, meeting of the Bolshevik Central Committee was held in Sukhanov's apartment (his wife was a Bolshevik), though Sukhanov was away at the time.

   For a readable, sound, and detailed account of the events of 1917, *see* William Henry Chamberlin, *The Russian Revolution, 1917–1921* (New York: The Macmillan Co., 1935), Vol. I. For a succinct popular treatment of the Bolshevik seizure of power, *see* Alan Moorehead, *The Russian Revolution* (New York: Harper & Brothers, 1958).

CHAPTER V

Leninism in Practice

1. Gorky, *op. cit.*, p. 30.
2. Lenin, *Sochineniya* (2d ed.), XXI, 378.
3. *Supra*, pp. 112–114.

4. Lenin, *Sochineniya* (2d ed.), XXI, 398 f.
5. *Ibid.*, XXI, 398.
6. *Ibid.*, XXI, 402.
7. *Ibid.*, XXI, 260.
8. *Ibid.*, XXI, 266.
9. Although trained in the law, Lenin adopted an attitude toward lawyers which was rather bilious. In a letter written in January, 1905, to Elena Stasova and other Party members who were in prison, Lenin offered the following words of advice in dealing with their defense counsels: "Lawyers must be ruled with an iron rod and placed in a state of siege because this intellectual riffraff often behaves disgustingly. Let them know ahead of time: 'If you, son of a bitch, permit yourself the slightest impropriety *or political opportunism* (to speak of the immaturity, of the falseness of socialism, of being carried away, *of the rejection of violence by Social Democrats,* of the peaceful character of their teachings and movements and the like, or anything the least bit similar), I, the accused, will cut you short in public, will call you an infamous wretch, will declare that I renounce such a defense . . .' " (Lenin, *Sochineniya* [4th ed.], VIII, 50 f.) In the same letter, he advised Communists who were brought to trial to "participate in judicial investigation . . . in order to catch witnesses and agitate against the court."
10. Gorky, *op. cit.*, p. 41.
11. For a discussion of the concessions, *see* Louis Fischer, *The Soviets in World Affairs* (Princeton, N.J.: Princeton University Press, 1951), pp. 300 ff. and 323 ff.
12. Lenin, *Sochineniya* (2d ed.), XXII, 36 f. The failures of the Socialist Revolutionaries in 1917 have been exhaustively analyzed in Oliver H. Radkey, *The Agrarian Foes of Bolshevism* (New York: Columbia University Press, 1958).
13. Lenin, *Sochineniya* (2d ed.), XXII, 38 f.
14. *Ibid.*, XXII, 552.
15. *Ibid.*, XXII, 57.
16. This accusation by Lenin renders inaccurate Nikita S. Khrushchev's assertion in the secret address at the Twentieth Party Congress in February, 1956, that "Stalin originated the concept 'enemy of the people.' " (*See* Bertram D. Wolfe, *Khrushchev and Stalin's Ghost* [New York: Frederick A. Praeger, 1957], p. 106.) Khrushchev's statement is simply not true, for it was Lenin who coined the term and first applied it by implication to fellow Party members.
17. Lenin, *Sochineniya* (2d ed.), XXII, 58 ff.
18. *Ibid.*, XXII, 600.
19. *Ibid.*, XXII, 201.
20. *Ibid.*, XXII, 277 f., 608 f., n. 123.
21. *Ibid.*, XXII, 327 f.

22. *Ibid.*, XXII, 331.
23. *Ibid.*, XXII, 334.
24. Others elected to full membership in the Central Committee at the Seventh Congress were: Lenin, Trotsky, Jacob M. Sverdlov, Zinoviev, Sokol'nikov, Stalin, Krestinsky, Smilga, Stasova, M. M. Lashevich, V. V. Schmidt, Dzierzynski, Mikhail Fedorovich Vladimirsky, and Artem (Fedor Andreyevich Sergeyev). In addition to the two Oppositionists, the candidate-members included A. A. Yoffe, A. S. Kiselev, Jan Antonovich Berzin, Peter Ivanovich Stuchka, G. I. Petrovsky, and A. G. Shlyapnikov.
25. Steinberg, who left the Soviet Union, wrote a general history of the SR's in the form of a biography—*Spiridonova, Revolutionary Terrorist* (London: Methuen, 1935).
26. Lenin, *Sochineniya* (2d ed.), XXII, 114 and 131 f.
27. *Ibid.*, XXII, 113.
28. *Ibid.*, XXII, 114.
29. I. Z. Steinberg, *op. cit.*, p. 196.
30. Karl Radek, *Portrety i pamflety* (Moscow: Sovetskaya literatura, 1933), Book I, p. 50.
31. Lenin, *Sochineniya* (2d ed.), XXIII, 202.
32. Gorky, *op. cit.*, p. 31.
33. *Ibid.*, p. 35.
34. Lenin, *Sochineniya* (2d ed.), XXIII, 220. This calumny against Kautsky was published in an article which appeared in the October 11, 1918, issue of *Pravda* under the same title as that given to Lenin's pamphlet.
35. *Ibid.*, XXIV, 121.
36. *V.K.P.(b) v rezolyutsiyakh* . . . (6th ed.), Part I, p. 285.
37. *Ibid.*, Part I, p. 289.
38. *Ibid.*, Part I, p. 293. For an English translation of the 1919 Party program, *see* James H. Meisel and Edward S. Kozera (eds.), *Materials for the Study of the Soviet System* (2d ed.; Ann Arbor, Mich.: George Wahr, 1953), pp. 100-121.
39. Lenin, *Sochineniya* (2d ed.), XXIV, 121 f.
40. *Ibid.*, VIII, 397.
41. *Ibid.*, XX, 37.
42. *V.K.P.(b) v rezolyutsiyakh* . . . (6th ed.), Part I, p. 299.
43. *Ibid.*, pp. 304 f.
44. Lenin, *Sochineniya* (2d ed.), XXIV, 135 ff.
45. *V.K.P.(b) v rezolyutsiyakh* . . . (6th ed.), Part I, p. 307.
46. *Ibid.*, Part I, p. 319.
47. *Ibid.*, Part I, pp. 321 f.
48. *Ibid.*, Part I, p. 322.
49. *Devyatyi s"ezd* (Moscow: Gosizdat, 1920), p. 79.
50. *Ibid.*, p. 81.

51. *Ibid.*, p. 118.
52. *Ibid.*, p. 203. Ironically, Bukharin was ultimately to fall into the cogs of this enormous machine created by Lenin and operated by Stalin.
53. *Ibid.*, p. 46.
54. *Ibid.*, p. 42.
55. *Ibid.*, p. 44.
56. *Ibid.*, p. 44.
57. Lenin, *Sochineniya* (2d ed.), XXV, 111.
58. *Ibid.*, XXV, 94.
59. *Ibid.*, XXV, 183 f.
60. *Ibid.*, XXV, 236.
61. *Ibid.*, XXV, 230 f.
62. *Ibid.*, XXV, 491.
63. *Ibid.*, XXVI, 232.
64. A. Kolontay (Kollontai), *The Workers' Opposition in Russia* (Chicago: Industrial Workers of the World), p. 9.
65. Lenin, *Sochineniya* (2d ed.), XXVI, 223, 225, 229.
66. *Ibid.*, XXVI, 227.
67. Robert V. Daniels, "The Kronstadt Revolt of 1921: A Study in the Dynamics of Revolution," *The American Slavic and East European Review*, X, No. 4 (December, 1951), 241-254. *See also* D. Fedotoff White, *The Growth of the Red Army* (Princeton, N.J.: Princeton University Press, 1944), chap. 5; and George Katkov, "The Kronstadt Rising," *Soviet Affairs, Number Two* (New York: Frederick A. Praeger, 1959), pp. 9-74.
68. Lenin, *Sochineniya* (2d ed.), XXVI, 284.
69. *Desyatyi s"ezd* (Moscow: Gosizdat, 1921), p. 39.
70. *Ibid.*, p. 42.
71. *Ibid.*, p. 164.
72. *V.K.P.(b) v rezolyutsiyakh . . .* (6th ed.), Part I, p. 367.
73. *Ibid.*, Part I, p. 366.

CHAPTER VI

Stalin's Rise to Power

1. *V.K.P.(b) v rezolyutsiyakh . . .* (6th ed.), Part I, p. 363.
2. Gorky, *op cit.*, p. 41.
3. Lenin, *Sochineniya* (2d ed.), XXVII, 226.
4. *Ibid.*, XXVII, 246.
5. *Ibid.*, XXVII, 239.
6. *Ibid.*, XXVII, 262.
7. *V.K.P.(b) v rezolyutsiyakh . . .* (6th ed.), Part I, p. 442.
8. Lenin, *Sochineniya* (2d ed.), XXVII, 13.
9. *Ibid.*, XXVII, 264.

10. Lenin's concern with physical health was confirmed by many of his associates and found expression in some of his own statements. Thus, Elena Stasova recounted that when Lenin noted that Alexander Dmitrievich Tsyurupa and Dzierzynski were overworking themselves, he insisted that they take a rest. In a communication to Tsyurupa, he referred to a "careless attitude toward state property," meaning that a Party member's health was really not his own but the state's.— *Vospominaniya o Vladimire Ilyiche Lenine* (Moscow: Institut Marksizma-Leninizma, Gospolitizdat, 1956), p. 320.

N. Valentinov (Vol'sky), who was associated with Lenin in the period following the Second Congress, noted that Lenin stressed the importance of a revolutionary's being able to row and to make haste on foot in order to either flee from exile or get rid of a police spy (*Vstrechi s Leninym*, p. 124).

In November, 1913, Lenin wrote to Gorky from Cracow the following observation regarding physicians: "Your news that a Bolshevik— although a former Bolshevik—was treating you by a new method has made me really very anxious. God preserve us from 'comrade' doctors in general and Bolshevik doctors in particular! But seriously, in 99 cases out of 100, 'comrade' doctors are asses, as a brilliant doctor once told me. I assure you that one should be treated only by first-class foreign specialists (except in unimportant cases). It is terrible to allow a Bolshevik to try his experiments on you."—*The Letters of Lenin*, trans. and ed. Elizabeth Hill and Doris Mudie (New York: Harcourt Brace, 1937), p. 323.

11. Stalin, *op. cit.*, V, 134 ff.

12. *See* Lenin, *Sochineniya* (2d ed.), XXVI, 187 f. and 191 ff.

13. A translation of the entire document—dictated by Lenin on December 30-31, 1922, and deposited in the Trotsky Archive at Harvard University—may be found in Richard Pipes, *The Formation of the Soviet Union; Communism and Nationalism, 1917-1923* (Cambridge, Mass.: Harvard University Press, 1954), pp. 273-277. The documents were later published in the Soviet Union; they were given to delegates at the Twentieth Congress in February, 1956, and were then published in the June, 1956, issue of *Kommunist* (No. 9). *See also* Wolfe, *op. cit.*, pp. 271-276.

14. Lenin's "Testament" was not published in the Soviet Union until June, 1956 (in *Kommunist* [No. 9]). It was published in *The New York Times* of October 18, 1926, as well as during the preceding year in Max Eastman's *Since Lenin Died*. For a recent publication of it, *see* Wolfe, *op. cit.*, pp. 260-263.

15. Krupskaya's letter of December 23, 1922, was quoted in its entirety by Khrushchev in his "secret" speech of February 24-25, 1956, at the Twentieth Party Congress. *See* Wolfe, *op. cit.*, p. 98.

16. Wolfe, *op. cit.*, p. 263.

17. *Ibid.*, p. 100. *See also* Robert H. McNeal, "Lenin's Attack on Stalin: Review and Reappraisal," *The American Slavic and East European Review*, October, 1959, pp. 295-314.

18. Lenin, *Sochineniya* (2d ed.), XXVII, 408 f.

19. Stalin, *op. cit.*, V, 211.

20. *Ibid.*, V, 266.

21. *Ibid.*, V, 219.

22. *Ibid.*, V, 226.

23. Leon Trotsky, *Stalin, An Appraisal of the Man and His Influence* (London: Hollis and Carter, 1947), p. 361.

24. Stalin, *op. cit.*, V, 266.

25. For a translation of the text of the "Declaration of the Forty-Six," see E. H. Carr, *The Interregnum, 1923-24* (New York: The Macmillan Co., 1954), pp. 367-373.

26. Stalin, *op. cit.*, VI, 13-22; contains that portion of the text of Stalin's speech dealing with the six errors.

27. *V.K.P.(b) v rezolyutsiyakh* ... (6th ed.), Part I, p. 543.

28. Stalin, *op. cit.*, VI, 46 ff.

29. *Ibid.*, VI, 105.

30. *Ibid.*, VI, 175.

31. *Ibid.*, VI, 182.

32. *Ibid.*, VI, 255.

33. *Ibid.*, VI, 227.

34. *Ibid.*, VI, 209.

35. *Ibid.*, VI, 209 f.

36. *V.K.P.(b) v rezolyutsiyakh* ... (6th ed.), Part I, pp. 578 f. *See also* Mark Neuweld, "The Origin of the Communist Control Commission," *The American Slavic and East European Review*, October, 1959, pp. 315-333.

37. Stalin, *op. cit.*, VI, 348.

38. *Ibid.*, VI, 350 f.

39. *Ibid.*, VII, 376.

40. *Ibid.*, VII, 388 f.

41. *Ibid.*, VII, 274.

42. *Ibid.*, VII, 328.

43. *Chetyrnadtsatyi S"ezd R.K.P.(b)* (Moscow, 1926), p. 165.

44. *Ibid.*, p. 321.

45. Stalin, *op. cit.*, VII, 365. At the Fourteenth Congress, Stalin gave a revealing definition of the NEP when he criticized Sokol'nikov for not understanding the "dialectics of development in the circumstances of the dictatorship of the proletariat, in the circumstances of the transitional period, in which the methods and weapons of the bourgeoisie are utilized by the socialist elements for the conquest and liquidation of the capitalistic elements."—*Ibid.*, VII, 369.

46. *Ibid.*, VII, 380.

47. *Ibid.*, VIII, 243.
48. *Ibid.*, VIII, 278.
49. *Ibid.*, VIII, 355 f. It was at the Twelfth Congress that Zinoviev had asserted that Communists "can hear the grass grow"—a figure of speech expressing the delusion of having mastered the so-called "laws of history." For a discussion of Zinoviev's arguments against Stalin's "socialism in one country" thesis, *see* William Korey, "Zinoviev's Critique of Stalin's Theory of Socialism in One Country, December, 1925–December, 1926," *The American Slavic and East European Review*, IX, No. 4 (December, 1950), 255-267.
50. Stalin, *op. cit.*, X, 52; Trotsky's letter is quoted at length here.
51. *Ibid.*, X, 368.

CHAPTER VII

Stalinism

1. The equating of the apparatus with the Party was expressed as early as November, 1926, at the Fifteenth Conference. The resolution concerning the Oppositionist bloc—adopted on the basis of Stalin's report —contained the following assertion: "The Party proceeds from the fact that the Party apparatus and the Party masses constitute a single whole, that the Party apparatus . . . embodies the leading elements of the Party as a whole, that the Party apparatus contains the best people of the proletariat who can and must be criticized for errors, who can and must be 'refreshed,' but whom it is impossible to defame without risking the decomposition of the Party and leaving it unarmed."—*V.K.P.(b) v rezolyutsiyakh* . . . (6th ed.), Part II, p. 152.
2. *V.K.P.(b) v rezolyutsiyakh* . . . (6th ed.), Part II, p. 30.
3. Stalin, *op. cit.*, VIII, 262 f.
4. *Supra*, pp. 104–106.
5. For a good discussion of the economic debate over industrialization between the Trotskyites and Stalinists, *see* Alexander Erlich, "Preobrazhenski and the Economics of Soviet Industrialization," *Quarterly Journal of Economics*, LXIV, No. 1 (February, 1950), 57-88.
6. Stalin, *op. cit.*, XI, 46.
7. *Ibid.*, XI, 42 f.
8. *Ibid.*, XI, 170.
9. *Ibid.*, XI, 208.
10. For a translation of most of Bukharin's article, *see* Wolfe, *op. cit.*, pp. 295-315.
11. Stalin, *op. cit.*, XI, 159. For a good brief account of Stalin's sleight-of-mouth abilities in the field of economic policy, *see* Alexander Erlich, "Stalin's View on Soviet Economic Development," and John D. Bergamini, "Stalin and the Collective Farm," in *Continuity and*

Change in Russian and Soviet Thought, ed. Ernest J. Simmons (Cambridge, Mass.: Harvard University Press, 1955), pp. 81-99, 218-236.

12. Stalin, *op. cit.*, XI, 231.
13. *Supra*, pp. 208–209.
14. Stalin, *op. cit.*, XI, 287.
15. *V.K.P.(b) v rezolyutsiyakh . . .* (6th ed.), Part II, p. 292.
16. *Ibid.*, Part II, pp. 316 ff.; also Stalin, *op. cit.*, XI, 318 ff.
17. Stalin, *op. cit.*, XI, 321.
18. *Ibid.*, XII, 1.
19. *Ibid.*, XII, 2.
20. *Ibid.*, XII, 27.
21. *Ibid.*, XII, 52 f.
22. *Supra*, p. 187.
23. Stalin, *op. cit.*, XII, 105.
24. *Ibid.*, XII, 106.
25. *Ibid.*, XII, 140.
26. *Ibid.*, XIII, 15.
27. *Ibid.*, XII, 305.
28. *Ibid.*, X, 301.
29. *Ibid.*, XIII, 39.
30. *Ibid.*, XIII, 302.
31. *Ibid.*, XIII, 293 f.
32. *Ibid.*, XIII, 347 f.
33. *Ibid.*, XIII, 369.
34. Stalin, *Voprosy leninizma* (11th ed.; Moscow: Gospolitizdat, 1952), p. 529.
35. Some of the basic facts concerning Kirov's assassination were confirmed by Khrushchev in his secret address delivered at the Twentieth Congress in February, 1956. *See* Wolfe, *op. cit.*, pp. 128 and 130.

    Details of the case which threw some suspicion on Stalin's role were made available at an earlier time by Soviet intelligence officials who had defected. For an example, *see* Walter G. Krivitsky, *In Stalin's Secret Service* (New York, 1939), pp. 184 ff.
36. For the record of false testimony, *see* John Dewey *et al., Not Guilty, Report of the Commission of Inquiry into the Charges Made Against Leon Trotsky in the Moscow Trials* (New York: Harper & Brothers, 1938).
37. For a thorough analysis of this aspect of the Moscow trials, *see* Nathan Leites and Elsa Bernaut, *Ritual of Liquidation* (Glencoe, Ill.: The Free Press, 1954), Part III.
38. Emilian Yaroslavsky, "K chistke partii," *Bol'shevik*, No. 7-8 (April 30, 1933), p. 12. Yaroslavsky pointed out that the Party had been lenient in admitting candidates to membership, with approximately 80 per cent gaining acceptance during the 1930-32 period (p. 17).
39. *V.K.P.(b) v rezolyutsiyakh . . .* (6th ed.), Part II, p. 636.

40. For the text of the resolution, *see Bol'shevik*, No. 5-6 (March 15, 1937), pp. 2-5.
41. *Ibid.*, p. 8.
42. Stalin, *Voprosy leninizma* (11th ed.), p. 633. Abdurakhman Avtorkhanov, an official of the CPSU at that time, has calculated that well over 1.5 million Party members were purged between 1933 and 1939.—*See* Avtorkhanov, *Stalin and the Soviet Communist Party* (New York: Frederick A. Praeger, 1959), pp. 241 f.
43. The Party recruited members during the latter part of the purge, in 1937 and 1938. But in a decision of July 14, 1938, the Central Committee criticized the delay in the processing of applications for membership. It was reported that between January and June, 1938, a total of 108,518 applicants had become candidates and 49,465 candidates had become members. (*See Partiinoe stroitel'stvo*, No. 15 [August 1, 1938], p. 63.) In March, 1939, the Eighteenth Congress eliminated the various categories of applicants, for whom the admission requirements varied in terms of the number and quality of the recommendations and the length of the period of candidacy. These categories, adopted in 1934 at the Seventeenth Congress, were designed to give preference to industrial workers and to tighten requirements. The 1939 Statutes provided for a one-year period of candidacy for all applicants and recommendations from three members of three years' standing who had worked with the applicant for at least one year.
44. Stalin, *Voprosy leninizma* (11th ed.), p. 517.
45. The execution of certain Zhdanovites was admitted by Khrushchev in his secret speech at the Twentieth Congress but was blamed not only on Stalin but in particular on Beria. *See* Wolfe, *op. cit.*, p. 192.
46. *Partiinaya zhizn'*, No. 20 (October, 1947), p. 83.
47. Quoted in Lenin, *Sochineniya* (2d ed.), XXV, 624, n. 141.
48. *Bol'shevik*, No. 18 (September, 1952), p. 5.
49. Stalin, *Sochineniya*, XI, 58.

CHAPTER VIII

Stalin's Heirs

1. *Pravda*, January 13, 1953.
2. Mikhail Suslov, a new member of the Presidium of the Central Committee and a Secretariat member, attacked Voznesensky by name in the December 24, 1952, issue of *Pravda*.
3. *See* Wolfe, *op. cit.*, p. 244. Other evidence which indicates that a general purging of the Party was in the offing in late 1952 is found in the new Statutes adopted by the Nineteenth Congress. A provision empowered the Committee of Party Control, which is responsible for the verification of Party discipline, to have its own plenipotentiary

representatives "independent of local Party bodies." This provision was abrogated by the Twentieth Congress in 1956.

4. *Bol'shevik,* No. 4 (March, 1953), p. 14.

5. *Ibid.,* p. 17. It should be noted that Beria mentioned Stalin's name only slightly more frequently than he mentioned Lenin in the funeral oration. In contrast, Malenkov and Molotov each mentioned Stalin four times as often as they did Lenin.

6. The best eyewitness account of the apparent events occurring immediately after Stalin's death is to be found in Harrison E. Salisbury, *American in Russia* (New York: Harper & Brothers, 1955), Chap. 10. *See also* Salisbury's account of these events published in *The New York Times,* September 21, 1954. Salisbury's treatment of the growing fear and terror which gripped Moscow during December of 1952 and January and February of 1953 is very revealing.

7. Stalin, *Sochineniya,* XIII, 107. Stalin also had told the Fourteenth Congress on December 23, 1925: "It is impossible to lead the Party other than collegially. It is foolish to dream of this after Ilyich [Lenin's death]—[*applause*]—it is foolish to speak of this." (Stalin, *Sochineniya,* VII, 391).

8. *Supra,* pp. 244–245.

9. *Pravda,* February 3, 1955.

10. *Pravda,* February 9, 1955.

11. *Pravda,* June 16, 1938.

12. *See The Anti-Stalin Campaign and International Communism* (New York: Columbia University Press, 1956). The Khrushchev secret speech was first published in the June 5, 1956, issue of *The New York Times.* It is available, with an excellent commentary, in Wolfe, *op. cit.* The text was also published under the title *The Anatomy of Terror, Khrushchev's Revelations about Stalin's Regime,* with an introduction by Nathaniel Weyl (Washington, D.C.: Public Affairs Press, 1956).

13. Published in the July 2, 1956, issue of *Pravda,* as well as in pamphlet form. The stenographic report of the Twentieth Congress includes the text of a resolution adopted on February 25, 1956, which states that the Congress heard Khrushchev deliver a report "Concerning the Cult of the Person and Its Consequences." (*See XX S"ezd Kommunisticheskoi Partii Sovetskogo Soyuza, 14-25 fevralya 1956 goda, stenograficheskii otchet* [Moscow: Gosizdat, 1956], II, 498. The biographical article on Khrushchev in *Bol'shaya Sovetskaya Entsiklopediya* [2d ed.; February, 1957], XLVI, 391, also states that Khrushchev delivered this report "at a closed session of the Congress.")

14. *O preodolenii kul'ta lichnosti i ego posledstvii, postanovlenie Tsentral'nogo Komiteta KPSS* (Moscow: Gosizdat, 1956), p. 18.

15. *Ibid.*

16. Wolfe, *op cit.*, p. 248.
17. That Khrushchev tended to identify himself with Stalin until shortly before the Twentieth Congress has been substantially documented in Myron Rush, *The Rise of Khrushchev* (Washington, D.C.: Public Affairs Press, 1958).
18. *See* Wolfe, *op. cit.*, pp. 130 and 180.
19. *Ibid.*, p. 184.
20. *See* Boris Meissner, *The Communist Party of the Soviet Union,* ed. John S. Reshetar, Jr. (New York: Frederick A. Praeger, 1956), pp. 90 ff. and 105 ff.
21. Molotov had allegedly committed an "ideological error" in February, 1955, at the time of Malenkov's resignation. This consisted in his having declared that only the "foundations" of a socialist society had been built in the Soviet Union, whereas he should have said that socialism had already been achieved in that country in 1936. He appropriately published a recantation in *Kommunist,* No. 14 (September, 1955), pp. 127 f. Much earlier, Molotov had admitted an error in quoting Lenin at the Fifteenth Congress. (*See Bol'shevik,* No. 12 [1928], pp. 89 f.)
22. *Pravda,* July 4, 1957. In addition to A. N. Kosygin and Pervukhin, the new candidate-members were: Peter N. Pospelov of the Secretariat, Dem'yan S. Korotchenko (Ukrainian Party organization), J. E. Kalnberzins (Communist Party of Latvia), A. P. Kirilenko (Sverdlovsk Province Committee First Secretary), K. T. Mazurov (Belorussian Central Committee First Secretary), and Vasilii P. Mzhavanadze (Georgian Central Committee First Secretary). In June, 1958, Khrushchev added two more candidates to the Presidium—Nikolai V. Podgorny and Dmitrii S. Polyansky—both of whom were former subordinates of his in the Ukrainian Party organization.
23. *Vneocherednoi XXI s"ezd Kommunisticheskoi Partii Sovetskogo Soyuza, stenograficheskii otchet* (Moscow: Gospolitizdat, 1959), II, 127.

CHAPTER IX

The Khrushchev Era

1. *XXII s"ezd Kommunisticheskoi Partii Sovetskogo Soyuza, stenograficheskii otchet* (*The Twenty-second Congress of the CPSU, stenographic report*) Moscow: Gospolitizdat, 1962), I, 105. Hereinafter cited as *XXII s"ezd.*
2. *Vneocherednoi XXI s"ezd Kommunisticheskoi Partii Sovetskogo Soyuza, stenograficheskii otchet* (*The Extraordinary Twenty-first*

Congress of the CPSU, stenographic report) (Moscow: Gospolitizdat, 1959), I, 65 and 113. Hereinafter cited as *Vneocherednoi XXI s"ezd.*

3. *Ibid.,* I, 105; Cf. II, 251.

4. Robert Conquest has contended that these differences reflected a basic disagreement within the Presidium and the Central Committee over the degree of repression to be employed against the "anti-Party group" and the number of additional persons to be included in the group. (*See* Conquest, *Power and Policy in the U.S.S.R.* [New York: St Martin's Press, 1961], pp. 372–381.)

5. *Vneocherednoi XXI s"ezd,* II, 161–162.

6. *Ibid.,* I, 463.

7. *Ibid.,* II, 141–142, 205, 369–370.

8. *Ibid.,* II, 385.

9. *XXII s"ezd,* I, 55. Khrushchev also announced that the Soviet Union had a 100-megaton bomb but would refrain from detonating it, because "even if [this were done] in the most remote places we could still break our windows."

10. *Ibid.,* I, 424.

11. *Ibid.,* I, 103.

12. *Ibid.,* I, 111, 422.

13. *Ibid.,* I, 112.

14. *Ibid.,* I, 134.

15. *Ibid.,* II, 353–354, 390; III, 19.

16. *Ibid.,* II, 217, 224, 355, 391, 405. Khrushchev also referred to their "criminal actions." (*Ibid.,* II, 589.)

17. *Ibid.,* II, 585.

18. *Ibid.,* I, 449; II, 107, 186, 216, 350–355, 390 f., 404.

19. *Ibid.,* I, 284 f., 291; II, 214, 404.

20. *Ibid.,* I, 279–281; II, 187, 215.

21. *Ibid.,* II, 107, 405.

22. *Ibid.,* II, 355.

23. *Ibid.,* II, 403.

24. *Ibid.,* II, 43.

25. *Ibid.,* II, 589.

26. *Ibid.,* II, 43.

27. *Ibid.,* II, 552–553.

28. *Ibid.,* II, 589–590.

29. *Ibid.,* II, 405.

30. *Ibid.,* III, 121. Following the interment of Stalin's body, a series of renamings occurred: Stalingrad became Volgograd, Stalino was renamed Donetsk, Mount Stalin (the highest in the Soviet Union) became Mount Communism, the Tadjik capital (Stalinabad) was given its former name of Dyushambe.

Despite the condemnation of the "cult of personality," the

Twenty-second Congress revealed surprisingly little about Stalin and his method of rule. Khrushchev, in his concluding speech, disclosed that Stalin had ordered the execution of Alyosha Svanidze, the brother of his first wife, allegedly on Beria's advice. He also revealed several of the mysterious circumstances surrounding the murder of Kirov in 1934 and hinted at Stalin's involvement; most of these facts had been generally known for some time. Khrushchev repeated a passage from his 1956 "secret speech": "Stalin could look at a comrade with whom he was seated at the same table and say: 'Your eyes are shifty today.' After this it could be assumed that the comrade whose eyes were supposedly shifty was suspect." (*Ibid.*, II, 583.) The underlying theme in these revelations was the alleged refusal of the "anti-Party group" to prevent a recurrence of the "cult of personality." Khrushchev posthumously rehabilitated the purged military figures (Tukhachevsky, Yakir, Uborevich, Kork, Yegorov, Eideman, Blucher) and the following Party officials: Chubar', Kosior, Rudzutak, Postyshev, Eikhe, Voznesensky, and A. A. Kuznetsov. He also expressed approval of the erection of a memorial to the innocent victims of the "cult of personality." (*Ibid.*, II, 587.) However, Khrushchev numbered these only in the "thousands" (*ibid.*, II, 585), which would exclude the far more numerous victims of Stalin's policies who were not rehabilitated.

31. *Ibid.*, I, 253.
32. *Ibid.*
33. *Ibid.*, II, 588, 592–593.
34. *Ibid.*, III, 337.
35. *Ibid.*, I, 122–123.
36. For a discussion of Khrushchev's russificatory policies in education, as well as some of the reactions elicited by them, *see* Yaroslav Bilinsky, "The Soviet Education Laws of 1958-59 and Soviet Nationality Policy," *Soviet Studies,* XIV, No. 2 (October, 1962), 138–157; *see also* Borys Lewytzkyj, *Die Sowjetukraine, 1944-1963* (Köln-Berlin: Kiepenheuer & Witsch, 1964).
37. *XXII s"ezd*, I, 217.
38. *Ibid.*, I, 226.
39. *Ibid.*, I, 109.
40. *Ibid.*, I, 325–326.
41. *Ibid.*, II, 579.
42. *See* William E. Griffith, *Albania and the Sino-Soviet Rift* (Cambridge, Mass.: The M.I.T. Press, 1963), pp. 26 and 263.
43. *See ibid.*, doc. 14, pp. 243–270, for an English translation of the most important parts of this significant address published in the November 8, 1961, issue of *Zëri i Popullit* (*The Voice of the People*), organ of the Albanian Workers' Party.

44. *Kommunisticheskaya partiya sovetskogo soyuza v rezolyutsiyakh i resheniyakh s"ezdov, konferentsii i plenumov Ts.K.* (7th ed.; Moscow: Gospolitizdat, 1960), IV, 622–624.

45. *Vneocherednoi XXI s"ezd,* I, 109. In denouncing Yugoslav "revisionism" at the Twenty-first Congress, Khrushchev claimed that Belgrade had been "spreading all sorts of fables" regarding Sino-Soviet differences. Speaking with something less than clairvoyance, he asserted: "The [Yugoslav] revisionists are seeking differences between our Communist parties, but their illusory hopes are doomed to failure."

46. *Ibid.,* I, 94–95. At the Twenty-first Congress, Khrushchev also declared, in apparent response to the Chinese decision to establish communes, that haste in proclaiming Communism would lead only to "distortion and compromising of our cause." (*Ibid.,* I, 95.) Communism would require a "highly developed modern industry, complete electrification of the country, scientific-technical progress in all branches of industry and agriculture, complete mechanization and automatization of all production processes, thorough use of new sources of energy. . . ." (*Ibid.,* I, 96.) These criteria were apparently designed to disqualify the Chinese from proclaiming the establishment of Communism in the near future. Khrushchev also criticized "leveling Communism" and demanded retention of incentives and material stimuli to increase productivity. He informed his listeners (and the Chinese) that socialist countries "successfully utilizing the potentialities established in the socialist structure will pass over into the higher phase of Communist society more or less simultaneously." (*Ibid.,* I, 107–108.)

47. For excerpts from these documents, *see* David Floyd, *Mao Against Khrushchev: A Short History of the Sino-Soviet Conflict* (New York: Frederick A. Praeger, 1963), pp. 266–271 and 278–281.

48. *Partiinaya zhizn',* No. 23 (December, 1960), p. 29.

49. *Pravda,* April 3, 1964. The Soviet decision to publish Suslov's February 14, 1964, denunciation of the Communist Party of China was explained in an unsigned article which appeared in the March, 1964, issue (No. 5) of *Kommunist,* the principal CPSU theoretical organ. The Chinese were said to have refused a CPSU invitation of March 7 to cease polemics and to meet in May preparatory to a meeting of all Communist parties to have been held in the autumn of 1964. Peking responded with intensified attacks, and Moscow declared that further silence on its part "not only would not do any good but would contribute to the desire of the leaders of the CPC to achieve their aims." (P. 15.) Moscow complained that the CPC leaders were "blinded by nationalist arrogance" and that the "Chinese press and radio call upon the Soviet people to struggle against the Central

Committee of our Party and the Soviet government." The CPSU
organ also complained of Chinese racism. (Pp. 31–32.) It noted
with alarm: "Today they [the CPC] have 'excluded' [*otluchili*]
Yugoslavia from socialism. Tomorrow the leadership of the CPC will
take it into their heads to do this with respect to other socialist
countries." (P. 20.) (*See* "Za splochennost' mezhdunarodnogo kom-
munisticheskogo dvizheniya na printsipakh marksizma-leninizma,"
Kommunist, No. 5 [March, 1964], pp. 13–52.) A subsequent *Kommunist* article, also unsigned, accused the Chinese of "violating
Leninist norms of Party life" by holding only two Party congresses
between 1928 and 1964. China's "great leap" forward was likened
to Trotskyite "super-industrialization," and the CPC was accused of
not having a program while engaging in "unprincipled and baseless"
criticism of the 1961 CPSU program. (*See* "O nekotorykh storonakh
partiinoi zhizni v kompartii Kitaya," *Kommunist,* No. 7 [May, 1964],
pp. 10–24.)

50. *Vneocherednoi XXI s"ezd,* I, 90.

51. *Ibid.,* I, 107; *XXII s"ezd,* I, 163.

52. *XXII s"ezd,* II, 470.

53. Indicative of the new image was the following statement made by
Khrushchev to the November, 1962, plenary session of the Central
Committee: "Once he [Stalin] came to the 'Dynamo' factory and
only then when there was a struggle against the Trotskyites and
Zinovievites. After that he did not go to factories. All of his journeys
were to his country home or to the Kremlin. The Kremlin was closed
to visitors. He was afraid to travel about the city, he was afraid of
the people. The man shut himself up in an armored chest. What kind
of life was that without contact with the people!" (*Pravda,* November 20, 1962, p. 7.)

54. Khrushchev's son-in-law, Adzhubei, endeavored to defend this aspect
of the "new diplomacy" in the following terms: "The ruling circles
of the U.S.A. have become accustomed to viewing the U.N. as their
patrimony. For years there has reigned there a nauseating atmosphere
of ostentation and so-called classical parliamentarism. The Soviet
delegation shattered this deadly boredom and firmly gave the
Western politicians to understand that they will not succeed in giving
orders there forever. In order to express its attitude to these gentle-
men who engage in the deception of peoples, to explode the hypo-
critical quiet, the Soviet delegation, the delegations of other socialist
countries organized disturbances when mendacious, provocational
speeches were made from the U.N. rostrum that offended the dignity
of the peoples of the socialist camp, the peoples of colonies and
states liberating themselves. When the fists the delegates of the
socialist camp drummed on the tables in protest grew tired, other

methods were found to restrain the pharisees and liars.

"Possibly this shocked the diplomatic ladies of the Western world, but it was simply splendid when Comrade N. S. Khrushchev, during one of the provocational speeches delivered by a Western diplomat, took off a shoe and began to bang the table with it. [*Laughter. Stormy applause.*] It at once became clear to everyone that we are resolutely against, that we do not want to listen to such talk! By the way, Nikita Sergeyevich Khrushchev placed his shoe in such a way (in front of our delegation sat the delegation of fascist Spain) that the tip of the shoe almost touched the neck of Franco's Foreign Minister, but not quite. In this instance, diplomatic flexibility was displayed! [*Laughter. Stormy applause.*]" (*XXII s"ezd,* II, 472–473.)

SUGGESTED READINGS

The purpose of the following listing is to provide the general reader with a reference to additional sources in English that treat certain phases of the Party's history and related aspects of the history of the Soviet Union in greater detail than was possible in the present volume.

The total sweep of Russian developments has been ably treated in standard works on Russian history. These include the histories by Sir Bernard Pares, George Vernadsky, and Sidney Harcave. Recent works are: Warren B. Walsh, *Russia and the Soviet Union: A Modern History* (Ann Arbor, Mich.: University of Michigan Press, 1958); Jesse D. Clarkson, *A History of Russia* (New York: Random House, 1961); and Donald W. Treadgold, *Twentieth Century Russia* (2d ed.; Chicago: Rand McNally & Co., 1964). These comprehensive works contain excellent bibliographies.

Among the works useful for a general understanding of the Communist Party of the Soviet Union, the Soviet regime, and Communism are the following:

ARMSTRONG, JOHN A. *Ideology, Politics, and Government in the Soviet Union: An Introduction.* New York: Frederick A. Praeger, 1962.

BAUER, RAYMOND A., INKELES, ALEX, and KLUCKHOHN, CLYDE. *How the Soviet System Works.* Cambridge, Mass.: Harvard University Press, 1956.

BLACK, CYRIL E. (ed.). *The Transformation of Russian Society.* Cambridge, Mass.: Harvard University Press, 1960.

BOCHENSKI, JOSEPH M., and NIEMEYER, GERHART (eds.). *Handbook on Communism.* New York: Frederick A. Praeger, 1962.

DANIELS, ROBERT V. (ed.). *A Documentary History of Communism.* New York: Random House, 1960.

FAINSOD, MERLE. *How Russia Is Ruled.* Rev. ed. Cambridge, Mass.: Harvard University Press, 1963.

GRIPP, RICHARD C. *Patterns of Soviet Politics.* Homewood, Ill.: The Dorsey Press, 1963.

HENDEL, SAMUEL (ed.). *The Soviet Crucible: The Soviet System in Theory and Practice*. 2d ed. Princeton, N. J.: D. Van Nostrand Co., 1963.

HOOK, SIDNEY. *Marx and the Marxists: The Ambiguous Legacy*. Princeton, N. J.: D. Van Nostrand Co., 1955.

HUNT, R. N. CAREW. *The Theory and Practice of Communism*. New York: The Macmillan Company, 1951.

INKELES, ALEX, and BAUER, RAYMOND A. *The Soviet Citizen*. Cambridge, Mass.: Harvard University Press, 1959.

KULSKI, WLADYSLAW W. *The Soviet Regime: Communism in Practice*. 4th ed. Syracuse, N. Y.: Syracuse University Press, 1963.

McCLOSKY, HERBERT, and TURNER, JOHN E. *The Soviet Dictatorship*. New York: McGraw Hill, 1960.

McNEAL, ROBERT H. (ed.). *Lenin, Stalin, and Khrushchev: Voices of Bolshevism*. Englewood Cliffs, N. J.: Prentice-Hall, 1963.

MEISEL, JAMES H., and KOZERA, EDWARD S. (eds.). *Materials for the Study of the Soviet System*. Ann Arbor, Mich.: The George Wahr Publishing Co., 1953.

MOORE, BARRINGTON, JR. *Soviet Politics: The Dilemma of Power*. Cambridge, Mass.: Harvard University Press, 1950.

MOSELY, PHILIP E. *The Kremlin and World Politics*. New York: Vintage Books, 1960.

PETERSEN, WILLIAM (ed.). *The Realities of World Communism*. Englewood Cliffs, N. J.: Prentice-Hall, 1963.

RAUCH, GEORG VON. *A History of Soviet Russia*. 4th rev. ed. New York: Frederick A. Praeger, 1964.

SCHUMAN, FREDERICK L. *Russia Since 1917*. New York: Alfred A. Knopf, 1957.

SWEARER, HOWARD R., and LONGAKER, RICHARD P. (eds.). *Contemporary Communism: Theory and Practice*. Belmont, Calif.: Wadsworth Publishing Co., 1963.

TOWSTER, JULIAN. *Political Power in the U.S.S.R., 1917–1947*. London and New York: Oxford University Press, 1948.

TREADGOLD, DONALD W. (ed.). *The Development of the U.S.S.R.* Seattle, Wash.: University of Washington Press, 1964.

VAKAR, NICHOLAS P. *The Taproot of Soviet Society*. New York: Harper & Bros., 1962.

WETTER, GUSTAV A. *Dialectical Materialism.* New York: Frederick A. Praeger, 1959.

The following works are helpful for an understanding of the matrix from which Bolshevism emerged:

BARGHOORN, FREDERICK C. "D. I. Pisarev: A Representative of Russian Nihilism," *Review of Politics,* April, 1948, pp. 190–211.

BARON, SAMUEL H. *Plekhanov: The Father of Russian Marxism.* Stanford, Calif.: Stanford University Press, 1963.

BERDYAEV, NICOLAS. *The Origin of Russian Communism.* London: Geoffrey Bles, 1948.

BILLINGTON, JAMES H. *Mikhailovsky and Russian Populism.* London and New York: Oxford University Press, 1958.

FISCHER, GEORGE. *Russian Liberalism.* Cambridge, Mass.: Harvard University Press, 1958.

FOOTMAN, DAVID. *Red Prelude: The Life of the Russian Terrorist Zhelyabov.* New Haven, Conn.: Yale University Press, 1945.

HARE, RICHARD. *Pioneers of Russian Social Thought.* London and New York: Oxford University Press, 1951.

———. *Portraits of Russian Personalities Between Reform and Revolution.* London and New York: Oxford University Press, 1959.

KOHN, HANS (ed.). *The Mind of Modern Russia: Historical and Political Thought of Russia's Great Age.* New Brunswick, N. J.: Rutgers University Press, 1955.

LAMPERT, E. *Studies in Rebellion.* New York: Frederick A. Praeger, 1957.

MENDEL, ARTHUR P. *Dilemmas of Progress in Tsarist Russia: Legal Marxism and Legal Populism.* Cambridge, Mass.: Harvard University Press, 1961.

PLAMENATZ, JOHN. *German Marxism and Russian Communism.* London and New York: Longmans, Green & Co., 1954.

WITTFOGEL, KARL A. "The Marxist View of Russian Society and Revolution," *World Politics,* July, 1960, pp. 487–508.

Yarmolinsky, Avrahm. *Road to Revolution: A Century of Russian Radicalism*. New York: The Macmillan Company, 1959.

Among the works that are useful for an understanding of Bolshevism prior to the seizure of power are the following:

Badaev, A. E. *The Bolsheviks in the Tsarist Duma*. New York: International Publishers, 1932.

Dudden, Arthur P., and von Laue, Theodore H. "The RSDLP and Joseph Fels: A Study in Intercultural Contact," *American Historical Review*, October, 1955, pp. 21–47.

Fainsod, Merle. *International Socialism and the World War*. Cambridge, Mass.: Harvard University Press, 1935.

Gankin, Olga Hess, and Fisher, H. H. (eds.). *The Bolsheviks and the World War*. Stanford, Calif.: Stanford University Press, 1940.

Haimson, Leopold H. *The Russian Marxists and the Origins of Bolshevism*. Cambridge, Mass.: Harvard University Press, 1955.

Hammond, Thomas T. *Lenin on Trade Unions and Revolution, 1893–1917*. New York: Columbia University Press, 1957.

Leites, Nathan. *A Study of Bolshevism*. Glencoe, Ill.: The Free Press, 1953.

Levin, Alfred. *The Second Duma, A Study of the Social-Democratic Party and the Russian Constitutional Experiment*. New Haven, Conn.: Yale University Press, 1940.

Pares, Sir Bernard. *The Fall of the Russian Monarchy*. New York: Alfred A. Knopf, 1939.

Seton-Watson, Hugh. *The Decline of Imperial Russia*. New York: Frederick A. Praeger, 1952.

Treadgold, Donald W. *Lenin and His Rivals: The Struggle for Russia's Future, 1898–1906*. New York: Frederick A. Praeger, 1955.

Wolfe, Bertram D. *Three Who Made a Revolution*. New York: The Dial Press, 1948.

A great deal has been written on the Bolshevik seizure of

power in 1917; the following works represent a balanced combination of eyewitness accounts, memoirs, documentary sources, and secondary sources:

ABRAMOVITCH, RAPHAEL R. *The Soviet Revolution.* New York: International Universities Press, 1962.

ADAMS, ARTHUR E. (ed.). *The Russian Revolution and Bolshevik Victory: Why and How?* Boston: D. C. Heath and Co., 1960.

BROWDER, ROBERT PAUL, and KERENSKY, ALEXANDER (eds.). *The Russian Provisional Government, 1917.* 3 vols. Stanford, Calif.: Stanford University Press, 1961.

BUNYAN, JAMES, and FISHER, H. H. (eds.). *The Bolshevik Revolution, 1917–1918: Documents and Materials.* Stanford, Calif.: Stanford University Press, 1934.

CARR, E. H. *The Bolshevik Revolution, 1917–1923.* 3 vols. New York: The Macmillan Company, 1950–53.

CHAMBERLIN, WILLIAM HENRY. *The Russian Revolution, 1917–1921.* 2 vols. New York: The Macmillan Company, 1952.

CHERNOV, VICTOR. *The Great Russian Revolution.* Translated and abridged by PHILIP E. MOSELY. New Haven, Conn.: Yale University Press, 1936.

CURTISS, JOHN S. *The Russian Revolution of 1917.* Princeton, N. J.: D. Van Nostrand Co., 1957.

DEUTSCHER, ISAAC. *The Prophet Armed: Trotsky, 1879–1921.* London and New York: Oxford University Press, 1954.

KERENSKY, ALEXANDER. *The Catastrophe.* New York: Appleton-Century-Crofts, 1927.

McNEAL, ROBERT H. (ed.). *The Russian Revolution: Why Did the Bolsheviks Win?* New York: Rinehart & Co., 1959.

MOOREHEAD, ALAN. *The Russian Revolution.* New York: Harper & Bros., 1958.

RADKEY, OLIVER. *The Agrarian Foes of Bolshevism: Promise and Default of the Russian Socialist Revolutionaries, March to October, 1917.* New York: Columbia University Press, 1958.

————. *The Election to the Russian Constituent Assembly of 1917.* Cambridge, Mass.: Harvard University Press, 1950.

REED, JOHN. *Ten Days that Shook the World.* New York: International Publishers, 1919.

SUKHANOV, N. N. *The Russian Revolution, 1917: A Personal Record.* Translated and edited by JOEL CARMICHAEL. London and New York: Oxford University Press, 1955.

TROTSKY, LEON. *The History of the Russian Revolution.* Translated by MAX EASTMAN. 3 vols. New York: Simon & Schuster, 1932.

ZEMAN, Z. A. B. (ed.). *Germany and the Revolution in Russia, 1915–1918: Documents from the Archives of the German Foreign Ministry.* London and New York: Oxford University Press, 1958.

Leninism, in theory and in practice, is treated in the following studies:

BALABANOFF, ANGELICA. *Impressions of Lenin.* Translated by ISOTTA CESARI. Ann Arbor, Mich.: University of Michigan Press, 1964.

DANIELS, ROBERT V. *The Conscience of the Revolution: Communist Opposition in Soviet Russia.* Cambridge, Mass.: Harvard University Press, 1960.

FISCHER, LOUIS. *The Life of Lenin.* New York: Harper & Row, 1964.

FISHER, H. H. *The Famine in Soviet Russia, 1919–1923.* New York: The Macmillan Company, 1927.

LOW, ALFRED. *Lenin on the Question of Nationality.* New York: Bookman Associates, 1958.

MEYER, ALFRED G. *Leninism.* Cambridge, Mass.: Harvard University Press, 1957.

PAYNE, ROBERT. *The Life and Death of Lenin.* New York: Simon & Schuster, 1964.

POSSONY, STEFAN T. *Lenin: The Compulsive Revolutionary.* Chicago: Henry Regnery Co., 1964.

RADKEY, OLIVER H. *The Sickle under the Hammer: The Russian Socialist Revolutionaries in the Early Months of Soviet Rule.* New York: Columbia University Press, 1963.

SCHAPIRO, LEONARD. *The Origin of the Communist Autocracy: Political Opposition in the Soviet State, 1917–1922.* Cambridge, Mass.: Harvard University Press, 1955.

SHUB, DAVID. *Lenin.* Garden City, N. Y.: Doubleday & Co., 1949.

STEINBERG, I. N. *In the Workshop of the Revolution.* New York: Rinehart & Co., 1953.

WESSON, ROBERT G. *Soviet Communes.* New Brunswick, N. J.: Rutgers University Press, 1963.

For discussions of Lenin's policies in dealing with the nationality question, see the following:

ADAMS, ARTHUR E. *Bolsheviks in the Ukraine: The Second Campaign, 1918–1919.* New Haven, Conn.: Yale University Press, 1963.

BORYS, JURIJ. *The Russian Communist Party and the Sovietization of Ukraine.* Stockholm, 1960.

KAZEMZADEH, FIRUZ. *The Struggle for Transcaucasia, 1917–1921.* New York: Philosophical Library, 1951.

PARK, ALEXANDER. *Bolshevism in Turkestan, 1917–1927.* New York: Columbia University Press, 1957.

PIPES, RICHARD. *The Formation of the Soviet Union: Communism and Nationalism, 1917–1923.* Cambridge, Mass.: Harvard University Press, 1954.

RESHETAR, JOHN S., JR. *The Ukrainian Revolution, 1917–1920: A Study in Nationalism.* Princeton, N. J.: Princeton University Press, 1952.

Various aspects of Stalin's rise to power are treated in the following works, most of which are rather tendentious in nature:

CARR, E. H. *The Interregnum, 1923–1924.* New York: The Macmillan Company, 1954.

———. *Socialism in One Country, 1924–1926.* 2 vols. New York: The Macmillan Company, 1958 and 1960.

DEUTSCHER, ISAAC. *Stalin: A Political Biography.* London and New York: Oxford University Press, 1949.

———. *The Prophet Unarmed: Trotsky 1921–1929.* London and New York: Oxford University Press, 1959.

ERLICH, ALEXANDER. *The Soviet Industrialization Debate, 1924–1928.* Cambridge, Mass.: Harvard University Press, 1960.

RESWICK, WILLIAM. *I Dreamt Revolution.* Chicago: Henry Regnery Co., 1952.

SERGE, VICTOR (pseudonym of VICTOR L. KIBALCHICH). *From Lenin to Stalin*. New York: Pioneer Publishers, 1937.

SPULBER, NICOLAS. *Soviet Strategy for Economic Growth*. Bloomington, Ind.: Indiana University Press, 1964.

———— (ed.). *Foundations of Soviet Strategy for Economic Growth: Selected Soviet Essays, 1924–1930*. Bloomington, Ind.: Indiana University Press, 1964.

TROTSKY, LEON. *My Life*. New York: Charles Scribner's Sons, 1930.

————. *Stalin: An Appraisal of the Man and His Influence*. Translated and edited by CHARLES MALAMUTH. London: Hollis and Carter, 1947.

The literature dealing with the quarter-century of Stalinist rule is vast and variegated. The following works cover the Party, cultural policies, police repression, treatment of non-Russian nationalities, and economic policies of the Stalinist period:

ARMSTRONG, JOHN A. *The Politics of Totalitarianism*. New York: Random House, 1961.

————. *Ukrainian Nationalism*. 2d ed. New York: Columbia University Press, 1963.

BARGHOORN, FREDERICK C. *Soviet Russian Nationalism*. London and New York: Oxford University Press, 1956.

BECK, F., and GODIN, W. *Russian Purge and the Extraction of Confession*. New York: The Viking Press, 1951.

BLACK, C. E. (ed.). *Rewriting Russian History*. New York: Frederick A. Praeger, 1956.

BROWN, EDWARD J. *The Proletarian Episode in Russian Literature, 1928–1932*. New York: Columbia University Press, 1953.

BRZEZINSKI, ZBIGNIEW K. *The Permanent Purge*. Cambridge, Mass.: Harvard University Press, 1956.

CAROE, OLAF. *Soviet Empire: The Turks of Central Asia and Stalinism*. London: Macmillan & Co., 1953.

CONQUEST, ROBERT. *The Soviet Deportation of Nationalities*. New York: St Martin's Press, 1960.

CURTISS, JOHN S. *The Russian Church and the Soviet State, 1917–1950*. Boston: Little, Brown and Co., 1953.

DALLIN, DAVID J., and NICOLAEVSKY, BORIS I. *Forced Labor in Soviet Russia*. New Haven, Conn.: Yale University Press, 1947.

DEUTSCHER, ISAAC. *The Prophet Outcast: Trotsky, 1929–1940*. London and New York: Oxford University Press, 1963.

DINERSTEIN, HERBERT S., and GOURÉ, LEON. *Two Studies in Soviet Controls: Communism and the Russian Peasant; Moscow in Crisis*. Glencoe, Ill.: The Free Press, 1955.

DJILAS, MILOVAN. *Conversations with Stalin*. New York: Harcourt, Brace & World, 1962.

DMYTRYSHYN, BASIL. *Moscow and the Ukraine, 1918–1953*. New York: Bookman Associates, 1956.

ERICKSON, JOHN. *The Soviet High Command*. New York: St Martin's Press, 1962.

FAINSOD, MERLE. *Smolensk under Soviet Rule*. Cambridge, Mass.: Harvard University Press, 1958.

FISCHER, LOUIS. *The Life and Death of Stalin*. New York: Harper & Bros., 1952.

FISHER, RALPH T., JR. *Pattern for Soviet Youth*. New York: Columbia University Press, 1959.

FRIEDRICH, CARL J., and BRZEZINSKI, ZBIGNIEW K. *Totalitarian Dictatorship and Autocracy*. Cambridge, Mass.: Harvard University Press, 1956.

GOURÉ, LEON. *The Siege of Leningrad*. Stanford, Calif.: Stanford University Press, 1962.

HOLZMAN, FRANKLYN. *Soviet Taxation*. Cambridge, Mass.: Harvard University Press, 1955.

JASNY, NAUM. *The Socialized Agriculture of the U.S.S.R*. Stanford, Calif.: Stanford University Press, 1949.

KOLARZ, WALTER. *Russia and Her Colonies*. New York: Frederick A. Praeger, 1952.

KOSTIUK, HRYHORY. *Stalinist Rule in the Ukraine: A Study of the Decade of Mass Terror, 1929–1939*. New York: Frederick A. Praeger, 1961.

LEITES, NATHAN, and BERNAUT, ELSA. *Ritual of Liquidation*. Glencoe, Ill.: The Free Press, 1954.

LEONHARD, WOLFGANG. *Child of the Revolution*. Chicago: Henry Regnery Co., 1958.

LUCKYJ, GEORGE S. N. *Literary Politics in the Soviet Ukraine, 1917–1934*. New York: Columbia University Press, 1956.

SCHUELLER, GEORGE. *The Politburo*. Stanford, Calif.: Stanford University Press, 1951.

SCHWARTZ, HARRY. *Russia's Soviet Economy*. 2d ed. New York: Prentice-Hall, 1954.

SCHWARZ, SOLOMON. *The Jews in the Soviet Union*. Syracuse, N. Y.: Syracuse University Press, 1951.

SHULMAN, MARSHALL D. *Stalin's Foreign Policy Reappraised*. Cambridge, Mass.: Harvard University Press, 1963.

SOUVARINE, BORIS. *Stalin: A Critical Survey of Bolshevism*. New York: Alliance Book Co., 1939.

STEINBERG, JULIEN (ed.). *Verdict of Three Decades: From the Literature of Individual Revolt Against Soviet Communism, 1917–1950*. New York: Duell, Sloan & Pearce, 1950.

SULLIVANT, ROBERT S. *Soviet Politics in the Ukraine, 1917–1957*. New York: Columbia University Press, 1962.

TROTSKY, LEON. *The Stalin School of Falsification*. New York: Pioneer Publishers, 1937.

WEISSBERG, ALEXANDER. *The Accused*. New York: Simon & Schuster, 1951.

WOLIN, SIMON, and SLUSSER, ROBERT M. (eds.). *The Soviet Secret Police*. New York: Frederick A. Praeger, 1957.

ZAWODNY, J. K. *Death in the Forest*. Notre Dame, Ind.: University of Notre Dame Press, 1962.

Of the growing literature on international Communism, the following works may be regarded as representative:

BORKENAU, FRANZ. *World Communism: A History of the Communist International*. Ann Arbor, Mich.: University of Michigan Press, 1962.

BRZEZINSKI, ZBIGNIEW. *The Soviet Bloc: Unity and Conflict*. Rev. ed. New York: Frederick A. Praeger, 1961.

CATTELL, DAVID T. *Communism and the Spanish Civil War*. Berkeley, Calif.: University of California Press, 1956.

CROSSMAN, RICHARD (ed.). *The God That Failed*. New York: Harper & Bros., 1949.

DALLIN, ALEXANDER (ed.). *Diversity in International Communism: A Documentary Record, 1961–1963.* New York: Columbia University Press, 1963.

DEGRAS, JANE (ed.). *The Communist International, 1919–1943.* Vol. I, *1919–1922*; Vol. II, *1923–1928.* London and New York: Oxford University Press, 1956 and 1960.

FISCHER, RUTH. *Stalin and German Communism.* Cambridge, Mass.: Harvard University Press, 1948.

GOODMAN, ELLIOT R. *The Soviet Design for a World State.* New York: Columbia University Press, 1960.

HULSE, JAMES W. *The Forming of the Communist International.* Stanford, Calif.: Stanford University Press, 1964.

KINTNER, WILLIAM R. *The Front Is Everywhere: Militant Communism in Action.* Norman, Okla.: University of Oklahoma Press, 1950.

MCKENZIE, KERMIT E. *Comintern and World Revolution, 1928–1943: The Shaping of Doctrine.* New York: Columbia University Press, 1964.

NOLLAU, GÜNTHER. *International Communism and World Revolution.* New York: Frederick A. Praeger, 1961.

NORTH, ROBERT C. *Moscow and Chinese Communists.* 2d ed. Stanford, Calif.: Stanford University Press, 1962.

OVERSTREET, GENE D., and WINDMILLER, MARSHALL. *Communism in India.* Berkeley, Calif.: University of California Press, 1959.

PAGE, STANLEY W. *Lenin and World Revolution.* New York: New York University Press, 1959.

POSSONY, STEFAN T. *A Century of Conflict: Communist Techniques of World Revolution.* Chicago: Henry Regnery Co., 1953.

RIEBER, ALFRED J. *Stalin and the French Communist Party, 1941–1947.* New York: Columbia University Press, 1962.

SALVADORI, MASSIMO. *The Rise of Modern Communism.* New York: Henry Holt & Co., 1952.

SERGE, VICTOR. *Memoirs of a Revolutionary, 1901–1941.* London and New York: Oxford University Press, 1963.

SETON-WATSON, HUGH. *From Lenin to Khrushchev.* New York: Frederick A. Praeger, 1960.

SWEARINGEN, RODGER, and LANGER, PAUL. *Red Flag in Japan.* Cambridge, Mass.: Harvard University Press, 1952.

ULAM, ADAM B. *Titoism and the Cominform*. Cambridge, Mass.: Harvard University Press, 1952.

Sources on the post-Stalin era of Soviet politics include the following:

ARMSTRONG, JOHN A. *The Soviet Bureaucratic Elite: A Case Study of the Ukrainian Apparatus*. New York: Frederick A. Praeger, 1959.

AVTORKHANOV, ABDURAKHMAN. *Stalin and the Soviet Communist Party*. New York: Frederick A. Praeger, 1959.

BARGHOORN, FREDERICK C. *The Soviet Cultural Offensive*. Princeton, N. J.: Princeton University Press, 1960.

BASS, ROBERT, and MARBURY, ELIZABETH (eds.). *The Soviet-Yugoslav Controversy, 1948–1958*. New York: Prospect Books, 1959.

BILINSKY, YAROSLAV. *The Second Soviet Republic: The Ukraine After World War II*. New Brunswick, N. J.: Rutgers University Press, 1964.

BRUMBERG, ABRAHAM (ed.). *Russia Under Khrushchev*. New York: Frederick A. Praeger, 1962.

CONQUEST, ROBERT. *Power and Policy in the U.S.S.R.* New York: St Martin's Press, 1961.

DALLIN, ALEXANDER. *The Soviet Union at the United Nations*. New York: Frederick A. Praeger, 1962.

DALLIN, DAVID J. *Soviet Foreign Policy after Stalin*. Philadelphia: J. B. Lippincott Co., 1961.

DINERSTEIN, H. S. *War and the Soviet Union: Nuclear Weapons and the Revolution in Soviet Military and Political Thinking*. Rev. ed. New York: Frederick A. Praeger, 1962.

EMBREE, G. D. *The Soviet Union Between the 19th and 20th Party Congresses*. The Hague: Nijhoff, 1959.

FEDENKO, PANAS. *Khrushchev's New History of the Soviet Communist Party*. Munich: Institute for the Study of the USSR, 1963.

GARTHOFF, RAYMOND L. *Soviet Strategy in the Nuclear Age*. Rev. ed. New York: Frederick A. Praeger, 1962.

GRULIOW, LEO (ed.). *Current Soviet Policies*. Vol. I, *The Documentary Record of the Nineteenth Communist Party*

Congress and the Reorganization After Stalin's Death; Vol. II, *The Documentary Record of the Twentieth Communist Party Congress and Its Aftermath.* New York: Frederick A. Praeger, 1953 and 1957. Vol. III, *The Documentary Record of the Extraordinary Twenty-first Communist Party Congress.* New York: Columbia University Press, 1960.

———, and SAIKOWSKI, CHARLOTTE (eds.). *Current Soviet Policies.* Vol. IV, *The Documentary Record of the Twenty-second Congress of the CPSU.* New York: Columbia University Press, 1962.

HAZARD, JOHN. *The Soviet System of Government.* 3d ed. Chicago: University of Chicago Press, 1964.

JACOBSON, HAROLD K. *The USSR and the UN's Economic and Social Activities.* Notre Dame, Ind.: University of Notre Dame Press, 1963.

KELLEN, KONRAD. *Khrushchev: A Political Portrait.* New York: Frederick A. Praeger, 1961.

KULSKI, WLADYSLAW W. *Peaceful Co-existence: An Analysis of Soviet Foreign Policy.* Chicago: Henry Regnery Co., 1959.

LEONHARD, WOLFGANG. *The Kremlin Since Stalin.* New York: Frederick A. Praeger, 1962.

MEHNERT, KLAUS. *Peking and Moscow.* New York: G. P. Putnam's Sons, 1963.

MEISSNER, BORIS. *The Communist Party of the Soviet Union: Party Leadership, Organization, and Ideology.* Edited and with a chapter on the Twentieth Party Congress by JOHN S. RESHETAR, JR. New York: Frederick A. Praeger, 1956.

MOSELY, PHILIP E. (ed.). "Russia Since Stalin," *The Annals of the American Academy of Political and Social Science,* CCCIII (January, 1956).

PISTRAK, LAZAR. *The Grand Tactician: Khrushchev's Rise to Power.* New York: Frederick A. Praeger, 1961.

RUBINSTEIN, ALVIN Z. *The Soviets in International Organization: Changing Policy Toward Developing Countries, 1953–1963.* Princeton, N. J.: Princeton University Press, 1964.

RUSH, MYRON. *The Rise of Khrushchev.* Washington, D.C.: Public Affairs Press, 1958.

SCHAPIRO, LEONARD (ed.). *The U.S.S.R. and the Future: An Analysis of the New Program of the CPSU.* New York: Frederick A. Praeger, 1963.

SCHOLMER, JOSEPH. *Vorkuta*. New York: Henry Holt & Co., 1955

SCOTT, DEREK J. R. *Russian Political Institutions*. Rev. ed. New York: Frederick A. Praeger, 1961.

SWAYZE, HAROLD. *Political Control of Literature in the USSR, 1946–1959*. Cambridge, Mass.: Harvard University Press, 1962.

TRISKA, JAN F. (ed.). *Soviet Communism: Programs and Rules*. San Francisco: Chandler Publishing Co., 1962.

TUCKER, ROBERT C. *The Soviet Political Mind: Studies in Stalinism and Post-Stalin Change*. New York: Frederick A. Praeger, 1963.

ULAM, ADAM B. *The New Face of Soviet Totalitarianism*. Cambridge, Mass.: Harvard University Press, 1963.

WHITNEY, THOMAS P. (ed.). *Khrushchev Speaks*. Ann Arbor, Mich.: University of Michigan Press, 1963.

WOLFE, BERTRAM D. *Khrushchev and Stalin's Ghost*. New York: Frederick A. Praeger, 1957.

ZAGORIA, DONALD S. *The Sino-Soviet Conflict, 1956–1961*. Princeton, N. J.: Princeton University Press, 1962.

Index

C M